PROFESSIONAL DEVELOPMENT
The Dynamics of Success

SECOND EDITION

PROFESSIONAL DEVELOPMENT
The Dynamics of Success

MARY WILKES
NATIONAL COLLEGE

C. BRUCE CROSSWAIT
SOUTH DAKOTA STATE UNIVERSITY

HBJ Media Systems Corporation
A Subsidiary of Harcourt Brace Jovanovich
Orlando   New York   San Diego   Chicago

Design by Anita Duncan
Cover and part opening photos by John Oldenkamp and Cynthia Sabransky

ISBN: 0-15-572004-X

Library of Congress Catalog Card Number: 83-81039

Printed in the United States of America

05-720040 / 10 9 8 7 6 5 4 3 2 1

Additional Illustration Credits:
Page 55: adapted from *Experiences in Biology*, Revised Edition by Evelyn Morholt,
copyright © 1967 by Harcourt Brace Jovanovich, Inc. Reproduced by permission of the
publisher.
Page 70: These photographs have been utilized with the express consent of Redken
Laboratories, Inc., the owner thereof, and any reproduction or other use is prohibited without its
prior consent.
Page 87: David Taylor Dance Theatre; Bryan Egelhoff Photo/Lynelle Mossholder and
Albert Adams
Page 126: Drawing by Lloyd Birmingham
Colorplates:
Plates 2 and 3: Drawings by Harriet Sherman
Plate 4: Makeup and photographs courtesy of Merle Norman Cosmetics
Plate 5: Bottom right photo by Bob Takis/American Airlines, Inc.
Plate 6: Fashions courtesy of The Broadway (So. Ca.)
Plate 7: Courtesy of Butterick Fashion Marketing Co.
Plate 8: Fashions courtesy of The Broadway (So. Ca.)
All uncredited photos, except those noted above, by John Oldenkamp and Cynthia Sabransky.

CONTENTS

PREFACE

Professional Development: The Dynamics of Success was written for a unique course—the professional or personal development course. Unlike many courses and textbooks that are intended to help students develop salable skills in a particular field, this course and this book aim to alert the students to the qualities and techniques needed both to *find* a good job and to be *successful* in that job.

The favorable response to the first edition, published in 1981, has been gratifying, and we now offer an improved and updated second edition. We continue to address the needs and concerns of both the men and women who take this course.

In this book we have tried neither to underplay nor to exaggerate the importance of personal appearance—"projecting your image." We have kept topics relating to grooming, cosmetics, and appearance to a reasonable minimum and always within the context of their importance to personal and professional effectiveness.

This book is organized around the premise that the techniques and personal qualities students need to find the best possible job in a particular field are identical to those that they must develop and refine in order to become effective and promotable employees. For this reason, we begin Part One, "Starting Out Right," with the elements of the job campaign—locating openings, evaluating companies, writing résumés and application letters, arranging for interviews, and presenting oneself effectively at interviews. In each of the succeeding Parts, we explore subjects touched upon in Part One in greater depth.

Part Two, "Projecting Your Image," covers grooming, personal hygiene, exercise, diet and nutrition, health, and wardrobe care and selection.

Part Three, "Working with Others," treats the communication process, personal effectiveness, group dynamics, personal values, and business ethics.

Part Four, "Planning for Success," focuses on goal setting, time management, social and business etiquette, travel, and personal money management.

Part Five, "Moving Up the Ladder," introduces the student to management and leadership styles, basic management theories, and opportunities in the field of management.

Each chapter opens with a comprehensive goal, followed by specific learning objectives. Text discussions are down-to-earth and relevant to the real world of the entry-level professional. Key vocabulary terms, review and discussion questions, application exercises, and suggested additional readings conclude each chapter.

The illustration program has been totally revised and includes a new full-color fashion insert, which highlights color coordination for men and women. The illustrations were planned to *teach* and *enhance* the text presentation. Approximately 350 photographs, drawings, and figures crystallize the topics under discussion.

Principal textual changes of the new edition include:

- The Application Exercises, which have been increased substantially, reinforce the concepts learned in each chapter by relating them to on-the-job situations

- An expanded treatment of résumés, with examples of functional and chronological styles

- New section on special grooming requirements for allied health occupations

- Expanded treatment on the benefits of aerobic exercise with an explanation of how to measure performance

- Addition to the fashion section of an explanation of the four seasonal color types and how skin tones affect wardrobe choices

- New topic, "Written Communication"

- New topic, "The Office Family"

- New section on universal life insurance

- Addition of new topics relating to banking and investment opportunities, such as interest plus checking, Super NOW accounts, and Individual Retirement Accounts.

- Addition of sections on group organization, situational leadership, and Theory Z

- New topic, "Management Prerequisites"

- An expanded glossary, with key terms used in each chapter

The authors appreciate the responses and specific suggestions from many users of the book. We would like to give special thanks to Ms. Deborah Walker Greene, Sullivan Junior College of Business, and to Ms. Donna Sandberg, Wisconsin Indianhead Technical Institute, who critically reviewed the manuscript for revision. Also, we are grateful to Dr. Clarita Eusebio-Kelly, HCA Institute, and Professor Harriet Strongin, Nassau Community College, both of whom contributed new information on good grooming techniques. Finally, we would like to acknowledge the staff members of HBJ Media Systems Corporation who worked on this project: Patricia Clarke, Editorial Assistant; Debra Ann Filbrandt, Administrative Assistant; JoAnn Fisher, Editorial Coordinator; William Gurvitch, Production Manager; and James Moulton, Director of Publishing, Business Books.

Mary Wilkes

C. Bruce Crosswait

PROFESSIONAL DEVELOPMENT
The Dynamics of Success

PART ONE

STARTING OUT RIGHT

The first phase of your professional development begins the minute you start to think about where to look for your first job. The tools you need to succeed are essentially the same tools you will need during your entire career: planning skills, communication skills, appearance, poise, and confidence.

1   THE JOB CAMPAIGN

2   THE INTERVIEW

1

THE JOB CAMPAIGN

COMPREHENSIVE GOAL
To instruct you in methods of finding job vacancies, preparing a résumé, and writing a letter of application.

SPECIFIC OBJECTIVES
After reading this chapter, you will be able to:

- locate job vacancies by using available source materials

- construct a résumé

- compose an application letter

- complete an application form

Starting a job campaign is the kind of adventure that can kindle both anticipation and apprehension. By its nature it involves encounters with the unknown—new people, new places of business—and resulting discoveries, both about the field you are entering and about yourself as well.

To compound the problem, you will be offered much well-meaning advice and free information, some of which can be more of a hindrance than a help. Your favorite uncle tells you to be aggressive. A friend says, "If you try to be aggressive, you might seem arrogant." Your instructor gives you pointers on how to negotiate salary, and then your father insists that you should accept the first offer. Confused, you turn to the experts. After reading some of their how-to-succeed-in-the-interview books, you may be more perplexed than ever.

Since you have invested much time, energy, and money in your formal education, you want the best possible returns. The first two chapters of this book are designed to help you succeed. They are organized to lead you through every step up to and through the job interview to your goal—your first job in your chosen field.

The Preliminaries

Before you ever meet an interviewer, some preliminary research and much paperwork are essential. The first step will be investigating various job markets on the basis of your skills and interests. Writing a résumé and an application letter and filling out the application form are also prerequisites to the interview.

You will find, when you embark on this phase of your job campaign, that you need organization, imagination, and determination. In fact, just tracking down the job openings is a job in itself. To

Job hunting requires research.

get started, look at the categories listed on the pages following. They will give you an idea of some of the avenues you can pursue.

JOB MARKET

The best jobs are not always advertised in the daily newspaper. A nationwide survey conducted by the Department of Labor revealed the following statistics about how successful job applicants located their job:

- 48%—Through friends or relatives
- 24%—Direct contact with employers
- 13%—Combination of the methods listed here
- 6%—Through school placement services
- 5%—In response to help-wanted ads
- 3%—Through public employment agencies
- 1%—Through private employment agencies and job-search firms

In today's competitive market it is best to consider all sources. The following guide to various employment sources could lead to a job that is right for you.

College Placement Office   Most schools maintain placement offices, and many employers prefer to work directly with them. This office is an excellent job source because it usually has a list of openings that closely match your qualifications.

College Placement Annual   This book lists all the names of companies in your field that are looking for entry-level applicants.

Trade Associations   Find the address of the appropriate trade association from the *Encyclopedia of Associations*, a reference book available in most libraries. Then write to the trade association and inquire about its placement service. If you belong to a student branch of a professional association, such as the National Secretaries Association, the Future Business Leaders of America, or the American Marketing Association, write and ask for tips and job leads.

Trade and Professional Journals   These are magazines such as *The Office, Computerworld, Hotel and Motel Management, Journal of Accountancy,* and *Secretary.* They usually have advertisements for job vacancies in their classified sections.

State Employment Service or Job Services Center   This is an agency that provides *free* statewide and local job placement, along with vocational counseling and testing. Additionally, the agency administers the state civil service exam that enables a person to qualify for jobs with the state government. You will find it listed as the *Job*

Placement services offer you personalized attention.

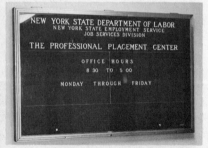
A job services center provides free job placement.

Look through the Yellow Pages.

Services Center in the telephone directory under your state's Department of Labor or Employment Department. Since it is a public service, it is often overcrowded and you may have to wait hours for assistance.

Federal Job Information Center If you have a federal personnel office nearby, it would be to your benefit to visit it. You can register for federal civil service tests offered on assigned dates. After taking the test, you will be given a rating that will qualify you for various government jobs.

Registers and Clearinghouses You may want to consider placing your name with a register or clearinghouse that specializes in the type of career that you are seeking. A *clearinghouse* is an agency that collects, classifies, and distributes information. You will have to pay a fee for a weekly or monthly newsletter, which will provide job vacancies in your field for a specified geographical area. One of the best compilations of jobs for the various regions of the United States is the *National Business Employment Weekly*, available % *The Wall Street Journal*, 420 Lexington Avenue, New York, NY 10170.

Professional Placement Services In contrast to state employment agencies, these are privately owned agencies. They offer you more personalized service, but they charge a fee. If the employer is willing to pay all the charges, the job is referred to as *fee paid*. If you accept a non-fee paid position, you will be obligated to pay the fee, which is usually based on your beginning salary. Some employers reimburse employees after six months or a year of employment.

CAREER SEARCH, INC.

Jobs in

* ★ Management
* ★ Banking
* ★ Retailing
* ★ Advertising

Call us for the right job.

50 S. Centre St.
889-1234

In this ad, a private employment agency lists fields in which it has job openings, but does not list specific jobs.

F/PD

BKPR	$250
SECS JR/SR	$200-300
CLK-TYPIST (temp)	$4.50

Success Agency
746-7885 17 E. Elm

These are all jobs for which the company will pay the agency's fee. Junior and senior refer to level of responsibility and salary, not to age. The first two salaries listed are weekly, the third hourly. The third job is a temporary one.

Manager Trainee
College background required. Must be willing to start at the bottom and work up. Company offers excellent salary/benefits to the applicant who is highly motivated and personable. EOE.
Send resume to:
Bellcrest
3000 Terrace
Hyattsville
MD 20784.

This is an entry-level position. Many management positions for college graduates are of this sort. EOE stands for Equal Opportunity Employer.

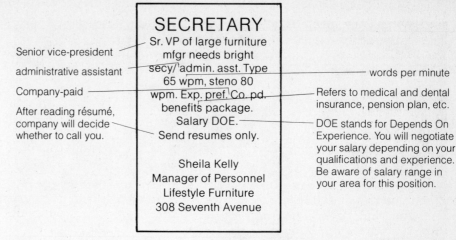

Figure 1–1
Typical help-wanted ads

Telephone Yellow Pages Decide what types of firms might suit your qualifications and interests. Look under these categories in the Yellow Pages. Call the companies listed there and secure the names of their personnel directors. Then send a résumé and application letter to each. Should you be interested in employment in another city, go to your local telephone company or public library, where the telephone books of other major cities are available.

Newspaper Help-Wanted Ads Remember, newspaper want ads are read by thousands of people. Your application will be one of many. Richard Bolles, author of *What Color Is Your Parachute?*, believes that the odds are stacked against you. But if you are one to cover all bets, he adds, this is another avenue of job sources. Moreover, this will be an excellent way to get an idea of the jobs available in your field and their salary range. Many students do not know how to read a want ad. Figure 1–1 illustrates several ads and features of which you should be aware.

Newspapers and Magazines Articles about business expansion and branch office openings appear frequently in local newspapers and sometimes in such national magazines as *Forbes, Fortune,* and *Business Week.* By following up on a news story you may get yourself a new job in a new area.

Friends and Relatives Be sure to spread the word around your family and circle of acquaintances that you are job hunting. Most companies make a practice of posting job openings for the convenience of their own employees. Ask your family and friends to check the latest listings in their companies and the names of the appropriate personnel director or supervisor.

Contact with Employers   This area is often overlooked by college graduates. They hesitate to walk in the door of a business and ask for an application blank. True, the applicant may have to face rejection in this situation, but it is a numbers game. The more businesses contacted, the better the chances for success.

Jobs listed on a company bulletin board.

RÉSUMÉ

Once you have located as many job sources as you can, your next step is to prepare your *résumé*. The résumé, sometimes called the data sheet or *vita*, is a well-organized summary of your educational and professional background, along with pertinent personal data. It gives an overview of your entire work history, education, and skills, and is so important in the job-getting process that some job seekers hire professionals to produce their résumés. You can, however, create a quality résumé on your own by considering the following points.

On scratch paper, write down answers to these questions:

Job Objective
What career goal do you have in mind?
Under what conditions do you work best?
What tasks do you like best? Least?
What are your skills and assets? (Include those that relate to people, machines, and materials.)

Education
What colleges and educational institutions have you attended?
What academic degrees do you have?
List the courses you have taken that relate to your career goal.
What is your cumulative grade point average?
What is your grade point average for your major?
Have you attended any seminars, workshops or in-service training courses?

Work Experience
What full-time and part-time jobs have you held? (List them all, even if you do not think babysitting and gas pumping are important.)
What were some of the duties involved in your past jobs? Do they relate to your job objective?

References
From whom can you obtain references? Consider school years, past jobs, community and religious organizations.

Personal Data
What awards, honors, and special recognition have you received?
What hobbies, special interests, and talents do you have?
What organizations do you belong to? Have you ever held an office in these organizations?

Writing a résumé.

What jobs have you held?

With these answers, you now have the raw material for your résumé. The next step is to organize this information.

The following guidelines can help you prepare an effective résumé:

1. Your raw data must be organized and placed under appropriate headings. Typical categories are job objective, education, work experience, personal data, and references. There is no one right format for the placement of these headings. Parallel arrangement and wording will provide the necessary uniformity.

2. Don't use abbreviations for academic terms or any other terms that may be foreign to the interviewer. Common educational abbreviations, such as *GPA (grade point average)*, Poli. Sci. (political science), and DP (data processing), may be confusing.

3. Be careful about the use of grade point averages. Some colleges use a 5-point scale (A equals 5 points) and others a 4-point scale (A equals 4 points). Should you claim a grade point average of 3.5, inform the reader if it is on a 4.0 or 5.0 scale.

4. If your grade point average is low cumulatively, but high for your major course of study, note that fact. For example, an accounting major could state: "grade point average of 3.4, on a 4.0 scale, in all accounting courses."

5. Confine your résumé to one page. Busy personnel directors have little time to read lengthy résumés.

Collect material for your résumé.

6. Use short phrases and active verbs. Avoid the use of the personal pronoun "I." Write "directed project," "supervised office," "reorganized books," instead of phrases such as "I was responsible for"; "I was in charge of."
7. Consider the arrangement of data. Because the eye is trained to read the top part of the page first, the more valuable selling points—work experience, education, and job target—should be on the upper half of the page. Job counselors believe that references placed at the bottom of the page provide a natural "lead in": After potential employers finish reading the résumé, their next step will be writing or telephoning the references.

Organize your data.

There are basically two types of résumé, the chronological and the functional. The *chronological résumé* is the most popular and widely accepted. It lists the most recent job or educational experience first, then the remaining data in reverse chronology. (See figure 1–2.) The *functional résumé* first presents the job or educational experience—not necessarily the most recent—that directly relates to the vacancy. (See figure 1–4.) This type of résumé concentrates on duties performed or skills acquired, and best serves the candidate who has a history of job responsibilities. However, it can be designed to fit the younger applicant who has acquired some marketable skills through educational training. For example, secretarial science majors might use this pattern for their functional résumés:

> Type at 70 wpm; take dictation at 110 wpm; operate memory typewriter, word processing equipment, ten-key; strong English background; experience in composing business letters

Whichever résumé form you choose, the guidelines above and the suggestions below will apply to its format.

Vital Information   Your name, address, and telephone number deserve the best visual position. Make it as easy as possible for the personnel director to contact you.

Frequently, students have their college addresses and phone numbers printed on their résumés. When they move after graduation, this information becomes obsolete. To avoid this problem, remember to include a permanent address and number on the résumé, such as your parents'. Be sure to indicate which is temporary and which is permanent. Give the dates when each will be valid. (See figure 1–2.)

Job Objective   What type of position are you seeking? List that goal near the top of the résumé. Notice that some job goals are stated in

Angela Marchesi

Temporary Residence
828 Fourth Street
Lincoln, Nebraska 68507
(402) 555-9087
(Before 6/30/84)

Permanent Residence
Star Route, Box 30
Columbus, Nebraska 68766
(402) 555-8907
(After 6/30/84)

Career Objective: Computer Programmer

Education: September 1982-Present:
Nebraska Wesleyan, Lincoln, Nebraska. Will receive Associate of Science degree in Computer Data Processing in June 1984. Current grade point average 3.5 on 4-point scale.

September 1978-June 1982:
Kramer High School,Columbus, Nebraska.

Experience: October 1983-Present:
Programmer, Nebraska Wesleyan. Designed and wrote program for college's off-campus housing system (BASIC). Wrote program to print 10-99 forms; revised program to print W-2 forms (COBOL).

September 1982-October 1983:
Operator, Nebraska Wesleyan. Responsible for running student programs in N-Mode (B3 Simulation), operating the college's computers and running production jobs (admissions reports and time analysis reports). Hardware used:

NCRI-9050 Interactive Resource Executive (IRX)
NCRI-8430 Interactive Resource Executive (IRX)
TI-990 Models 4 and 29
IBM Keypunch

June 1981-September 1982:
Office Assistant, Data Corporation, Columbus, Nebraska. Responsible for data entry filing, typing, and keypunching.

Honors and Activities: Dean's Honor List since beginning Nebraska Wesleyan. Graduated with honors Kramer High School. Captain Women's Tennis Team. Enjoy racquetball, acting, and playing guitar.

Personal Data: Health excellent.

References: See enclosed Reference sheet.

Figure 1–2
Chronological Résumé

specific detail, whereas others are vague and general. For example:

General	Career Goal:	Sales Manager
Specific	Career Goal:	Sales Manager in the computer hardware field
General	Career Goal:	Executive Secretarial Position
Specific	Career Goal:	Executive Secretarial Position utilizing my experience in public relations

For an entry-level position, a general statement is sufficient. However, if you have special talents that would qualify you for a more advanced position, or you wish to indicate a career path, be more specific. Stay away from broad general terms such as "seek opportunity for advancement," "want position with an expanding company," and "desire challenging position." Personnel directors read these vague, nondescript statements so frequently that the effectiveness of such phrases is minimal.

Education and Work History The placement of education and work history depends upon which aspect of your background pertains most directly to your job target. If your vocational training prepared you well for a particular objective, your education credentials should precede the work section. A list of pertinent college courses will demonstrate that although you lack experience, you have the requisite knowledge. On the other hand, if you have held past jobs that demonstrate your ability in similar work responsibilities, your work history should receive major emphasis.

Courtesy of SCM Corporation

What are your skills?

Don't forget to include your phone number.

REFERENCES FOR
ANGELA MARCHESI

EDUCATIONAL

Mr. G. W. Bare, Professor of Computer Science   (402) 555-3481
Nebraska Wesleyan
2310 Huron Street
Lincoln, Nebraska 68507

Mr. Gene Hosiaux, Athletic Coach   (402) 555-7643
Kramer High School
1900 Elm Street
Columbus, Nebraska 68767

Mrs. James Crowe, Principal   (402) 555-7643
Kramer High School
1900 Elm Street
Columbus, Nebraska 68767

OCCUPATIONAL

Dr. Ken Coddington, Chairman   (402) 555-8954
Data Processing Division
Nebraska Wesleyan
349 Parker Street
Lincoln, Nebraska 68507

Mr. Bob Conner, Senior Programmer   (402) 555-3274
Computer Center
Nebraska Wesleyan
338 Parker Street
Lincoln, Nebraska 68507

Ms. Zelda Winner, Engineer   (402) 555-2510
Data Corporation
33 East Main Street
Columbus, Nebraska 68763

PERSONAL

Ms. Betty Drake   (402) 555-3980
9808 Tenth Street, SE
Columbus, Nebraska 68762

Mrs. Agnes McClellan   (816) 555-4999
8902 Burgermeister Road
Kansas City, Missouri 83306

Mr. Bob Williamson   (402) 555-0984
5987 Cedardale Drive
Waterloo, Nebraska 68790

Figure 1–3
Reference Sheet

Hobbies, Special Interests, Special Abilities You may reason that your outside interests have very little relationship to your job target. Don't be too certain. One young woman, applying for a secretarial position, noted on her résumé that she had artistic ability. Unknown to her, the employer was looking for someone who could handle blueprints, and hired her because of that talent.

List hobbies that indicate you are a doer. Employers will wonder about your ability to relate to people if all of your hobbies are sedentary and nonsocial, such as macrame, stamp collecting, and reading. Include some active pastimes in your list, such as skiing, running, and boating.

List your credentials.

Personal Data The only time personal data can be required is when it is a *bona fide occupational qualification* (BFOQ); for example, the job of flight attendant necessitates certain physical standards. Under the Civil Rights Act of 1964 and its amendments, you are not required to include any personal data on your résumé that does not directly apply to the position you seek; however, you can volunteer such information.

References Choose individuals who know you well and can give you a good recommendation. Many college graduates make the mistake of giving professors as their only references. This choice does not give the employer a complete picture of your total personality. Instead, to provide a balance, select references from various aspects of your background. Include at least three references. Be sure to obtain permission from the individuals you choose as references. If you plan to distribute copies of your résumé widely, you might decide to state "references available upon request." If employers are interested in hiring you, they will ask for your references.

Some graduates list as many as nine references, which is a great psychological ploy for many reasons. First, it demonstrates that the applicant must be respected to be able to find that many individuals to vouch for the person. Also, busy personnel directors or employers find this time saving when they try to phone references. Often the first contact will be a dead end because the reference is on vacation, in a meeting, or otherwise unavailable. If several sources are provided, three can probably be contacted on the first try.

If you decide to provide this many references, your résumé entry under "References" should direct the reader to your Reference Sheet. (See figure 1–2.) The Reference Sheet (see figure 1–3) should be prepared on a separate page. Group references into appropriate categories—occupational, educational, and personal. In the first two categories, give the person's title. All references should include name, address, and phone number.

What are your hobbies?

ARTHUR BATES
980 Fifth Street
Ventura, California 92345
(813) 555-9865

CAREER OBJECTIVE

A public service position in the travel industry.

WORK EXPERIENCE

Reservationist, Travel Unlimited, 404 South Street, Ventura, California 98632. Wrote tickets, planned itineraries for customers, made phone contacts with potential customers, helped with weekly accounting reports, developed Hawaiian sales campaign.

Alumni Coordinator, Ventura Travel School, Ventura, California. Kept records current, contacted graduates by phone, organized filing system for alumni school newspaper.

Host, Rudy's Restaurant, Ventura, California. Handled customer service, coordinated seating arrangements, planned banquets.

EDUCATION

Associate of Science degree, Travel and Airlines, Ventura Travel School, Ventura, California, 1984.

Relevant Classes:

Computer Concepts	Tariffs and Ticketing
Computerized Reservations	Reservations
Marketing	Accounting I, II
Tourism Marketing	First Aid
International Travel	Cruise Study Program

San Diego High School, San Diego, California, 1981. Graduated with honors.

PERSONAL DATA

Hobbies: Skiing, Swimming, Tennis, Piano.
Health: Excellent

REFERENCES

Will be furnished upon request.

Figure 1–4
Functional Résumé

Appearance   Even if your résumé is well organized and your credentials excellent, the résumé will go unread if it is unattractively arranged. Center the data to insure a picture frame of white on all four sides of the paper., Avoid strikeovers, discernible erasures, and smudges. An eye-catching quality is sometimes helpful when your résumé competes with many others. Striking résumés can be composed and produced very inexpensively by a printer.

After you have arranged all your information in correct order, read the entire résumé objectively. Does it describe an individual you would like to hire? It should!

Now proofread it. Make sure it contains no spelling or grammatical errors. With the résumé carefully typed or printed, you are ready to compose a personal sales letter, usually referred to as an application letter.

Proofread your résumé.

APPLICATION LETTER

Every résumé mailed should be accompanied by an *application letter*. Application letters cannot be mass-produced like the résumé. Each letter must be written specifically for the organization being applied to. Your cover letter and résumé can be either solicited or unsolicited. Solicited replies are a response to an advertised or publicly announced job vacancy. (See figure 1–5.) Unsolicited letters refer to letters and résumés sent to companies that are not actively recruiting new employees. (See figure 1–6.) Unsolicited résumés and letters can be as effective as solicited letters, so send both types out to employers.

What may sound like an overwhelming task can be reduced to a workable plan by following the three-paragraph pattern described below. As you read the description, refer to the sample application letters in figures 1–5 and 1–6.

Anne Robertson

Commercial printers can produce striking résumés.

Step One: The First Paragraph This paragraph must get the reader's attention and keep it. Remember, employers read dozens of letters for each job vacancy, and you want yours to stand out. A thought-provoking question, the name of a person referring you to the company, or a brief statement of your qualifications is a good way to start. Note the following examples.

Question
Do you need a highly motivated, self-starting individual for your company?

Are you looking for a secretary who can take dictation at 100 wpm and transcribe at 80 wpm?

Name of Person Referring
Mr. Hanson, your sales manager, has informed me that you will soon be looking for an accountant.

Mr. Allan Smith spoke to me about the vacancy in your chemistry department.

When using the name of someone who has referred you to the company, be sure to have that person's permission. Try to make sure that he or she is held in high regard within the firm.

Statement of Qualifications
My ability to speak two foreign languages fluently could give RMC an advantage in foreign sales.

My two years experience as part-time accountant at the Kramer Company can be an asset to your new firm.

Another effective method of drawing attention to yourself is to first thoroughly research the company. Then demonstrate your knowledge and interest in the company by referring to something significant.

I read with interest that MARC is opening a new branch in Denver, Colorado, which happens to be my hometown.

Step Two: The Second Paragraph This is the longest of the three paragraphs. It should amplify one or two of your major qualifications that are pertinent to the position you are seeking. Within the paragraph, reference to the résumé you have enclosed will remind the reader of your other qualifications. Here are two examples:

I have studied computer programming for the past four years at Catron University. During that time, I have maintained a grade point average of 3.5 on a 4.0 scale in all my subjects. My instructor, Professor John Arthur, hired me as a tutor for his freshmen and sophomore students. While pursuing my studies, I acted as a part-time computer operator in the Catron University Data Proc-

Courtesy of Dictaphone Corp.

The second paragraph of your letter should describe your qualifications.

324 E. Adams Street
Waverly, NE 68114

June 10, 19--

Ms. Sharon Hame
Business Manager
Consolidated Tools, Inc.
125 Third Place
Fullerton, NE 68302

Dear Ms. Hame:

Mr. Hanson, your sales manager, has informed me that you will soon be looking
for an accountant. Please consider me an applicant for that position.

I will receive a B.S. degree in Accounting in August 19-- and feel that my
experience with tax accounting can be an asset to your firm. As you can see from
my resume, I worked as a tax preparer for R & C Tax Service, which provided me
with a first-hand knowledge of taxes. In addition to this experience, I have been
responsible for accounts payable, member billings, and supply inventory for the
last two years at the Waverly Chamber of Commerce.

I am willing and eager to put my skills to work. I am available for a personal
interview at your convenience. I can be reached at (402) 555-4802 any day after
5:00 p.m.

Sincerely,

Russell Hanks

Russell Hanks

Enclosure

Figure 1–5
Solicited Application Letter (Modified-Block Style)

125 Parker Street
Wesston Springs, AZ 85501
April 2, 19--

Mr. Mac Hull
Operations Manager
Holland Laboratories
168 Lawrence Avenue
Phoenix, AZ 85027

Dear Mr. Hull:

Do you need a programmer who has mastery of three computer languages: COBOL, FORTRAN, and NEAT/3? If so, I wish to be considered for the position.

I have studied computer programming for the past fours years at Catron University. During that time, I have maintained a grade point average of 3.5 on a 4.0 scale for all my subjects. My instructor, Professor John Arthur, hired me as a tutor for his freshman and sophomore students. While pursuing my studies, I acted as a part-time computer operator in the Catron University Data Processing Center. Please refer to the enclosed resume for additional information about my background and experience.

For further discussion, you may telephone me at (603) 555-4055 before May 5, 19--. After that date, I can be reached at (602) 555-7224. I will be available for a personal interview at your convenience. Thank you for any consideration given my candidacy.

Sincerely,

Sue Ann Smith

Sue Ann Smith

Figure 1–6
Unsolicited Application Letter (Full-Block Style)

Mailing a résumé.

essing Center. Please refer to the enclosed résumé for additional information about my background and experience.

I will receive a B.S. degree in accounting in August 19–– and feel that my experience with tax accounting can be an asset to your firm. As you can see from my résumé, I worked as a tax preparer for R & C Tax Service, which provided me with a firsthand knowledge of taxes. In addition to this experience, I have been responsible for accounts payable, member billings, and supply inventory for the last two years at the Waverly Chamber of Commerce.

Step Three: Concluding Paragraph   This paragraph can be short and to the point.

I will be available for a personal interview at your convenience.

A statement like this will be sufficient to demonstrate your interest in the position. Ask for an interview and state where you can be reached. Include a telephone number.

After carefully typing your letter, examine it for misspelled words, errors in grammar, and misplaced punctuation. Scrutinize its appearance for erasures, smudges, and strikeovers. This letter demonstrates your professionalism. Mistakes or sloppiness will harm your chances for obtaining an interview.

TELEPHONE INTRODUCTIONS

After all of your résumés and application letters are mailed, it is time to begin the second phase of the job campaign. Approximately ten days after the letters have been mailed, start telephoning the employers to inquire as to the opportunities with that particular company. This is the time to practice your diplomacy. Don't ask direct questions such as:

Do you like my résumé?
Did you read my résumé?
Do you have a position for me?
When can I have an interview?
Are there any job openings?

Instead, ask questions that will not lead to an immediate "no" and thus end the conversation. Ask questions or make statements similar to the following:

I mailed your company a résumé about ten days ago. I was hoping to determine if you have had a chance to review it yet.
In following up on my résumé, I was wondering if it has reached your desk.
After reviewing my résumé, do you find that my qualifications meet your company's requirements?

The follow-up phone call is probably one of the most powerful facets of the job campaign. It shows the employer that you are an achieving, organized, and responsible individual.

Application Form

Sometimes you will be asked to complete an application form before the interview. Be prepared with complete and appropriate information. Following are some pointers to help you in your task.

- Most of the information required will repeat what is on your résumé, so bring along a copy for reference.

- Follow directions. If you write your name when the form instructs you to print it, you may give the employer the impression that you can't follow directions.

- If there is a section that doesn't apply to you, mark it N/A for "not applicable," indicating that you haven't overlooked the section.

- Questions dealing with race, religion, sex, age, marital status, or legal convictions are potentially discriminatory in nature. (For further discussion of this subject, see table 2–1 in Chapter 2.) You do not have to answer these questions, but you can write N/A to indicate that you have read them. (Figure 1–7 is an example of a nondiscriminatory application form.)

- Should the question of salary be raised on the application,

Fill out your application form carefully.

APPLICATION FOR EMPLOYMENT

Date _____

Position Desired _____ Salary Desired _____ Referred by _____

LAST NAME	FIRST	MIDDLE	SOCIAL SECURITY NO.

PRESENT ADDRESS STREET	CITY	STATE	ZIP CODE	APT. NO.	TELEPHONE NO. AREA CODE

ARE YOU PREVENTED FROM LAWFULLY BECOMING EMPLOYED IN THE UNITED STATES BECAUSE OF VISA OR IMMIGRATION STATUS ☐ NO ☐ YES CURRENT VISA STATUS	HAVE YOU EVER BEEN CONVICTED OF A CRIME

EDUCATIONAL RECORD

SCHOOLS	NAME & LOCATION	COURSES	ATTENDED FROM MO.	YR.	TO MO.	YR.	DEGREE
HIGH OR PREP		ACAD. COMM. VOC.					
COLLEGE		MAJOR MINOR					
POST GRADUATE, BUSINESS SCHOOL, OR OTHER							

EMPLOYMENT RECORD

NAME OF EMPLOYER (PRESENT OR MOST RECENT) ADDRESS	STARTED: DATE
YOUR POSITION NAME AND TITLE OF IMMEDIATE SUPERIOR	SALARY
DESCRIPTION OF DUTIES	LEFT: DATE
REASON FOR LEAVING	SALARY

NAME OF EMPLOYER ADDRESS	STARTED: DATE
YOUR POSITION NAME AND TITLE OF IMMEDIATE SUPERIOR	SALARY
DESCRIPTION OF DUTIES	LEFT: DATE
REASON FOR LEAVING	SALARY

NAME OF EMPLOYER ADDRESS	STARTED: DATE
YOUR POSITION NAME AND TITLE OF IMMEDIATE SUPERIOR	SALARY
DESCRIPTION OF DUTIES	LEFT: DATE
REASON FOR LEAVING	SALARY

Figure 1–7
Nondiscriminatory Application Form

23

If a section of the form does not apply, mark it N/A.

put "to be discussed" or "negotiable." Don't give the impression of avoiding the issue by leaving it blank.

- When filling out the form, be conscious of its possible permanence. If hired, your form will go into the company's personnel file, so keep it free of crossouts or strikeovers.

- In the employment section of most forms there is usually a space for the applicant to state the reason for leaving a previous position. (See figure 1–7.) This can be a difficult section to answer, particularly if you have been released or fired from a position. If the position you were terminated from was not held for any appreciable length of time, it may be better to not list it at all. Your answer in this section should be brief and honest. You should be careful not to give an employer any reason to believe you are an undesirable employee. Some answers are self-explanatory—"laid-off due to a reduction in force," "part-time position," or "work for hire on temporary assignment." If you were terminated for a personality conflict, you may state as much. This sometimes is the case in terminations, and you are not to blame for the circumstances.

In general, you will find that the application form is yet another opportunity for you to assess yourself, your skills, and your personal qualities, and to communicate them to others. It would be a good idea for you to study the questions asked on the application form shown in this chapter; the forms you will be asked to fill out when you go for interviews will usually list the same questions. If you are well prepared, your application form will reinforce your application letter and résumé, and add to your confidence as you meet the interviewer.

KEY TERMS

job services center
clearinghouse
fee paid
DOE

EOE
résumé
GPA
chronological résumé

functional résumé
bona fide occupational
   qualification (BFOQ)
application letter

TEST YOURSELF:
QUESTIONS FOR REVIEW AND DISCUSSION

1. If your school did not have a placement service and you wished to apply for a job in a certain major city, what would be your sources of information concerning job vacancies?
2. Describe the two forms of résumé. What are the advantages of each?
3. As a recent graduate, which résumé form would you choose? As an experienced professional?
4. What are three good ways to start an application letter?
5. Describe the three important paragraphs of an application letter.
6. How should you deal with illegal questions on an application form?

APPLICATION EXERCISES

The following letters have many errors in content and mechanics. There are at least five mistakes in each letter. Circle the mistakes.

1.   March 8, 19––

   Potomac Research
   1200 Mt. Vernon Avenue
   Alexandria, VA 22308

   Dear Sirs:

   I happened to be reading the newspaper and say your ad for a receptionist. Could I have an interview with you?

   I feel I would make a godo receptionist for you company because I like to work with people. I've had very little experience but I'm willing to learn.

   If you are interested, give me a call.

   Best wishes,

   Janet Marker

2. June 5, 19‑‑

Walker Enterprises
55 West Indiana Street
Chicago, Illinois 60620

To Whom It May Concern:

I'm about to graduate from college and I'm in need of a job. Do you have any openings?

My major in college was accounting, but I'm also interested in management or sales. I'm sure I could fit into any of those areas.

My grade point average was low, but that's because I had to work besides go to college so you can see I am ambitious.

For an interview, call me at (612) 555‑0449.

Yours forever,

Mark Gerber

Suggested Readings

Bolles, Richard Nelson. *What Color Is Your Parachute?* Berkeley, Calif.: Ten Speed Press, published annually.

College Placement Annual. College Placement Council: 62 Highland Ave., Bethlehem, Pa. 18017, published annually.

Corwen, Leonard. *Your Job—Where to Find It, How to Get It.* New York: ARCO Publishing, Inc., 1981.

Irish, Richard K. *Go Hire Yourself an Employer.* Garden City, N.Y.: Anchor Books, 1978.

Kocher, Eric. *International Jobs—Where They Are, How to Get Them.* Reading, Mass.: Addison–Wesley, 1979.

Lewis, Adele. *How to Write Better Résumés*, rev. ed. Woodbury, N.Y.: Barron, 1983.

McLaughlin, John E., and Stephen K. Merman. *Writing a Job-Winning Résumé.* Englewood Cliffs, N.J.: Prentice-Hall, 1980.

Molloy, John T., *Live For Success*. New York: William Morrow & Co., Inc., Perigord Press, 1981.

Reed, Jean. *Résumés That Get Jobs*, 3rd. ed. New York: Arco Publishing, Inc., 1981.

2

THE
INTERVIEW

COMPREHENSIVE GOAL
To prepare you for a job interview

SPECIFIC OBJECTIVES
After reading this chapter, you will be able to:

- anticipate and respond to an interviewer's questions

- choose appropriate dress for the interview

- display the qualities of initiative, attitude, and courtesy looked for by interviewers

- conduct an interview

- distinguish between lawful and unlawful questions

- evaluate the interview process

If your résumé and application letter have created a good impression, you will be invited for an interview. This screening process often creates mental images of stern-faced executives firing complex questions at you. Erase that thought and compare the interview to the discovery stage of a new friendship; consider it as a get-acquainted session. Basically, interviewers are strangers who want to get to know you. Their purpose is to find the right person for the job.

Before the Interview

Although "be yourself—act natural" is valid advice, this does not excuse you from thorough preparation for the interview. After all, you've spent a considerable amount of time developing marketable job skills. The short time spent in the interview can determine your future use of those skills. Don't be like the confident graduate whose uncle arranged an interview for her. This young woman felt her high grades, good references, and strong educational background were sufficient for gaining employment. She did not bother to prepare for the interview. She did not get the job. On her return, the rejected niece had a sad tale for her uncle. When he asked her why the interview had gone so badly, she could only reply, "I guess I didn't know what an interview was all about." Don't let great jobs slip by because you are unprepared. In order to present yourself successfully, you should project a professional, businesslike image. Consider the following points on preparation, appearance, attitude, initiative, and courtesy.

Think of the interview as a getting-acquainted session.

PREPARATION

An interview requires more time than just that spent in the personnel or interviewer's office. Thought should be given to questions that might be asked during the session. One difficult but frequently asked question is, "What are your weaknesses?" It requires more than a snappy reply. Another favorite query of employers is, "Why should I hire you?" Be ready with a convincing answer.

One good way to prepare yourself for your interview is to practice answering the questions listed here. Ask a friend or member of your family to play the roler of interviewer while you run through a mock interview. You might also find it helpful to tape-record the session and play it back.

TYPICAL INTERVIEW QUESTIONS

1. Tell me about yourself.
2. Why are you looking for a job?
3. Why do you feel qualified for this job?
4. Why should I hire you?
5. Why would you like to work for our company?
6. What is there about this job that appeals to you?
7. What academic subjects did you like best? Least?
8. Why did you major in this field?
9. Describe the traits of a good boss.
10. What have you learned from your previous job?
11. What are your goals for the next two years? The next five?
12. Name three accomplishments you've achieved in the last two years.

Rehearsing with a friend will help you prepare for your interview.

13. What do you do in your spare time?
14. What are your weaknesses?
15. Are you willing to relocate?
16. Have you ever held a position of authority or responsibility?
17. Are you active in any organizations?
18. Will you be able to travel?
19. Will you be able to work overtime on occasion?
20. Why did you choose this career?
21. Can you describe a typical day on your present (or previous) job?
22. Have you ever been fired or asked to resign?
23. What is the ideal job for you?

Learn to be specific in your answers. In order to be convincing, you must know your subject, and general statements are no evidence of knowledge. One young woman was asked, "Why do you want this job?" She replied, "Because I like people." The interviewer came back with, "If you like people so well, why don't you get a job as a waitress?" "I like people" is the sort of vague general statement that an interviewer hears many times. It would have been better for the applicant to illustrate her liking for people by citing pertinent work experience or activities involving people.

Don't memorize answers, but have an idea of what you might say to a particular question. It is possible that very few of the listed questions will be asked, but the mental preparation is still not in vain. The time you spend in planning will give you a confidence that will be reflected in your manner during the interview.

APPEARANCE

Appearance is important. Certainly, it is superficial and unfair to be judged by how you look and dress, but it is one of the few factors by which the interviewer can assess you. Remember, you are a complete stranger. If you walk into a personnel director's office wearing sloppy clothes, how will this person perceive you? Why should he or she bother with you, when fifty other well-groomed applicants are waiting for the job? You may be far more qualified than the other fifty, but if you neglect your appearance, the interviewer may assume that you will neglect your work. Why take chances? Clothes and grooming do make a statement about you.

What attire is acceptable for the interview? The answer varies from one type of company to another and from one geographical location to another. If, before the interview, you can determine what employees typically wear at the firm in question, you have a guide for your apparel. A company's *dress code*, which spells out acceptable office attire, may be formal or informal. Find out if three-piece vested suits are preferred for the male employees or if casual sport

Do you consider this applicant appropriately attired for an interview?

A tailored, well-fitting suit will make a good impression.

jackets are permitted. See if the women wear pantsuits or skirts and dresses. Dress according to the image of the company and the demands of the job. For example, a woman who is being interviewed for a public relations position would be wise to wear a tailored jacket and skirt. On the other hand, if she is to be in a cubicle handling paper instead of dealing with people, casual clothes might be suitable for an interview.

If you still feel unsure about how to dress for a specific interview, you might want to consult one of the popular guides published on this subject. Among them are *Dress for Success* and *The Woman's Dress for Success Book*, both by John T. Molloy, and *You Are What You Wear*, by William Thourlby.

If you cannot find out what clothing style is generally accepted, then choose conservative business attire. Disregard your high-fashion clothes, and select a tailored, well-fitting suit in a neutral or dark color. Complement this suit with a white or pastel shirt or blouse, and accessorize conservatively.

Bearded males must decide whether to have a complete shave or an expert trim. A clean-shaven face was a must years ago, but in a national college survey, nearly half the firms queried said they would now accept beards and mustaches if they were well-trimmed and not extreme. Handlebar mustaches, for example, were considered extreme. One graduate claims that he landed his position as systems analyst for a sporting goods manufacturing firm because of his beard. When he went to the interview, he was met by a bearded personnel director, who later introduced him to the president of the company, who also had a beard. It became obvious to the young man that the corporate image was one of casualness and rugged individualism; his bearded appearance fit the corporate style.

Be conservative with make-up and jewelry, and pay attention to details. A well-coordinated outfit can go unnoticed if there is a distracting spot on the collar. One interviewer said she notices a person's hair, nails, and shoes. She maintains that if applicants don't take care about details such as these for a special appointment, their day-to-day appearance will be sloppy. Moreover, concern for the details of physical appearance can indicate carefulness about work-related duties.

ATTITUDE

During the interview, you communicate to the interviewer your feelings about yourself, about the company, and about the job. You have to demonstrate an attitude of confidence and competence. Remember, the company is not out there waiting to give you a job. It is looking for someone who will be an asset to the firm and who will help increase its profits. Some of the qualities an employer looks for in a job candidate are enthusiasm, confidence, and organizational skills. Don't enter the interview with the attitude "I need a job" or, on the other hand, "You owe me a job." Rather, go in intending to prove that the business will benefit from hiring you.

As Molloy states in *Live for Success:*

Your attitude makes a difference.

> It doesn't make any difference what question they ask. The answer they want is always the same. The answer is the 'can-do' answer. They will smile and hire you if you say I want to work at this company because I can do X, Y, and Z. If you give them a realistic set of goals that fit the job, you're likely to get it. I believe I can help this company accomplish its sales goals. I believe I can sell widgets, computers, or anything else. This is what they're looking for, a can-do attitude.[1]

[1]John T. Molloy, *Live for Success* (William Morrow & Co., Inc., Perigord Press, 1981), p. 82.

Communicate your feelings about yourself, about the company, and about the job.

Sometimes the attitude a company is looking for is an unconventional one. During the course of one interview, the personnel director asked the young man he was interviewing, "What is your philosophy of life?" After some thought, the applicant responded, "That's a dumb question." He got the job. This is *not* a recommended procedure, but in this instance the young man displayed an aggressive quality needed for the difficult position of bill collector for a bank.

One specific area where your attitude toward yourself as a professional can be evident is in the area of illegal questioning. If the interviewer asks a personal question (as discussed later in this chapter and in table 2–1) that you do not feel is pertinent to the job's duties, you do not have to answer it.

Occasionally you will be asked to take a skills test in an area that does not apply to the job for which you are being interviewed. Feel free to question the interviewer about the purpose of the test.

INITIATIVE

Employers today find that many graduates with excellent grades lack the initiative needed to take over a responsible job. Consequently, interviewers are alert for any display of this quality. You can demonstrate initiative both prior to the interview and during the interview.

An applicant who has researched the company and is prepared with specific questions and comments that indicate his or her ability to make a contribution to the company demonstrates initiative. Sometimes, of course, this preliminary research will not be possible,

Reading annual reports is a good way to demonstrate initiative.

as in cases where you go to an employment agency and are sent by them directly to an interview. But even company recruiters on college campuses where interviews have been set up ahead of time complain that the majority of student applicants know nothing about the company that is recruiting them. The recruiters find that most graduating seniors are interested only in getting a job and are not really concerned about the company itself. Frequently students will hurry from a class to a campus-based interview without advance planning. Some interviewees hardly know the name of the company, much less its products or services. Why should a firm show interest in an applicant of this nature?

Television and radio personality Paul Harvey told of an unemployed man during the Depression, when hundreds of thousands of people were out of work, who managed to secure three job offers in two days. He did this by first researching the companies thoroughly. Then he astonished interviewers by showing how his expertise could help them.

There is no easy formula for the applicant to follow in order to demonstrate initiative during the interview. But be aware of its importance and utilize any opportunity to display it. You may be able to bring up aspects of your work or educational experience that show an ability to take charge or to work independently. Skills tests during an interview may provide you with a chance to show initiative. For example, one employer makes a practice of dictating a letter to all secretarial applicants. He then has the applicants type the letter. He has found that nine out of ten applicants will return a finished copy that contains misspelled words. (What he is looking for is not good spellers, but people with initiative. For this reason, he puts a dictionary beside the typewriter.)

COURTESY

Courtesy is more than just the social graces, proper dress, and polite manners, although all of these can influence the interview.

Hazel Hankin

Shake hands firmly.

A follow-up letter will show courtesy and interest.

Courtesy means being aware of the other person's feelings. For instance, learn the interviewer's name and its correct pronunciation. If the last name is an unusual one and you pronounce it correctly, you are not only courteous, but you will also leave a good impression.

During the introductions, shake hands firmly. Wait for an invitation or a gesture to be seated. Plunging into the nearest chair could cause some awkward moments if the interviewer had another seating arrangement in mind.

Don't light a cigarette unless invited to do so, and don't chew gum. Be careful not to dominate the conversation; let the interviewer lead it.

After an interval of questions and answers, you may conclude that the interview is winding down. However, let the interviewer initiate the closing remarks, rather than suggesting yourself that it is time to go. Remember, the interviewer is in control of the situation. Some interviews last thirty minutes, some last for hours, depending on circumstances and company policies. When the interviewer stands and extends his or her hand, follow the cue, offer your thanks, and then leave.

The next day, write a thank you note expressing your appreciation for the interview. Such a letter exhibits courtesy on your part and also keeps your name up front with other contenders.

The follow-up letter need not be elaborate, but should be sincere. Note the following example:

Dear Mr. Brewer:

Thank you for giving me the opportunity to interview for the position of staff accountant with Black & Black, Inc. After considerable evaluation, I wanted to inform you that I'm very interested in employment with your firm.

I appreciate your thorough explanation of the company and its policies. Black & Black, Inc. has much to offer an ambitious young person. I await your decision and can be contacted at (402) 555-3944.

Sincerely,

If you do not receive a response from the employer after a reasonable period of time, you can telephone. The follow-up phone call was discussed in chapter 1. There is no reason to be afraid of inquiring about the status of a position you have been interviewed for.

The Right Company for You

Your main concern to this point has been how to prepare and present yourself successfully. But you are not the only one up for inspection. You are evaluating an organization in which you are going to invest a major part of your future. You want to work for a firm that gives you a sense of pride, self-respect, and satisfaction.

KNOWLEDGE OF THE COMPANY

An excellent way to investigate a company is to study its *annual report*. This report will tell you about the firm's financial standing, growth, types of products and proposals for new products, its history, the location of its home and branch offices, and the image it wishes to project to the public. You may find some annual reports in your local library. If the one you want is not there, ask for *Standard & Poor's Register of Corporations, Directors and Executives* to get the address of the corporation, as well as the name of its personnel director or the head of the division in which you are interested.

If the company is a privately owned firm, information about it may be a bit more difficult to uncover. If possible, ask questions of the firm's employees about its policies, its growth, and its products, or talk to competitors' employees about their impressions of the firm.

CORPORATE IMAGE

Matching personality with company is just as important as matching skills with job duties. Will your attitudes, values, and beliefs coincide with those of the company's *corporate image*—the mental conception people have of it? This is an area that should be explored before accepting a job.

A publication of Standard & Poor's Corp.

You can research companies with the aid of this reference.

Figure 2–1
A corporate symbol is a visual means of conveying a company's image.

Ask yourself, "What does this company represent? What type of image does it project to its public? Is it one of dignity, stability, and dependability? Does it have a reputation for being modern and progressive? Is its atmosphere formal or casual? Does its image fit my values?"

There are several ways you can judge a company's image. Check its advertising and the quality of its products or services. When you go to the interview, notice the building and office furnishings. If the offices have antiquated equipment and run-down furnishings, would you be happy working there? True, you don't need plush carpeting or expensive wall paneling to work effectively, but a well-equipped office makes a nine-to-five job a little easier.

Going to the interview ten or fifteen minutes early is good advice for numerous reasons. First, if you don't allow ample time and something unexpected happens, you may be late for the inter-

While waiting for your interview, you can absorb some of the company's atmosphere.

view. Second, arriving early gives you a chance to organize your thoughts before you go into the interviewer's office. Finally, the few minutes wait provides some time for absorbing the company's atmosphere and listening to the conversation of the employees. Do they sound happy, pressured, or hostile? Is there a predominantly positive or negative attitude displayed?

Encourage the interviewer to talk about the firm, perhaps by asking questions about its products and services. This serves two good purposes. You learn about the company, and you exchange personal opinion. The more of these exchanges, the better are your chances. Eli Djeddah advises in *Moving Up*, "When your executive is talking never take the stage away from him. A good interview, in fact, is one in which the other man talks for two hours and you talk for ten minutes."[2]

Evaluate the environment and ask yourself if you really want to work for the firm. Don't sell your self-esteem for a monthly paycheck.

FINANCES

Before you participate in an interview, have a good idea of the typical starting salary for the job you want. Such information is not difficult to obtain. Review the want ads, question teachers in your major, ask professionals in the field, or inquire at your state employment office about the range offered in your area.

Besides knowing the general salary range, determine how much you will need for your fixed expenses. Prepare a budget that covers all monthly living expenses. Your salary should provide you with the essentials plus some extras, or you won't be content with the job.

Generally, you do not bring up the subject of salary during the interview. Let the interviewer do that. He or she may introduce the topic by asking, "What kind of salary do you expect?" Answer with a noncommittal, "I know what the average starting salary for this position is in other companies. What is your range?" If you mention a specific salary first, you may go too high or, worse, too low. Be ready to negotiate and discuss. Don't take the first offer. In your negotiations, explore the company's policy regarding raises. Perhaps these will compensate for a low starting salary.

Have confidence in your self-worth, your training, talent, and enthusiasm. One young woman learned the value of self-esteem quite by chance. During the interview, she learned that the salary was much lower than she had expected. Believing her time was worth more than the salary offered, she declined the job. Two days later, she was again offered the job, but with a higher salary, a better title, and her own office. If you truly believe you are worth more

[2]Eli Djeddah, *Moving Up* (Berkeley, Calif.: Ten Speed Press, 1978), p. 91.

Check salary ranges in the help-wanted ads.

than the salary offered, don't settle for less. But one word of caution: Some students have an inflated idea of their abilities. They expect an executive pay scale for entry-level experience and education. Be realistic.

COMPANY EMPLOYMENT POLICIES

Salary should not be the only factor in your decision. The company's promotion policies, probationary periods, evaluation systems, self-improvement programs, and employee benefits are increasingly important. Be sure to ask about medical and dental coverage.

Find out what the company's promotion policy is. Will management review your work and then promote you on the basis of your ability and productivity? If the company is family owned, are all the key positions filled with relatives? Will promotions be regular or will you be in the same position until your supervisor retires?

Does the company have a *probationary period*? How long does it last? How long are you considered a trainee—two weeks, three months, six months? In short, when are you considered a regular member of the staff?

Are workers evaluated by a logical method or according to the boss's preferences for blue eyes and flattering comments? Is work performance checked regularly or only when things are going wrong? If your interviewer answers your inquiry about promotion policy with "We use the MBO method," there is no need to be puzzled. MBO (*management by objectives*) is a popular evaluating technique. On a one-to-one basis, you and your supervisor arrive at the objectives or goals that you would like to achieve over a period

David Moskowitz

Insurance is usually among the fringe benefits companies offer their employees.

An in-house workshop may be used to evaluate the quality of work performance.

of time. After that predetermined time, the supervisor reviews your work to determine if you are approaching these prescribed goals. MBO is generally considered a very effective approach to employee evaluation.

Ask the personnel director if the company offers any self-improvement programs. Does the firm hold in-house workshops to improve the quality of work performance? If you wanted to take a college course that related to your job duties, would the company pay for the course?

Near the end of the interview inquire about employee benefits. Most companies offer *fringe benefits*, such as vacations, retirement plans, and insurance programs that can mean money in your pocket but never show on the weekly or monthly paycheck. Does this company offer a paid vacation after a year's employment? What is its sick-leave policy? How about group insurance benefits? Expense accounts? Company car?

You should ask these questions not only to protect yourself but also to remind the interviewer that you are seeking the company that best suits your needs.

The Other Side of the Desk

The last section of this chapter will show you how to conduct an interview. At first, this information may appear unnecessary to the entry-level applicant, but by placing yourself in a different vantage point you can better understand the interviewer and his or her

A company car is a fringe benefit of some jobs.

expectations, techniques, and procedures. Besides, these skills may be useful in your future, whether you have your own business, manage an office, or become a personnel director.

PREPARING FOR THE INTERVIEW

Just as the applicant must prepare, so must the interviewer. Before the interview begins, interviewers should familiarize themselves with the résumé and the application letter, as well as the job description and requirements, and prepare suitable questions relating to the position.

A seating arrangement should be considered before the interviewee arrives. Following are two popular seating arrangements that tend to remove barriers between applicant and interviewer. Because the participants are placed on an equal basis, both arrangements enhance communication.

Some interviewers prefer a massive desk between themselves and the applicant, as a symbol of authority and power, or possibly as a protective partition. Whatever the reason for the arrangement, communication can be somewhat inhibited.

Other seating arrangements include such casual ones as two easy chairs or a couch and an easy chair. Most interviewers try to make the interviewee as relaxed as possible: In a friendly, non-threatening atmosphere, the candidate is likely to respond more fully and honestly to questions.

After an applicant has entered the room, it is up to the interviewer to extend some courteous gestures—a hand of greeting, an invitation to be seated, or perhaps an offer of a cigarette or coffee. After introductions, light conversation will help put the newcomer at ease and lead into the serious business of the interview.

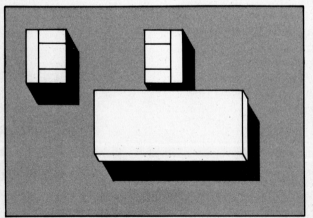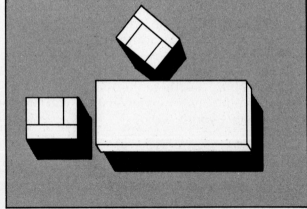

Figure 2–2
These seating arrangements promote unimpeded communication between interviewer and applicant.

INTERVIEWING TECHNIQUES

Most skilled interviewers develop a combination of approaches designed to draw the applicant out. These techniques are used not only by personnel directors, but also by salespeople, counselors, and good communicators of any kind.

Open-Ended Questions *Open-ended questions* are broad, general questions, such as "What did you like about college?" "What do you do in your spare time?" "What do you consider were your most valuable college courses?" They give the job seeker a chance to display his or her strong points, and special skills and aptitudes, and help the interviewer to uncover personality traits that may not be revealed otherwise.

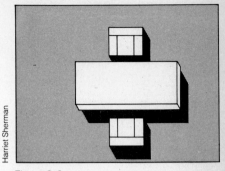

Figure 2–3
This seating arrangement can be intimidating to the applicant.

Close-Ended Questions *Close-ended questions* are very narrow and specific. For example, "Can you type?" "Have you had a course in computer science?" "Do you speak a foreign language?" "Would you be free to travel?" are queries that zero in on one significant point. They may put the interviewee at a disadvantage because he or she might be weak in those areas, but they are necessary for the interviewer to put the right person in the right job.

Probing Questions *Probing questions* may be asked when the interviewer is suspicious that information is being withheld. The following is an example:

Mrs. Miller: What was your grade average in your major field?
Mr. James: Ah, mostly B's.

A casual seating arrangement encourages easy communication.

Surprise questions are designed to test the applicant's ability to handle pressure.

Mrs. Miller:	What were the rest of your grades, then?
Mr. James:	A few A's and C's.
Mrs. Miller:	Would you describe yourself as a B or a C student?
Mr. James:	A high C student.
Mrs. Miller:	What prevented you from doing better?

Mrs. Miller suspects that Mr. James's average for his major is lower than he implies, so she probes more deeply to determine the extent of the problem.

Surprise Questions   *Surprise questions* are used to judge how well a person can handle pressure. Questions like "Why should I hire you?" "Why did you select this firm?" "Tell me about yourself," posed at an unexpected point in the interview, can unsettle the best of applicants *unless* they are prepared.

Mirror Technique   The *mirror technique* is best explained by using a sample dialogue:

Ms. Rourke:	What do you plan to be doing in five years?
Ms. Trebbie:	Studying for my *doctorate* in psychology.
Ms. Rourke:	Oh, are you interested in getting your *doctorate*?
Ms. Trebbi:	Yes, it is one of my *goals*.
Ms. Rourke:	Why have you selected this as a *goal*?
Ms. Trebbi:	I want to *help other people*.
Ms. Rourke:	What do you mean, *help other people*?
Ms. Trebbi:	I think I'm a humanitarian person. I want to put my *talents* to work for other people.
Ms. Rourke:	What are some of your specific *talents*?

Notice that throughout the discourse Ms. Rourke doesn't comment favorably or unfavorably; she sends ideas right back to Ms. Trebbi. Follow the italicized words through the dialogue, and see how Ms. Rourke picks the key concept, repeats it, and develops it into another question.

Block of Silence   Mastering this technique isn't as difficult as it may seem. Somewhere in the middle of the interview, the interviewer deliberately discontinues the dialogue, then observes how the interviewee handles the *block of silence*. Generally, an insecure person will feel obligated to chatter away or fidget with something. On the other hand, a confident person will remain calm and patiently wait for the next question. (This silent pause can also provide the interviewer with the opportunity to organize his or her thoughts for more questioning.)

Nonverbal Communication   Good interviewers are aware of what is being communicated by *nonverbal communication*—the interviewee's body movements, gestures, and facial expressions—and are careful to control their own. (For example, a hunched-over posture says "I'm depressed" or "I'm afraid.") On their own part, they try not to influence the applicant's answers by their own posture, gestures, or facial expressions. They keep note taking to a minimum to prevent unnecessary distraction.

Would you hire this applicant?

How you present yourself during an interview is important.

Areas for Questioning

The questions an interviewer asks should be developed in order to uncover as many aspects of the applicant's personality as possible. Note in the following table the possibilities for both open- and close-ended questions.

Subject	Sample Questions
Work background	What did you learn from your previous job?
	What were your duties as mail clerk?
Educational background	Do you feel you received a good education at your school?
	In what way did that education prepare you for this job?
	What courses did you take?
	What was your favorite course?
Motivation	What are your goals?
	Why did you choose this particular career?
Personality	How would you describe yourself?
	What qualities do you most admire in other people?
	What qualities do you most admire in a boss?

UNLAWFUL QUESTIONS

Since passage of Title VII of the Civil Rights Act of 1964, the Equal Pay Act of 1963, the Age Discrimination in Employment Act of 1967, and the publication of executive orders related to them, an interviewer must be careful in his or her choice of questions.

Any questions on the subject of religion, sex, color, race, age, or national origin are potentially discriminatory and unlawful. If such questions are asked and the applicant is not hired, he or she may feel justified in filing a complaint at the local office of the Equal Employment Opportunity Commission (EEOC). You should therefore consider each question carefully before asking it in an interview.

If you are asked an illegal question that you don't care to answer, be tactful in your reply. One young lady used the following reply: "I'm here because I feel I'm well qualified for the position. My personal life will not have any bearing on my work performance, therefore I don't feel I need to answer that particular question."

However you answer, keep the statement honest and sincere. Watch the tonal quality of your voice so that you don't sound angry or threatened. If the message is delivered well, you will still be considered a contender for the position.

Consult table 2–1 for a list of possibly illegal questions.

After the Interview

The interview is over. You have followed the preceding suggestions. You have produced a professional résumé, a persuasive application letter, worn appropriate clothing to the interview, remembered the correct pronunciation of the interviewer's name, answered the questions fully. Now you wait for an affirmative sign.

Instead, you hear, "Sorry, we chose a more qualified applicant." Don't consider this rejection a personal veto. There could be many reasons why you weren't hired, none of which reflect on you personally. The principle reason could be, very simply, that you weren't the right person for this particular job. Perhaps you lacked skills or experience. Or perhaps a completely unpredictable reason could have caused the interviewer to decide against you. One interviewer may be seeking a vivacious kind of person, another a more quiet sort. You cannot be "all things to all people"; first of all, you must be yourself.

Use the experience gained from one interview to prepare yourself for the next one. Remember the difference between success and failure is often your degree of stubbornness. A failure accepts defeat, or blames someone else; a success will use defeat as a lesson and begin again.

When you do hear the two words "You're hired," a part of your world will change. You will find yourself working with a group of

Table 2–1

QUESTIONS THAT MAY BE DISCRIMINATORY

Problem Areas	Potentially Dangerous Questions	Reason for Discriminatory Nature
Marital status	Are you married? What is your spouse's occupation? What is your spouse's full name?	Questions of this nature tend to discriminate against women. Some firms do not like to hire married women, but will hire married men.
Dependents	Do you have children? What ages are your children? Do you plan to have children?	This is another area in which discrimination against women may occur. The number of children and their ages would be of little significance in the hiring of a man, but many employers hesitate to hire a woman with small children because they fear frequent absenteeism.
Credit	Do you have any debts? Have you saved any money? Do you have a good credit rating? Do you own your own home?	Minority-group incomes tend to be lower than the national average; therefore, these questions may discriminate against minorities.
Age	How old are you? What is your birth date?	As a result of the Age Discrimination in Employment Act, it is unlawful to ask a person's age. The reason for this is to protect qualified applicants over forty from being bypassed for younger employees. However, if there is a minimum age requirement, such as eighteen or twenty-one, it is permissible to ask age of younger applicants.
Religion	Do you attend church? Can you work on Saturday or Sunday? How do you usually spend Sundays?	Some religions forbid their members to work on Saturday or Sunday. This form of questioning could therefore be directly discriminatory. However, if there is a proven need for the employee to be available for work on weekends, the question can be asked.
Arrests or convictions	Have you ever been arrested?	If is unlawful to ask about arrests, but not about convictions if they relate to specific jobs.
Bonding	Have you ever been refused bond? Are you bondable?	These questions are unlawful if they are used to elicit information about the applicant's character. However, they are permissible if the employee must be bonded.
Citizenship	Are you an American citizen?	Lawfully immigrated aliens have every right to employment in the United States. Any questions designed to reveal a person's nationality are discriminatory and potentially unlawful. Direct questioning is permitted, however, if the job has national security implications.
Lowest salary	What is the lowest salary you will accept?	This question has frequently been directed toward women applicants, in the hope that they would accept lower pay than men for the same job. Discussion of salary is permissible, but to phrase the question in this manner is unlawful.
Garnishment	Have your wages ever been garnisheed?	In some states, garnishment of salary is illegal. The answer in any case has no bearing on work performance and serves to discriminate against minorities.
Relatives working for same firm	Do you have any relatives working in this firm?	Sometimes company policy prohibits more than one family member from working for the firm. This policy usually discriminates against women, as it is most often a male family member who is already employed.
Handicaps or health problems	What is the state of your health? Do you have any handicaps?	Only if these questions relate directly to the job may they be asked.

Leaving the interview.

unfamiliar people. You will be faced with a new set of challenges. Your life-style will change; even your wardrobe and appearance will assume a different significance.

The following chapters will help you prepare for those changes. However, preparation for the career world is not the only message of this text. It also places strong emphasis on how to develop your personal qualities and skills in order to become an effective, promotable employee who will eventually become a successful executive or manager.

The experience that you have gained in going through the interview process will prepare you for comparable situations on the job. You will be involved daily in interpersonal encounters. Be prepared. Be confident. Be yourself.

KEY TERMS

dress code
annual report
corporate image
probationary period
management by
    objectives (MBO)

fringe benefits
open-ended questions
close-ended questions
probing questions
surprise questions

mirror technique
block of silence
nonverbal
    communication

1. What is meant by the term "dress code"?
2. How should you decide what to wear to an interview?
3. What is a block of silence? How should you respond to it?
4. If an interviewer asks you a question that you feel is an infringement on your privacy or is an illegal question, how would you answer it? If you felt you were not selected for a job as a result of discrimination, what could you do?
5. Many job counselors say the time to be looking at promotion is during the interview. What questions could you ask during the interview to determine promotion possibilities? In what ways can you display qualities that will demonstrate your growth potential?
6. After the interview is completed, how should you follow up? How can even an unsuccessful interview be useful to you?

APPLICATION EXERCISE

Pick out the mistakes that the interviewee has made and discuss them.

Interviewer:	Why should I hire you?
Interviewee:	Because I like people.
Interviewer:	Why do you think you like people?
Interviewee:	I don't know. I just like to be around people better than I like being alone.
Interviewer:	What would you say are your strengths?
Interviewee:	I'm dependable, hard working, and have a good education.
Interviewer:	What are your weaknesses?
Interviewee:	Ah, er, I don't have any.
Interviewer:	When could you start working for us?
Interviewee:	Well, I would like to take a vacation first. I've been busy with college studies, and I think I deserve a break. I suppose I would be ready in about a month and a half.
Interviewer:	What do you know about our company?
Interviewee:	I am, I, well let's see. I do know you sell wieners and cold meat because I've seen your commercial on TV.

Suggested Readings

College Placement Annual. College Placement Council: 62 Highland Ave., Bethlehem, Pa., 18017, published annually.

Djeddah, Eli. *Moving Up*. Berkeley, Calif: Ten Speed Press, 1978.

Molloy, John T. *Dress for Success*. New York: Warner Books, 1975.

Molloy, John T. *Live for Success*. New York: William Morrow & Co., Inc., Perigord Press, 1981.

Molloy, John T. *The Woman's Dress for Success Book*. New York: Warner Books, 1978.

Olson, Richard F. *Managing the Interview*. New York: John Wiley & Sons, Inc., 1980.

Stewart, Charles J. *Interviewing Principles and Practices*. Dubuque, IA: Wm. C. Brown Co., Kendall-Hunt, 1980.

Thourlby, William. *You Are What You Wear*. New York: New American Library, 1978.

PART TWO

PROJECTING YOUR IMAGE

Throughout your career, your success will be influenced by the visual image you project to others. That image is determined by grooming, poise and posture, dress, and physical condition—in other words, your overall appearance. Looking good and feeling well will give you a confidence that communicates itself to those around you.

3

THE LOOK OF SUCCESS

COMPREHENSIVE GOAL
To provide information on the care of skin and hair and the principles of body cleanliness and to help you wisely purchase and use cleaning products, grooming aids, and cosmetology services.

SPECIFIC OBJECTIVES
After reading this chapter, you will be able to:

- explain the physical and chemical structure of the skin and hair
- identify skin types and determine the best cleansing methods for each
- name the causes of and treatments for acne
- understand the body chemistry involved in the tanning process
- understand the principles involved in hair grooming
- evaluate the various methods of facial and body hair removal
- differentiate between deodorants and antiperspirants
- manicure nails
- apply makeup

Just as you found it important to present an attractive appearance while securing your job, you will find it even more important to continue to present yourself attractively as you advance in your career.

You are now a professional. Does your mirror reflect a professional image? The adage, "To be successful, look successful," applies very particularly to the contemporary business world. Unhealthy hair, blemished skin, excessive or poorly applied makeup, and dirty fingernails do not send out signals of competence. A well-groomed appearance projects an image of success and an aura of self-confidence. In fact, personal appearance is often a criterion for professional evaluation. Therefore, it is important to spend some time evaluating the visual image you project and, if necessary, taking steps to improve your appearance.

This chapter will not teach you how to be handsome or beautiful. It is intended to help you take advantage of your natural features and cultivate an attractive personal and professional appearance through skin and hair care and body grooming, as well as the proper use of makeup.

Skin Care

Achieving and maintaining a healthy, attractive complexion is important to everyone. The basic principles of proper skin care are the same, no matter what your race or sex.

A short lesson on skin structure will give you a better appreciation of the eighteen square feet of living tissue that protects your body.

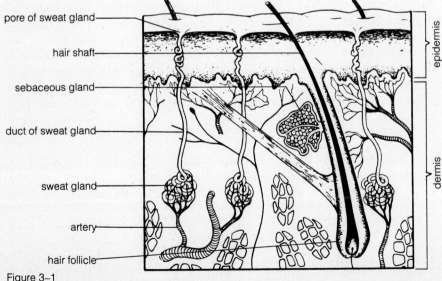

pore of sweat gland

hair shaft

sebaceous gland

duct of sweat gland

sweat gland

artery

hair follicle

epidermis

dermis

Figure 3–1
Cross Section of Skin

Figure 3–1 shows the outer skin, which consists of two layers, the epidermis and the dermis. The *epidermis*—the surface of the skin—is a layer of dead cells that serves to protect the living tissue underneath. The dead cells push up from below and gradually flake off, so this layer is in a constant state of change. (In the epidermis is found *melanin*, the brown pigment that determines the darkness of the skin. The sun can activate melanin, causing the skin to darken temporarily.)

The *dermis* is living tissue. It contains nerves, blood vessels, smooth muscles, hair follicles, sweat glands, and sebaceous glands. *Sweat glands*, which secrete liquid waste material through the pores, act as a cooling system for the body. *Sebaceous glands* secrete oil through pores containing hair follicles. When one of these pores becomes clogged, a blackhead or a whitehead forms.

Under the dermis, and not shown in the diagram, is a layer of *subcutaneous* ("beneath the skin") tissue.

THE ACID MANTLE

A great deal of controversy has focused on the subject of *pH balance* (or *acid mantle*) of the skin. Shampoos and skin preparations have chemicals that can range from high acidity (low pH balance) to high alkalinity (high pH balance).

0	4.5–5.5	14
Acid	Skin's Chemical Range	Alkaline

Many skin products today boast of being close to the skin's acid mantle range of 4.5 to 5.5. Their advertisements claim that cosmetics that are too acidic or too alkaline are harmful to the skin. On the other hand, some doctors and researchers maintain that, while the natural state of the skin is slightly acidic, a temporary change in the skin's mantle will not destroy or harm the tissue. The controversy is far from settled, and until any conclusive statement is issued, you will have to decide how important pH balance is for your skin.

SKIN TYPES

It is necessary to know your skin type in order to give it the proper cleansing and moisturizing treatment. There are four categories: dry, oily, combination, and normal. By answering these questions, you can identify your skin type.

DRY SKIN
1. Do you have small pores?
2. Is little perspiration evident on a hot day?
3. Does your face chap easily?

4. Does your skin feel taut after you cleanse it?
5. Do you sunburn easily?

An affirmative answer to all five questions indicates dry skin. Sun, wind, and extreme cold can be very unkind to such skin, so it needs additional protection from the elements.

OILY SKIN
1. Do you have large pores?
2. Do you frequently develop whiteheads or blackheads?
3. Do you perspire easily?
4. In the morning, does your face have a slick film?
5. Does your skin have a coarse texture?

If you answered "yes" to these five questions, consider yourself in the oily skin category. However, chances are good that by the time you pass the age of twenty-five, your skin will lose some of its oil.

COMBINATION SKIN
1. Are large pores evident in the forehead, nose, and chin areas?
2. Are small pores evident in the cheek and eye areas?
3. Do you find blackheads or whiteheads in the forehead, nose, and chin areas?
4. Does the skin on your cheeks feel dry after cleansing?

Three or four positive responses to the above questions indicate combination skin. This type of skin usually has an oily T-zone across

Hazel Hankin

What is your skin type?.

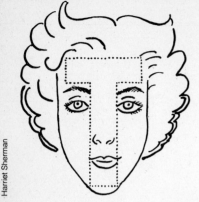

Figure 3–2
The T-Zone

the forehead and in the nose and chin areas, while the remainder of the face is dry. See figure 3–2 for an illustration of the T-zone.

NORMAL SKIN
1. Does your face have a healthy, glowing look?
2. Do you seldom have eruptions of whiteheads and black-heads?
3. Do you have smooth skin with no visible pores?
4. Does your skin feel taut after washing?
5. Does your skin have an oily film in the mornings?

If you can answer yes to the first three questions and no to questions 4 and 5, consider yourself lucky: You have perfect skin. With daily care, moderate amounts of sun, a balanced diet, and regular cleansing and moisturizing, you can continue to have the benefits of good skin.

The male reader may be beginning to feel that none of this applies to him. In fact, recent research has shown that the skin of men is different from that of women. At puberty, the production of *androgens,* or male hormones, by the male endocrine system causes men's skin to become thicker and oilier than that of women. It therefore may wrinkle and age less quickly; on the other hand, the androgen output makes many men prone to acne. The sections of this chapter on oily skin and on acne will accordingly be of particular interest to men.

A healthy, glowing look

SKIN CLEANSING

Each of the four skin types requires a special method of cleansing. The abundance of skin-care products marketed makes your choice of the correct product a difficult task.

In purchasing a soap or cleanser, don't assume that the most expensive product will give the best results. A publication of the Food and Drug Administration states, "Basically they are all similar in composition. . . . In the expensive creams you may be paying for a pretty jar, an appealing fragrance, extensive advertising and promotion or a feeling about the product which is esthetically pleasing to you."[1]

Soap is an excellent skin cleanser, especially for oily skin. However, because there are so many types on the market, the choice of soap may be confusing. The following will help clarify differences among soaps and aid you in purchasing the right soap for your skin.

Pure soap	Made from animal and vegetable fats, pure soap leaves a soap scum but is preferred to synthetics by some people.
Transparent soap	A mild soap that dissolves rapidly; it has added fat and glycerin for translucency, and is usually expensive.

[1]Margaret Morrison, "Cosmetics: The Substances Beneath the Form," *FDA Consumer,* HEW Publication No. (FDA) 78-5007 (Washington, D.C.: Government Printing Office).

Hazel Hankin

Cleansing the skin

Pure soap

Transparent soap

Detergent soap	The majority of soaps on the market are detergent. Because they do not contain fats, detergent soaps do not leave a ring around the wash basin.
Deodorant soap	This contains a fragrance and sometimes an antiseptic agent to reduce body odor.
Antibacterial soap	Extra chemicals are added to inhibit bacterial growth. Some doctors maintain, however, that certain bacteria are beneficial and that these soaps may be too strong.

While soap is an excellent cleansing product, especially for oily skin, cleansing cream is often preferred by people with dry skin. Cleansing products can be broadly categorized as dry-skin cleansers and oily-skin cleansers. Dry-skin products replace the oils lost in cleansing, whereas oily-skin products are designed to remove the natural oils. For maximum benefit, you should choose one formulated for your skin type.

No matter what your skin type, *exfoliation*—the removal of dead skin cells from the epidermis—is an important aspect of cleansing. This can be done by lightly rubbing a terry washcloth, a soft-bristled brush, or an abrasive sponge over the skin. Be careful not to scrub too hard; the purpose is to remove dead skin cells, not to take off the top layer of skin. All skin types require exfoliation because it stimulates circulation and helps cleanse the pores.

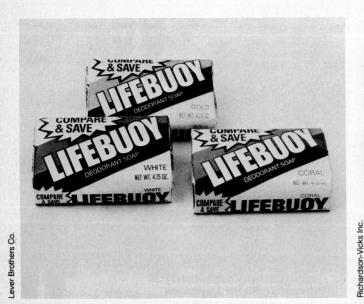

Deodorant soap

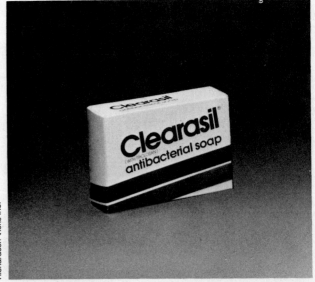

Antibacterial soap

Cleansing and care of facial skin varies according to the four types of skin. Each of the following sections prescribes specific procedures for a particular complexion.

Dry Skin A dry-skin cleanser or a transparent soap is best. Two daily washings, one in the morning and one in the evening, are sufficient for dry skin. More frequent cleansing will further dry the skin and cause it to flake.

After cleansing, rinse many times with warm water to remove soap or cleanser residue. If you want, you may next apply a skin freshener. Do not use an *astringent*—a liquid cosmetic for cleansing the skin and contracting the pores. Astringents generally contain large amounts of alcohol, which may be harsh on dry skin. Skin fresheners contain less alcohol but are not as effective in removing soap, oil, or dirt.

Oily Skin Soap is the recommended cleanser for oily skin. Frequent cleansings, four to five times a day, will remove oil from the face and help prevent clogged pores.

After a soap and water cleansing, rinse well to remove any traces of soap. Then apply an astringent to remove excess oil and to dry the skin. Contrary to popular belief, there is no evidence that use of an astringent can shrink the size of pores. It will contract the pores temporarily after application, but the effect is not permanent.

Combination Skin Read the sections both on dry and on oily skin and treat the respective areas accordingly.

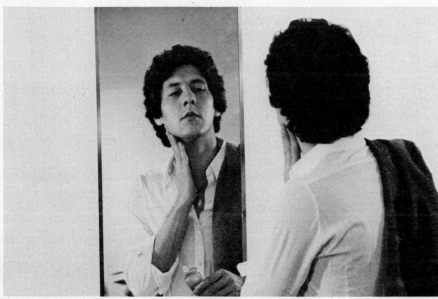

HBJ Photo

Applying a skin freshener

Applying a moisturizer

Normal Skin Continue to treat your skin with thorough cleansings. Use an astringent or a skin freshener after cleansing.

The last step in the cleansing routine for *all* skin types is moisturizing or *hydrating*. To hydrate something means to cause it to take up or to combine with water. Some skin consultants suggest hydrating the skin by splashing on warm water, then, while the face is still slightly damp from the water, applying a moisturizer to seal in the water temporarily.

A moisturizer, or skin conditioner as it is called in men's cosmetic lines, should be applied after the astringent or skin freshener. Contrary to what its name implies, a moisturizer does not put moisture back into skin; it acts as a seal and prevents moisture loss. It also helps keep the skin soft and supple. The application of a moisturizer is also important for oily skin. Oily skin has an excess of oil, not moisture. Choose a light moisturizer that does not contain heavy oils.

A special message to people with normal skin: You may not feel a need for a moisturizer, but a gradual drying process takes place as you grow older. If you do not add a moisturizer when you're young, early wrinkles formed by the natural drying process may age your complexion prematurely.

ACNE

The dictionary defines *acne* as a common skin disease characterized by chronic inflammation of the sebaceous glands. As the afflicted will agree, the definition gives no indication of the grief that even a relatively mild case of acne can cause.

Unfortunately, there is no miracle to make acne disappear. A clean face may help, but little can be done to prevent a new blemish from popping out. A change in the body's hormones causes the sebaceous glands to secrete more oil than is necessary, and as yet nothing has been discovered to regulate this inordinate flow.

Knowing the cause of acne provides little consolation, but perhaps the following suggestions can help in dealing with the inflammation and minimizing its effects.

1. Watch your diet. Although there is no scientific evidence that specific foods cause or aggravate an acne condition, certain foods should be avoided in many cases. Eliminate greasy foods, chocolates, sugars, and nuts. Snack on fresh fruits and vegetables. Healthful foods and proper nutrition benefit your skin.
2. Try to avoid stressful situations.
3. Frequent washing with soap and water or an acne cleanser will help.

4. Try steaming your face over hot water to stimulate circulation; follow with a thorough cleansing. This should be done at least three times a week. A word of caution about this method: Results have been excellent for some people, but for others steaming aggravates the acne problems.
5. Don't squeeze pimples; this often spreads infection below the skin's surface. (This is particularly important advice for black people because scar tissue builds up easily in their facial skin, resulting in permanent damage.)
6. When buying over-the-counter acne cleansers, buy products that contain sulfur, resorcinol, salicylic acid, or benzoyl peroxide. Benzoyl peroxide is the strongest of these chemicals and may be too harsh for sensitive skin. Be careful to follow the directions accompanying the cleansing product.

If the acne shows no sign of clearing up, see a *dermatologist* (skin doctor). After analysis, the dermatologist can prescribe medicating drugs, or a special diet related to your skin type and skin problems. Some doctors may prescribe a cisretinoic acid, a derivative of vitamin A, which is taken in pill form and which has proven very effective in many cases. Cortisone, cryotherapy, and cryosurgery are among the other methods that can be used by the specialist to help clear up your skin.

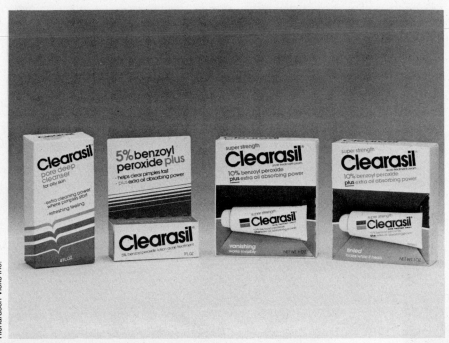

Richardson-Vicks Inc.

Over-the-counter preparations used to combat acne

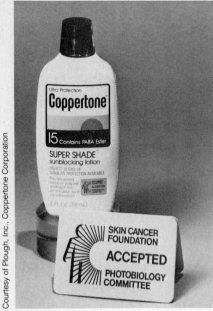

Courtesy of Plough, Inc., Coppertone Corporation

This preparation provides maximum protection from the sun's rays.

SUNTAN

A suntan has not always been considered a mark of distinction, and current medical warnings may again lead society to view deep tans as unfashionable. Chronic overexposure to the sun may rob the skin of moisture, cause premature aging and wrinkling of the skin, and increase the chances for skin cancer. On the other hand, hiding under a beach umbrella all day to protect the skin doesn't sound appealing. With the proper use of sunscreens, based on your skin type, you can enjoy outdoor activities without a sunburn and help prevent the effects of long-term overexposure to the sun.

If you want to participate in summer activities, exposure to ultraviolet rays is unavoidable. Fortunately, you can buy products that contain varying amounts of sunscreens designed to protect particular skin types from sunburn. You can determine how much protection a sunscreen product will give by looking at the number on the container. This number refers to its *Sun Protection Factor* (SPF); it will range from 2 (minimal sun protection) to 15 (ultra sun protection). If you sunburn easily, choose a product numbered between 8 and 15; if you tan easily and rarely burn, you will be safe with a 2 or 4. Most studies indicate that an SPF of 15 is the best choice for all skin types. It does not prevent tanning, but it increases the time you can be out in the sun with minimal risk. Do not use baby oil, cocoa butter, or any product without a sunscreen because they do not help filter the ultraviolet rays of the sun.

Florida Division of Tourism

Our attitudes toward suntans have changed over the years. Compare this picture with the one opposite.

ELEVEN NATURALS FOR GOOD EATING.

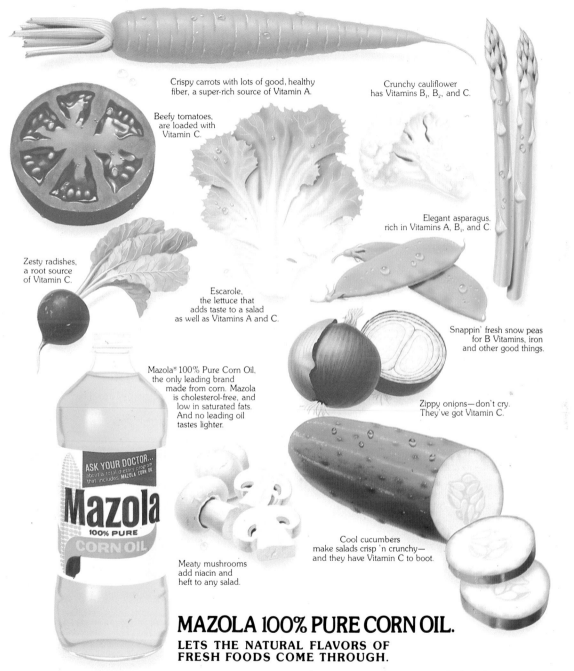

Crispy carrots with lots of good, healthy fiber, a super-rich source of Vitamin A.

Crunchy cauliflower has Vitamins B$_1$, B$_2$, and C.

Beefy tomatoes, are loaded with Vitamin C.

Elegant asparagus. rich in Vitamins A, B$_1$, and C.

Zesty radishes, a root source of Vitamin C.

Escarole, the lettuce that adds taste to a salad as well as Vitamins A and C.

Snappin' fresh snow peas for B Vitamins, iron and other good things.

Mazola® 100% Pure Corn Oil, the only leading brand made from corn. Mazola is cholesterol-free, and low in saturated fats. And no leading oil tastes lighter.

Zippy onions—don't cry. They've got Vitamin C.

ASK YOUR DOCTOR... about a total dietary program that includes MAZOLA CORN OIL.

Mazola 100% PURE CORN OIL

Cool cucumbers make salads crisp 'n crunchy— and they have Vitamin C to boot.

Meaty mushrooms add niacin and heft to any salad.

MAZOLA 100% PURE CORN OIL.
LETS THE NATURAL FLAVORS OF FRESH FOODS COME THROUGH.

What you eat makes a difference in how you look. A well-balanced diet, low in sugars, additives, and cholesterol, and high in natural ingredients, can improve all the facets of your appearance—hair, eyes, complexion, and body tone. The advertisement shown here indicates some dietary elements you need to look and feel your best.

Diamond—soft bangs, curls around chin.

Oblong—fluffy fullness to slightly below ears.

Square—soft curls at jawline and temple.

Oval—anything goes, depending on hair type and texture.

Heart shape—fullness at chin, height at forehead.

Oblong—fullness at sides extending to ears.

Round—height at top, not much fullness at sides.

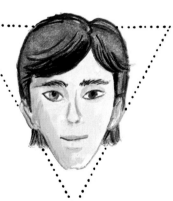

Inverted triangle—height at top, width at chin.

Pear shape—width at temples, hair back at forehead.

Your face shape and hairstyle should be compatible, whether you want to accentuate your facial contours or disguise them. Here are some suggestions.

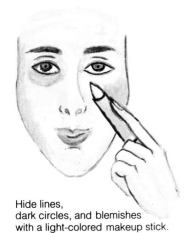

Hide lines,
dark circles, and blemishes
with a light-colored makeup stick.

Judicious use
of darker makeup helps to
downplay overprominent areas.

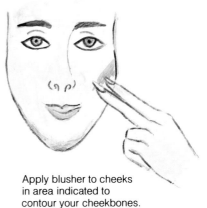

Apply blusher to cheeks
in area indicated to
contour your cheekbones.

Eyeliner

Separate lashes with an eyelash comb.

Outlining lips

When you are finished, your face
should look glowing, healthy, and
natural.

Your facial undertones affect and are affected by the makeup you apply, the clothes you wear, and the tint of hair coloring you choose. The facial undertones of the two women in the pictures at top are predominantly yellow, while those of the woman below are predominantly blue. Yet see how the rosy pinks worn by the woman at top left affect her complexion tones.

Because of your particular facial undertones, you may find that certain colors and color combinations are becoming, while others do nothing to flatter you. With a little time and experimenting, you can discover your own unique good looks and the colors that enhance them, the hairstyles that flatter them, and the clothes that show them off.

Tanning products that brown the skin without the aid of the sun can be purchased. Their ingredient, dihydroxyacetone, is considered a nontoxic agent and is safe to use. Remember, when applying this type of lotion, to spread it evenly or you will find yourself with a spotty tan.

The tanning process occurs when ultraviolet rays penetrate the epidermis. The melanin in the epidermis begins to increase with exposure to the rays, turning the skin brown. This is nature's way of protecting the body against sunburn. If you are dark-skinned, remember that although you have more melanin in your epidermis than do light-skinned individuals, you too can suffer from overexposure to the sun.

Hair Care

Hair is one of the most important single factors in your overall image. The style, color, and condition of your hair make a definite statement about your appearance.

Hair grows from follicles beneath the skin's surface. Figure 3–1 depicts the hair shaft and follicle. Hair is made of a protein substance called *keratin*. Each hair shaft has three parts: the *medulla*, a soft inner core that looks like a tube running through the hair shaft; the *cortex*, which contains melanin that gives hair its color and

HBJ Collection

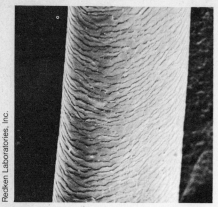

A healthy hair shaft

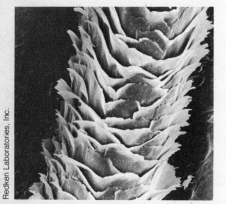

A damaged hair shaft

keratin protein that gives hair its elasticity; and the *cuticle*, a transparent, protective outer layer of scales.

When hair emerges from the scalp, its protein cells have hardened and the hair is dead. Sebaceous glands surrounding the follicle secrete oil that coats the cuticle, causing its cells to lie smooth and flat and giving hair its luster. The amount of secretions can create an oily, dry, or normal hair condition. Hair will become dull-looking if the cuticle is deprived of oil due to clogged glands or a dandruff condition or if chemical processes and harsh environmental exposure cause the position of the cuticle's cells to be distorted and raised instead of flat and smooth. The photos on the following page show the difference between a damaged and a healthy hair shaft.

Many times, hair is cut, curled, permed, straightened, colored, or exposed to extremes in weather and temperature without its owner realizing the damage these effects can cause. Damaged hair can never be restored to its original, healthy condition. Treatments and conditioners can be used to improve the appearance while you wait for new hair growth. For healthy, attractive-looking hair, you need to establish a hair care routine.

HAIR AND YOUR DIET

The best hair care begins with a good diet. Gayelord Hauser, the health food authority, declares that eating the proper foods can greatly improve the appearance of your hair.

There is one way to correct a multitude of hair troubles, and that is to replace empty starches and sugars, cakes, candies, soda pops, and nutritionless cereals with food that will nourish your hair. Most important are the first-class proteins like lean meat, fish, eggs, cottage cheese. Use only whole grains, good bread, fruit juices, and honey. Cut to a minimum all animal fats with the exception of butter. But be generous with the golden vegetable oils. You have a wide choice to fit your taste and pocketbook; sunflower oil, sesame oil, soya oil, wheat germ oil, corn oil, and many others. These oils make tasty salad dressing. Cook with these oils and bake with them, and if your hair is especially dry and mousey, take a tablespoonful of oil every day.[2]

In the course of time, you will begin to notice the difference a good diet makes in your hair's texture and appearance.

THE HAIRCUT

The main business requirement for hair is that it appear neat. What a good diet means to your hair's health, a good haircut means to its style. If it is not cut correctly or kept trimmed, your hair will

[2]Gayelord Hauser, *Treasury of Secrets* (New York: Crest, 1963), p. 263.

appear untidy. A good haircut can give your hair body, manageability, and line, so take this snipping seriously. Go to a trained hairstylist. Your most visible feature deserves the best care.

A wet cut produces a better style than a dry cut. Make sure the hairdresser not only wets the hair, but gives you a complete shampoo to remove dirt, hair spray, setting lotion, and oil.

Whether a razor cut is better than a scissor cut is debatable. The type of cut you receive depends both on the particular hairstyle you want and your hairdresser's training. After your hair has been cut and dried, let the mirror reveal if it is a good cut. Ask these questions:

1. Are there any holes or gaps?
2. Does it have a choppy, uneven appearance?
3. Does it lie well?
4. Will it fall back into place after you shake your head?

If you can answer "no" to the first two questions and "yes" to the last two questions, you should have a good haircut.

Some customers bring pictures of a hairstyle to show their hairdresser. This is a good idea, but don't expect your finished hairstyle to look exactly the same. Your facial structure and your hair's color, texture, and density will influence the finished look.

THE HAIR CARE ROUTINE

For good-looking hair, a hair care routine is a must. This advice is not solely for women. As Charles Hix points out in his popular guide for men, *Looking Good*, "A strand of hair from a man is not

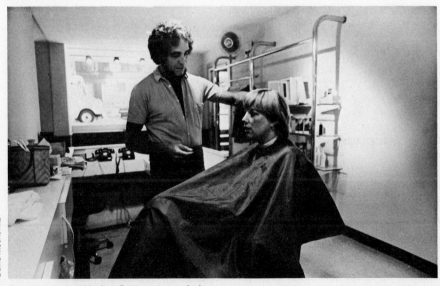
David Moskowitz

Choose a trained hairstylist to cut your hair.

different in any way from that of a woman."[3] A good hair care routine for both sexes should consist of brushing, shampooing, and conditioning.

Brushing Brushing the hair before shampooing will help loosen dirt and distribute the natural oils. There is no need to brush your hair 100 strokes a day. This can cause damage, especially if the brush you use does not have natural bristles or rounded ends. A daily brushing is good for the scalp, but there is no reason for a lengthy brushing session.

Shampooing The frequency of your shampoos depends upon your hair type. Oily hair requires shampooing every day or every other day. Weekly or biweekly shampoos may be sufficient for dry hair.

How do you know if you have oily or dry hair? Oily hair will separate into stringy strands within a day or even hours after washing. It will look greasy and dirty within a short time. Dry hair doesn't collect dirt as fast, but it can appear dull and lifeless. Extremely dry hair has a strawlike texture.

When washing your hair, wet it thoroughly. Then apply a small amount of shampoo. Use the pads of your fingers to rub the scalp. This is a good time to give your scalp a massage. While the shampoo is on the hair, place your hands firmly on your scalp and in a circular motion move your fingers over the entire hair area. Be careful to continue using the pads of your fingers, because fingernails will

[3]Charles Hix, *Looking Good* (New York: Hawthorn, 1978), p. 22.

Brushing your hair daily helps distribute the natural oils.

You can choose from a variety of shampoos.

scratch the scalp and tear your hair. Keep in mind that wet hair is susceptible to damage.

After shampooing, rinse hair well, and gently blot it dry with a towel. Do not vigorously rub it; this too can cause damage.

In selecting a good shampoo, you want one that will cleanse your hair and produce body, smoothness, sheen, luster, highlights, and manageability. But can you buy all this in one package? Most likely, you can't. If you buy a shampoo that gives your locks body, it may also leave your hair lusterless. Purchase a shampoo for the "frizzies" and the frizzies will be corrected at the expense of manageability. One solution is to select two or three brands, each possessing a different feature, then alternate brands with each shampoo. Check *Consumer's Research Magazine* or *Consumer Reports*; these magazines will give you an idea of what is the best shampoo for the money. As you will note, the most expensive shampoos are not necessarily the best.

Most shampoos today are made with synthetics, and the vinegar and lemon juice rinses of grandmother's day are are no longer necessary to eliminate soap scum. However, hairdressers still use these rinses occasionally for stripping the hair of buildup from hair spray and conditioners. Moreover, lemon juice and vinegar have been found to close the fraying scales of the cuticle, giving hair a shiny look. Blondes are advised to use ¼ cup of lemon juice in rinse water; brunettes should use ¼ cup of vinegar.

David Moskowitz

Conditioners

Conditioning Conditioners will not correct the damage caused by poor diet, overprocessing, and too much sun. But they can temporarily alleviate your hair problem. After you shampoo, apply conditioner to your hair with the palms of your hands. Leave it on for about a minute; then rinse well. The following list can assist you in finding the right conditioner:

Problem	Solution
Fine hair	Use a protein conditioner to coat the hair shaft, thus giving the hair a little more thickness. Check the label; protein should be listed first.
Dry hair	Use a product with lanolin or oil. Water will be the first ingredient on the label; lanolin or oil will be listed third or fourth. Some products suggest applying heat to help the conditioner penetrate the hair shaft.
Drab hair	Lemon juice or vinegar will close the cuticle scales to create a glossy look.
Limp hair	Try rinsing the hair with stale beer to give it body. A protein conditioner can add life to tired hair.

The Wella Corporation

Massage your scalp with the pads of your fingers while shampooing.

HAIR CARE   73

DANDRUFF

Dandruff is the flaking of scalp scales. Mild cases can be controlled with the proper shampoo, daily brushing, and gentle massage. Severe cases of inflammation, redness, or oozing should be treated by a doctor. No one knows for certain what causes dry scalp scaling. Medications, cold climates, the extreme heat of hair appliances, and emotional problems are sometimes considered to be responsible, but no sound evidence has proven these theories. Shampoos that contain selenium, zinc, tar, sulfur, or salicylic acid are good dandruff fighters.

HAIR COLORING

At some point in almost everyone's life, a change in hair color seems appealing. A change to a few shades lighter or darker can be very becoming, but a drastic switch is not advised for many reasons.

1. Skin tones may not complement the new hair color. A dark-haired person with dark skin tones, for example, who changes from black to blond may find the total look rather strange because complexion and hair color may not blend together.
2. Hair growth means touch-ups on tattletale roots every four to six weeks. This can be expensive.
3. A drastic chemical change in the hair shaft may leave the hair dry and brittle.
4. The National Cancer Institute has found that some chemicals in permanent dyes have caused cancer in laboratory

Hazel Hankin

Dandruff shampoos

animals. If you purchase an over-the-counter dye, the label will carry a warning about this possibility.

For these reasons, you should think twice before a friend or advertisement convinces you that another color is better than your natural one.

If you want to experiment with a new color before adopting it permanently, investigate home products such as shampoo-in colors, temporary rinses, and semipermanent rinses. These are safe to use if directions are followed. Bleaching and dyeing are best left to the trained stylist, who will know how much chemical change your hair can take without damage.

Frosting, tipping, and painting are bleaching processes that add highlights to the hair. Frosting is usually done for the purpose of achieving a natural sunbleached look. To frost hair, bleach is applied to strands of hair pulled through holes in a tight rubber cap. In the tipping process, just the ends of the hair are bleached. Painting, which changes hair color only minimally, is done with a brush to highlight random areas.

Chesebrough-Pond's

You can successfully give yourself a home permanent if you follow directions.

CURLING AND STRAIGHTENING

The same process is used in both permanently curling and straightening the hair. A chemical solution is applied to the hair. effecting a permanent change in the chemical bonds of the hair shaft. The solution continues to work until a neutralizer is applied to stop the action. By checking the hair every few minutes, a trained person can tell when to apply the neutralizer. If the solution is left on too long, the hair will be overprocessed and feel mushy. The only difference between the curling and straightening processes is in the tools: Permanent rods are used for curling; a comb is pulled through the hair for straightening.

If directions are followed closely, you can achieve satisfactory results with home permanents. Do not curl or straighten hair that is bleached or extremely dry; it cannot take additional stress.

HAIR REMOVAL

American women, unlike those of most other cultures, consider any exposure of body hair to be untidy. Shaving, tweezing, waxing, electrolysis, and the use of depilatories are satisfactory methods of removing body hair. An explanation of each method and its advantages and disadvantages can be found in table 3–1.

The section on "Appearance" in chapter 2 discussed the growing acceptance of moustaches and beards in contrast to the once mandatory clean-shaven male face. Nevertheless, a clean-shaven appearance is still the norm in the business world.

For most men, shaving once in the morning is sufficient; how-

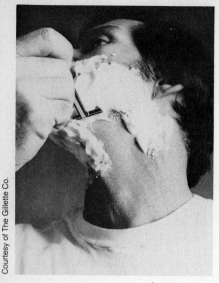

A razor shave

ever, some men are forced to shave twice a day to avoid a "five o'clock shadow." Daily shaving is hard on facial skin. Fortunately, the last few years have seen an increasing emphasis on the availability of male skin-care products. Most male skin-care lines are found at major department stores. However, the increased interest in and market for male cosmetics has resulted in the introduction of new ingredients in men's basic shaving products. Many shaving creams and gels now contain lanolin. Lanolin-based shaving lotions are more lubricating and less drying than conventional shaving creams. Lanolin's lubricating properties provide a protective coating for the face and allow the razor to glide over the skin more easily, thus minimizing the potential for nicks and cuts. The following lists include shaving tips for men.

RAZOR SHAVE
1. A good time to shave is after a shower, when the warm water has softened the hairs.
2. To soften the beard and hydrate the hairs, apply a hot, moist towel.

Table 3–1

HAIR REMOVAL METHODS

Method	Procedure	Advantages	Disadvantages
Razor	Lather or soap should be applied to wet skin; shave with long, upward strokes.	Inexpensive and quick.	There is rapid regrowth of hair; skin may be nicked or cut. Not intended for use on women's faces.
Electric shaver	Preshave lotion should be applied, preferably after warm shower or bath.	Quick, and usually nonirritating.	There is rapid regrowth because hairs are not cut close to skin. Not intended for use on women's faces.
Waxing or zipping	Warm wax is applied to skin; when the wax hardens, it is pulled away with hairs imbedded.	Results in a smooth look, since hair is removed below skin surface.	Hair must be fairly long before wax can be applied, and the process is painful and time-consuming.
Electrolysis	An electric needle is inserted into hair follicle; electricity kills the hair root.	*Generally* removes hair permanently and painlessly.	Because scarring is possible, a professional should administer this treatment, which is expensive. Permanent removal may require several treatments.
Depilation	Chemical depilatory is applied and left on for ten to fifteen minutes; then, chemical and hair are rinsed off.	Removes hair close to the skin; the process is simple.	Skin irritation is possible.

3. Depending on your skin type, choose an aerosal foam, lathering shaving cream, or gel. Foams and lathering creams may be applied with hands or a brush. Men with dry skin should avoid the use of a brush, which may further irritate sensitive skin.
4. Shaving should be done in the direction in which the hair grows, using short, up-and-down strokes.
5. Leave the chin and upper lip areas until last. The cream, gels, or aerosol foams will need more time to soften the coarse hairs in these areas.

ELECTRIC SHAVE
1. Wash face to remove excess oil, then dry thoroughly.
2. Apply a preelectric shave lotion or talcum powder.
3. Shave in the direction of the hair growth, using short strokes.

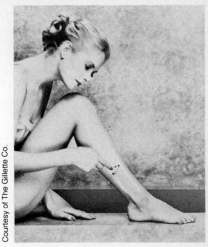

Courtesy of The Gillette Co.

Shave legs with long, upward strokes

After either kind of shave, apply an aftershave lotion, skin bracer, or skin refresher. Aftershave lotion does not have as high an alcohol content as do skin bracers and skin refreshers. Aftershave lotions are therefore better for dry skins; skin bracers or refreshers are more effective on oily skins.

Some men must struggle with painful ingrown hairs. One solution to the problem is to use a *depilatory* (a chemical agent for hair removal) and a razor or shaver on alternate days. (Note the discussion of depilatories in table 3–1.)

Stray eyebrow and nostril hairs can be removed by tweezing.

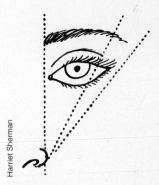

Harriet Sherman

Figure 3–3
Follow these imaginary lines when tweezing eyebrows.

Body Care

Daily bathing, whether a soothing soak in the tub or an invigorating shower, can be a time of relaxation and recharging. Bubble baths, scented soaps, whirlpool attachments, pulsating hand-held shower massages, and loofahs can all make cleansing more enjoyable. Indulge yourself with one thorough cleansing a day.

After your bath, apply a lotion or emollient cream to replace the natural oils depleted by the water. Body talc, powder, or fragrant body splash may complete the ritual. Although a scent is very nice, be careful not to put too much fragrance on. Almost nothing is more offensive than an overpowering scent.

Scents are available in a wide range, from leather or lime to floral or fruit. Have you wondered how cologne, toilet water, and perfume differ?

Perfumes contain more oil than do colognes and toilet water, and therefore they last longer on the skin. Cologne and toilet water have a higher alcohol content and lighter scent than do perfumes, and can be applied more generously.

S. C. Johnson & Son, Inc.

Applying aftershave lotion

A deodorant

An antiperspirant

Several minutes after bathing, apply a deodorant or antiperspirant. Don't apply these immediately after washing, while your body is still warm. Wait until your skin returns to normal temperature, when you will be perspiring less; this permits the application to penetrate better.

The choice between deodorant and antiperspirant depends upon your bodily needs and your personal preference. Both contain ingredients to reduce body odor. Antiperspirants also contain special chemicals to retard the flow of perspiration. If you perspire freely, you should use an antiperspirant. If not, a deodorant will serve you best.

Most products currently on the market are identified as either deodorants or antiperspirants. By law, an antiperspirant must have its ingredients listed on the label; deodorants do not have to list their ingredients.

FOOT CARE

Foot odor is a problem for some people. Although the soles of feet are tough, feet are prone to viral, fungal, and other infections caused by poor hygiene and ill-fitting or restrictive footwear.

Take the time in your bathing routine to wash feet carefully, being sure to cleanse between your toes. Failure to completely dry feet before putting on footwear provides a perfect environment for the growth of fungus. Athlete's foot is a common source of foot odor. Self-treatment with the use of over-the-counter medications available at your local drugstore will often solve the problem. If the odor problem persists and is severe, consult a *podiatrist* or foot doctor.

Although less visible, your feet should receive as much care as do your hands. Get into the habit of giving yourself a regular pedicure. In performing a pedicure you can follow the manicure guidelines provided in the next section with one exception: Toenails should be trimmed straight across, instead of rounded, to prevent them from becoming ingrown.

HAND CARE

Whether you are making phone calls, pointing out sections of a contract, or handling papers, your hands are a highly visible extension of your body. Dirty fingernails or grease lining the creases will draw the kind of attention that a career-minded person doesn't want.

Manicure your nails once a week to insure a well-groomed appearance. Start with clean hands, then trim your nails into the desired shape. Women generally strive for an oval shape, whereas men keep their nails short with rounded corners. Use an emery board to shape the nail—this is better for it than cutting. Next, soak

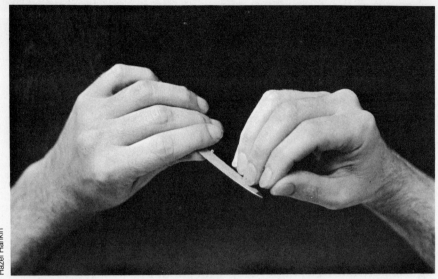

Hazel Hankin

Nail care

your fingers in warm water or take your daily bath, letting your hands soak. After the *cuticle* (the small strip of hardened skin that touches the nail) has been softened, take an orange stick or a cotton-tipped swab and push the cuticle back. Clip the cuticle only if it has been broken. Dry your hands and apply lotion, or buff with a chamois buffer. If you apply nail polish, stay away from bright colors, which are not appropriate for office wear.

Grooming for a Health Profession

If you have a job in any of the allied health professions, special attention will be required in your grooming and attire. Anyone in a medical job needs to be *impeccably* clean and neat in *every* detail. In addition to the grooming advice in this chapter and chapter 4, and the fashion advice in chapter 5, here are some special pointers for the medical or health services professional.

ATTIRE

Most jobs require that you wear a standard uniform and clinical shoes. Your uniform should be freshly laundered, spotless, and wrinkle-free every day. Some offices will allow women to wear pastel-colored smocks, which will allow you to vary your dress occasionally.

Clinical shoes may be mandatory and are a good idea in any case. They are constructed to provide cushioning and back support

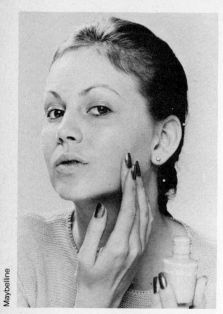

Applying a foundation

Highlighting

to withstand long periods of time on your feet. Clinical shoes are always preferred over high heels, which are impractical because they increase the possibilities of your tripping. Stockings should always be worn, and they should always be white.

Although a uniform minimizes the chances of overdressing, care should be taken in accessorizing. No dangling earrings, necklaces, or bracelets should be worn. In fact, jewelry should be limited to a wedding or engagement ring and a watch. Your watch should have a second hand for timing, especially if you are responsible for administering medications.

PERSONAL HYGIENE

Because of close patient proximity, your hygiene should be above reproach. A clean body, clean teeth, and fresh breath are very important. Hair should be clean and worn off the collar and away from the face. Women with long hair can pull it back into a chignon or ponytail. Hair caps for both men and women are often the rule.

Fingernails should be kept short. Gloves may be required. If long nails are allowed, dark nail polish should be avoided.

It is always a good idea to carry an emergency kit. Some suggested items to include in your kit are: an extra pair of white nylons, toothbrush, toothpaste, small bottle of mouthwash, a sewing needle and thread, and shoe polish to touch up shoes scuffed in the course of the day.

Facial Coloring

Facial coloring can add dimension to a face, hide flaws, and accent your best features. If you apply it well, the result will be an interesting but natural-looking face. Keep in mind that a tiny bit of color is enough.

MEN

Coloring bronzers and blemish cover-ups are sometimes used by today's male executives. A favorite facial cover is a bronzer sold in gel form, which is spread evenly over all of the face to achieve a healthy athletic look. This gel usually has moisturizing agents to give the face extra protection from the elements.

WOMEN

The following is a basic explanation of how to enhance your features. Its purpose is not to make you a model, but to improve your natural look. If you want to explore the subject more thoroughly, Way Bandy's book, *Styling Your Face*, is a good source.

FOUNDATION

Start with a clean face; never put makeup on a dirty face. Choose a foundation shade that closely matches your skin color. A radical color change will look artificial in daylight and office light.

Foundations are available in liquid, cream, pancake, or solid form. Oil-based foundation is best for dry skin, water-based for oily skin. Some foundations have a moisturizer already mixed in. If this is not the case, mix your foundation with a little moisturizer, then spread it evenly over the entire face. Be certain to cover all areas, getting right to the hairline and under the chin. Foundation is seldom applied to the neck because it stains clothes. Blend carefully wherever the foundation stops so that there is no visible line of demarcation. The mixture of moisturizer and foundation will give your face a slick look, but this will be corrected later.

FACIAL CONTOURING

Facial contouring means accenting certain areas by means of light tones and de-emphasizing others by means of dark. It gives your face dimension and makes it more interesting. It is not designed to make everyone's face resemble an oval; your own distinctive face shape and features can be enhanced to create your individual style of beauty.

1. With light makeup or a light-colored makeup stick, gently dot areas that you want highlighted, accented, or corrected.
2. Apply a darker makeup or brown eye shadow to features you want to minimize.
3. Apply blusher to the upper cheek area, to accent the cheekbones and give the effect of a healthy glow. Because high cheekbones are considered to be a mark of good bone structure, many women accent them. See colorplate 3 for the proper placement of blusher.

The eyes   Your eyes are your most expressive feature. Give them the emphasis they deserve.

Eyebrows look best with their natural growth line, so leave them alone with the exception of tweezing any stray hairs that extend beyond the imaginary lines shown in figure 3–3.

If you use eyeliner, apply it as close as possible to the edge of the upper lid, but never inside the lid. You might want to experiment with drawing a line on the bottom lid. Some cosmetologists say this accents the eye, but others contend that the bottom line makes the eye look smaller.

Next, apply mascara to your eyelashes both underneath and on top of the lash. Use black mascara if your hair is dark; use brown if

Use darker makeup to minimize features

Applying eyeliner

Applying mascara

Maybelline

Outlining the lips

your hair is light. After the mascara dries, curl your lashes with an eyelash curler to make them look longer and your eyes look bigger. If your lashes are very short, apply a coat of mascara, let it dry, then dust the lashes lightly with powder, then apply a second coat.

Use eye shadow sparingly for day wear. The safest colors for day are muted earth and flesh tones.

The lips Your lips are also a dominant facial feature. Give them dimension by using a brush or a colored lip pencil to outline your mouth with a darker shade. After outlining, apply your usual color of lipstick. No one can tell the difference, but the effect is striking.

FINAL TOUCHES

The last step is application of translucent powder. Blot the powder over your face with clean cotton balls. This will give a matte finish and take away the greasy shine. A buffed look, popular for both dark and light skin, can be achieved by taking a small soft cloth and making circular movements over the face.

Look in the mirror. Are there any lines or obvious color changes? To be very certain, take your mirror and stand in the sunlight. If your face looks natural, you have passed the test.

Grooming is seldom mentioned in business circles. Don't interpret this lack of communication as permission for sloppy grooming habits. One of the most important factors in getting ahead is projecting a professional image. So much so, that a visual image may cause employers to reject a candidate that they might otherwise hire or promote. Some employers feel that your appearance will reflect your job performance. Your professional image means looking good, feeling well, acting poised, and communicating confidence to those around you. The following checklist of good grooming "musts" is offered as a guide:

- A clean appearance and hygiene beyond reproach

- Clean, manicured nails

- Clean teeth and fresh breath

- Clean hair that is neat, attractively styled, and practical for the job

- Unobtrusive and natural-looking makeup appropriate for the office

- Good posture

- Spotless and proper attire

The last two items will be discussed in greater detail in the following chapters.

The test: Is the look natural?

KEY TERMS

epidermis	androgens	keratin
melanin	exfoliation	medulla
dermis	astringent	cortex
sweat glands	hydrating	hair cuticle
sebaceous glands	acne	depilatory
subcutaneous	dermatologist	podiatrist
pH balance	Sun Protection Factor	nail cuticle

TEST YOURSELF:
QUESTIONS FOR REVIEW AND DISCUSSION

1. What are the three layers of the skin?
2. What does pH balance mean?
3. What are the best methods of controlling acne?
4. What happens to your skin when you tan? What are the dangers of tanning?
5. What are the characteristics of oily skin? Dry skin?
6. What is meant by the T-zone?
7. What is an astringent?
8. What are the differences between an antiperspirant and a deodorant?
9. Describe the hair curling and straightening process.
10. How would you describe the visual qualities of a good-looking person?
11. A sloppy appearance affects the way others perceive you. Have you ever experienced poor treatment from store clerks or waitresses because of a sloppy appearance? Is your attitude toward strangers affected by their appearance?
12. If a co-worker had bad breath or body odor, would you tell the person of the problem? How could you be tactful in discussing the matter with the co-worker?
13. Hair care—haircuts, shampooing, styling, curling, straightening, coloring—can be done by yourself or by a professional. Weigh the pros and cons of personal care versus professional care for each process.

APPLICATION EXERCISES

1. Answer the following questions about your facial features.

   What do you think is your best facial feature?
   What do you consider a facial flaw?
   What do you do to enhance your good features?
   What do you do to correct or to camouflage your flaws?
   What facial feature does a friend consider to be your best asset?
   What facial feature does a classmate consider to be your best asset?
   Do you find that you perceive yourself differently than others do?

2. Answer the following questions about your hair.

   Name one feature that you like about your hair (for instance, texture, color, style)
   What do you dislike about your hair?
   What do you do to enhance the good qualities of your hair? (for instance, use of special hair care products, regular cuts, special diet)
   How do you correct your hair problems? (for instance, regular cuts, coloring, curling)
   What aspect of your hair does a friend consider to be its best feature?
   What aspect of your hair does a classmate consider to be its best feature?
   Do you find that you perceive yourself differently than others do?

Suggested Readings

Bandy, Way. *Styling Your Face.* New York: Random House, 1981.

Coffey, Barbara, and the editors of *Glamour. Glamour's Success Book.* New York: Simon & Schuster, 1979.

Kingsley, Philip. *The Complete Hair Book.* New York: Grosset & Dunlap, 1979.

McNair, Barbara, and Stephen Lewis. *The Complete Book of Beauty for the Black Woman.* Englewood Cliffs, N.J.: Prentice-Hall, 1972.

Meredith, Bronwen. *Vogue Body and Beauty Book.* New York: Harper & Row, 1979.

Powlis, La Verne. *The Black Woman's Beauty Book.* Garden City, N.Y.: Doubleday, 1979.

Sassoon, Beverly, and Vidal Sassoon. *A Year of Beauty and Health.* New York: Simon & Schuster, 1979.

Schoen, Linda Allen, ed. *The AMA Book of Skin and Hair Care.* New York: Avon, 1976.

Zacarian, Setrag A. *Your Skin.* Radnor, Pa.: Chilton, 1978.

Zizmor, Jonathan, and Sharon Sabin. *The Complete Guide to Grooming Products for Men.* New York: Playboy Press, 1982.

4

PERSONAL AND PROFESSIONAL POISE

COMPREHENSIVE GOAL
To instruct you in good exercise and nutritional practices and show how physical conditioning can produce personal and professional poise.

SPECIFIC OBJECTIVES
After reading this chapter, you will be able to:

■ list the benefits of exercise

■ explain the terms "aerobic," "isotonic," and "isometric," and differentiate among these forms of exercise

■ practice muscle-relaxation exercises

■ identify good posture principles

■ understand and apply the principles of good nutrition

■ explain the functions of vitamins in the diet

■ choose a reducing plan based on an understanding of calorie counting and food needs

■ define and evaluate "health" foods

■ understand the significance of various parts of the food label

While it is true that success cannot be measured by appearance, a well-toned body projects a successful image. Moreover, when you are physically fit, you have more energy to perform effectively on the job, and you are less likely to miss work on account of illness.

Physical fitness, or lack of it, affects your personal life as well. If you are overweight or underweight, you are likely to feel tired; as a result, you may turn down invitations, snap at friends. When your body is not fit, your mind is often not as alert as it should be: You question your judgment; you procrastinate instead of acting decisively. But when you feel well and know you look well, you convey a maturity, a confidence, and a capability that your friends and associates will recognize.

Poise

Physical fitness has many rewards, and one of the foremost of these is *poise*—a word that is almost as elusive in definition as the word "success." The dictionary defines poise as balance and stability, but the word has a far more personal meaning to most people. One person may consider poise to be dignity and grace, whereas to another it is charm and spontaneity. As it will be considered here, poise has two separate but related meanings, which can be classified as "physical poise" and "mental poise." The following paragraphs will discuss these terms and describe briefly how each type of poise can be attained.

Physical poise is smoothness and grace of movement. It is sitting down in a chair with a fluid motion; it is ascending and descending stairs with ease; it is reaching across a desk in an unbroken movement. Exercise can give you the muscle control needed for physical poise. If you are not already participating in some physical activity, it is time to start stretching and bending all the muscles of your body. Physical poise and exercise are so important that half of this chapter is devoted to the subject.

Mental poise is the confidence of knowing you are the best you can be. To illustrate the point, ask yourself if, on a morning when your mirror reflects a dull, messy mop of hair, dark circles under the eyes, a budding new pimple, and a sallow complexion, you are ready to run out and meet the world. On such a morning, do you say "Hi" to everyone you meet, or do you go meekly through the day hoping that no one will notice you? But on another day, when your hair sparkles, your complexion glows, and you've had enough sleep, don't you feel more like greeting people and stopping to say hello to friends? When you know you look good, you become more outgoing. Mental poise is that assurance of looking and feeling good.

Poise is the product of exercise and diet. The two complement

Physical poise means grace of movement.

each other and contribute to physical and mental well-being. This well-being carries over into your professional effectiveness.

Exercise

The rewards of exercise are so numerous that the first few moments of discomfort at the beginning of any exercise are quickly forgotten. These rewards include the following:

Better posture	Better distribution of weight
Increased agility	More energy
Increased body awareness	Improved self-image
Better complexion	Release of anger, frustration, and stress
Improved appearance	
Appetite regulation	Better sleep habits
More effective burning of calories	Increased awareness of surroundings
Strengthened heart	Improved circulation
Weight loss	

Researchers have found that athletes tend to be superior to nonathletes in leadership, self-confidence, dominance, enthusiasm, toughmindedness, emotional stability, and sociability.

This chapter will discuss three forms of exercise: aerobic, isotonic, and isometric. *Aerobics* refers to strenuous physical activities such as those involved in sports, which are most often performed in the open air. These activities stimulate the *cardiopulmonary system* (heart and lungs), so that in time the heart is strengthened and the *vascular system* (blood vessels) improved. *Isotonics* and *isometrics* are less strenuous, but necessary exercises if you want to work on flexibility and muscle control.

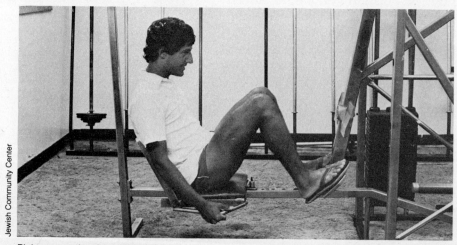

Jewish Community Center

Pick an exercise that you enjoy.

AEROBIC EXERCISE

True aerobic exercise is not merely vigorous activity, but *sustained* vigorous activity that works the heart. Regular aerobic exercise helps build a stronger heart and benefits the circulatory system. Like any muscle, the heart must be used regularly to its capacity to maintain its strength. The stronger the heart muscle, the more efficiently the blood is pumped through the veins and arteries. By exercising the cardiopulmonary system, aerobics improve blood circulation and help burn calories.

Aerobics also promote deep breathing, which helps exchange the air in your lungs. Shallow breathers use only the upper portion of their lungs to breathe. Deep breathers fill their lungs so that all of the tiny air sacs function, permitting more oxygen to enter the blood.

To test your breathing, place your hands on your lower ribs and take a deep breath. If you are a deep breather, the lower part of your rib cage will expand. If you are a shallow breather, you might regularly practice deep breathing until it becomes a habit. When exercising vigorously, deep breathing is especially effective for endurance; conversely, endurance effects deep breathing.

Aerobic exercises help participants work their hearts to capacity through continuous, sustained movements that demand uninterrupted output from the body for 12 to 30 minutes. By strengthening your heart through such regular workouts, you can reduce your normal heart rate. Stronger hearts do not have to work as hard to circulate blood.

The benefits of true aerobics can be measured. Here's one way to do it: Before you begin your aerobics regimen, calculate your *resting* (normal) *heart rate* by taking your pulse. Do this by placing your index and third finger over the artery in your inner wrist and counting the number of times your heart beats over a ten-second interval. Multiply that number by six to determine what your pulse rate is per minute.

To give your heart an adequate workout during 12 to 30 minutes of your exercise program, you need to bring your heart rate up to its capacity. You can determine what your capacity range or *target zone* is by subtracting your age from the number 220 and multiplying the balance by 70 percent (to determine your minimum capacity, or the number of heartbeats per minute necessary for an effective workout) and by 80 percent (to learn your maximum capacity, or the number of beats per minute that your heart can safely handle). Your pulse rate while exercising should fall within the minimum and maximum range you have established. By checking your pulse periodically during your exercise routine you can determine whether you need to work harder or to slow down. If you do aerobics regularly you should eventually find that it takes longer for you to reach the limits of your target zone. People who pursue a regular program of

Deep breathing

Courtesy of Shirley Boyle/Pat Stirmac Photo

Aerobic dancing
is vigorous exercise set to music.

aerobics using this and other available methods of measurement have found that eventually their resting heart rates are lower—indicating that the heart doesn't have to pump as fast because it has, in effect, become stronger.

How a 30-year-old can find his/her target zone:

1. Subtract your age (30) from 220.

$$220 - 30 = 190$$

2. Multiply 190 by 70% to determine your minimum capacity.

$$190 \times .70 = 133 \text{ beats per minute}$$

3. Multiply 190 by 80% to determine your maximum capacity.

$$190 \times .80 = 152 \text{ beats per minute}$$

If your pulse rate during your exercise break is only 125, you need to exercise harder or longer; if your rate is 160, you need to slow down.

Regardless of whether you are trying to reach your maximum capacity and lower your resting heart rate or whether you are simply aiming for better physical health, at least three weekly, 30-minute aerobics sessions are recommended. Be sure that your physical condition can support strenuous activity. A thorough medical examination prior to embarking upon any exercise program is a good idea.

Some good aerobic exercises are aerobic dancing, jogging, jumping rope, cross-country skiing, bicycling, and swimming. Each of these will be discussed in the following sections.

Aerobic Dancing   Aerobic dance classes are so popular that most health clubs and fitness centers, as well as many private instructors, offer them regularly. *Aerobic dance* is exercise set to music that combines the fun of dance with the benefits of jogging, while making the heart rate stay within its target zone for approximately 20 minutes.

It can be an energizing workout that leaves you feeling revitalized and full of energy. Tapes and records are also available for those who want to pursue aerobic dancing privately. Instructions accompanying these packages are generally complete and easy to follow.

Jogging   This sport, sometimes referred to as an epidemic because of its popularity, is appropriate for all ages. A good pair of running shoes is the only requirement. Make certain that the shoes provide a cushion between your feet and the running surface. Fancy jogging outfits are not necessary, although colorful attire may enhance the mood of the sport.

When you first start to jog, be sensible. Do not plan to jog for

In jogging you will build up endurance gradually.

two miles the first time out. Jogging two miles a day, or ten miles, is a goal that requires gradual building up of endurance. One advantage of the sport is its flexibility in terms of scheduling. Although setting a regular time for jogging is best, sometimes events of the day necessitate a change, and adjustment of time is relatively easy with this sport.

A word of caution to females: In some cases, jogging has been harmful to women's internal organs. You may want to consult your doctor before starting a jogging program.

Jumping Rope Jumping rope is nearly as popular as jogging. It also is inexpensive—requiring only a good pair of shoes and a jump rope—and can easily fit into a busy schedule. In fact, 15 minutes of jumping rope can equal a half hour of jogging.

Most likely you will not start jumping for a continuous 15 minutes. Jump a minute or two, rest, then repeat. Just as with jogging, you should allow yourself time to build up endurance. You might want to measure your level of fitness on the Los Angeles firemen's scale. The low level is 100 turns a minute for two minutes; medium is 110 turns a minute for two minutes; high is 125 turns a minute for three minutes.

Cross-Country Skiing Another exercise that burns calories effectively is cross-country skiing. This cold-weather sport requires good equipment as well as training, which adult education classes and sports shops often provide free for the novice. These classes are necessary to ensure your safety in the winter wilderness.

Cross-country skiing exposes you to the beauty of the outdoors.

Cycling with a group can add to your fun.

Cross-country skiing is often considered winter's counterpart to summer cycling. It exposes many people to the outdoor beauty that they would otherwise never experience. Marked trails exist in many of the recreational parks across the United States.

Cycling   Another activity that gets you around the countryside is bicycling. A good bicycle is essential, but it might be wise to borrow or rent one at first instead of investing. If you find you like the sport, purchase a bike equipped with gears for hill climbing and high speeds.

A beginning goal of a mile or two a day is sufficient; as your back and leg muscles strengthen, you can increase the distance. Some cities have excellent bike paths. If you prefer a road or are forced to use one, ride with traffic, keep to the right, and watch out for cars. Legally, you may have the right of way, but many motorists are not aware of this. Remember, bicycles are moving vehicles and are governed by the same traffic regulations that apply to automobiles.

Swimming   Many physical fitness enthusiasts prefer swimming over any other sport. Some of the reasons for their preference are:

1. Swimming is considered the safest form of workout.
2. Every muscle is involved.
3. The cardiovascular system gets superior exercise.
4. A swimmer does not get overheated.
5. Swimming seldom produces muscular aches and pains.
6. People any age can participate.

Set a certain number of meters a day as your goal, then strive to increase that number a little more each time you swim. Use a variety of strokes, such as the Australian crawl, butterfly, breaststroke, backstroke, and sidestroke in order to work on all of your muscle groups.

In addition to being a good all-around exercise, swimming is exhilarating: It lifts the spirits and relaxes the body. The flotation of the body gives a swimmer a real mental lift. Gliding through the water, ducking under, or lazily kicking around on your back can bring out the child in you.

All aerobic exercises are strenuous and require some self-discipline. The beginning few minutes are the toughest; you may feel cold, tired, lethargic, and wonder if it is all worth it. However, after the first minutes of exercise, the stimulation of your body will start to change your attitude. The glow of contentment after the exercise is over is an incomparable feeling. If you hesitate to begin, push yourself into motion. The lasting pleasure and healthful results surpass the first moments of discomfort.

ISOMETRICS

Isometric exercises, sometimes called lazy man's exercises, require little effort or movement. Business people can practice these while at their desks, standing in line, talking on the telephone, waiting for an elevator, or during any other small block of free time. These "silent" exercises pit muscle against muscle, and require no noticeable movement. Read the instructions provided for each exercise in figure 4–1 to help you understand the muscle-against-muscle concept.

If you can condition yourself to do these exercises every time you have a few free minutes, you can tone up specific muscle

Swimming lifts the spirit and relaxes the body.

American Red Cross

groups. While driving to and from work, one commuter practiced sitting exercises while stopped at red lights. The results of this isometric exercising were evident to friends within one month's time.

ISOTONICS

These exercises, not as strenuous as the cardiopulmonary exercises, are necessary for flexibility. *Isotonic* means "equal tension." Calisthenics and weight lifting are examples of isotonic exercise. The exercises described in this text are modifications of both types.

If you are not practicing any form of isotonic exercise at this time, start at the rate of five repetitions per exercise. As your muscles strengthen, increase the number of repetitions by five each time until you reach at least 20 repetitions per exercise. This does not have to be your limit; some individuals do 50 to 100 repetitions for each exercise, each day. At a minimum, isotonics should be done five times a week.

You may want to add small weights to your limbs for maximum benefit. Small barbells, weighing three pounds for women and five pounds for men, can be held in the hands. Strap-on leg weights, weighing about three pounds, can be attached to the ankles. These weights can be purchased at most sporting goods stores.

Remember, while doing these exercises, it is important to breathe properly. Exhale at the beginning of the exercise, and inhale deeply near completion. If you don't breathe correctly, your *thoracic* (chest) muscles will "fight" against your cardiopulmonary muscles. If you practice breathing out at the beginning, your muscles will work together and you will breathe more deeply. Try to develop a rhythm that coordinates your movements and your breathing. Music may help you establish a pattern. Read the instructions provided for each exercise in figure 4–2.

Figure 4–1
Isometrics

1. While sitting straight in chair, pull stomach muscles in tight; hold to the slow count of five; then release. This is an abdomen tightener.

2. From standing position, rise up on toes and stretch; push flat palms up toward ceiling. Stretch as long as it feels good. The most overt isometric exercise, this is good for posture.

3. Place both hands behind head; push backwards with head while pushing forward with hands. This strengthens upper back and neck muscles.

4. With arms and hands in "prayer" position, push them against each other. This is good for bosom and chest muscles.

Drawings by Harriet Sherman

YOGA

Many people think that yoga involves sitting in an awkward or contorted position for long periods of time in a darkened room filled with incense as the participant meditates and chants. Actually, *yoga* is a physical discipline with mental benefits that is practiced at many different levels. Basically it is a series of postures and exercises that are designed to stretch the muscles, induce deep breathing, and promote mental relaxation.

Beginners start by learning basic postures and good breathing techniques. Although meditation is one aspect of yoga, it is not mandatory for obtaining the many benefits of yoga, and is in fact an advanced aspect of the discipline.

Yoga movements are not intended to be strenuously athletic. Instead the movements are slow and precise. Yoga is convenient because it can be practiced alone for a few minutes a day and will provide maximum results for the time and energy expended.

If you want to try this form of exercise, consider buying a book for beginners. Rachael Carr's *Yoga for You* is a good choice. Taking an introductory class is a good idea, because the movements are precise. If done incorrectly they could be ineffective and even dangerous.

Posture

Although exercise will improve your posture, you need to make a conscious effort to maintain good posture. The strong nonverbal impact conveyed by good posture should be sufficient motivation for most professional people. Which individual in figure 4–3 would you prefer to consult for business advice?

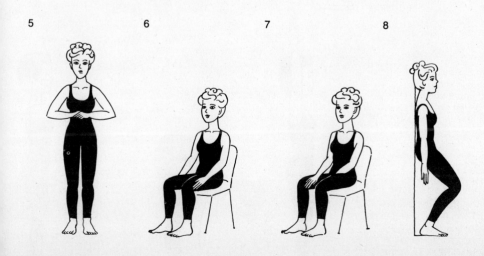

5. Keeping arms and hands in the same position, grasp hands and pull them away from each other. This is good for bosom and chest muscles.

6. Sit with feet flat on floor; place hands against outside of knees, then push knees outward while pushing in with hands. This is good for leg and arm muscles.

7. Using the same position as in exercise six, place hands on inside of knees and push out with hands and in with knees. This is also good for leg and arm muscles.

8. With back against wall and feet about four inches from wall, try to get back of head, shoulders, small of back, and buttocks all against wall. If you find this too difficult, bend knees and lower body about six inches; then slowly straighten knees as you push back up against wall.

Figure 4–2
Isotonics

1. Stand with arms at sides, feet on floor and about twelve inches apart. Raise arms so back of hands touch each other above head. Breathe in as arms are raised, exhale as arms are lowered. (This breathing procedure is an exception to the rule.)
2. Extend arms out to side, shoulder high. Slowly bring them forward to meet in front, then swing them back as far as possible. Return to starting position.
3. With arms extended, shoulder high, rotate wrists rapidly for one minute. Enlarge circles, rotating arms.

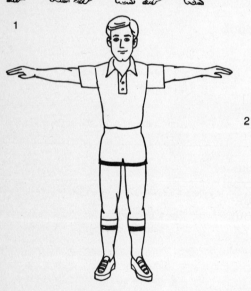

4. With left arm down at side, extend right arm over head. In short movements, bend upper body over toward floor on left side. Reverse, and repeat on right side.

5. On the count of one, extend arms above head; bring them down on the count of two to extend in front of body; on the count of three touch toes; on four bring arms up to front of body. Start again on the count of one.

7. With hand touching chair, swing leg out to the side as far as possible. Swing leg as far forward as possible, then as far backward as possible. Repeat as desired.

6. With hand touching chair for balance, do deep knee bends.

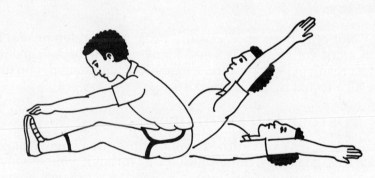

8. Lie on floor with arms extended above head; bend knees to protect back muscles. On the count of one, raise arms over head while bringing upper body to sitting position; on the count of two, touch toes; on three, return to sitting position; on four, lower body to floor. On the count of five you should again be lying flat on floor with arms extended above head.

9. Lie on floor; raise both legs slowly until perpendicular to floor; then slowly lower legs.

10. Lie on right side with head on right arm; then raise left leg as high as possible; repeat on left side.

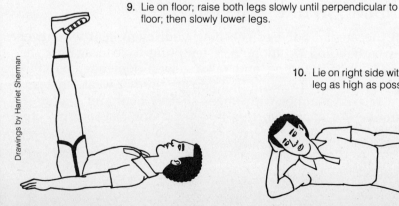

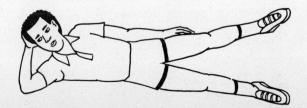

Figure 4–3
When you stand, check your body alignment; don't slump. When walking, keep your head up and shoulders back.

Drawings by Harriet Sherman

Not only does good posture project a positive image, but it is important for health reasons. Many painful back ailments are a direct result of poor posture. Circulation, elimination, and breathing are all affected by improper posture.

POSTURE AND ATTITUDE

In chapter 2 you learned about attitude as a mental quality. One way this quality is communicated is through your bodily movements and posture. The way you stand or sit makes your attitude obvious to others. Look in the mirror and ask yourself what attitude you are expressing to the world. If it is less than desirable, stretch up that backbone, tuck in your buttocks, suck in your stomach, pull back those shoulders, keep your head up, and relax your arms at your sides. Feel better already?

STANDING, SITTING, WALKING

Form the mental habit of checking your alignment whenever you are in a standing position. It is tempting to lean against the nearest wall when standing and talking with someone, but this attitude projects the impression that you are tired or weak. Instead, stand in a relaxed manner with knees slightly bent and feet at an angle. But stay on your own two feet—you don't need any extra support.

Smooth, graceful movement while walking requires, first, good muscle structure, and second, practice. Keep your shoulders back and your head up. There is no need to examine the ground before each step. Move your legs from the pelvic sockets in a fluid motion. Your heel should touch the ground first; then transfer the weight across the arch to the ball of the foot. You should be able to walk a straight line without toeing in or out. Relax your arms at your sides with a slight swing accompanying each stride.

Sitting at a desk for eight hours a day can be detrimental to good posture. It you keep your back straight and shoulders back, it will prevent unsightly rolls from emerging beneath the rib cage. Getting up and moving around occasionally will help relieve tired muscles. How many times have you seen someone at a desk hunched over paperwork? It is not a very attractive sight, is it? Remember, when writing or reading at your desk, keep your backbone straight. Pull your chair up close for added support and as a posture reminder. Avoid the habit of curling up over the telephone; instead, lean back in the chair or move around a bit.

When lowering yourself into or rising from a chair, keep your back straight, placing one foot ahead of the other for stability. (See figure 4–4.) Do not depend on the arms of the chair for support; let your leg muscles do the work. This is a time when you reap the benefits of regular exercise: You need strong thigh muscles for good balance.

Ascending and descending stairs also requires muscular strength, especially in the thighs. Those knee bends mentioned in the isotonics section will help develop the thigh muscles. As you ascend and descend the stairs, place your hand lightly on the hand-

Figure 4–4
Let your leg and thigh muscles do the work when seating yourself or rising from a chair. Keep your head up when going up and down stairs.

rail for protection against a fall. Keep your head up; there is no need to watch every step as you move up and down the stairs. (See figure 4–4.) Your mind can be compared to a computer that can gauge the depth and width of the steps and measure the motion accordingly.

Posture does make a difference! Posture has a strong subliminal impact on others. An expensive suit can look shabby on a slouching figure. Rounded shoulders and lowered eyes do not project a professional image.

Muscle Relaxation

Busy people often find their muscles tensing from the demands of a hectic schedule. A good way to avoid tenseness is to practice a form of muscle relaxation that is sometimes called the five-minute-two-hour nap.

When muscles start to tense across the shoulders and in the jawline or neck, it is a signal to seek privacy and relax for five minutes. Close your eyes and picture a restful scene that makes you feel peaceful. Then follow the steps in muscle relaxation described below and illustrated in figure 4–5.

- Breathe deeply, and fill the air sacs all the way to the bottom of your lungs with oxygen.

- Tighten the muscles in your right arm by clenching your hand into a fist and contracting all the muscles throughout

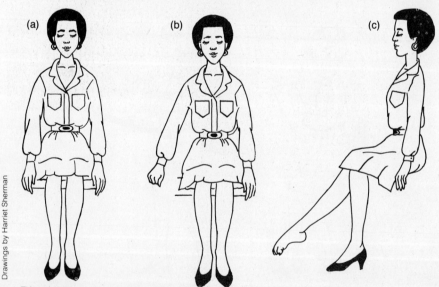

Drawings by Harriet Sherman

Figure 4–5
The steps in muscle relaxation include:
(a) closing eyes and breathing deeply
(b) clenching fist and contracting muscles in each arm
(c) contracting muscles in each foot and leg

the arm. After twenty seconds, release and relax the muscles. Notice the warm tingling sensation in your fingers caused by the release of tension. The palms of your hands should feel relaxed. How does the lower arm feel? The upper arm?

- Repeat the procedure on the left arm.

- Clench the muscles in your right leg and foot. Curl your toes under and tighten up those muscles until the leg muscles start to quiver. After twenty seconds, relax and feel the tingling sensation throughout your leg. Do your toes feel relaxed? The muscles in your foot should feel warm and calm. Check your lower leg: Does it feel relaxed? How about your upper leg: Are the muscles relaxed?

- Repeat the procedure on the left leg.

- Now tighten your facial muscles. Clench your jaw, tighten your forehead muscles. After twenty seconds, relax and feel the tension release in the facial muscles.

- Tighten the muscles in the pelvic region. Then relax and experience the calming sensation.

- Next, concentrate on the upper back. This is an area that usually needs much attention. Tighten the muscles across the shoulders and in the neck. Really clench those muscles, then relax and experience the release of pressure.

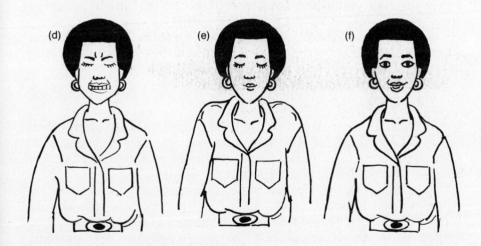

(d) contracting facial muscles, then relaxing them
(e) contracting shoulder and neck muscles, then relaxing them
(f) opening your eyes and smiling

A fast-food counter is not the best place to fill your nutritional needs.

- Your whole body is now relaxed. Remain still and feel the calming sensation. Your eyes should still be closed.
- After several seconds, if you haven't fallen asleep, open your eyes and smile. You are ready to face the remainder of the day.

Mental Benefits of Exercise

Exercise can make a difference in your life. The preceding portion of this chapter has emphasized the physical rewards of regular exercise; sometimes overlooked are its positive psychological effects. Studies show that exercise consistently relieves depression and anxiety, and is more effective than tranquilizers as a muscle relaxant.

Nutrition

Exercise alone will not make your body strong, attractive, and healthy. Nutrition is equally important. You have probably heard this advice so much from your parents, teachers, doctors, and coaches that the words are becoming meaningless.

But have you stopped to think of the consequences of a steady diet of fried fast foods and carbonated beverages? Consistently eating like this can lead to such problems as dry skin, dull and lifeless hair, poor teeth, lack of energy, eye irritation, muscle spasms, and depression. Your body is a complicated machine, and in order for it to function properly you must give it the proper fuel. Otherwise, you can expect some sort of breakdown after a period of time.

Read the following information, then question yourself. Do you want to satisfy your nutritional needs with the best, or are you going to settle for empty calories and junk foods?

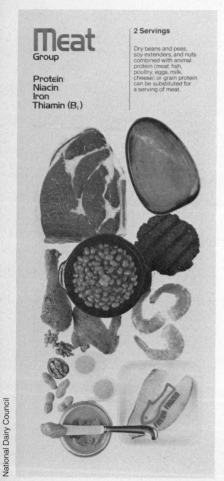

Meat
Group

Protein
Niacin
Iron
Thiamin (B₁)

2 Servings

Dry beans and peas, soy extenders, and nuts combined with animal protein (meat, fish, poultry, eggs, milk, cheese) or grain protein can be substituted for a serving of meat.

Protein-rich foods

PROTEINS

Because of their structure, these vital nutrients are often called the building blocks of the body. *Proteins* improve reflexes; give energy; promote healthy skin, hair, and nails; replace old cells; fight disease; heal fractures; and replace body tissue.

According to the United States Senate Select Committee on Nutrition and Human Needs, 12 percent of the daily diet should consist of protein. This nutrient can be stored in the body only to a limited extent; therefore, the body requires a daily intake of proteins to function properly.

Good sources of protein are fish, poultry, peanuts, butter, cheese, dried peas, beans, nuts, milk, eggs, and beef. It is the contention of many experts that Americans rely too heavily on beef as their primary source of protein. Beef does provide protein; however, it also supplies a lot of fat. For example, a five-ounce piece of beef will contain about 130 calories of protein and 400 calories of fat. In contrast to the American diet, seafood diets like those of the Oriental cultures provide sufficient protein plus the benefits of shiny hair, clean complexions, and lean bodies.

FATS

Fats are fundamental to the diet. Although many people mistakenly think all fat is bad and should be avoided, a *limited* amount of fat is vital because fats are the carriers of vitamins A, D, E, and K. Without fat in the bloodstream, these vitamins would not be distributed throughout the body. Fats also supply the essential fatty acids that the body cannot manufacture and that are responsible for the formation of cell membranes. Fat, which provides twice as many calories per gram of food as do protein or carbohydrates, is the most concentrated source of energy for our bodies.

HBJ Photo

Saturated and unsaturated fats

Fats can be divided into two categories, *saturated fats* and *unsaturated fats*. Saturated fats are found in meats, dairy products, and lard. These fats have the characteristics of hardening at room temperature. Unsaturated fats, which are considered by many nutritionists to be better for you than saturated fats, are oils such as safflower oil, sunflower oil, and corn oil. The United States Senate Select Committee on Nutrition and Human Needs recommends a diet that contains 10 percent saturated fat and 20 percent unsaturated fat.

Although fats are essential to your daily diet, moderation should be applied to your daily fat intake. Ideally, it should be around 30 percent of your total daily diet. If more than 42 percent of your diet is fat, you may find yourself with a weight problem. Unfortunately, fats are rather difficult to measure because so many are hidden in items such as baked goods, cheeses, fried foods, nuts, and mayonnaise.

CARBOHYDRATES

The most economical food source for energy and body heat are *carbohydrates*. These starches and sugars should make up about 58 percent of a balanced diet.

Carbohydrates, which can be found in a wide range of foods, can be divided into two categories, fattening carbohydrates and quality carbohydrates. A small amount of sugar is needed daily to provide quick energy, but many individuals consume more sugar than necessary. Candy, jam, honey, molasses, and syrup are some sources of fattening carbohydrates. The quality carbohydrates come from starches and natural sugars. Grains, rice, beans, fruits, and vegetables are excellent sources.

Fattening carbohydrates

WATER

Water is the most essential nutrient of all. You can live for weeks without food, but only a few days without water. Your total body weight is 64 percent water.

You need water to digest foods, to regulate body temperature, and to carry away body waste. Although the body manufactures some of its own water, you need to replenish the system with at least four glasses of water a day. Remember, water is a component of many beverages, fruits, or soups. Best of all is pure water: Get in the habit of drinking it.

Some cities have delicious water; others cannot boast of such a claim. If you find the water in your area not to your taste, you might consider buying bottled water. Because of its growing popularity, you can find an array of different types of bottled water, such as mineral, spring, and carbonated.

VITAMINS

Don't disregard the real importance of vitamins and minerals. Have you ever stopped to think of what might happen if your body lacked these nutrients?

The most essential nutrient is water.

A lack of vitamin B2, or riboflavin, will cause the eyes to become bloodshot or itchy. A lack of vitamin D will prevent your body from absorbing the calcium needed to maintain strong bones and teeth. A lack of vitamin A causes your skin to become dry. It also can cause night blindness. The problems that can occur as a result of vitamin or mineral deficiency are many. For easy reference to vitamins and minerals, their functions and sources, see table 4–1.

Popping a vitamin pill into your mouth once a day, however, does not insure you against vitamin deficiency. Vitamins cannot function if your diet lacks protein, fat, and carbohydrates, because these nutrients are necessary to carry the vitamins to all parts of the body. The best insurance against vitamin deficiency is a balanced diet.

Vitamin Overdose If a few vitamins are good, more must be better? This can be dangerous reasoning. An overdose of vitamin D, for example, can lead to liver and kidney damage. Contrary to what some vitamin salespeople say, vitamins A, D, and E are stored in the body. A build-up of such vitamins may cause ailments varying from high blood pressure and kidney problems to muscle weakness.

Therefore, if you feel you need a vitamin supplement, or if you are considering taking massive doses of a particular vitamin, consult your doctor first. He or she will be able to advise you about what is best for your particular needs.

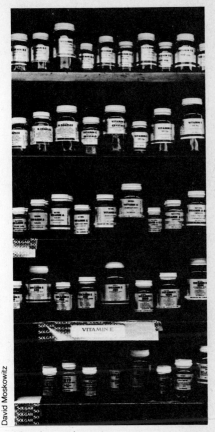

David Moskowitz

Vitamin supplements

THE BALANCED DIET

A balanced diet simply means one that is composed of the right amount of foods from each of the four food groupings shown in figure 4–6. Neglecting to eat foods from any of the four categories will cause your diet to be lacking in one or more valuable nutrients.

When you first glance at the food chart, you may feel that the recommended daily amount of food is too much to eat. However, large quantities of food are not necessary. In fact, you should feel satisfied sooner when eating a balanced meal than when eating a meal of junk food.

Weight Control

If you think you need to gain or lose weight, and are considering a *structured* diet, check table 4–3 to see what your ideal weight *should* be. People who want to maintain their weight or who want to lose only a few pounds may find that they can achieve results with minor modifications of their dietary habits. For instance, eliminate more starchy foods from an erstwhile nutritious, well-balanced diet. Prepare foods differently, by steaming vegetables and eliminating heavy sauces or by roasting rather than frying meats.

Common sense, increased exercise, monitoring of caloric intake, and general moderation through self-discipline is all many people really need to maintain or lose weight.

If you are extremely over- or underweight, you may need to try a more structured diet. Since weight control is a complicated bodily process, however, you should consult a doctor before starting any structured diet—and particularly any of the quick-weight-loss diets that are being ballyhooed today.

Table 4–1 NUTRIENTS AND HEALTH

Name of Nutrient	Some Reasons Why You Need It	How Much You Need Daily	Foods That Supply Important Amounts
Vitamin A	To keep skin smooth and soft To help keep mucous membranes firm and resistant to infection To protect against night blindness (when going from light to dark)	Adults: 5,000 International Units	Liver, yellow fruits, deep green and yellow vegetables, whole milk, cheddar-type cheese, cream, butter, margarine, watermelon, fresh asparagus, tomatoes, eggs
Thiamine (vitamin B₁)	To keep appetite and digestion normal To keep the nervous system healthy and prevent irritability To help body release energy from carbohydrates	Men: .9 to 1.2 milligrams Women: .8 milligram	Pork, lamb, other meats, enriched and whole grain breads and cereals, milk, white and sweet potatoes, dry beans and peas, fruits and vegetables
Riboflavin (vitamin B₂)	To help cells use oxygen To keep vision clear and prevent sensitivity of eyes to light To help keep skin and tongue smooth To help release energy from food	Men: 1.3 to 1.7 milligrams Women: 1.2 to 1.3 milligrams	Milk, liver, all kinds of cheese, lean meats, fish, poultry, eggs, leafy green vegetables
Niacin (another B vitamin)	To help body use carbohydrates, fats, and proteins For smooth skin and healthy digestive tract To keep nervous system healthy	Adults: 13 to 19 milligrams	Lean meats, poultry, peanuts, other nuts, enriched and whole-grain breads and cereals, potatoes, dried fruits
Ascorbic acid (vitamin C)	To make cementing materials that hold body cells together To make walls of blood vessels firm To help resist infections and to prevent fatigue To help heal wounds and broken bones	Men: 70 milligrams Women: 70 milligrams	Oranges, grapefruit, limes, tangerines, strawberries, cantaloupes, tomatoes, green peppers, broccoli, raw cabbage, lightly cooked greens, white potatoes

CALORIES

The kinds of food you eat and how much are the first things to consider if you wish to lose weight. Weight control can be better understood if you know what *calorie* means. In nutrition, one calorie equals the amount of heat needed to raise the temperature of one kilogram of water one degree centigrade. To get a clearer picture of the meaning of calorie, think of it as a measure of potential energy.

Table 4–1 (continued)

Name of Nutrient	Some Reasons Why You Need It	How Much You Need Daily	Foods That Supply Important Amounts
Vitamin D	To help the body absorb and use calcium and phosphorus to build bones and teeth	Children: 400 International Units	Vitamin D milk, fish liver oil, salmon, tuna, herring, mackerel, sunshine action
Calcium and phosphorus	To help build bones and teeth To help blood to clot (cal.) To help release energy from proteins, fats, and carbohydrates (phos.) To help blood neutralize acids and alkalies (phos.) To help muscles contract and relax For normal response of nerves to stimulation	Adults: .8 gram calcium .8 gram phosphorus Children: 1 to 1.4 grams calcium 1 to 1.4 grams phosphorus	Milk, cheese, ice cream, kale, turnip and mustard greens, collards, dried fruits
Sodium and potassium	For osmosis (passage of substances back and forth between cells and body fluids To help keep normal balance of water between cells and the fluids For normal response of nerves and contraction of muscles	Unknown (Intake is estimated to be 3 to 7 grams per day)	Table salt, milk, meat, fish, poultry, cheese, seafood, beets, celery, carrots
Iron	To build red blood cells which carry oxygen to all parts of the body	Adults: 10 to 12 milligrams	Liver, egg yolk, red meat, green leafy vegetables, dried fruits, enriched bread and cereals
Iodine	To help make thyroid hormones which regulate rate of body metabolism	Adults: .1 to .2 milligram	Seafood, iodized salt, some in all plants
Magnesium	To help build bones and teeth To help chemical reactions take place To have healthy nerves	Adults: .3 gram	Nuts, legumes, cereals, meats, milk, dried fruit

Source: Chart adapted from materials furnished by the U.S. Department of Agriculture Cooperative Extension Service, South Dakota State University, and from Edwina Morris, "Why Vitamins Are Vital to Life," Publication 469, Cooperative Extension Service, Mississippi State University.

MILK GROUP

Milk in some form
(1⅛″ cube cheese = 1 cup milk)
Children under 9   2–3 cups
Children 9–12   3 or more cups
Teenagers   4 or more cups
Adults   2 or more cups

MEAT GROUP

2 or more servings

beef, veal, pork, lamb, poultry, fish, eggs

dry beans, dry peas, nuts

VEGETABLE FRUIT GROUP

4 or more servings

citrus or other fruit for Vitamin C
dark green or deep yellow vegetable
   for Vitamin A
other vegetables and fruits

BREAD CEREAL GROUP

4 or more servings

whole grain or cereal

Drawing by Harriet Sherman

Figure 4–6 The Four Food Groups and Recommended Daily Allowances

When consumed, a calorie can be turned quickly into energy; if energy is not needed, the calorie is stored as fat. Body fat is actually potential energy stored for future use.

The number of calories you need is based on your energy level and size. If you are an active person, you will require more calories than a person who has a desk job. The activity chart in table 4–2 shows how many calories you burn while participating in various activities.

The number of calories you require to maintain your current weight varies according to your activity level. To get an idea of the approximate amount you need, figure that it takes 18 calories a day to maintain one pound of weight for a male. About 16 calories a day are needed to maintain one pound of a woman's weight. To find out how many calories you require for one day, multiply your weight by the appropriate amount. For example, a man weighing 160 pounds should consume 2,880 calories a day to maintain his weight (160 lbs. × 18 calories = 2,880 calories).

Consult your doctor before dieting.

Table 4–2

ENERGY EXPENDITURE BY A 150-POUND PERSON IN VARIOUS ACTIVITIES

Activity	Gross Energy Cost (cal. per hr.)	Activity	Gross Energy Cost (cal. per hr.)
Rest and Light Activity	50-200	Badminton	350
Lying down or sleeping	80	Horseback riding (trotting)	350
Sitting	100	Square dancing	350
Driving an automobile	120	Volleyball	350
Standing	140	Roller skating	350
Domestic work	180		
		Vigorous Activity	over 350
Moderate Activity	200-350	Table tennis	360
Bicycling (5½ mph)	210	Ditch digging (hand shovel)	400
Walking (2½ mph)	210	Ice skating (10 mph)	400
Gardening	220	Wood chopping or sawing	400
Canoeing (2½ mph)	230	Tennis	420
Golf	250	Water skiing	480
Lawn mowing (power mower)	250	Hill climbing (100 ft. per hr.)	490
Bowling	270	Skiing (10 mph)	600
Lawn mowing (hand mower)	270	Squash, handball, and racquetball	600
Fencing	300	Cycling (13 mph)	660
Rowboating (2½ mph)	300	Scull rowing (race)	840
Swimming (¼ mph)	300	Running (10 mph)	900
Walking (3¾ mph)	300		

Source: The President's Council on Physical Fitness and Sports, *Exercise and Weight Control* (Washington, D.C.: Government Printing Office, 1980).

Table 4–3

WEIGHTS OF PERSONS 25 to 59 YEARS OLD

	Men				Women		
Height	Small Frame	Medium Frame	Large Frame	Height	Small Frame	Medium Frame	Large Frame
5 ft. 2 in.	128-134	131-141	138-150	4 ft. 10 in.	102-111	109-121	118-131
5 ft. 3 in.	130-136	133-143	140-153	4 ft. 11 in.	103-113	111-123	120-134
5 ft. 4 in.	132-138	135-145	142-156	5 ft. 0 in.	104-115	113-126	122-137
5 ft. 5 in.	134-140	137-148	144-160	5 ft. 1 in.	106-118	115-129	125-140
5 ft. 6 in.	136-142	139-151	146-164	5 ft. 2 in.	108-121	118-132	128-143
5 ft. 7 in.	138-145	142-154	149-168	5 ft. 3 in.	111-124	121-135	131-147
5 ft. 8 in.	140-148	145-157	152-172	5 ft. 4 in.	114-127	124-138	134-151
5 ft. 9 in.	142-151	148-160	155-176	5 ft. 5 in.	117-130	127-141	137-155
5 ft. 10 in.	144-154	151-163	158-180	5 ft. 6 in.	120-133	130-144	140-159
5 ft. 11 in.	146-157	154-166	161-184	5 ft. 7 in.	123-136	133-147	143-163
6 ft. 0 in.	149-160	157-170	164-188	5 ft. 8 in.	126-139	136-150	146-167
6 ft. 1 in.	152-164	160-174	168-192	5 ft. 9 in.	129-142	139-153	149-170
6 ft. 2 in.	155-168	164-178	172-197	5 ft. 10 in.	132-145	142-156	152-173
6 ft. 3 in.	158-172	167-182	176-202	5 ft. 11 in.	135-148	145-159	155-176
6 ft. 4 in.	162-176	171-187	181-207	6 ft. 0 in.	138-151	148-162	158-179

Figures include 5 lbs. of clothing for men, 3 lbs. for women, and shoes with one-inch heels for both.

FIGURING OUT THE SIZE OF YOUR FRAME

■ Extend arm and raise forearm to 90-degree angle.

■ Hold fingers straight, turn palm away from body.

■ Put other thumb and index finger on protruding bones on either side of elbow, then measure the distance between thumb and forefinger.

■ Find your height (with 1-inch heels) in the table below. If your elbow measurement falls within the corresponding range, you have a medium frame. If it is larger, you have a large frame. If it is smaller, you have a small frame.

	Men		Women	
Height		Measurement	Height	Measurement
5′2″-5′3″		2½-2⅞	4′10″-5′3″	2¼-2½
5′4″-5′7″		2⅝-2⅞	5′4″-5′11″	2⅜-2⅝
5′8″-5′11″		2¾-3	6′	2½-2¾
6′-6′3″		2¾-3⅛		
6′4″		2⅞-3¼		

Source: Metropolitan Life Insurance Company.

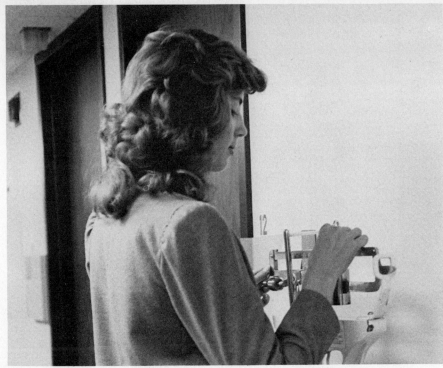

Weigh yourself at regular intervals but not more often than once a week.

LOSING WEIGHT

If you wish to lose weight, first decide how much you *should* weigh. See table 4–3 for ideal weight according to height and body frame. If you are a woman who wishes to weigh 110 pounds, multiply 110 by 16 to arrive at 1,760 calories per day (110 lbs. × 16 calories = 1,760 calories).

Do not let your daily calorie count drop below 1,200 calories; if you do, it may mean that you are *not* getting the necessary nutrients for a balanced diet.

A safe weight loss is in the range of one to three pounds a week. One pound of fat equals 3,500 calories. If you consume 1,000 fewer calories than usual each day and maintain the same activity level, it will take you three and a half days to lose one pound of weight. Should this sound too slow, consider increasing your activity level.

Counting calories can sometimes be deceiving. The types of foods you choose will also affect your weight loss. Sugary and starchy foods and alcoholic beverages have a high caloric value but little nutritional worth. Soda pop, candy, potato chips, sweet rolls, and cakes are examples of *empty-calorie foods*. These foods provide energy for a short time, then drop you into a mental slump. They also contribute to your total daily caloric intake without providing your system with necessary nutrients.

Phillips-Ramsey

An active sport

If your typical diet resembles the following, then you are heading for disaster.

Breakfast	Coffee
Snack	Coffee and sweet roll
Lunch	Hamburger and a cola drink
Snack	Candy bar
Evening meal	Tacos and beer

Dieting—even if it is unstructured—is not easy, but it can be done. You can accomplish a lot by decreasing without necessarily eliminating flour- and oil-based preparations and starchy foods; by eliminating raw sugar intake; by decreasing or eliminating alcoholic intake; and by increasing your intake of water, raw vegetables and fruits for snacks—a few among many examples of common sense calorie-control techniques that also may have positive effects on your mental condition.

CHOOSING A STRUCTURED DIET

The dozens of diets that are published in the popular press can be confusing to the prospective dieter. The Banting (fasting) diet, the fructose diet, the rice diet, and the grapefruit diet, for example, all promise near-instant results. If you want to determine which diet will work best for you, consult Consumer Guide's *Rating the Diets*, which describes and evaluates popular diets. You should be careful not to extend any diet beyond the time suggested by its source. Many, if not all, quick-weight-loss diets are highly *imbalanced* in order to achieve those rapid results, and as such they are safe only if you follow them for the relatively short periods of time recom-

Hazel Hankin

Diet pills can be dangerous.

mended. Many of these kinds of diets are accompanied by follow-up, well-balanced, *maintenance* plans to help you stay at the weight level you reached during the quick-weight-loss interval. Others recommend that you return to the quick-weight-loss diet after you've been on a more normal routine for a healthy length of time. Regardless, you should consult your doctor before launching any structured—and particularly a quick-weight-loss—diet.

Also beware of diet pills. These harmless-looking pills can cause increased pulse rate, nausea, nervousness, irritability, and insomnia. Certain pills do decrease the appetite at first, but become less effective after a few days. Some dieters, without their doctor's consultation, will then double the dosage; an act that can lead to serious physical and mental problems.

Find a doctor who practices good nutrition in his or her daily habits. A doctor who knows the value of exercise and a balanced diet can best direct you.

David Moskowitz

Dieting is not easy.

THE SEMI-FAST DIET

Because it conforms easily to the business schedule, an often-successful diet for a career person is the *semi-fast diet*. This diet is simple and easy to follow. Eat a large breakfast, then a very late lunch. These two meals will provide you with all the energy you need for the working day. You eliminate the evening meal, which usually provides unused energy that is stored as fat.

A good sample diet might be:

Breakfast	Fruit juice
	Milk and cereal
	Eggs and bacon
	Toast and butter
	Coffee
Lunch	Vegetable soup
	Salad with cheese chunks
	Fish
	Whole-wheat roll
Bedtime snack	Apple

This diet, of course, requires self-discipline and a change in your routine. But its basic principle is useful for any diet plan: Eat a good breakfast and keep your evening meal light.

SUCCESSFUL WEIGHT LOSS

On how many Mondays have you started a new diet? How many times have you failed to stick with the diet? Setting a goal and planning a diet is the easy part. Sticking with it is frequently another matter. It is easy to propose a diet plan and carry it through the first few days, but then emotional factors may start to weaken your

Hazel Hankin

Dozens of diet books promise instant results.

resolve. Or perhaps after a few days of success you will begin to rationalize that since you have been so faithful, you deserve a reward. Sound familiar? Look at the following list of excuses to see if any fit you:

- To be sociable, you must indulge.
- You are sad and need a pick-me-up.
- You are happy and want to celebrate.
- You feel nervous and need something to eat.
- You must not disappoint the hostess.

You can use all kinds of emotional arguments and rationalizations to defeat your diet plan. Following a diet takes daily self-discipline. It is a step-by-step process of self-denial.

Dieting means dealing with hunger pangs. Don't let the first signals of hunger weaken your resolve. Go hungry for a while. Experience the hunger and ask yourself if it is really so terrible. Remember that every time you feel hunger, it's a sign that you are losing weight. Learn to handle hunger pangs; don't ignore them for long periods of time, but remember that a few hours of hunger is not starvation.

It's possible to diet sensibly, even on a business schedule.

Snack machines test a dieter's self-discipline.

Health Foods

Health food is a broad term that is often liberally applied to various food products. In general, it can be said that the superior nutritional value of these products is unsubstantiated. The Food and Drug Administration (FDA) has not established any guidelines governing the use of the term "health food" or its contents. *Health food* is intended to mean food that is nutritionally sound and which contains *all* natural ingredients, as opposed to food that contains chemicals and preservatives. Although truth in advertising is required by the government, buyers still need to beware of misleading claims that may appear on products ranging from soups and jams to breads and cereals.

If you see the word "natural" displayed on an item in the supermarket, be aware that the product may contain only one or some natural ingredients, and that it may still contain additives or preservatives. Many commercially packaged foods do have unnecessary, if not harmful, additives and preservatives. Let your own nutritional values and common sense determine what you buy. Many people who patronize health or natural food stores today do so to avoid additives more than they do to necessarily gain extra nutritional value from alternative food products.

Organically grown is a term that is usually applied to foods—especially fresh produce—grown without chemical fertilizers or pesticides. The FDA finds no nutritional difference between the usual commercial foods and the higher-priced organically grown foods. Even foods that are grown without chemical fertilizers are not always completely pure. Soil that has been untreated for several

A health food store

years may still retain chemical fertilizer residue. Moreover, rainfall and winds can also carry chemicals from surrounding fields. Finally, consumers must rely on the honesty of the health food company. Foods are passed from grower to wholesaler to retailer with nothing but a verbal guarantee that all the products were grown on chemical-free land.[1]

Many commercial foods do have unnecessary additives in the form of artificial coloring, artificial flavoring, and sweeteners. As much as possible, avoid these.

Reading a Label

Any packaged food claiming nutritional value is required by law to carry a nutrition label. These labels provide a listing of ingredients, calorie count, and nutritional values.

The ingredients of a can or carton are listed in order of amount from the largest to the smallest. For example, check the ingredients listed on cereal boxes. Frequently, sugar will be first, meaning that sugar is the major ingredient in that package. (See figure 4–7 for an illustration.)

The nutrition label will also show the number and size of servings per container, calorie count, and amount in grams of protein, carbohydrates, and fat. Accompanying this information is the percentage of the *recommended daily allowance (RDA)* for vitamins. If the label states "vitamin C—25," this means that, if you eat the

[1]"It's natural! It's organic! Or is it?" *Consumer's Report* (July 1980), p. 410.

Crunchy Crispies

FORTIFIED WITH VITAMINS AND IRON

Product Information

A nutritious breakfast consists of juice or fruit, cereal with milk, toast with butter or margarine, and milk to drink.

NUTRITION INFORMATION PER SERVING
SERVING SIZE: 1 OZ. (ABOUT ⅞ CUP) (28.35 g)
SERVINGS PER PACKAGE: 12

Nutrients listed are for one serving.

Number of servings per container.

	1 OZ. (28.35 g) CEREAL	WITH ½ CUP (118 mL) VITAMIN D FORTIFIED WHOLE MILK
PERCENTAGES OF U.S. RECOMMENDED DAILY ALLOWANCES (U.S. RDA)		
PROTEIN	4%	10%
VITAMIN A	25%	30%
VITAMIN C	*	*
THIAMINE	25%	30%
RIBOFLAVIN	25%	35%
NIACIN	25%	25%
CALCIUM	*	15%
IRON	25%	25%
VITAMIN D	10%	25%
VITAMIN B₆	25%	30%
FOLIC ACID	25%	25%
VITAMIN B₁₂	25%	30%
PHOSPHORUS	8%	20%

Percentages of U.S. Recommended Daily Allowances.

*CONTAINS LESS THAN 2% OF THE U.S. RDA OF THESE NUTRIENTS.

INGREDIENTS: SUGAR, WHEAT, MALTED BARLEY, SALT. FORTIFIED WITH THE FOLLOWING NUTRIENTS: VITAMIN A PALMITATE, NIACIN, IRON, VITAMIN B₆, RIBOFLAVIN (VITAMIN B₂), THIAMINE MONONITRATE (VITAMIN B₁), FOLIC ACID, VITAMIN B₁₂, AND VITAMIN D₂. BHA ADDED TO PACKAGING MATERIAL TO PRESERVE FRESHNESS.

Sugar is listed first among ingredients.

CONTAINS 1.7% NON-NUTRITIVE CRUDE FIBER BY WEIGHT.

CARBOHYDRATE INFORMATION

	1 OZ. (28.35 g) CEREAL	WITH ½ CUP (118 mL) VITAMIN D FORTIFIED WHOLE MILK
CALORIES	100	180
PROTEIN	3 g	7 g
CARBOHYDRATE	18 g	24 g
FAT	0	4 g
STARCH AND RELATED CARBOHYDRATES	12 g	12 g
SUCROSE AND OTHER SUGARS	6 g	12 g
TOTAL CARBOHYDRATES	18 g	24 g

Notice throughout that the addition of milk changes the nutritional and caloric values of the cereal.

Nutrients in metric weights as grams (1 ounce = 28 grams).

suggested serving size, you will receive 25 percent of your needed daily amount of vitamin C.

Start reading labels; they can reveal some surprising facts, as well as help you learn the basics of good nutrition.

Does the routine of exercise and balanced eating sound irrelevant to the business career? On the contrary, more and more corporations are finding that a healthy employee is a productive employee. Many American firms have health facilities and employ full-time fitness directors to guide employees through exercise programs. Many other corporations set aside a conference room during lunch hour for calisthenics. "The list of firms committed to employee fitness reads like a Who's Who of the Fortune 500."[2]

KEY TERMS

poise	target zone	carbohydrates
aerobics	aerobic dance	calorie
cardiopulmonary system	thoracic	empty-calorie foods
vascular system	yoga	semi-fast diet
isotonics	proteins	health food
isometrics	saturated fats	organically grown
resting heart rate	unsaturated fats	RDA

[2]Kathy Megan, "Business Offering 'Thin' Fringe Benefits," Columbia News Service, Rapid City *Journal* (April 30, 1973), p. 13.

HBJ Photo

Participants in a company-sponsored athletic program.

TEST YOURSELF:
QUESTIONS FOR REVIEW AND DISCUSSION

1. Explain physical poise and mental poise. Can you have one without the other? Apply the concepts to office life.
2. What is meant by aerobic exercise? Name your favorite aerobic exercise and explain why.
3. Differentiate between isotonic and isometric exercises.
4. How does posture communicate attitude? Why is good posture so important in the business world? List some of the physical and mental benefits of good posture.
5. What are some good sources of protein? Of fat? Of carbohydrates? What percentage of your daily diet should consist of protein? Of fat? Of carbohydrates?
6. Name some saturated fats; some unsaturated fats.
7. Are vitamin pills worth the investment? What are the benefits of vitamin pills? The dangers?

APPLICATION EXERCISES

1. Physically fit people are becoming more appreciative of the importance of strong heart muscles. As a result, the timing of heartbeats has become a popular activity for the participants in various sports activities.

   A normal pulse rate is considered to be between 60 and 100 beats per minute. Generally, the better a person's physical condition, the lower the pulse rate. To make certain that you are not over-exerting yourself, count your pulse five minutes after exercising. It should be below 120. Ten minutes after exercising, it should be below 100.

   To count your pulse, count the number of heartbeats in a ten-second interval and multiply by six to determine the number of beats per minute.

   Listed below is a guide to recommended target heart rates during exercise. Try to achieve the appropriate heart rate while exercising in order to give your heart a workout.

AGE	HEART RATE
Under 30	160
35–39	150
40–44	145

   Source: Jeanette Farnsworth, The National Lifestyle Institute, Bountiful, Utah.

2. Keep a record of everything you eat for one week. At the end of the week, evaluate your diet on the basis of caloric intake and fulfillment of the recommended daily allowances from the four food groups. Make adjustments to your diet where needed.

Suggested Readings

Anderson, James L., and Martin Cohen. *The Competitive Edge: The West Point Guide for the Weekend Athlete*. New York: William Morrow & Co., Inc., 1981.

Carr, Rachel. *Yoga for You*. Englewood Cliffs, N.J.: Prentice-Hall, 1981.

Fixx, James F. *Jackpot!* New York: Random House, 1982.

Jacobs, Don T. *Getting Your Executives Fit*. Mountain View, Calif.: Anderson World, Inc., 1981.

Kirschmann, John D. *Nutrition Almanac*. New York: McGraw-Hill, 1979.

Mason, L. John. *Guide to Stress Reduction*. Culver City, Calif.: Peace Press, Inc., 1980.

Winckler, Isabel. *The Encyclopaedia of Diets*. England: State Mutual Bank, 1981.

Wynder, Ernst. *Book of Health: A Complete Guide to Making Health Last a Lifetime*. American Health Foundation, 1981.

5

PLANNING AND BUYING A WARDROBE

COMPREHENSIVE GOAL

To examine the importance of "visual packaging" in the business world, and to instruct you in color coordination, correct use of clothing lines, wardrobe shopping, and clothing care

SPECIFIC OBJECTIVES

After reading this chapter, you will be able to:

- understand color theory
- understand the visual effects of various clothing "lines"
- understand the principles of proper clothing proportion
- identify various weaves and materials
- plan a personal wardrobe, based on the principles of color, line, and proportion
- make informed judgments about color, line, construction, and price when shopping for a wardrobe
- use accessories to complete an ensemble
- apply the rule of fourteen to an outfit
- understand and apply the principles of clothing care

Does clothing make the person or vice versa? One statement can generally be made: A successful business person is a well-dressed person.

The importance of wise clothing choice has been documented in John T. Molloy's *Dress for Success*. In his survey of 100 top executives of major corporations, 96 percent answered that the employees of their firms had a much better chance of getting ahead if they knew how to dress; 72 percent indicated they would hold up the promotion of a person who didn't dress properly; 84 percent said they turned down people who showed up at job interviews improperly dressed.[1]

In *You Are What You Wear*, clothing expert William Thourlby writes, "When you step into a room, even though no one in that room knows you or has seen you before, they will make ten decisions about you based solely on your appearance." Thourlby further states: "To be successful in almost any endeavor, you must be sure that these decisions about you are favorable, because in that first impression you make—you are what you wear."[2]

First impressions are largely visual. True, clothes will not compensate for weak credentials, poor work records, and bad habits; but a person who is neat in appearance can open doors where a sloppy one will not be admitted.

Wardrobe Analysis

A good business wardrobe need not be extensive. Many well-dressed people have amazingly few articles of clothing. They build a wardrobe around a few good articles that can be used in several ways, starting with one basic outfit in a neutral color, then adding coordinating pieces.

The first step to a good wardrobe is to analyze your current clothing inventory. Begin by sorting through your closet and discarding any clothes you haven't worn in the last eighteen months. Be realistic; if you haven't worn an item in that length of time, chances are good you never will wear it again.

After you have removed the space wasters, take a pen and refer to the chart in table 5–1. Place a check in each box that describes an article of clothing you now have.

After completing the chart, look it over and ask yourself if one color is predominant. A basic wardrobe should be organized around one neutral color (for example, gray or beige) or dark color (for example, navy or brown). Use pastels and bright colors for variety and accent.

E. I. Du Pont de Nemours & Co., Inc.

A successful business person is a well-dressed person.

Fashions courtesy of The Broadway (So. Ca.)

[1]John T. Molloy, *Dress for Success* (New York: Warner Books, 1982).

[2]William Thourlby, *You Are What You Wear* (New York: New American Library, 1980).

For example, using gray as the basic color, see how many possible outfits you can coordinate with the following clothing articles:

Item	Color
1 Suit with vest	Gray
1 Sport coat or blazer	Gray tweed
5 Shirts or blouses	White, white on white, light blue, blue pinstriped on white, pale yellow
5 Ties or scarves	Navy blue, striped, patterned gray, green polka dot, print
1 pr. Trousers or slacks	Muted gray plaid

Table 5–1

WARDROBE INVENTORY

	Black	Gray	White	Beige	Tan	Brown	Camel	Red	Pink	Maroon	Yellow	Light Green	Dark Green	Light Blue	Navy	Orange	Lavender	Turquoise	Magenta	Purple	Chartreuse	Golden Yellow
Basic suit, skirted suit, pantsuit																						
Shirts, blouses																						
Trousers, pants																						
Sport jackets, blazers																						
Dresses																						
Ties, scarves, belts, etc.																						
Shoes																						
Belts																						
Coats																						
Socks																						

As limited as this amount of clothing may seem, it can produce a number of attractive combinations. By adding a few items from time to time, such as a solid-colored skirt or pants to match or blend with the suit coat or blazer, you can continue to extend your basic wardrobe indefinitely.

Later in this chapter, color consultants are recommended as a good resource for helping you plan a wardrobe around your "right" color. The gray used in the preceding example may not be *your* color. If not, you can apply the same concept to building your wardrobe around a color that *is*.

Sort through your closet
and eliminate space wasters.

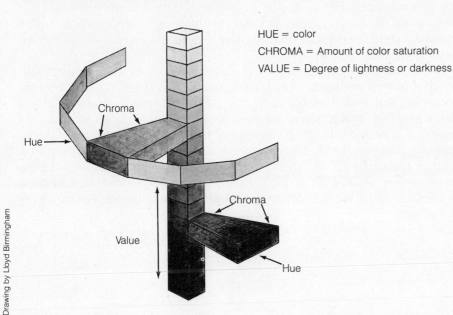

HUE = color
CHROMA = Amount of color saturation
VALUE = Degree of lightness or darkness

Chroma

Hue →

Chroma

Value

Hue

Figure 5–1
Cutaway Scheme of the Munsell Color System

Color

As you have seen, by mixing and matching a few items you can create several new combinations. But you need to know the basics of color theory to create well-coordinated outfits.

Your first step is to review some standard terms. *Hue* refers to the characteristics that differentiate one color from another. *Value* indicates the range of light and dark in a color. *Chroma* or saturation are terms that refer to the purity of a color; a color in its strongest chroma is devoid of white. (See colorplate 5 and figure 5–1 for an illustration of these terms.) *Shade* means that black has been added to the pure pigment; *tone* refers to various modifications of a color; and *tint* means that white has been added.[3]

[3]The definitions of these terms vary among color companies.

What clothes can be
coordinated with others?

The *primary colors* are yellow, blue, and red. *Secondary colors* are green, violet, and orange. You can blend equal amounts of yellow and blue to produce green, equal amounts of blue and red to produce violet, and equal amounts of red and yellow to produce orange. Combinations of the primary and secondary colors create the *intermediate colors* of orange, green, and violet as shown in figure 5–2.

Refer to the color wheels for help in understanding the following color schemes:

A *monochromatic* scheme utilizes one color in various shades, tints, and tones. For example, a navy suit with a blue shirt and blue tie would be monochromatic. A pink blouse, maroon skirt, and a scarf in shades of pink and maroon would also make an attractive monochromatic outfit.

A *complementary* color scheme uses two colors that are opposite each other on the color wheel, such as green and red. The two colors complement and intensify each other. For instance, red makes green look greener, and green makes red look redder. Strong color combinations, like red and green, are great for billboards and party decorations, but not for clothing. Instead, use a shade of one color and a tint of the other color. An interesting color combination would be a dark-green skirt with a pink blouse. A rust-colored suit with a light-blue shirt would also make an attractive complementary combination.

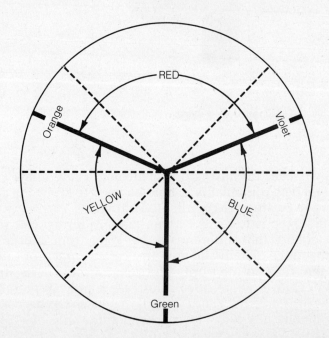

Figure 5–2
This diagram of a color wheel will help you understand the color schemes described in the text.

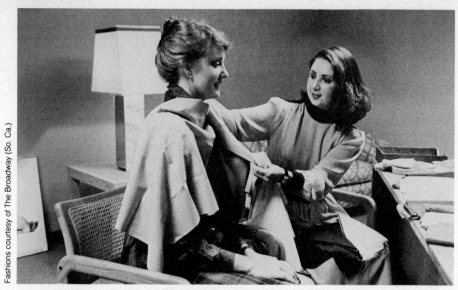

Color consultants also help clients select their best fashion shades.

Analogous color schemes are created by using two colors side by side on the color wheel. Red and orange, blue and violet, or yellow and green are examples. Again, the colors should be placed together in a range of shades, tints, and tones. A muted-gray plaid suit with small stripes of green and blue running through the plaid utilizes the principle of analogous color harmony. A shirt in either a tint of blue or green would be appropriate with this suit. The tie could have a subtle arrangement of blue and green.

A *split-complement* color scheme is a combination of one color with another next to its complement on the wheel. For example, blue could be matched with either red or yellow. A yellow dress with accents of blue is an example of the split-complement color scheme, as is a neutral suit with flecks of blue and red worn with a white shirt and a navy and maroon striped tie.

A *triadic* color scheme is a combination of three colors that are equidistant on the color wheel. One color should be the basic one, with the other two used as accents. Using yellow, blue, and red to form a triad, you might wear a navy suit, a white shirt, and a striped tie of red and yellow on navy.

If you choose a multicolored plaid, print, or stripe as the principal item in an ensemble, you will usually find that it falls into one of the color schemes listed previously. Pick one or two colors in that fabric to accent the costume. If you wear a plaid jacket, you might repeat one or two of its subordinate colors in the tie and pants.

Now apply these fundamentals of color to your wardrobe. Can it be expanded with a few additional pieces in the right color? Possibly you have some previously overlooked articles that could be coordinated.

THE PSYCHOLOGY OF COLOR

Color has a language of its own. Red reminds people of warmth, passion, or anger; blue represents depression or calm and peace; white stands for purity and innocence. Each of the colors of the spectrum communicates moods, feelings, and emotions. Can you think of other examples of colors that communicate?

Color consultants are aware of the effect of colors on people's moods; therefore, they are careful to choose colors appropriate to the mood they want a setting or a product to convey. For example, the interior colors of passenger planes are purposely coordinated to make the passengers feel relaxed and cheerful. Beauty products are seldom packaged in brown jars. The recreational vehicle industry knows the value of color. A camper design can be reproduced in models with the same floor plan and the same features but different color schemes, and one color scheme will outsell the others.

When John Molloy tested business clothing, he found green and certain shades of brown disliked by most people for office wear. He strongly advocates conservative colors such as gray, beige, and navy for business wear by men.[4] These colors, as well as being easily coordinated in your wardrobe, tend to inspire confidence in others.

Color makes a statement about you and the firm you represent. Notice the different professions and the predominant colors worn by their members. Have you seen many stockbrokers in flashy reds and electric blues? On the other hand, how many artists do you find in three-piece gray suits?

COLOR AND YOUR COMPLEXION

Your hair, eyes, and skin tones affect your wardrobe color choices. You probably already know this from your shopping experiences. However, many individuals do not realize the effect that facial skin undertones have on clothing color. *Facial undertones* can be divided into two broad categories, blue and yellow. People with predominantly blue undertones cannot wear most hues of orange, while individuals in the yellow undertone category find some shades of red and blue-green impossible to wear. To determine if you are a blue- or yellow-undertoned person, take two relatively large pieces of material, one in purplish red and the other in orange. Put one, then the other, near your face. If you look good with the purplish red, you have blue facial undertones. If you find orange does wonders for you, you have yellow undertones.

Some color consultants have divided the personal color categories into four seasonal types: summer, winter, autumn, and spring. The summer and winter seasonal types are the blue undertones; the autumn and spring types are the yellow undertones. The same principle of blue and yellow undertones still applies; however,

[4]Molloy, *Dress for Success*.

the four categories give more detail for the various personal color keys. *Color Me Beautiful*, by Carole Jackson, is a good book about the seasonal color types.

This coloring remains consistent from childhood to old age. What does change from day to day is the amount of blue or yellow in the skin. Your skin is a living organism that reacts to your body chemistry. When you are healthy, pinkish tones will be splashed across the facial canvas. When you feel tired and run down, gray tones will predominate in your complexion, and normally flattering colors can look wrong on certain days.

Wardrobe Planning

Look at your wardrobe inventory (table 5–1) again. What additional colors could be added to your wardrobe? Place X's in the columns if you plan to purchase that item in that particular color.

Table 5–2

A MAN'S BUSINESS WARDROBE

Item	Quantity	Colors	Fabric
Suit	2	Grays, navy, beige	Wool, wool blends, cotton, cotton blends
Sport jackets	2	Gray, blue, beige, plaids	Wool, wool blends, linen, corduroy, tweeds, cotton, cotton blends
Pants	3	Solid colors	Wool, wool blends, gabardine, flannel, cotton, cotton blends
Belts	2	Brown, black	Leather
Shirts	10	White, white background, pastels	Cotton, cotton blends, synthetics
Ties	10	An assortment of colors and patterns	Varied
Socks	10 pr.	Dark	Wool, nylon, cotton
Shoes	3 pr.	Black, brown	Leather
Overcoat, topcoat, or raincoat	1	Beige or dark	Wool or, for raincoats, cotton or cotton blend

There is another point to consider before you make your shopping list: How many suits, dresses, shirts, etc., do you need? Study tables 5–2 and 5–3 for suggestions for the individual entering the business world. The kinds of clothes you need will vary, of course, depending on the part of the country you live in.

Shopping

With carefully prepared lists of your needs and color choices, you are now ready to go shopping. But there is one more important matter to be covered before the shopping trip: money. Certainly,

Table 5–3
A WOMAN'S BUSINESS WARDROBE

Item	Quantity	Colors	Fabric
Suit	1	Grays, blue, brown, beige	Wool, wool blends, linen, cotton, cotton blends
Jackets or blazers	2	Variety of colors, plaids	Velvet, corduroy, wool tweeds, linen, cotton, cotton blends
Skirts	5	Variety of colors, muted plaids	Wool, wool blends, tweeds, linen, cotton, cotton blends
Pants	2	Shaded colors	Gabardine, wool, wool blends, linen, cotton, cotton blends
Dresses	3	Tinted colors, prints, and designs	Wool, polyester, jersey, synthetics, cotton, cotton blends
Blouses	8	Tinted colors, prints, and designs	Cotton, cotton blends, synthetics
Scarves	10	All colors	Silk, cotton, synthetics
Stockings	6 pr.	One shade darker than skin	Nylon
Shoes	4 pr.	Black, brown, matching colors	Leather
Coat	1	Dark neutral color	Wool, wool blend
Belts	Several	Various	Leather, fabric, metal

A knowledgeable salesperson can be helpful to shoppers.

your budget will dictate how much you can spend for a certain clothing item, but even within the confines of a budget you will probably have some flexibility. Therefore, another consideration should enter into the final decision. This is whether you are going to purchase the more expensive version of a garment or the cheaper version. In other words, are you going to spend $200 for a suit or $75? At first, the $75 suit may sound like a real bargain, but that is not always the case. Compare the quality of workmanship, the material, the styling, and the buttons. Consider how you feel in each suit. If you feel better dressed in the higher-priced suit, chances are you are going to want to wear it more frequently. In contrast, the lower-priced suit may hang in the closet after only a few wearings. By applying simple mathematics, you can decide which suit is really the more expensive:

$75 suit worn five times in one season = $15 a wearing
$200 suit worn twenty times in one season = $10 a wearing

Of course, the higher-priced suit is not always the better-quality garment. Many times the extra money buys you a fancy label and little else. Smart shoppers know how to look for quality without the crutch of a label. They also watch for sales. Toward the end of a season, you will be able to spend the same amount you would have spent at the beginning, while getting better-quality items. Moreover, if you can forecast your needs, you may be able to outfit yourself for the next season at a considerable savings. Shopping at discount stores and factory outlets is another way to find bargains. These places often carry overstock from excellent manufacturers at bargain prices.

SHOPPING CHECKPOINTS

Wise shopping takes some training. The following points should be considered when shopping for clothing items:

1. Examine the fabric. Will it wear well? Does it have body? Twist the sleeve of the garment to see how easily it wrinkles. Pull the fabric one way and then another to check the weave and amount of ''give.'' See if the garment has been preshrunk.
2. Consider whether the garment requires dry cleaning or is washable. If it is a garment that has to be dry-cleaned after every wearing, add more money to the cost of the garment. If it is washable, will it wash easily? Will it withstand many washings?
3. Check seam allowances and hemlines. Generous seam allowances of at least ¼ inch are important to prevent the material from splitting under stress.
4. Look at the buttons and buttonholes. Are the buttons of good quality? How securely are they attached to the fabric? Is the stitching around the buttonholes even?

Fashions courtesy of The Broadway (So. Ca.)

Examine garments carefully before buying.

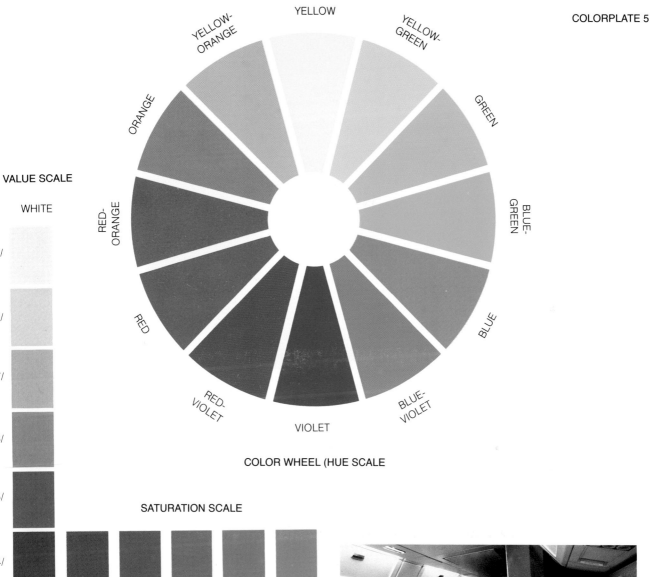

YELLOW

YELLOW-ORANGE

YELLOW-GREEN

ORANGE

GREEN

RED-ORANGE

BLUE-GREEN

RED

BLUE

RED-VIOLET

BLUE-VIOLET

VIOLET

COLOR WHEEL (HUE SCALE

VALUE SCALE

WHITE

9/

8/

7/

6/

5/

4/

3/

2/

1/

BLACK

SATURATION SCALE

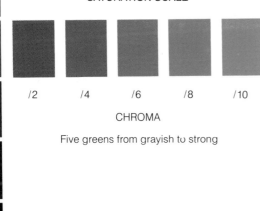

/2   /4   /6   /8   /10

CHROMA

Five greens from grayish to strong

The interior of this airplane has been decorated in warm colors intended to make riders feel cheerful.

In coordinating your wardrobe, choose two to three basic colors, such as taupe and black as featured here. These colors are neutrals, and the rust color provides the accent. Neutral colors lend themselves well to a variety of accents that can help extend your wardrobe.

Monochromatic need not be dull. The major colors in this wardrobe are in blues and grays, but the rich accent tones dramatize the overall effect. By choosing accent pieces that have both colors, it is possible to mix and match to create many different looks.

Men's wardrobes can also be color-coordinated. The tans and blues shown here can complement each other when used together. They can also be used separately, in differing tones, to create a monochromatic look.

Top left, analogous color scheme of violet and red. Here the violet predominates; the intensity of the red is muted by the shades and tints of violet in the plaid.

Top right, a complementary color scheme of blue-green and red-orange. Employing red-orange only in the piping and the shoes makes it possible to use it at full intensity.

Bottom left, a split complement color scheme of blue and red. White piping intensifies the colors.

Summer is winter's sister, and summer skin tones are also flattered by blue undertones. Soft shades, rather than true, vivid colors, look best on a summer-toned person.

Winter skin tones wear black and white well. Vivid colors and icy pastels with blue undertones also enhance people with winter coloration.

Autumn skin tones are enhanced by warm colors that have golden undertones. Colors, such as this "red," should be gold- or orange-based rather than blue-based.

Spring skin tones have delicate coloration that is enhanced by clear, warm colors and some brights, but all colors should have yellow undertones. Peach, coral, salmon, camel, honey, and golden tan are among the many choices a spring-toned person can wear well.

Every season introduces a "new" rainbow of fashion colors that are expected to be popular. Color choices should be based on the wearer's right "season." A color consultant can help you to determine the many colors you can wear in order to enhance your own coloring while being "in fashion."

5. If the fabric is patterned, checked, or plaid, see if it is matched well at the seams.
6. Consider the color. Is it flattering? Can it be coordinated with the rest of your wardrobe? If the material has a design or print, are the colors stamped on or woven into the fabric? Look at the back side of the fabric. A good woven fabric will look good on its reverse side. A stamped-on color will appear solid on the reverse side unless some colors have bled through.

Using these checkpoints as a guide for wise shopping, you will soon develop an "eye" for quality. Moreover, each category of apparel has special features that should be evaluated to insure a good buy.

When you go shopping, wear an outfit much like the one you plan to buy. There are three good reasons for this. First, if you are shopping for a relatively expensive article of clothing, you may receive more courteous attention from salesclerks if you are not in your favorite old jeans. Second, you can get a more accurate indication of fit if, for example, you try on a jacket over a blouse or shirt. Finally, you can better judge the overall appearance of the new clothes if you are wearing appropriate shoes and accessories.

In conclusion, remember the primary principle of wise shopping. Don't purchase *anything*, even at a rock-bottom price, if it is not absolutely perfect for you. If the color is wrong, the fit a little tight, the collar too loose, the slacks too baggy, you will never feel good in the garment.

Sport jackets and blazers are constructed similarly.

JACKETS, BLAZERS, SPORT COATS

The basic construction of these garments is similar. When trying on a jacket, check the collar and lapels to make sure they lie flat. There should be no rolls or bulk, and the material should be well-pressed. Now raise your arms and swing them forward. Is there enough material across the back to allow freedom of movement? Are the armholes large enough? Turn and look at the back of the jacket in the mirror. Does it hang properly or is there an excess of material, causing a fold?

Next, check the sleeve. Make sure it is not too long or too short. Sleeves should usually reach to about five inches from the thumb tip. Men should remember to allow for about a half inch of the shirt sleeve to show.

Button the front of the jacket. For a comfortable fit, the jacket should touch the body, not bind it.

Make one last test of fit to see that the length of the jacket is just "right." The bottom line of the jacket produces a very noticeable line and a jacket that is an inch too long or too short will unbalance the total look.

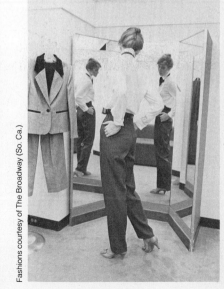

Check fit and length of pants.

PANTS AND TROUSERS

Try on pants or trousers with a blouse or shirt to give you an accurate idea of fit and appearance. Look closely in the mirror to make sure a blouse or shirt line does not show. If it does, the pants are too tight. Now check the waistband. You do not want this band too tight, because it will fold over and appear sloppy. Next, sit down. Is there enough material across the back? Stand and bend to check for freedom of movement. The crotch should be neither too tight nor too baggy. Note the length. Men's pants with cuffs should lightly touch the shoe. Without cuffs, they should have a slanted leg that is longer at the heel and shorter in front. If the fit is not perfect, ask for alterations.

SKIRTS

When trying on a skirt, make certain that the waistband fits comfortably. If the band is too tight, it will fold over. Moreover, a tight waistband makes you look fatter, because it causes bulges above and below the belt line. Examine the skirt for ample seam and hem allowances. Don't buy a skirt that is too short; even if it can be lengthened, the original factory hemline is likely to show. If the skirt is too long, have a tailor make alterations or, if you alter the skirt yourself, ask a friend to mark the desired length with chalk or pins to ensure an even hemline.

BLOUSES AND SHIRTS

For a crisp, fresh look, washable cotton blends are generally the most satisfactory. One hundred percent cotton wrinkles easily, whereas a blend of cotton and polyester gives you the feel of cotton

Skirt lengths vary from year to year. Choose a length in which you are comfortable. Remember, it is easier to shorten a skirt than to lengthen it.

Silky, lightweight materials are excellent for blouses.

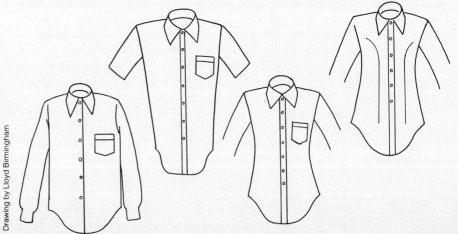

Figure 5–3
Men's Shirt Styles

and the wrinkle-free quality of polyester. One hundred percent polyester fabric is another good choice: It washes well, wrinkles very little, and has a silky texture. Many other lightweight materials, such as Qiana and Arnel, are excellent for shirts and blouses. Silk sometimes is difficult to wash and iron properly and often requires dry-cleaning.

Check the workmanship of the shirt or blouse. Examine the buttons, buttonholes, and seams. Make sure that the material allowance permits freedom of movement without bagginess. The collar size of men's shirts is measured around the neck, starting at the Adam's apple. Men's shirt sleeves are measured from the bone at the base of the neck to the wrist. The cuffs should button comfortably at the wrist. Figure 5–3 shows the various styles of men's shirts.

Shirts should permit freedom of movement without being baggy.

DRESSES

To give yourself a good idea of fit and correct length when you try on dresses, wear the appropriate undergarments and shoes. Examine the dress to make certain the neckline lies flat and smooth. Notice the seams and where they fit on your body: The shoulder seam should fall at the end of the shoulder and the bodice darts should end at the fullest part of the bust. The waistline should rest correctly on your figure. The zipper should be of good quality. Figure 5–4 demonstrates the points to look for in achieving a good fit.

COATS

Unless you have an unlimited supply of money, you will probably only purchase one good coat every two or three years. This

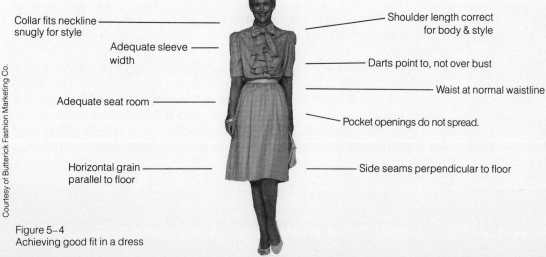

Collar fits neckline snugly for style

Adequate sleeve width

Adequate seat room

Horizontal grain parallel to floor

Shoulder length correct for body & style

Darts point to, not over bust

Waist at normal waistline

Pocket openings do not spread.

Side seams perpendicular to floor

Figure 5–4
Achieving good fit in a dress

investment requires careful shopping. The following guidelines can help you choose a good basic coat that will wear well through several years' use:

- Wear a suit when you try on coats. This will give you an idea of how the coat fits over your suit jackets.

- Purchase a coat that is simply designed. Don't buy a coat that has many buttons, straps, pockets, etc. You will quickly tire of this detailing. Also, unusual buttons, straps, and unique accents are difficult to replace if lost.

- Choose a coat in a neutral or dark color that doesn't show dirt easily and one that will match most of your wardrobe.

- Be sure the weight and warmth of the coat are suitable for the climate in which you live.

- Pick an easy-to-clean cloth coat. Leathers and suedes are attractive, but are expensive to have cleaned.

- Select a coat you feel good in. It should fit right; the color should complement your face; and the style should become you.

SHOE SHOPPING

Another clothing category that deserves attention is shoes. Don't be guilty of spending all your grooming time and wardrobe money on clothing and forgetting that scuffed, run-down shoes can ruin an otherwise attractive appearance.

When you go shoe shopping, remember that the foot can expand during the day by as much as one full size. Consequently, the best time to shop for a good fit is late afternoon. Try on the shoes and walk around on the store's carpet for a while. Does the heel slip away from your foot as you walk? Wiggle your toes to check for adequate space. When trying on a leather shoe, you may find it a bit tight, but leather will give and conform to your foot after several wearings. An imitation leather or vinyl shoe, because it is less pliable, may never conform; instead, your foot has to conform to the shoe, an uncomfortable solution which leads to calluses and bunions. Generally, you will find that leather is the best material for shoes: It is long-wearing, looks stylish, and allows the foot to breathe.

If you are buying shoes for office wear, pick subtle colors and conservative styles, such as tie shoes for men and closed pumps for women.

ACCESSORIES

Accessories can stretch your wardrobe and add sparkle to it. Moreover, these extra wardrobe pieces—scarves, ties, belts, jew-

Burberrys®

A simply designed coat, in a neutral color, is the most practical choice for the professional wardrobe.

Fashions courtesy of The Broadway (So. Ca.)

Women's shoe styles change as often as clothing fashions, but a comfortable "classic" in a neutral color is a good choice for limited budgets.

Men's shoe styles are also varied, but leather in a subdued style works best in office environments.

Three ways to tie a scarf

elry, even the glasses you wear—can enable you to express your individual style in any attire.

Scarves   These have endless uses, ranging from head coverings to attractive suit decorations. They are a particularly effective way of dressing up or toning down an outfit. You can use an assortment of solid and printed scarves interchangeably with suits, dresses, and blouses to make your wardrobe look bigger and brighter.

Ties   There are seven types of tie: solid, polka-dot, club, rep, foulard, paisley, and plaid. A solid tie in a dark, conservative color tends to give the wearer a distinguished appearance, and is a safe choice with patterned shirts. A polka-dot tie is elegant. The material should have a high sheen; the smaller the polka dots, the more elegant the look. A *club tie* has a minute repeating pattern woven in the material. A *rep tie* is conservatively colored, with diagonal stripes. A *foulard* is imprinted with a very small geometric design. Because the design of a *paisley tie* is rather busy, with many colors in its teardrop-shaped motif, paisley ties leave and return to the fashion scene. Plaid ties are frequently worn with casual clothes and are often sold in wool or cotton fabrics.

The knot shown in figure 5–5 can be useful for both ties and scarves.

Belts   Belts are a versatile and often inexpensive way to update or change a look. You may choose belts from a wide variety of materials—leather in all widths, fabric sashes, and metallic, to name a few. Here are a few keys to wearing belts attractively. If you are petite or full-busted, your belts should not be more than two inches wide. If you are long-waisted, a belt in a contrasting color can give you a shorter look. To achieve a long or tall appearance, choose a belt in the same color family as your dress or separates.

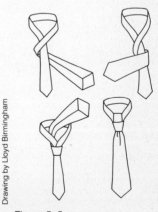

Figure 5–5
Tying a necktie

Hats can be fashionable, but they are generally worn outside of the office.

Jewelry In the office, the rule of moderation applies to jewelry. Jewelry that dangles or jingles is distracting to others and gets in your way. Save it for the evening or the weekend when you want to look dramatic or glamorous.

Glasses Glasses, if chosen wisely, will enhance your features and your wardrobe. If you do need glasses, you should first of all consult a good ophthalmologist. Then take the prescription to a reputable optician. As well as filling the prescription to the specifications of your doctor, the optician will help you select frames appropriate for your face shape and your life style. Figure 5–6 shows some examples.

Contact lenses now come in a variety of types. There are hard lenses, soft lenses, and even tinted lenses, if you want to enhance your eye color. If you wish to wear contact lenses, consult an ophthalmologist, who will judge from the health of your eyes and the type of prescription you require whether you can wear contact lenses successfully. If you wear contact lenses, take care to avoid exposing them to hair sprays, creams, soaps, or lotions. Don't wear them while sleeping or swimming. If you have any eye problems, consult your doctor immediately.

Gloves Twenty years ago, a woman was considered improperly dressed if she did not wear gloves for almost any occasion. Today, practicality has replaced protocol, and people rarely wear gloves except in the cold winter months, when bare hands look and feel uncomfortable.

Hats Always sensible in cold weather, hats today are popular accessories for men and women on a variety of formal and casual occasions. Although some professions may require headgear for practical purposes, such as hard hats and nurses' caps, hats are generally inappropriate accessories indoors.

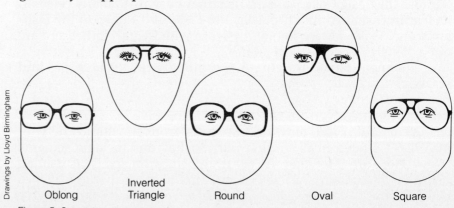

Oblong   Inverted Triangle   Round   Oval   Square

Figure 5–6
Eyeglass frames appropriate for various face shapes

THE RULE OF FOURTEEN

With a wide choice of accessories, you may have a tendency to overdress. A final check, using the *Rule of Fourteen*, will help prevent this. Count everything visible, using the following point system. The total should not exceed fourteen points. If your total is under eight points, consider adding an accessory.

Table 5–4

THE RULE OF FOURTEEN

Item	Points
Suit	
solid color	1
plaid	2
Dress	
solid color	1
print	2
noticeable trim	1
Jacket and slacks or trousers	
same color	1
two colors	2
different materials	2
Blouse or shirt	
white	1
patterned	2
colored	2
Shoes	
dark colors	1
bright colors	2
two-toned	2
open toe or heel	2
Socks	
dark color	1
light color	3
Nylons	
flesh-toned	1
dark or patterned	2
Jewelry	1 each item
Scarves or ties	
solid color	1
two or more colors	2
Belt	1
Attaché case	1
Purse	
dark color	1
two-toned or light color	2

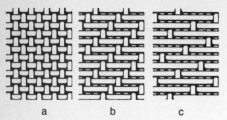

Figure 5–7
Woven Fabrics
a. Plain—The yarns are regularly intermeshed so that they form a racquetlike pattern.
b. Twill—The yarns are intermeshed to form a diagonal pattern.
c. Satin—The yarns are intermeshed so that one direction dominates the face of the cloth to form a soft, smooth surface.

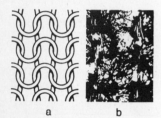

Figure 5–8
Nonwoven Fabrics
a. Knit—One loop of yarn is pulled through another.
b. Nonwoven—Fibers are interlocked or bonded by chemicals, heat, or mechanically.

Fabric

A knowledge of fabrics and their properties and weaves is essential if you want to choose a garment that will look well, clean well, and wear well. Consult figures 5–7 and 5–8 and table 5–5 for information on the characteristics of various weaves and fabrics.

Lines

Fabric and fit are not the only factors to be considered while shopping. Well-dressed people also understand the importance of *lines* and are conscious of what lines are best for them.

You most likely are already familiar with some of the optical illusions that lines can create. Depending upon their placement, lines can appear long, short, or curved. If you can use this principle, you can put the power of lines to work for you.

Clothing lines can be obvious, or they can be almost subliminal. The subtle lines produced by garment seams, button rows, and contrasting colors have an effect on the eye in the same way as do bold stripes or eye-catching, bright-colored borders.

HORIZONTAL LINES

Horizontal lines generally have a shortening and fattening effect; however, some horizontal lines are kinder to the figure than others. The line across the shoulder is an interesting one that can be worn by everyone except a broad-shouldered person. The lines across the chest or under the bust is a good accent line for all except large-busted women. The line at the waist, because it divides the

E.I. Du Pont de Nemours & Co., Inc.

Courtesy of Butterick Fashion Marketing Co.

Effects created by horizontal lines

body in half, is flattering for tall, thin people, but not good for short or fat people. A line at the hip is not complimentary to wide-hipped people; however, a loose-fitting jacket that ends at the hip can sometimes hide figure problems. Borders on dresses and skirts can actually lengthen the look if the remainder of the attire is of one color. On the other hand, a hemline that ends at mid-calf tends to be very shortening to any woman under five feet, six inches.

VERTICAL LINES

Vertical lines for the most part are slimming and lengthening. The single line down the front—a bold stripe, a row of buttons, or a decorative seam—is the most slimming of all. Two lines down the front, however, will often make a person look heavier, depending on the colors used. White and bright colors enlarge the appearance of an object, and black and dark colors diminish its size. Thus, a dark-colored jacket worn open over a white shirt is slimming, but a light-colored jacket over a dark shirt has the opposite effect.

Off-center vertical lines are broadening and unflattering to all but near-perfect figures. However, a vertical line on the side of clothing, such as a stripe on the arm extending from wrist to neck or a stripe on the side of the pants from ankle to waist, is an interesting and slimming one.

When buying a jacket, remember that a long jacket will visually shorten the body and a short jacket will give length to the body. When a suit jacket is buttoned, it forms a V that draws attention to the face. A V-line broadens at its open ends and slims at its point. Invert the V, and women can use this attractive and slimming line in a dress.

Two effects created by vertical lines.

V-lines

PROPORTION AND BALANCE

In any discussion of line, it is important to be aware of the principle of proportion. Sometimes called the *Golden Mean*, this principle rules that the smaller space should have the same relationship to the larger space as the larger space has to the whole.

Formal and informal balance are concepts important to the design of clothes. *Formal balance* in a garment means that it is identical on each side of an imaginary line drawn vertically down the middle of the figure. For example, a patch pocket on the right side of a jacket will be balanced by a pocket of the same size on the left.

Table 5–5

FABRICS

Name	Qualities	Clothing Use	Name	Qualities	Clothing Use
Broadcloth	Fine-ribbed, lustrous, closely woven wool, cotton, or cotton blend	Shirts, blouses, dresses	Poplin	Cotton or cotton blend with fine crossribbing	Suits, jackets, coats, raincoats
Corduroy	Pile fabric with narrow or wide ridges	Sport jackets, dresses, pants, sport clothes	Seersucker	A crinkled lightweight cotton or cotton blend	Shirts, blouses, suits
			Serge	Twill weave with diagonal rib	Suits
Cotton	Lightweight material; wrinkles easily; absorbent	Shirts, blouses	Silk	Natural fiber; smooth, rich look; often requires dry cleaning	Dresses, shirts, blouses, ties, scarves
Flannel	Made of cotton, wool, or wool blend; has nap	Suits, pants, shirts	Suede	Leather with brushed nap; easily soiled; expensive to clean	Sport coats, coats, vests
Gabardine	Closely woven fabric with high sheen	Suits, jackets, dresses			
Herringbone twill	Zigzag effect created by different weave directions	Suits, coats, skirts, jackets	Tweed	Rough fabric with unfinished appearance; flecks of color are mixed in weave	Jackets, suits, coats, skirts
Hopsacking	A coarse basket weave	Casual shirts and clothes	Ultrasuede	Washable suedelike fabric; expensive	Sport jackets, women's suits
Jersey	Soft knitted fabric; hugs body	Dresses, shirts, blouses	Velour	Soft material with look of velvet, yet washable	Dresses, jackets, sport coats, casual clothes
Lawn	Sheer cotton	Dresses, blouses			
Linen	Cool, lustrous cloth made from flax	Dresses, sportswear	Velvet	Rich looking, short cut, close pile; must be dry-cleaned	Jackets, women's suits, evening clothes
Polyester	Versatile synthetic fabric used alone or in blends	Suits, dresses, coats, shirts, blouses	Wool	Animal fiber; lightweight wool is cool in summer, heavyweight is warm in winter; holds shape	Coats, suits, dresses, pants, trousers

Can you tell which of these pictures illustrates the fad, fashion, and the classic?

Fashions courtesy of The Broadway (So. Ca.)

Burberrys®

Hartmarx

Informal balance means the sides are not identical, but are balanced in their proportions. A large pocket on one side of a jacket, for example, might be balanced by two small pockets on the other side.

Fad, Fashion, or Classic?

If you can distinguish each of these from the others, you will save both money and closet space.

The label *fad* is given to any clothing concept that becomes enormously popular. Its popularity, in fact, is usually the cause of its quick death. Nearly everyone purchases some version of it; the market becomes saturated; the public tires of it; and the fad lasts hardly longer than a season. Hot pants, mood rings, and tie-dyed materials are good examples of fads. If you want to join the crowd and spend money on a fad, pick a version that is inexpensive.

A *fashion* is a style that stays popular for several years. You can afford to invest a larger sum of money in a fashion. Knee-high boots and three-piece suits are examples of fashions.

A *classic* is a style that has been accepted for years and will probably never go off the market. Blazers, pleated skirts, and herringbone weaves are examples of classics that may be nearly obsolete for seasons, but return years later to strong demand.

Clothing Care

A well-chosen wardrobe is a valuable investment. Caring for such an investment requires a little time and organization.

Harry Rinehart

Is your closet well-organized?

Examine your closet, asking yourself the following questions: Do you have the proper hangers? Are your clothes grouped conveniently, with ample hanging space—for example, blouses, skirts, and tops together; slacks and trousers in another section; and full-length items in another? Are your shoes arranged neatly or scattered about the floor of the closet? Now check your drawers. Are your sweaters, underwear, and accessories organized or in disarray? If you feel guilty when answering these questions, then it's time for a system.

If you don't have sturdy hangers, plan to purchase some soon. After spending money on a good wardrobe, you would be foolish not to spend a few cents for good hangers. Wire hangers are fine for light cottons, but they will put an undesirable crease in the shoulders of heavier garments. Padded, wooden, or heavy plastic hangers are better for most clothing. Pants and trousers should be hung on pants hangers from the cuff end. For skirts, use skirt hangers or attach clothespins to wire hangers. A belt hanger is nice, but this too can be made by slipping belt buckles over the hook of a wire hanger.

Hang suits on a wishbone-shaped hanger. Remove all items from the pockets, button the front of the coat, and smooth the lapels. Do not put a suit away immediately after wearing; instead, air it first. If possible, hang it outside for a short time.

Blouses and shirts should be laundered after each wearing, since perspiration stains can become difficult to remove if left in the fabric too long. Besides, a freshly laundered blouse or shirt can give you a sense of cleanliness.

Shoe trees belong in any well-organized closet. Insert them into your shoes after each wearing to restore shoe shape. Shoe racks hold a large number of shoes; however, they do not maintain the shape of the shoes as well as do shoe trees. Do you have high boots that tend to wrinkle around the ankles? Invest in boot trees.

Both shoes and boots should be cleaned and polished regularly. Don't wear the same shoes day after day—for the sake of both your shoes and your feet.

Neckties should be checked for stains after wearing, and hung on tie racks.

LAUNDRY HINTS

An expensive garment can be cheapened quickly if it does not receive the proper laundry or dry-cleaning care. Not knowing how to care for clothes is no excuse; you can learn. The following suggestions may help.

With the many synthetic fabrics and fabric blends now available, washing clothes is not as simple as it used to be. Each clothing item can require a different temperature, soap, and treatment. Manufacturers are legally responsible for putting washing instructions on a garment, but sometimes these instructions are imprecise. The American Apparel Manufacturers Association has prepared a chart, shown in table 5–6, to clarify the terms used in these *care labels*.

Sweaters can be washed at home in cool water. To brighten light colors, put a drop of ammonia in the wash water. Squeeze the wash water gently through the sweater. When rinsing, add one-quarter cup of white vinegar to the rinse water to restore life to the sweater. Then block the sweater on a towel and let it dry. (Blocking a sweater means shaping it to its original form.)

If the label reads "dry clean," do so. Don't try to save money by taking short cuts. You can either take the garment to a professional cleaner or to a laundromat that has dry-cleaning machines. Do-it-yourself dry cleaning is less expensive, but you also must be capable of expert pressing to restore the garment to wearability.

Treat stains promptly. Before you use a chemical cleaner or a detergent on a stain, test it on a hem or seam of the garment to make sure it won't damage the garment. If the stain is nongreasy, soak it in cold water for a half an hour before you treat it.

If you are trying to remove a stain at home, here are some tips from the Neighborhood Cleaners Association, located in the eastern United States.

First, test the effect of water or cleaning fluid on a seam or hem. Place a towel under the stain to absorb excess moisture. With a soft cloth, rub gently from the outside of the stain to the center. Never apply water to ink or lipstick stains—it may release dyes and stain the fabric permanently. Avoid heat: It sets stains. If you spill fruit juice or a drink on a fabric, rinse it promptly. This kind of stain may be invisible at first, but with the application of heat it may turn yellow and be impossible to remove.

Your Wardrobe Reflects You

Every time you dress, you are making a personal statement: "I'm a professional who is serious about getting ahead in the world"; "I'm not much; I'm a very insignificant person"; or "I don't care about anything." The condition of your clothes, their lines, their colors, their fabric—all reflect your personality and your attitude toward your career. Give your wardrobe the attention *you* deserve.

PPG Industries, Inc.

No matter how you get that spot on your clothes, be sure to treat it quickly.

Courtesy of Butterick Fashion Marketing Co.

Your clothes reflect your personality and attitude toward your career.

Table 5-6

CONSUMER CARE GUIDE FOR APPAREL

	When Label Reads:	It Means:
Machine Washable	Machine wash	Wash, bleach, dry, and press by any customary method including commercial laundering and dry cleaning.
	Home launder only	Same as above, but do not use commercial laundering.
	No chlorine bleach	Do not use chlorine bleach. Oxygen bleach may be used.
	No bleach	Do not use any type of bleach.
	Cold wash Cold rinse	Use cold water from tap or cold washing machine setting.
	Warm wash Warm rinse	Use warm water or warm washing machine setting.
	Hot wash	Use hot water or hot washing machine setting.
	No spin	Remove wash load before final machine spin cycle.
	Delicate cycle Gentle cycle	Use appropriate machine setting; otherwise wash by hand.
	Durable press cycle Permanent press cycle	Use appropriate machine setting; otherwise use warm wash, cold rinse, and short spin cycle.
	Wash separately	Wash alone or with like colors.
Non-Machine Washing	Hand wash	Launder only by hand in lukewarm (hand comfortable) water. May be bleached; may be dry-cleaned.
	Hand wash only	Same as above, but do not dry-clean.
	Hand wash separately	Hand wash alone or with like colors.
	No bleach	Do not use bleach.
	Damp wipe	Surface clean with damp cloth or sponge.

Table 5–6 (continued)

	When Label Reads:	It Means:
Home Drying	Tumble dry	Dry in tumble dryer at specified setting—high, medium, low, or no heat.
	Tumble dry Remove promptly	Same as above, but in absence of cool-down cycle remove at once when tumbling stops.
	Drip dry	Hang wet and allow to dry with hand shaping only.
	Line dry	Hang damp and allow to dry.
	No wring No twist	Hang dry, drip dry, or dry flat only. Handle to prevent wrinkles and distortion.
	Dry flat	Lay garment on flat surface.
	Block to dry	Maintain original size and shape while drying.
Ironing or Pressing	Cool iron	Set iron at lowest setting.
	Warm iron	Set iron at medium setting.
	Hot iron	Set iron at hot setting.
	Do not iron	Do not iron or press with heat.
	Steam iron	Iron or press with steam.
	Iron damp	Dampen garment before ironing.
Miscellaneous	Dry-clean only	Garment should be dry-cleaned only, including self-service.
	Professionally dry-clean only	Do not use self-service dry-cleaning.
	No dry-clean	Use recommended care instructions. No dry-cleaning materials to be used.

Note: This care guide was produced by the Consumer Affairs Committee, American Apparel Manufacturers Association, and is based on the Voluntary Guide of the Textile Industry Advisory Committee for Consumer Interests. Federal labeling requirements pertaining to clothing care are being revised. For instance, it is proposed that if an item may safely be washed at any temperature, a specific temperature would not be recommended. If an item would be damaged if washed at a temperature other than the one recommended, the label must be explicit. Such changes may affect some of the references in Table 5–6. Apply your best judgment when referring to this useful guide.

KEY TERMS

hue

value

chroma

shade

tone

tint

primary colors

secondary colors

intermediate colors

monochromatic

complementary

analogous

split-complement

triadic

facial undertones

club tie

rep tie

foulard

paisley tie

Rule of Fourteen

lines

Golden Mean

formal balance

informal balance

fad

fashion

classic

care labels

TEST YOURSELF:
QUESTIONS FOR REVIEW AND DISCUSSION

1. Pick someone you know who is well dressed and describe his or her wardrobe. What type of wardrobe will you choose for your profession?
2. List and define monochromatic, complementary, analogous, split-complement, and triadic color schemes. Give examples of each, other than those used in the text.
3. What is the predominant color of your wardrobe? What colors can you use to accessorize your wardrobe? What additional clothing items could you buy to expand your wardrobe?
4. Pick one of the colors suggested in the text as the basis for a wardrobe and build an outfit around it.
5. When shopping for clothing, what factors should you consider in order to make a wise purchase?
6. What should you look for when trying on a jacket? Pants? Shoes?
7. What are some ways to calculate the true cost of an article of clothing?
8. Analyze the clothing you're wearing now in terms of the Rule of Fourteen. How many points do you score?
9. Give some examples of clothing lines. Are all vertical lines slimming and lengthening? Are all horizontal lines broadening?
10. Give some specific examples of the Golden Mean, formal balance, informal balance.
11. Explain how fad, fashion, and classic differ.

APPLICATION EXERCISE

Using the appropriate grouping, depending upon your gender, coordinate as many ensembles as you can from the clothing items pictured.

White Blouse
Gray Jacket
Gray Skirt

Navy Dress
Navy Jacket

Camel Jacket
Cream Blouse
Camel Skirt

Gray Suit
White Shirt

Navy Jacket
Navy Trousers
Pale Blue Shirt

Camel Suit
Cream Shirt

Suggested Readings

Jackson, Carole. *Color Me Beautiful.* New York: Ballantine Books, 1981.
Jones, Mablen. *Taking Care of Clothes.* New York: St. Martin's Press, 1982.
Keith, Judith. *I Haven't a Thing to Wear!* New York: Avon, 1981.
Molloy, John T. *Dress for Success.* New York: Warner Books, 1982.
Molloy, John T. *The Women's Dress for Success Book.* New York: Warner Books, 1978.
Thourlby, William. *You Are What You Wear.* New York: New American Library, 1980.
Wallace, Joanne. *Dress With Style.* Old Tappan, N.J.: Revell, 1982.

6

MAINTAINING GOOD HEALTH

COMPREHENSIVE GOAL
To provide factual information on potential physical and emotional problems, and to help you make intelligent decisions in these areas.

SPECIFIC OBJECTIVES
After reading this chapter, you will be able to:

- make an intelligent choice of a personal doctor and dentist

- know the signs of cancer

- recognize the symptoms of venereal disease

- evaluate the consequences of the use of tobacco, alcohol, and drugs

- recognize the effects of daily stress and the need for proper rest and nutrition

As an entry-level professional, you will not only encounter opportunities, but you will also be faced with responsibilities. Perhaps your new job will mean a major move to a big city, which entails being away from your family and friends for the first time, renting an apartment, managing your time and money, making new friends, and in general just coping with everyday problems. You will encounter new situations that call for mature decisions.

When a difficult situation first arises, you may be tempted to give up and go home. That solution is not only expensive but immature. As an adult, you want to demonstrate your capabilities in handling a range of matters, including finding a personal physician and dentist and deciding what is right for you in the areas of smoking, drinking, and drug use. You also have to deal with annoying, even troubling, problems of everyday stress, and you have to plan for proper rest and good nutrition.

Intelligent choices can be made only after thought and research. The information presented in this chapter is not intended to sway your judgment—only to clarify your alternatives.

Choosing the Right Physician and Dentist

It is easy to delay choosing a physician or dentist until sickness or a toothache prompts immediate action. However, under those circumstances it can be difficult to make wise choices. Your body deserves better care than emergency treatment, so find a physician or dentist before the emergency occurs.

FINDING A GOOD PHYSICIAN

Asking a respected friend's opinion is one way of finding a doctor, but lay people do not always have a foundation for judgment other than the doctor's bedside manner and personality. For a more reliable source of names, call your local medical society, your local hospital, or a nearby medical school. If you are in the process of moving to a new location, ask your present doctor for a recommendation.

Some corporations that recognize the monetary benefit of having healthy employees will not only encourage annual checkups, but also will pay for the examination. Other firms have a company doctor on staff. Some large organizations even have their own complete medical facility, usually referred to as a Health Maintenance Office (HMO).

The First Appointment Your first appointment with your new doctor will involve a thorough interview, during which the doctor or medical assistant takes down your medical history, as well as that of your immediate family. Be as open, frank, and specific as pos-

A thorough examination will include recording your weight.

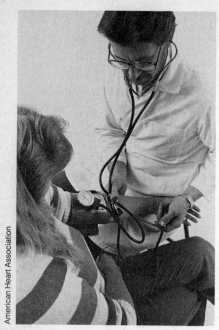

A blood pressure check

sible. The exchange of questions, answers, and comments enables the doctor to gain valuable clues as to what to look for in the examination.

A good examination will include checks for vital signs—among them, blood pressure, temperature, weight, and pulse rate. As the examination proceeds, try to relax, and be sure to ask questions. One of the doctor's most important roles is to help you understand your body and how it functions. Dr. Isadore Rosenfeld's book *The Complete Medical Exam* addresses the issue precisely: "What your doctor knows is critical; what *you* know is crucial."

The doctor will carefully examine every part of your body, noting, for example, the appearance and texture of the skin, including the condition of nails and hair; feeling the lymph glands in the neck, armpits, and groin; and checking the breasts' genital organs, and rectum for any irregularities.

In addition, certain laboratory tests of blood and urine samples are required, as they are indispensable aids to the doctor in diagnosing any abnormal symptoms.

As a professional, you do not want to be kept waiting too long in the reception room. Unless the doctor is called away for a medical emergency, a long wait should not be necessary. If it does occur, either the receptionist is scheduling incorrectly or the doctor has a complete disregard for time. For an annual physical, make an appointment several weeks, even months, in advance and let the receptionist know that you cannot afford long delays. Try to get the first appointment of the morning or afternoon.

Visits to the Doctor's Office   Aside from an annual physical checkup, you may wonder what necessitates an office visit. A nasty cold, stomach flu, or nagging headache can elicit this question. Many people make unnecessary visits to the doctor's office. When in doubt, it is wisest to call the doctor and let him or her decide whether the visit is necessary. This will save you both time and money. Of course, the doctor cannot help someone over the phone who has never been in the office before; this is another reason for that initial checkup. If you follow up with an annual physical examination, you may find that you have few reasons to see the doctor throughout the intervening year.

CHOOSING A DENTIST

Finding the right dentist requires the same kind of investigation as that involved in finding the right doctor. Ask faculty members at a nearby dental school, your doctor, or your pharmacist to recommend a dentist; or check the American Dental Association's *American Dental Directory,* which can be found in most public libraries.

Your new dentist should give you a thorough examination, including a full set of X-rays, unless he or she has received a recent

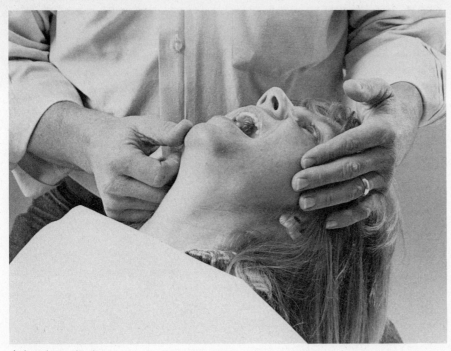

A dental examination

set from your former dentist. A good dentist encourages preventive care: proper brushing and flossing of your teeth and regular six-month checkups. During your six-month's examination, your teeth should be cleaned to remove *plaque*, a thin, transparent film on the enamel that contains harmful bacteria.

Preventing Tooth Decay

Three basic steps are involved in the prevention of tooth decay: proper diet, good hygiene, and fluoridation.

DIET

A proper diet is a balanced diet, which you can achieve with the guidance of your doctor or dentist. Try to regulate your consumption of foods high in sugar and starches; these foods stimulate the growth of organisms in the mouth associated with dental decay. Instead of depending on "fast" foods for your meals, or snacking on candy bars, carbonated sodas, coffee with cream and sugar, and cakes or cookies, substitute an orange or an apple, celery or carrot sticks, or other fresh fruits or vegetables. The sprig of parsley on your luncheon plate is more than just decorative. It contains chlorophyll, which is excellent for the breath. Parsley is also a good source of vitamin C.

Cookies and candy may be tempting, but they promote tooth decay.

HYGIENE

Most people use a toothbrush and toothpaste every day. The question is: Do you really *clean* your teeth, or do you merely brush them?

It is important that microorganisms that lodge on the surfaces of teeth and between teeth be removed. They contribute to the buildup of plaque, cavities, and tooth decay. Dental floss is a great help in getting rid of food particles and plaque.

Everyone's mouth configuration, substance or texture of teeth (particularly the enamel), and sensitivity of gums are different. Ask your dentist or the dental hygienist to advise you on the type of toothbrush to use and to teach you how to brush so that you will really *clean* your teeth, and how to use dental floss correctly. Brushing with baking soda is excellent for removing the tartar formation on teeth and brightening them.

Fluoride   Many years of research have shown that when *fluoride*, a chemical compound, is added to drinking water, people's teeth tend to be stronger and less susceptible to cavities. Thousands of communities in the United States now add fluoride to their water systems.

Fluoride is also available in other forms. When you were a child, your doctor may have prescribed fluoridated vitamin tables for you, and your dentist may have painted your teeth with a fluoride application. Fluoridated toothpastes may be helpful for continued dental decay prevention in adulthood.

In many communities, fluoride is added to the water system.

Personal Health—A Look at Some Specific Problems

This section of *Professional Development* is not intended to be an encyclopedia of patients' symptoms. Our aim is to give you a few clues about *practical* matters. If one theme recurs, it is: Get the best medical advice possible.

There are many illnesses we could discuss, but we will limit our discussion to a few specific problems that might come up in your new life and your personal and professional development: cancer; venereal disease; the effects of tobacco, alcohol, and drugs; stress-related health problems; and the need for rest and proper nutrition.

CANCER

Numerous deaths result yearly from an incompletely understood disease—cancer. It is known that cancer cells, once growth occurs, multiply rapidly and invade healthy tissue, taking the food needed from the normal cells. Though research continues, experts

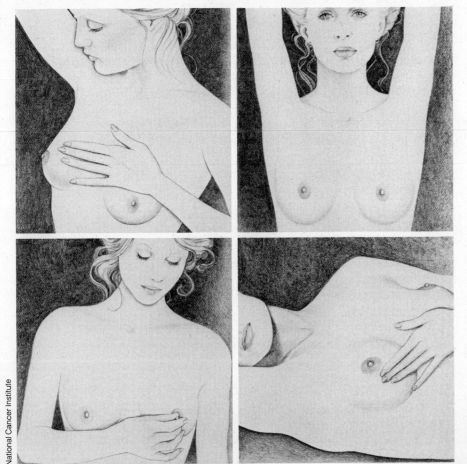

National Cancer Institute

Figure 6–1
Breast self-examination is simple.
1. In a standing position, raise one hand in the air. Use two or three fingers of the other hand to explore gently the opposite breast in a clockwise motion, feeling for any unusual lump or mass under the skin. Repeat on the other side. (Many doctors suggest doing this in the shower, since soapy fingers glide easily over the skin, making it easy to concentrate on the texture underneath.)
2. Towel off before a mirror and inspect both breasts for anything unusual. Then bend forward to check for abnormalities in shape.
3. Press each nipple gently and look for discharge.
4. Repeat fingertip inspection while lying flat on back with one arm behind the head.

One cancer you can give yourself.

Horrible isn't it?

American Cancer Society

AMERICAN CANCER SOCIETY

Cigarette smoking has been linked to lung cancer.

are still uncertain as to the exact causes of cancer. However, cigarette smoking, excessive exposure to the sun, X-rays, and the fumes of industrial chemicals are suspected to be among the causes.

Any sign of cancer should send you to the doctor's office immediately. As a guide for your protection, the National Institutes of Health list these seven warning signals of cancer.

- Unusual bleeding or discharge

- A lump or thickening in the breast or elsewhere

- A sore that does not heal

- Change in bowel or bladder habits

- Indigestion or difficulty in swallowing

- Persistent hoarseness or cough

- Change in a wart or mole

These seven warning signals may be imperceptible or unaccompanied by any pain. (Pain is rarely an early symptom of cancer.) Thus, any questionable symptom should prompt a visit to a doctor for medical diagnosis.

Women should check their breasts for unusual lumps regularly. Most doctors recommend shortly after menstruation. Figure 6–1 demonstrates the correct procedure for breast examination.

It is also important for women to have a Pap smear at least once a year in order to detect any symptoms of cervical cancer. Women over forty years of age may want to have a semiannual Pap smear as a precaution.

VENEREAL DISEASE

Venereal disease is a health problem that has reached epidemic proportions in America. Mandatory VD tests are administered in some states when a Pap smear is taken. Although most strains can easily be cured or controlled with penicillin and other antibiotics, VD, if left untreated, can lead to sterility, blindness, paralysis, and death. The most common venereal diseases are gonorrhea, genital herpes, and syphilis, and transmission is usually through sexual relations.

If you think you have symptoms of a venereal disease, *you must visit your doctor or local health clinic*. To ignore these symptoms could mean death or severe disability, as well as transmission of the disease. Because the disease can be cured if detected in the early stages, it doesn't make sense to let shame or guilt prevent you from getting medical assistance.

Gonorrhea   The most common of all venereal diseases, *gonorrhea* is a contagious, pus-producing inflammation of the genital mucous membranes. Microorganisms called *gonococci* cause gonorrhea.

Gonorrhea manifests itself in males by frequent and painful urination that is accompanied by a discharge of pus. If left untreated, gonorrhea can spread to the prostate and testes. The result is often sterility in the early stages, because the disease seals off the tubes that carry sperm from the testes.

In females, the external genitalia are affected first, though frequently, in the early stages of the disease, a woman may not experience the common symptoms. If gonorrhea remains undetected and untreated, it usually spreads to the reproductive organs, causes inflammation of the Fallopian tubes and ovaries, and results in sterility.

Both men and women may experience further complications in the bladder, rectum, mouth, joints, kidneys, and heart.

A doctor must prescribe the usual medication—penicillin. But while this powerful drug can give you early relief, don't relax and stop seeing your doctor regularly. Penicillin can also mask the symptoms of syphilis, which frequently accompanies gonorrhea.

Syphilis   *Syphilis* is a highly infectious venereal disease caused by microorganisms called *Treponema pallidum*. It is acquired through oral transmission, sexual intercourse, or by inheritance (congenitally).

The congenital factor is both sad and, in today's world of medicine, unnecessary. An infected pregnant woman may pass the

time for a showdow... ...VD

syphilis and gonorrhea can be completely cured if treated early by a doctor

HBJ Collection

If you suspect you have contracted a venereal disease, see your doctor or go to a public health clinic right away.

Treatment of VD requires antibiotics administered under a doctor's supervision. You can find out where to go by consulting a telephone directory.

bacteria on to her unborn child; this sometimes causes the mother to have a miscarriage or a stillbirth. Many babies survive, however, and enter this world with advanced stages of syphilis.

Diagnosis of syphilis is complicated; the best detector is a blood test. The first symptom is the appearance of a *chancre* (small, hard, painless sore), usually located in the genitals, mouth, or anus. The lymph glands located near the sore may swell and become tender. This sore can appear between nine and ninety days after exposure, but at this stage, the bacteria have already invaded the blood. This stage of syphilis can go undetected, especially in a woman.

Even after the sore heals, syphilis, if left untreated, travels through the bloodstream to other parts of the body. A skin rash may develop, along with a slight fever, sore throat, headache, sores in the mouth, throat, and nose, and possibly, loss of hair.

After that time, if the disease remains undetected, it will go into a dormant stage that may last for years, or it may even die out. If syphilis activates in the final stage, it can affect the central nervous system, the spinal cord, the brain, the heart and blood vessels, and the lungs. Blindness, paralysis, insanity, and even death can result.

The usual treatment for syphilis is penicillin or another antibiotic—always under a doctor's careful supervision. However, damage already done is irreversible.

Genital herpes   One of the most rampant of the venereal diseases was not diagnosed as such until the mid-1960s. It is *genital herpes*, and it is caused by a virus whose technical term is *herpes simplex virus type 2.*[1] It is estimated that over 20 million Americans now have genital herpes, and nearly half a million new cases occur a year.[2]

A most painful disease, genital herpes first manifests itself, according to Dr. Benjamin Kogan, as "a slight tingling in the genital area. Then one or a group of small (sometimes itchy) blisters appears."[3] These blisters can be extremely painful, especially during urination, and the pain may be compounded by swelling of the lymph nodes in the groin area.

Genital herpes does not usually respond to penicillin and antibiotics. Until quite recently, the normal treatment has been for a doctor to coat the blisters with a medicated solution that would give relief—the sore and blisters appear to heal—but would not necessarily effect a permanent cure for the disease.

At this time there is no known permanent cure for herpes 2. The disease seems to flare up when the victim becomes stressed or angry. Some victims attempt to keep the disease arrested by maintaining a positive mental attitude.

If a pregnant woman has a history of the disease, it is imperative that she inform her doctor. The virus, even if dormant, can do harm to the fetus, and a Caesarean section may have to be performed so that the child does not contract the disease during passage through the birth canal.

Vaginitis This overall term, *vaginitis*, means inflammation of the vagina and encompasses a number of diseases and disorders that are not venereal but are transmitted sexually. Men as well as women can have the symptoms and be carriers of the infections. Most prominent among them are moniliasis, trichomoniasis, and nonspecific vaginitis.

Moniliasis is a yeast fungal infection that causes severe itching and a white, curdy discharge. It can occur in women who are diabetic, pregnant, on birth-control pills, or on antibiotics. Moniliasis spreads to sex partners and frequently recurs; in males, the infection affects the oral, penile, and anal areas.

Trichomoniasis is caused by a single-cell parasite that lives in the vagina or urethra and is transmitted sexually. The symptoms in women (usually absent in men) are a foul-smelling, greenish-yellow discharge, coupled with itching and irritation.

Nonspecific vaginitis is a bacterial infection that causes increased vaginal secretions, a white or gray discharge, inflammation and swelling of the vagina, and pain during intercourse. Some gynecological specialists believe that this infection is the result of poor hygiene. Daily bathing and clean underwear are simple pre-

HBJ Photo

A laboratory technician makes a culture to identify a VD organism.

---

[1]Cold sores, fever blisters, and other lesions are caused by *herpes simplex virus type 1.*
[2]"Hunting for the Hidden Killers," *Time* (July 4, 1983), p. 51.
[3]Benjamin A. Kogan, M.D., *Health, Third Edition* (New York: Harcourt Brace Jovanovich, Inc., 1980), p. 80.

American Cancer Society

Too many young people take up
smoking for foolish reasons.
In this ad, the American Cancer
Society points out some of them.

ventives. On the other hand, some doctors attribute the problem to a variety of causes, such as wearing tight jeans, the constant wearing of nylon underwear, sensitivity to deodorant or perfumed bath products, and excessive use of douches and other feminine hygiene items.

Tobacco, Alcohol, and Drugs—Their Effects on Your Body

Tobacco, alcohol, and drugs all affect the normal functioning of your body. Your own set of values—built up over a number of years and reflecting the influence of your family, friends, teachers, and clergy—will determine how you handle cigarettes, alcohol, and drugs in personal, social, and business situations.

SMOKING

Until recently, smoking was socially accepted—considered pleasurable, relaxing, and, by some, a mark of adulthood. Because of medical discoveries that link smoking with lung cancer, however, smoking is no longer looked on as sophisticated and glamorous. In fact, many smokers are beginning to suffer casual harassment from nonsmokers.

Statistics favor nonsmokers, as is evident in the various reports by the United States Surgeon General of the Public Health Service. One of the findings included in a recent report is that the death rate for all age groups is almost 70 percent higher for cigarette smokers than for nonsmokers. Furthermore, it reports that because of illness, smokers spend over one third more time away from their jobs than do nonsmokers.[4]

What Happens When You Smoke Consider what happens when you smoke. Your lungs are meant to draw in oxygen and expel carbon dioxide. The lining of the lungs is filled with *cilia*, hairlike extensions that whip back and forth at 900 times a minute and force pollutants and mucous from the lungs. Smoke slows this cilia action, increases the amount of mucous, and gradually causes tissue degeneration. Cancer, emphysema, and bronchitis are lung diseases that afflict smokers at a much higher rate than nonsmokers.

Because it carries carbon monoxide into the lungs, smoking also puts a strain on the heart. Carbon monoxide enters through the bloodstream via the tiny air sacs in the lungs and travels through the blood. Body tissue requires oxygen instead of worthless carbon monoxide, and it signals the heart to pump harder to supply the

[4]*Smoking and Health*, Report of the Surgeon General, U.S. Public Health Service (Rockville, Md.: Dept. of Health, Education, and Welfare).

Many social events revolve around the consumption of alcoholic beverages.

needed oxygen. This call for oxygen taxes the cardiopulmonary system. In addition, the lack of oxygen may cause the complexion of heavy smokers to take on an unhealthy, grayish-white cast.

For many, smoking is a relaxing, pleasurable habit, but the evidence is clear: Tobacco does harm your body and shorten your life. Is is worth it? You must decide.

ALCOHOL

Cocktail parties, happy hours, and social events frequently revolve around liquor. This means that you will be faced with decisions about whether you should drink and how much.

An occasional drink will not harm your body, but chronic drinking can. True, it is a long path from the first drink to alcoholism, but the latter is a disease that afflicts only drinkers. Twenty to twenty-five million people either have or had a serious drinking problem. One out of every nine persons is an alcoholic probability. One survey has found that one out of every fifteen young drinkers will become an alcoholic.[5] Another study concludes that one out of ten top executives is an alcoholic.[6]

What's in a Drink?   Alcoholic beverages differ in the amounts of alcohol they contain. Two twelve-ounce cans of beer are equal in alcoholic content to five and a half ounces of wine or one and a half

[5]Margaret O. Hyde, *Alcohol: Drink or Drug?* (New York: McGraw-Hill, 1974), p. 3.
[6]Jack B. Weiner, *Drinking* (New York: Norton, 1976).

An occasional drink will not impair your health, but chronic drinking can.

ounces of whiskey or vodka. Therefore you can consume more beer or wine before feeling their effects. For this reason, many people think that drinking beer or wine will not lead to alcoholism. This is untrue; it just requires a larger quantity.

Another way of measuring alcoholic content is by *proof*. Proof indicates the alcoholic strength of a beverage by a number that is twice the percent by volume of alcohol present. A bottle of liquor must have a proof degree on its label. If the label reads "100 proof," it means that it contains 50% alcohol.

How Much Can You Drink? How much you can drink before losing control depends upon many factors. Drinking quickly, drinking on an empty stomach, and using carbonated mixes all contribute to quick intoxication. Your mood and your physical size also affect the amount of liquor you can drink. Some social drinkers have a glass of milk before going to a party to coat the stomach lining and permit alert thinking for a longer period of time. Responsible drinkers know their personal limits. Unfortunately, after several drinks "no" gets harder to say.

What Happens When You Drink? Consider the effect of various liquors on a man weighing 150 pounds who is drinking on an empty stomach. Each of the following quantities of alcohol will put the man's blood alcohol level at .03%.

1½ oz.	Distilled spirits
3½ oz.	Sherry
5½ oz.	Wine
24 oz.	Beer

What happens when more alcohol is consumed? You can judge from the scale above how many drinks you would need to reach the various blood alcohol levels described below.

.03% Judgment impaired
.05% Carefree, mellow behavior; inhibitions disappear
.10% Loss of equilibrium and coordination
.20% Drinker becomes quiet, or angry, boisterous, and
      argumentative
.30% Blurring of vision; confusion; disorientation
.40% Coma
.50% Heart and respiratory failure; death

The highest point on the scale, .50%, is seldom reached because before that point the drinker becomes unconscious. However, on occasions, such as fraternity initiations when participants have been forced to drink at a fast rate, the results have sometimes been fatal.

A driver whose blood alcohol level rises above the .08–.15% level (state laws vary) is considered intoxicated. Driving while intoxicated is a serious offense that will go on your driving record and affect your insurance rates. A new organizaton, MADD (Mothers Against Drunk Drivers), has been very effective in getting stricter laws passed. Mandatory jail terms are now frequently given to offenders.

How Alcohol Affects Your Body   Not only your blood composition, but your whole physiology is affected by drinking. The alcohol in your highball or cocktail is swiftly absorbed by the stomach and small intestine into the bloodstream, where it quickly passes to the liver. But the liver can only *detoxify* (to remove a poison or toxin from) a small amount of the alcohol at a time. Most of the alcohol continues to circulate unchanged through the body for some time, until detoxicated by the liver. That is why people can feel the effects of alcohol hours after they have consumed it.

Excessive drinking can result in irreparable damage to the body. It can affect the central nervous tissue: Memory loss and mental impairment are prevalent among alcoholics. Alcohol also damages the kidneys, which are overstimulated by the liquor and pass off large amounts of wastes.

When Does Drinking Become a Problem?   An occasional drink does not harm the body, unless that occasional drink is replaced with many drinks. The National Institute on Alcohol Abuse and Alcoholism has prepared the following quiz to identify problem drinkers.

1. Do you think and talk about drinking often?
2. Do you drink more now than you used to?
3. Do you sometimes gulp drinks?
4. Do you often take a drink to help yourself relax?
5. Do you drink when you are alone?
6. Do you sometimes forget what happened while you were drinking?
7. Do you keep a bottle hidden somewhere—at home or at work—for quick pick-me-ups?
8. Do you need a drink to have fun?
9. Do you ever just start drinking without really thinking about it?
10. Do you drink in the morning to relieve a hangover?

If you answer "yes" to four or more of the questions, you may have a drinking problem.

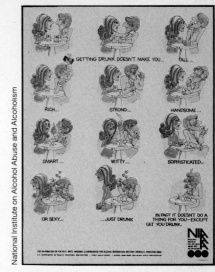

National Institute on Alcohol Abuse and Alcoholism

Alcohol abuse is a matter of national concern, as this poster indicates.

The Alcoholic—A Business Problem A discussion of alcoholism in a book of this type may seem irrelevant, but the disease is a business problem as well as a personal problem. In the business world, alcoholism causes increased absenteeism, decreased proficiency, and increased human error. "Conservatively, it costs a firm or corporation $2,500 per year per alcoholic employed."[7] In a large company, this can add up to a multimillion-dollar loss. Some corporations have rehabilitation programs for their employees who are problem drinkers. One corporation contends that it saves $10 for every $1 invested in the program.[8] Remember, alcoholism affects people of all levels, from entry-level positions to top executive positions.

In fact, the higher the position, the more vulnerable the person who holds it. Business luncheons, evening entertaining, and rigid deadlines are among the factors that contribute to alcoholism in the executive suite.

For whatever reasons, there are alcoholics in every company. Occasionally co-workers will recognize a problem drinker and try to protect that person by hiding the problem. This protection helps neither the individual nor the business.

DRUGS

Drugs, as well as cigarettes and alcohol, are a part of many individual's lifestyles. Does this sound hard to believe? The mention of drugs often causes one to think of underworld dealings, but caffeine, aspirin, and prescription and over-the-counter medicines are all substances that affect body chemistry. You can overdose on any one of these if you use it indiscriminately.

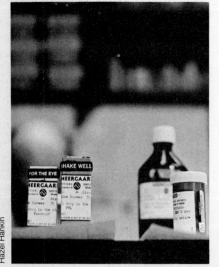

Hazel Hankin

Prescription medicines affect the body's chemistry.

Drug Terms and Their Meanings For purposes of this instruction, which necessarily is an overview, the word *drug* means "any substance that by its chemical nature alters the structure or functioning of the living organism." To understand the consequences of using drugs, you should be familiar with certain terms and classifications. The World Health Organization Expert Committee on Drugs recommends substituting *drug dependence* for terms that were previously used: "drug addiction" and "drug habituation." The committee defines drug dependence as "a state of psychic or physical dependence, or both, on a drug, arising in a person following administration of that drug on a periodic or continuous basis."[9] *Drug abuse* is defined as a "persistent or sporadic [occasional] exces-

[7]"Conservatively, it Costs a Firm or Corporation $2,500 Per Year Per Alcoholic Employed," *South Dakota*, Vol. 9, No. 1.
[8]Data from Weiner, *Drinking*, p. 45.

[9]Cited in Kogan, *Health*, p. 190.

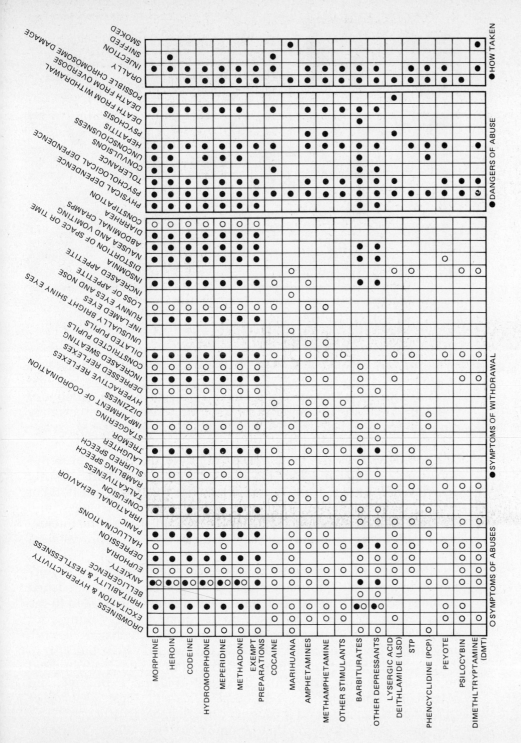

Figure 6–2
Common Symptoms of Drug Abuse

169

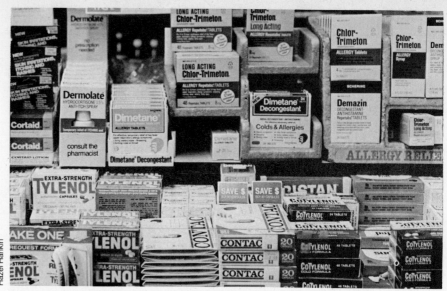
Hazel Hankin

Even over-the-counter drugs can be harmful if used indiscriminately.

sive drug use inconsistent with or unrelated to acceptable medical practice."

With these terms in mind, look at figure 6–2 to familiarize yourself with some of the most common drugs and the effects they can produce in physical and psychological dependence.

Be Careful With Drugs The misuse of any drug, even a prescription drug, can cause problems if the doctor's directions are not followed or if the medicine is combined with the use of alcohol. For example, antihistamines frequently will produce drowsiness, and the effect may be intensified if alcohol is also consumed. The interaction of antibiotics and alcohol may result in vomiting, drowsiness, or flushing.

Prescription drugs and over-the-counter medications purchased in a reliable pharmacy must pass high standards established by the Food and Drug Administration before they can be sold to the American public. *But a warning:* You are quite literally taking your life in your hands if you purchase drugs illegally. The hazard lies not only in the drug's unpredictable effect on your system but also in the possibility of becoming infected from an unsterile or adulterated preparation. Buying drugs "on the street" is illegal, expensive, and potentially dangerous to your body. *You don't know what you're getting for your money,* and if caught, you are liable to arrest.

There is an old saying that ignorance is bliss. Where drugs are concerned, ignorance can lead to serious disability, jail, or even death.

STRESS

We live in a mobile, active, and sometimes aggressive society. We travel to work; we stand in lines at the bank, the grocery store, the airport; we hear noise all day long (from beeping cars and building construction); we make reservations for dinner at a nice restaurant, only to arrive on time and have to wait forty minutes.

We have big and little problems at work. Usually, intelligent, responsible, and mature people can cope well with the important matters; it's the minor inconveniences—like a battery going dead in your hand calculator as you're working on your taxes or a typewriter ribbon getting snarled as you're just finishing the first draft of a report—that tend to upset you.

Then there's major stress—death of a loved one; divorce; being mugged and having your wallet stolen. (The lost money doesn't matter as much as the violation of your person and the aggravation of having to call your bank to stop credit, to notify department stores where you have charge accounts, and to request and wait for credit cards or a driver's license to be replaced.)

"*Stress*," says Dr. Kogan, "is the body's reaction to any demand made of it. . . . It is the *kind* of stress, and the way a person *copes* with stress that decides whether health will be harmed or even life endangered."[10]

It is not our purpose here to delve into a detailed psychoanalytic analysis of stress or to discuss its major manifestations, but rather to alert you to the day-to-day problems of meeting deadlines, entertaining business associates, worrying about next month's rent, and coming home to a TV set that blurts out the troubles of the world.

[10]Kogan, *Health*, p. 156.

We live in a mobile and aggressive society.

Noisy city streets can be a cause of stress.

Handling Stress   You can avoid some stress by taking better care of yourself. The following are a few suggestions for avoiding unnecessary stress.

1. Plan ahead—Don't wait until the last minute to get something done. If you have a deadline for a report and you wait until the last minute to type it, you may find yourself in an upsetting situation, especially if your typewriter breaks down.
2. Wear comfortable clothes—Clothes that are too tight or pinch can cause stress.
3. Exercise—Exercise is a great tension reliever and also strengthens your body so that you can handle some problems better.
4. Eat a balanced diet—Doctors have found that lack of certain nutrients or too much caffeine can cause jangled nerves.
5. Get plenty of rest—Sleep enough hours each night in order to face the stress of the next day. Different people need varying amounts of sleep. Know what you need in order to perform efficiently on the job.
6. Play soft background music, if possible, during work—Research has shown music to be a soothing aid.
7. Learn to laugh at life's little problems—If plans don't turn out as you wish, and nothing can be done about it, try to find some humor in the situation.

Taking personal management of your health and your career is difficult; it's a challenge, but with intelligence and patience it's a challenge well worth taking. Ask for help when you need it—from

Hazel Hankin

Choose nutritious snacks.

your supervisor, your doctor, your co-workers, friends, and family—but above all depend on your own resources and your own common sense.

KEY TERMS

plaque	genital herpes	nonspecific vaginitis
fluoride	herpes simplex	cilia
venereal disease	virus type 1	proof
gonorrhea	herpes simplex	detoxify
gonococci	virus type 2	drug
syphilis	vaginitis	drug dependence
Treponema pallidum	moniliasis	drug abuse
chancre	trichomoniasis	stress

TEST YOURSELF:
QUESTIONS FOR REVIEW AND DISCUSSION

1. What are some ways to judge a doctor's ability? A dentist's? Does the personality of the professional often influence the patient's judgment of the professional? Is personality a good basis for judgment of professional ability?
2. Why is it important to see a doctor regularly?
3. What are some warning signals of cancer?
4. Why do some people smoke? Why do they drink alcohol? Take drugs?
5. If a person wants to break the habit of smoking, what are some steps he or she can take to overcome the problem? How can an alcoholic break away from alcohol dependence? How can a drug user eliminate drug dependence?
6. Why is alcohol a business problem? If you think one of your co-workers drinks too much or is dependent on drugs, what should you do?
7. List some ways to cope with stress.

Get plenty of rest.

APPLICATION EXERCISE

Fill out the following form, then review it to see if there are any things you should attend to, such as finding a physician or scheduling a dental checkup or another kind of physical examination.

Health Care Questionnaire

1. Physician's name _____
2. Date of your last medical examination _____
3. Dentist's name _____
4. Date of your last dental checkup/cleaning _____
5. Names of other doctors (optometrist, podiatrist, etc.) _____
    _____
6. Shots received within the last 2 years _____
7. Allergies, if any _____
8. Health problems _____
9. List any family history of diseases _____
10. Childhood diseases you have had _____
11. Blood type _____
12. Date of last blood test _____
13. Date of last breast examination (women) _____
14. Date of last Pap smear (women) _____
15. Date of last eye examination _____
16. Date of last hearing check _____
17. List any medication you are currently taking _____
18. List any surgery you have had within the past five years _____

Suggested Readings

Barker, Patricia W. *The Quitting Game: How to Beat Your Smoking Habit.* Piscataway, N.J.: New Century Publishers, Inc., 1981.

Califano, Joseph A., Jr., *The 1982 Report on Drug Abuse and Alcoholism.* New York: Warner Books, 1982.

Emerson, Haven, and Gerald N. Grob. *Alcohol & Man: The Effects of Alcohol on Man in Health & Disease.* New York: Arno Press, Inc., 1981.

Kogan, Benjamin A., M. D. *Health.* New York: Harcourt Brace Jovanovich, Inc., 1980.

Soloman, Joel, and Kim Keeley. *Alcohol & Drug Abuse: Similarities & Differences.* Littleton, Mass.: John Wright PSG, Inc., 1981.

Van Impe, Jack. *Alcohol: The Beloved Enemy.* Nashville, Tenn.: Thomas Nelson, Inc., 1981.

Woodward, Nancy H. *If Your Child Is Drinking . . . What You Can Do to Fight Alcohol Abuse at Home, at School & in the Community.* New York: Putnam, 1981.

PART THREE

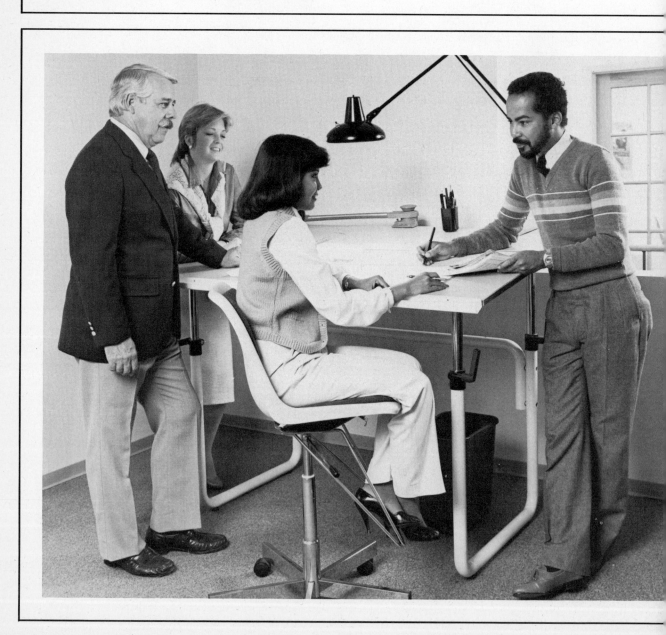

WORKING WITH OTHERS

The most important of all professional skills are those that involve your relationships with other people. The resources you need for success in human relations are insight, understanding, the willingness to assert your ideas and values, and the ability to communicate effectively both one-to-one and in groups.

7

COMMUNICATING: THE LIFELINE OF BUSINESS

COMPREHENSIVE GOAL
To instruct you in the principles and techniques of clear communication

SPECIFIC OBJECTIVES
After reading this chapter, you will be able to:

- define the communication cycle and describe each of its four parts
- explain and give examples of body language and nonverbal communication
- understand some basic elements of effective written communication
- explain and give examples of static
- identify the following communication problems: two-value thinking, singular perception, generalities, thinging, slanting
- distinguish between fact, inference, and opinion
- apply the principles of transactional analysis to human reactions
- understand and apply the Johari Window principle

Communicating is the lifeline of business. Without communication, no orders would be placed, no contracts signed, no advertisements circulated, no letters dictated. There would be no need for telephones, copiers, typewriters, tape recorders, or reports.

Communication can build a business or destroy one. Poor communication—whether in the form of a badly phrased memo or a misinterpreted telephone order—can cost a company thousands of dollars. Consistently poor communication can lead a company to financial ruin.

Because communication is serious business, employers value people who have good communication skills. In fact, surveys have shown that inability to communicate is one of the leading reasons for rejecting an applicant. Moreover, even if he or she passes the screening and secures a job, there is little chance for advancement for the careless communicator. And for managerial positions, the ability to speak and write clearly is essential.

Many colleges now require a communication skills course for undergraduates, and you should take one if you have the opportunity. This chapter is not intended to duplicate that course. It is concerned solely with the verbal and nonverbal communication skills needed in the business world.

The Communication Cycle

Communication is a complex transaction of thought in which two or more people can take part. The act of talking and the act of hearing do not ensure communication: Communication is a cooperation between individuals. It takes the form of a cycle, as illustrated in figure 7–1.

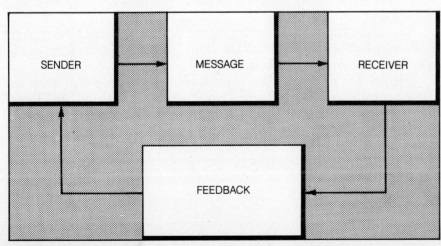

Figure 7–1
The Communication Cycle

"I have a pet at home"

"Oh, what kind of a pet?"

"It is a dog."

"What kind of a dog?"

"It is a St. Bernard."

"Grown up or a puppy?"

"It is full grown."

"What color is it?"

"It is brown and white."

"Why didn't you say you had a full-grown, brown and white St. Bernard as a pet in the first place?"

"Why doesn't anybody understand me?"

Figure 7–2
A Lesson in Specificity

The *communication cycle* has four basic components: sender, message, receiver, and feedback. Each component is necessary to complete the cycle; if one unit is missing, there is no communication.

The Sender

The *sender* begins the cycle when he or she wants someone to react, respond, or behave in some manner. A good sender is specific, considerate, and discriminating.

SPECIFIC

Good senders realize the value of words and choose their words carefully. Vague messages like the following can cause problems and delays in business:

- "I'll meet you around 3:00."
  (This message is a time waster. If the receiver thinks "around 3:00" means ten minutes to three, and the sender arrives at ten minutes after three, a total of twenty minutes is wasted for the receiver.)

- "It doesn't cost much."
  (What is not much to one person may seem like a large sum to another.)

- "He's tall."
  (How tall? What is tall to a five-footer is not tall to a six-footer.)

- "We will have the shipment sent soon."
  (When is soon? A day, a week, a month?)

Business cannot allow for inexactness. "He will send the report soon" may cause uncertainty; "Mr. Johnson will send the June sales report on August third" will not.

The misuse of "they" can cause problems. Statements such as "They said it was going to be the worst winter in history" or "They told us to report over here" are not acceptable in business. If you do not say who "they" are, your statement will lack credibility.

Learn to be specific. It can save time and money for you and your employer. Figure 7–2 demonstrates the importance of specificity.

CONSIDERATE

Considerate senders are sensitive to the receiver's needs and problems. Don't be so busy trying to impress others that you forget that your purpose is to convey a message.

Choose your words carefully when sending messages.

As a considerate sender, you should know your audience and choose an appropriate vocabulary. In general, avoid superficial displays of knowledge. Keep the message simple: Unnecessarily long or complex words confuse more than impress. If one specialist is conversing with another, jargon typical of their profession may be in order. Otherwise, choose simple language stated with sincerity.

DISCRIMINATING

Discriminating senders know there is no place in good business communication for slang, careless usage, or profanity. Slang words are so highly informal and often so far outside the experience of the person to whom they are addressed that their meanings are lost or misinterpreted. Careless usage and bad grammar reflect poorly on the sender. Try to listen to your own speech patterns. You may have fallen into annoying and distracting habits: For example, do you clutter sentences with unnecessary words or phrases, such as "like," "I mean," "you know," and "OK," or overuse emphatic adjectives, such as "fantastic" or "wonderful," until they have lost all meaning?

Some people use profanity in the belief that it adds emphasis to the message. However, they seem to forget they are taking a chance of offending others to the point of losing a business deal or a good employee. Actually, all that profanity does is indicate lack of control over the emotions, show poor taste, and weaken the professional image.

If you have *empathy*, you possess all three sending skills. Empathy is defined as "the projection of one's personality into the personality of another in order to understand him better." To improve your communication skills, try looking at the world from another's point of view.

Good verbal communication can improve business as well as personal relationships.

The Message

The *message* is the vehicle for the sender's thoughts. This vehicle may be the spoken or written word, body gestures, or facial expressions. In other words, the message can be verbal or nonverbal.

VERBAL COMMUNICATION

A verbal message consists first of all of words. Words, of course, do not exist apart from their meanings. Without meanings, words are just sounds. But words don't always mean the same things to all people. It's too simple to assume that merely because you as the sender attach a certain meaning to your words, the receiver will attach the same meaning to them—or will even recognize them at all.

The words, in turn, must be put into a pattern that shows good organization and sound reasoning. There are many textbooks that show how to accomplish this in the area of written communication; here, we will concentrate on spoken communication. The five Cs—Concise, Complete, Cohesive, Clear, and Courteous—are terms that describe all effective communication. They are always evident in good business correspondence, and should carry over into spoken transactions.

THE FIVE Cs OF VERBAL COMMUNICATION

You can eliminate many communication problems by applying the five Cs to your message.

Concise   Keep to the business at hand. One supervisor complained that on many occasions subordinates and clients would drop by his office, chat a while, then, just before leaving, state the real purpose of their visit. Socializing is an essential human activity, but it should not take up the major portion of a business conversation. This is not to say that you should walk into your boss's office and abruptly announce, "I want a raise!" Some preliminary exchange is necessary, but keep it from becoming a time-waster.

Complete   Give all, not half or part, of the necessary information. The shoe store owner who says, "I want to order a dozen of those red shoes," raises many questions for the shoe wholesaler, who needs to know style numbers, sizes, and many other details. The boss who hands a secretary a report and says merely, "Type this," without giving instructions about style, format, and number of copies, will probably not get the report back exactly as expected.

Cohesive   Don't jump from one subject to another. Transition and thought development are needed to keep the receiver's attention. Perhaps you have witnessed a conversation similar to the following one:

> Speaker: I want to order a dozen sheets of . . . Oh, and before I forget, will you send me a sample of that special tape? And did you ever see your competitor's new line of stationery? It's a quality product.

Ideally this sender should place the order first, and then follow up with the questions.

A vague order from the shoe store owner can cause problems for the wholesaler.

Hazel Hankin

To make a message cohesive, use transitional words such as "furthermore," "otherwise," "accordingly," "instead," "moreover," and "besides." Watch your thought progression so that your receiver can follow your message.

Clear   Speak clearly. Clarity is perhaps the most important of the five Cs. A clear message is logical and understandable. A clear verbal message is one that is enunciated carefully. Each word has a beginning and an end. Words are not run together.

When speaking, keep objects out of your mouth. That means hands, pencils, cigars, jewelry, and so forth. If you have ever taken dictation from someone who is smoking a cigar or chewing gum, you can understand the importance of this advice.

One letter or digit mispronounced can be costly in time and money for a company. Sometimes "fifteen" can sound like "fifty," or a "B" can sound like "D" or "V." Imagine the consequences of making dinner reservations for fifteen when the restaurant manager understands you to say fifty!

To improve your diction, practice with the tape recorder. The playback can be a revelation. Listen to hear if you actually said what you thought you said.

Courteous   Be thoughtful and considerate in the way you phrase your message. Notice the difference between these messages:

Who's calling	May I tell Miss Gallagher who's calling?
What do you want?	May I help you?

A little courtesy can smooth the way for pleasant human and business relationships.

Keep objects out of your mouth when you talk.

Body language includes gestures and facial expressions.

Figure 7–3
What is this man's body language communicating?

NONVERBAL COMMUNICATION

The term *nonverbal communication* embraces a number of categories: body language, vocal intonations, physical objects, and space, among others.

Body Language   *Body language*—the messages conveyed by body movements and facial expressions—is the subject of a branch of study called *kinesics*. Since kinesics is not an absolute science, however, misinterpretation of body language occurs frequently. The man standing with arms crossed in figure 7–3, for example, could be communicating rebellion or unreceptivity to new ideas. On the other hand, he could be chilled and hugging himself for warmth.

Body language can refer to the whole body or to one significant part. The eyes, for example, are a very expressive human feature: A frown indicates displeasure; raised eyebrows indicate surprise. You have often heard the term "shifty-eyed" used to describe someone who seems dishonest. "Look me in the eye and say that" challenges a person's sincerity. A direct gaze can also be a signal of interest. The "two-second eye lock"—holding another person's eye for longer than two seconds—has been cited by body language authority Julius Fast as an indication of interest."[1]

Hand movements also convey meaning. Tapping fingers, clenching fists, and sweeping gestures can indicate different degrees of tension, anger, or openness.

[1]Julius Fast, "What Is a Two-Second 'Eye Lock'? Know the Body Language of Sex, Power, and Aggression," *People* (February 13, 1978), p. 64.

THE MESSAGE   185

What are these people saying by their body language?

During a business meeting, watch for nonverbal cues. For example, suppose you are in a planning session regarding expansion of your department. If division vice-president Anthony DiNardo leans back in the chair and puts his hands behind his head, he may be saying he feels superior. If sales manager Jim Cain sits up and places one leg over the arm of his chair, he may be showing hostility, indifference, or dominance. If personnel director Mary Collier leans forward, she may be hearing something that pleases her. If marketing coordinator Dave Williams unbuttons his jacket, he may be showing agreement. Administrative assistant Lynn Fowler, exposing her palms, indicates sincerity and openness.

Both Ms. Collier and Mr. DiNardo wear eyeglasses. If Ms. Collier pauses to clean her glasses, she may be taking time for thought. An earpiece in the mouth may indicate a desire for more information. Touching both ends together could be a sign of stress. Mr. DiNardo might express anger by throwing his glasses on the table.[2]

Julius Fast maintains that people who are in agreement will adopt congruent positions. They will tilt their heads at the same angle, cross their legs similarly, hold their hands in similar positions. In a group setting, their bodies will be turned slightly toward each other.[3]

Voices, Objects, Space Vocal intonations and inflections communicate even when words are not spoken. "M-m-m" can convey doubt or enthusiasm, depending on the tone.

Physical objects are another very effective means of nonverbal communication, especially in the office. Take, for example, the desk chair, which ranges in size and bulk according to the status of the person sitting in it from the high-backed leather seat of the department director to the small swivel chair of the typist. A secretary with a back problem who asks for permission to use an executive's sturdy chair may find her request greeted with suspicion and nervousness on the part of her superiors.

Every business has unwritten rules regarding space, or *proxemics*, as it is sometimes called in business communications. By instinct, you know you cannot walk into a supervisor's office and perch on top of the desk, or grab a chair, sit down, and prop your feet up.

Each firm has a code that should be respected by its employees. The new employee who parks in the boss's parking space soon learns of the mistake. An invisible caste system may dominate the company lunchroom or cafeteria. If you do not believe it, try sitting at the table that your supervisor always uses.

[2]Adapted from Gerard I. Nierenberg and Henry H. Calero, *How to Read a Person Like a Book* (New York: Pocket Books, 1975), p. 51.
[3]Fast, "What Is a Two-Second 'Eye Lock'?", p. 65.

The kind of desk you have may be a nonverbal expression of your status.

A person's status in a firm can be measured in square feet: the larger the office, the greater the person's prestige. Location is also important. Corner offices are more desirable than side offices. Also notice desk sizes. The low-ranking employee with piles of paperwork usually has a small desk, whereas the president of the company sits behind a massive desk with hardly a paper on it.

As a new employee, be observant. Pick up the nonverbal cues

This executive's tastefully furnished corner office communicates his status.

of your associates and respect the company's unwritten rules of space.

WRITTEN COMMUNICATION

Learning to write well is hard work, but the importance of written communications in business cannot be overemphasized. The written word is a permanent record of transactions of any importance. Everything of significance should be written. The entry of the computer into the office and the expanding use of information-processing technology makes the importance of written communication even more significant.

The letter, memo, and report are the three most common forms of written business communications. Each form follows certain conventions with regard to content and physical preparation. The details of each form cannot be adequately covered here. You would be wise to invest in a basic reference book on business communications. In addition, you should read a few books on clear writing techniques. The following points are some basic guidelines for effective written business communications.

In order to write effectively, you need to plan what you want to say. Before you do anything else, outline the major points you need to convey. A simple list is a good starting point. Note: If you are responding to correspondence, check the points that need answering and be sure to include them in your list.

Try to address your reader by name instead of using "Dear Sir" or "Dear Madam." Your first paragraph should tell the reader what your correspondence is about. If you are answering a letter, refer the reader to the date of his or her letter.

Write for your intended audience. Use familiar words and avoid technical language or jargon, unless you know that the recipient is familiar with the terminology you are using. Above all, don't write at a higher or lower level than your intended reader.

Use the active versus the passive voice. Try to use active verbs and nouns and avoid unnecessary descriptive adjectives. Use good English, be clear, stick to the point, and be as brief as possible.

Use paragraphing to make the communication easier to read by breaking it into distinct, logical parts. Underline important words for emphasis, if necessary. Distinguish facts from opinions. And, be honest.

In the last paragraph tell your reader exactly what you expect of him or her or what you are going to do. If the correspondence is informational, summarize the main points.

Make your communications as attractive as possible. Type on good quality paper and keep it free from smudges and erasures. Your finished product should be perfect; it should not contain any misspellings, typos, or factual errors.

Remember, whether communication is verbal or nonverbal, the message is only a vehicle for thought exchange. To this point, we have discussed how the message is created, organized, and sent; but the completion of communication depends on whether the message is received correctly.

The Receiver

Receiving is the most frequent communication activity of any working day. *Receivers*—the recipient of the sender's message—can be divided into two types, passive listeners and active listeners. Passive listeners absorb some of the messages directed to them, but never receive others. Active listeners develop good habits of concentration, evaluation, and mental participation and thus succeed in absorbing most of the intended message.

This travel agent needs to concentrate on the details of a customer's itinerary.

CONCENTRATION

The average listener can comprehend at the rate of 300–400 words per minute, whereas the sender can only speak at the rate of 125–150 words per minute. With this difference, it is easy for the mind to begin to wander to last night's date or next weekend's ski trip. In a business situation, however, all your attention is required in order that no important part of the message is missed.

For example, an airline ticket agent cannot chance missing a single detail when a traveler asks for two economy class, round-trip tickets on January 11th to the Bahamas, with a one-day stopover in Miami on the return trip on January 27th. A bank teller must practice active listening when a customer presents a hundred-dollar bill and wants it changed for three twenties, one ten, five ones, ten dollars in dimes, and fifteen dollars in quarters.

Successful people are good listeners, according to one professional lecturer. After presenting a lecture to company sales people, he claims he can pick out the top ones without knowing their names, sales records, or backgrounds. Amazingly, his choices are usually accurate. Merely by observation, he has found that the most attentive listeners in the audience are generally the top performers in the sales force.

EVALUATION

Learn to be a critical listener. Evaluate what is being said and the motive behind the statement. Frequently people will use inferences and opinions as substitutes for *facts*—anything that can be supported by evidence. Learn to recognize the difference between fact, inference, and opinion.

For example, note how the following three statements differ:

A thermometer gives documented evidence of the temperature.

Fact

"The thermometer registers 104 degrees."

This statement is a fact because it can be supported by evidence.

Inference

"This is one of the hottest days of the year."

This statement is an inference because additional information is needed before it is recognized as a fact.

Opinion

"Today is hot."

This is a personal judgment about the weather.

Look at another example:

Fact

"The President is 54 years old *today*."

This is a fact that can be readily supported by proof. Remember, though, that what is fact today may not be a fact a year from now.

Inference

"The President is the youngest political leader in the world."

This is an inference; it needs evidence before it can be used as fact.

Opinion

"The President looks young for his age."

This is one person's appraisal of the President's appearance.

An active listener learns not to accept every statement at face value. Develop the habit of evaluating statements. Be aware, also, that people do not always say what they mean. By asking "Why did the sender make that statement?" you can sometimes find the real meaning behind the words. The following dialogues illustrate this point:

A teenage boy comes home from high school and tells his mother, "Mike is really babied. His parents give him too much. He just got a brand new car for graduation." How might his mother interpret what he says? Is he telling her that Mike is babied? Or is he saying that he feels envious of Mike?

A colleague says to you, "I have so much work to do that I don't know if I can get it all done. The boss wants me to do everything for him. He recently asked me to take charge of the arrangements for the national sales meeting next month." Is your colleague complaining or bragging?

One friend tells another, "We had so much fun at Larson's

party last night. It's too bad you weren't invited." What is this friend really saying?

Be an evaluative listener. Teach yourself to listen not only for the words but also for the meanings and the motives behind them.

MENTAL PARTICIPATION

A good listener takes notes, either mentally or physically. The bank teller and the ticket agent keep pads handy for jotting down details. Note taking in a social conversation would be considered rude, but in a business transaction it shows concern about getting the job done right and on time.

When you listen to speakers, pick out their central themes and main points. Ask yourself the following questions:

- What is the main idea of the speech?

- Is the speaker sticking to the main idea?

- What are the major points of the speech?

- Do the major points directly relate to the main idea?

- Is the speaker using good examples to prove the points?

- When is the speaker using facts? Inferences? Opinions?

- Is the speaker covering the material too quickly or too slowly?

- Does the conclusion of the speech relate logically to the main points?

- Does the speaker accomplish the goals set in the beginning of the speech?

Keep a pad handy for jotting down details of business transactions.

Note taking during a conference shows concern about getting the job done right.

Do not sit passively. Absorb and analyze the speaker's presentation and persuasiveness.

Feedback—the response the receiver returns to the sender—is necessary for a complete communication cycle. Without feedback, there is no communication.

Feedback comes in many forms. It can be either verbal or nonverbal: The speaker can acknowledge the sender by words or by action. Television networks use ratings for feedback. Teachers use tests for feedback. Businesses use suggestion boxes, questionnaires, coupons, and surveys for feedback. In face-to-face communication, speakers rely on the spontaneous reactions of the receiver for feedback.

Feedback is the sender's responsibility as well as the receiver's. It is difficult to determine what has gone wrong when a communication problem occurs, but the blame should not always be on the receiver. When an employer complains that employees do not follow the rules, the problem may not necessarily be in the feedback. The rules may not have been well stated or sufficiently stressed. When a consumer sends letters to a manufacturer and receives no response, one cause could be an incorrect address.

Feedback does not always take the form of an overt action or response. It can be transmitted through the medium of deliberate silence, as in the following situations:

Someone in a group of teenagers makes the suggestion that they all go to the beach. No one stirs.

An employee makes a written request for a raise in salary. The company administrators make no reply.

Feedback may not take the form the sender anticipates, but it nevertheless completes the cycle.

Breakdowns in Communication

All four components—sender, message, receiver, and feedback—are essential for a complete communication cycle. Each component has requirements that must be fulfilled before clear communication can take place. Unfortunately, even when a sender tries to produce an understandable message and a receiver listens carefully and responds with proper feedback, misunderstandings sometimes result. In this section, some of the causes of communication breakdown will be discussed.

STATIC

Static is any interference with the exchanges between sender and receiver (see figure 7–4) that distorts the intended message or feedback in such a way that misinterpretation results. Physical static, such as the annoying electrical interference on radio or television, or a loud noise that disrupts a conversation, is easier to remove than internal static. The reason for this is that internal static involves human factors.

Internal static is caused by the knowledge, emotions, and background of both the sender and the receiver. In the following section, look at what happens to communication between a boss and a new employee on the first day of work. The boss, Mrs. Johnson, intends

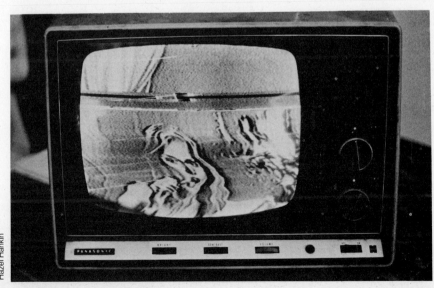

Hazel Hankin

Interference with communication

to personally train the new employee, Jim Carter, because the employee Jim is replacing has already left the company.

Knowledge Static   Mrs. Johnson has a large technical vocabulary and forgets that others may not be familiar with the words she uses. While instructing Jim Carter, she tells him:

> "Put this in the *tickler file*."
> "This goes into *escrow*."
> "This is a *satisfied mortgage*."
> "Take the papers over to *PR*."
> "Call this into *word processing*."
> "*R&D* will want this."
> "Mark this *ASAP*."
> "*FYI* this envelope and send it over to Mr. Smith."

If Jim is unfamiliar with these terms, he will naturally feel very confused. To correct this communication problem, he should ask questions about the things he doesn't understand. He will thus alert Mrs. Johnson to the fact that she is going too fast and assuming too much. He will also demonstrate his willingness to learn. Employers are a little suspicious of new employees who never ask questions. A lack of such feedback makes them wonder if the employee comprehends the information.

Emotional Static   Mrs. Johnson may feel rushed, pressured, and bored with the familiar details of the work she is explaining. She may be anxious to get back to her own job duties. Jim may be

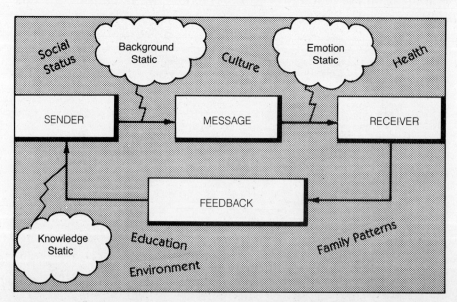

Figure 7–4
Communication Interference

nervous and worried about making a good impression. The two emotional states are not complementary.

Background Static   If Mrs. Johnson comes from a background of wealth and Jim comes from a lower-middle-class background, problems can develop. For example:

- She sends him to the post office to buy stamps, expecting him to purchase a roll. He buys a few and brings back the change.

- She asks him to buy typewriter ribbon. He chooses the economical nylon fabric instead of the more expensive film ribbon used.

Background static may have caused the misunderstanding that resulted in the purchase of a few stamps instead of a roll.

- She has a valued client in the hospital. She tells Jim to send flowers to the hospital. She was thinking of a bouquet of flowers, but Jim sends a single rosebud.

These barriers can be overcome as Mrs. Johnson and Jim get to know each other. However, the first few weeks of training can produce a great deal of internal static.

MENTAL TRAPS

Not only do knowledge, emotions, and background affect communication, but faulty logic on either the part of the sender or the receiver can also produce static. Mental traps such as two-value thinking, singular perception, generalization, "thinging," and slanting can snare unsuspecting communicators.

Two-Value Thinking   *Two-value thinking* is the belief that if a particular quality does not exist in someone or something, then its opposite must. For example, if a young woman does not seem to be ambitious, she must be lazy. If a young man is not strong, he is weak. If you do not deny my statement, you must agree.

For practice, try to find terms that fall between the extremes listed below. Although it is easy to group ideas into either-or categories, you will find that there are gradations between opposites; learning to allow for these ranges can help you to better understand others.

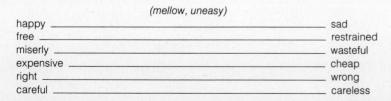

(mellow, uneasy)

happy _____	sad
free _____	restrained
miserly _____	wasteful
expensive _____	cheap
right _____	wrong
careful _____	careless

Figure 7–5
What do you see?

In two-value thinking, you may allow one desirable or undesirable trait to distort the whole picture. As an illustration, imagine that a new neighbor, Jane Smith, is moving into your neighborhood. Before you meet Ms. Smith, you hear that she is:

An excellent cook	Unemployed	A mother
An artist	A divorcée	Attractive
30 years old	An ex-public-relations manager	A gardener

Would a single factor influence your judgment of Jane Smith to the point of overriding all the other factors? Be careful about making judgments on the basis of one point.

Singular Perception   Have you ever been eager to meet someone because of what you had heard about him or her? What happened when you were finally introduced? Did you find your impression of the person much different from the reports of others? Why did this happen? It may have happened because of *singular perception*, which often influences one person's impression of another. Singular perception can be compared to tunnel vision: If you do not allow for other people's perceptions of events, persons, or ideas, you will view these as if you were wearing blinders.

Behavioral scientists agree that we are the sum total of all our experiences. Backgrounds, family patterns, education, and social values all affect the way we perceive life. Each of us is a unique individual with our own set of life experiences, and no one, not even our brothers and sisters, can have the same experiences.

Your viewpoint of the world will be different from another's. For a demonstration of this point, see figure 7-5. What did you see the first time you looked at the figure? Ask a friend to look at it. What did your friend see at first glance? You may have seen the white chalice, while your friend saw the two black silhouettes. Both of you were looking at the same figure yet saw two different images. Therefore, each of you had a different perception of the same scene.

The following incident is a good example of how different perceptions of the same event can cloud communication.

A supervisor approaches two clerks and asks if one would be willing to work overtime on the weekend. One clerk, Sue, responds that she would be most happy to work overtime. How do each of the three persons involved in the incident perceive Sue's eager volunteering?

Supervisor: Sue is an ambitious, hard-working girl.
Co-worker: Sue is apple-polishing.
Sue: I need the extra money to pay my debts.

Often, you see what you expect to see. Your mind determines your perceptions. "I saw it with my own eyes" is a phrase intended to

Tunnel vision

ensure validity, but it is not always accurate. Look at the photo at the bottom of this page. What do you see?

Backlogs of experience often dictate the manner in which you hear, see, taste, and judge. Singular perception is difficult to overcome. Remember that your view of the world is different from anyone else's. With a little effort, you can look at ideas, people, and events without preconceptions and, thus, achieve a broader view of the world.

Generalizations *Generalizations* group people, things, or ideas under one label, making no exception for individuality. For example, have you ever listened to a conversation during which people from various sections of the country were categorized: Texans are egotistical; New Yorkers are snobs; Southerners are easygoing; Floridians are rich; Midwesterners are conservative; and so on. If one of these labels has been applied to you, how did you feel about the generalization?

Analyze and research all areas of a situation before making a conclusion. Careful analysis is not only evidence of good reasoning, but is also a sound business practice.

Thinging In our fast-paced society, people can work side by side and still not get to know one another as humans. George R. Bach and Ronald Deutsch, authors of *Pairing*, call this dehumanization of personal relationships *thinging*. "Thinging" happens when you begin to think of another human as merely an extension of a machine. Grocery clerks, bank tellers, waitresses, all become "things" to serve you. "Thinging requires [deceiving] oneself by shutting out

Hazel Hankin

Do you make generalizations about people from other parts of the country?

Jeremiah B. Lighter

People looking at this photo will have different perceptions of the same scene.

"Thinging" is seeing people merely as generators of service.

the nonuseful part of the person. (The waitress with the tired feet may be a Ph.D. student whose scholarship funds have run out or a mother of three whose husband has deserted her. The thinger does not want to know such facts.)"[4]

Co-workers, subordinates, and supervisors are more than generators of a product or service. Get to know their feelings, attitudes, strengths, weaknesses, likes, and dislikes. The human interest you show will help promote better communication between you and your office mates.

Slanting *Slanting* can be defined as shading the truth a bit to benefit someone. Maybe you have been guilty of such an act without knowing what it is called. For example, imagine an avid skier who has just found that the the chill factor on the ski slopes is 20° below zero. The skier wants to go skiing in spite of the cold, and he wants his girlfriend to accompany him. When she asks him how cold it is outside before she decides whether to go skiing or not, he replies, "It's not cold. A little brisk, but not cold."

In another instance, a supervisor may encourage a junior executive to accept an additional duty. The subordinate wants to know if this additional responsibility will require much time. The supervisor replies that it will take very little time, but knows that the contrary is true. After accepting the additional duty, the subordinate finds that it involves much more work than the supervisor had implied. The supervisor has been guilty of slanting.

[4]George R. Bach and Ronald M. Deutsch, *Pairing* (New York: Avon, 1970), p. 77.

Statistics can be slanted. A manufacturer can claim that nine out of ten housewives in Los Angeles prefer its product to any similar product. This statement is true, but what might not be mentioned is the product's unfavorable reception in other cities.

A commercial might slant the truth by citing a survey that finds Brand X better than any other brand on the market. The commercial doesn't mention the number of people polled. Were there 10 or 100 or 1,000 questioned? What about the circumstances surrounding the polling? Were free gifts, discounts, or favors offered to the persons polled? Commercials sometimes gloss over the truth.

AVOIDING COMMUNICATION BREAKDOWN

How can breakdowns in communication be avoided? As you have learned, good communication begins with good reasoning. Courses in logic, popular years ago, are returning to campuses. Another college course that provides excellent training in reasoning is composition. Writing is thinking, and composing a well-constructed paragraph or essay is an exercise in thought. Learning to state an idea and supporting that idea with relevant arguments or evidence is good discipline in any professional field. And this kind of formal training not only helps you to present your own ideas clearly and logically, but also equips you to analyze the thinking of others.

Two rules can help you avoid faulty reasoning. First, allow for different viewpoints on the same issue. Second, avoid hasty conclusions. Keep these two simple rules in mind as you send and receive ideas.

Self-Awareness and Communication

"Know thyself" is excellent advice for the communicator. A better understanding of self and others will mean better communication.

9 out of 10 Doctors Surveyed Recommend

When you look at an advertisement, analyze it to see if it is guilty of slanting its statistics.

It is the child in you who loves cuddly animals.

The principles of transactional analysis and the Johari Window are helpful in gaining that understanding.

TRANSACTIONAL ANALYSIS

Eric Berne, the originator of *transactional analysis*, states that our personalities are divided into three parts: the parent, the child, and the adult. Our actions and thoughts come from one or the other of these three selves. Sometimes we respond and speak as the parent within us, sometimes as the child or adult.

The parent part of you is the authoritarian part. Your mother, father, ministers, teachers, grandparents—all the authority figures of your childhood told you how to behave. "Brush your teeth," "Hang up your clothes," "Don't get dirty," "Raise your hand if you want to speak," and "Cover your mouth when you cough" are their expectations persisting in your mind.

The child is the responsive, spontaneous, and emotional part of you. When you laugh or cry, that is the child in you. The child is also the part of you that enjoys walking in the rain; buys surprise presents for friends; participates in sports; likes shiny new things, puppies, and kittens; and eats fattening foods.

The adult is the part of you that listens to the expectations of the parent and the desires of the child, assesses the situation at hand, and decides what action is appropriate.

The following are examples of transactions between parent, child, and adult.

Office Worker
P: I've finished all my work. I should help Helen. She has so much work.
C: Why do I always have to help her?
A: I'll help her. I have nothing to do at present, and it might make time go faster.

Business Person
P: I should get to work early this morning. I have a lot to do.
C: It's a beautiful day. I'd rather go to the park.
A: I'll try to get my work done early. If I do, I'll take the afternoon off.

These examples give the impression that the adult always wins out and makes the final decision, but that is not always the case.

When two people are involved in a conversation, six selves are actually present.

If the communication between these two individuals is parallel, then the transaction can be called complementary.

But sometimes communications get crossed and problems occur. When this happens, it is called a crossed transaction.

Since transactional analysis is a concept that requires more in-depth coverage than is possible here, you might want to refer to

What Do You Say After You Say Hello? and *Games People Play*, both by Eric Berne, or *I'm OK—You're OK*, by Thomas A. Harris.

JOHARI WINDOW

Joseph Luft and Harry Ingham compare the human personality to that of a four-paned window, with each pane representing a segment of the total individual. (See figure 7–6.) Their theory is called the *Johari Window*.

Each pane is defined as follows:

Open   Section of self that is known to self and to others

Hidden   Section that is known to self but is kept hidden from others

Blind   Section that is unknown to self but is known to others

Unknown   Section that remains unknown to both self and others

To apply this principle, let us examine the case of Dennis, who wants to be regarded as intelligent. In the open section, Dennis chooses actions and words that help create this image. In the hidden section is Dennis's insecurity about his intellectual competence. In the blind section is his unawareness of the pretentious mistakes he makes that show his intellectual failings. In the unknown section is the reason why Dennis has a great need to be thought of as intelligent.

Figure 7–6
The Johari Window

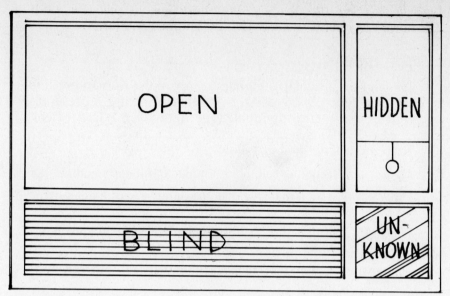

Figure 7–7
An ideal Johari Window

Ideally, as Dennis becomes more self-accepting, he will begin to disclose parts of himself to others. He will be able to express his ideas without fear of looking stupid. As this openness increases, so will his self-confidence.[5] His personality diagram will look like the one in figure 7–7.

Communication flows more freely among confident, open people who are not afraid of making a mistake or facing rejection. The communication process would be much smoother if everyone's open section were the largest section of his or her Johari Window.

Good communication should be considered an art. But, perhaps because it is one of the first skills developed as a baby, communication is frequently taken for granted. However, as a career-minded individual, you cannot afford to let poor communication habits slow you down. As you advance in your career, you will need to become more and more skilled in communicating your ideas, values, and attitudes to others.

[5]For further information, see Joseph Luft, *Of Human Interaction* (Palo Alto, Calif.: National Press, 1969).

KEY TERMS

communication cycle

sender

empathy

message

nonverbal communication

body language

kinesics

proxemics

receivers

facts

feedback

static

internal static

two-value thinking

singular perception

generalizations

thinging

slanting

transactional analysis

Johari Window

TEST YOURSELF:
QUESTIONS FOR REVIEW AND DISCUSSION

1. Define communication in terms of its importance to business.
2. What are the parts of the communication cycle?
3. Give an example of a situation in which a supervisor is a good sender. A poor sender.
4. Cite some examples of nonverbal communication that occur in office situations.
5. Give examples of slanting, singular perception, generalities, and thinging.
6. Give an example of a statement that the receiver interprets in a completely different way from that which was intended.
7. What is a generalization? Give an example, applying it to an office situation.
8. Describe a communication transaction, using Eric Berne's terms "adult," "parent," and "child."
9. Give an example of a hidden motive in a business transaction.
10. What is static? Cite ways in which static can hinder business communication.
11. Give an example of a fact, an inference, and an opinion.

APPLICATION EXERCISE

Use the following steps to complete the communication grid that follows.

Step 1   List your favorite expressions or slang terms at the top of the grid. (If you have trouble thinking of terms, ask your friends what words or phrases they notice you using repeatedly. Frequently, slang terms are used subconsciously.)

Step 2   List persons with whom you have frequent conversations along the left side. (Do not list just friends. Include people from various areas of your life, such as instructors, ministers, employers, parents, etc.)

Step 3   Consider how each individual would respond to your use of the expressions listed at the top of the chart. If the person's reaction would be positive, put a plus mark (+) in the appropriate column. If the person's reaction would be negative, put a minus symbol (−) in the appropriate column. If the person might not understand your expression, place a question mark (?) in the appropriate column. If the person has heard the term so many times that it would not convey anything, put a zero (0) in the appropriate column.

Step 4   When you have finished, look over the grid. Can you see how some of your slang vocabulary might be inappropriate for the business world?

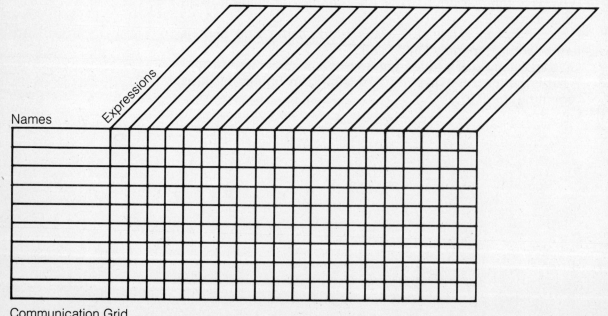

Names | Expressions

Communication Grid

Suggested Readings

Bach, George R., and Ronald M. Deutsch, *Pairing*. New York: Avon, 1970.

Berne, Eric. *Games People Play*. New York: Ballantine, 1978.

Berne, Eric. *What Do You Say After You Say Hello?* New York: Ballantine, 1975.

Fast, Julius. *The Body Language of Sex, Power & Aggression*. New York: M. Evans, 1977.

Fast, Julius, and Barbara Fast. *Talking Between the Lines.* New York: Pocket Books, 1980.

Flesch, Rudolf. *A New Guide to Better Writing*. New York: Popular Library, 1982.

Goffman, Erving. *Interaction Ritual: Essays in Face-to-Face*. New York: Pantheon, 1982.

Gunning, Robert. *Technique of Clear Writing*. New York: McGraw-Hill, 1968.

Harris, Thomas A. *I'm OK—You're OK*. New York: Avon, 1973.

Hayakawa, Samuel I. *Language in Thought and Action*. New York: Harcourt Brace Jovanovich, Inc., 1978.

Luft, Joseph. *Of Human Interaction*. Palo Alto, Calif.: Mayfield, 1969.

Machotka, Paul, and John P. Spiegal. *Articulate Body*. New York: Irvington, 1982.

Nierenberg, Gerard I. *Meta-Talk*. New York: Cornerstone, 1981.

Nierenberg, Gerard I., and Henry H. Calero. *How to Read a Person Like a Book*. New York: Cornerstone, 1972.

Nierenberg, Gerard I. *Meta-Talk*. New York: Cornerstone, 1981.

8

PERSONAL EFFECTIVENESS

COMPREHENSIVE GOAL
To make you aware of your own motives and needs and of the motives and needs of others; and to help you to act both assertively and with consideration for others.

SPECIFIC OBJECTIVES
After reading this chapter, you will be able to:

- diagram Maslow's Needs Hierarchy
- describe Thomas Harris's theory of the four life positions
- identify members of an office family
- distinguish between a victim and a nonvictim
- describe ways to avoid victim status
- discuss Manuel Smith's Bill of Assertive Rights
- give examples of assertiveness techniques

When one college graduate was asked how he liked his new job, he remarked, "I love my job; it's the people I can't stand." This is a problem that faces many employees. Government statistics reveal the the major reason for dismissing employees is not lack of skills but the inability to work well with other people. One employee complaint checklist is excerpted in table 8–1. Notice that most of the complaints listed are people-related ones.

Your career may place you in a situation that requires constant contact with people not of your choice. The quicker you learn the importance of compatibility with all types of personalities, the better your chance for job success. Professional compatibility means maintaining a fine balance: cooperating with others without becoming a "yes" person. A personally effective person has concern for others *and* a respect for self.

Concern for Others

The old Indian prayer, "Let me not criticize my brother until I've walked a mile in his moccasins," is good advice for everyone. Often we pass judgment too hastily—concluding, for example, that a new employee is uncommunicative and aloof, only to discover later that he or she is shy. Good methods for exploring what makes you and others tick can be found in the theories of Abraham Maslow and Thomas Harris, which will be discussed in this section. As you study these theories, test them in daily life situations.

HBJ Photo

Understanding others will help you work with them effectively.

Table 8–1

WORKING CONDITIONS WE FIND ANNOYING

- A bad boss

- Too long a commute, and/or difficult access to job site

- Hot, stuffy working conditions—rooms without windows, poor ventilation

- Too many people in the same space—bull-pen offices, cramped quarters

- No quiet space

- Being stuck in the office all day, being confined to desk

- Inflexible hours, rigidly observed

- Working in neutral or hostile working-space

- Unclear job description

- Male chauvinistic environment; women treated as second-class citizens

- No sense of purpose

- Too much pressure, constant deadlines, and crash programs or tasks

- Not having control of our own work

- Not allowed to experiment and try new things

- Frenzied work patterns

- Regimentation

- No challenges

- No sense of working on a team

- No friends among co-workers; too much rudeness, lack of tact, or sensitivity

- Being asked to work past the time we're supposed to be able to leave

- No opportunity to talk with people

- Having no time for reflection; emphasis on action

- Never being able to see concrete results of our work

- Incompetent co-workers

- Too severe dress code

- Coffee not readily available

- Dishonest, false, or hard-sell representation of company or product

- Not being given recognition, appreciation, or chance for advancement

- Never being given feedback, or being subject to too many evaluators

- Being asked to do tasks we hate (e.g., accounting for some)

- Meetings held for no significant purpose

- Dissatisfied co-workers, who won't do anything beyond the minimum

- Having always to go through established channels

- Too much paperwork; record-keeping at the expense of people-helping

- Not being given enough resources or resource persons

- Power struggles within the company

- Economic cliff-hanging about future; no job security

- Underpaid

- Co-workers' personal agendas consistently blocking group goals and action

- Unhealthy competition among co-workers: game-playing, back-stabbing

- Not being given the chance to grow on the job

- Lack of fairness and justice in way employees are treated

- Bureaucratic philosophy insensitive to human need and variability

- Underutilization of employees' skills

- Never being involved in the decision-making process

- Meaningless, routine busy work

- Smokers nearby to nonsmokers

- Nonsupportive staff situations

- Antagonistic supervision

Source: Excerpted and adapted from Richard N. Bolles, *The Three Boxes of Life* (Berkeley, Calif.: Ten Speed Press, 1981), pp. 307–8.

MASLOW'S NEEDS HIERARCHY

According to Abraham Maslow, all people share the same basic physiological needs and human drives. He explained these needs and drives by placing them on a pyramid-like scale, with the basic drives at the bottom of the scale and the need for self-actualization at the top (see figure 8–1). He called this pyramid a *Needs Hierarchy*.[1]

Before humans can function well in society, their basic drives must be satisfied. The primary drive of all humans is the satisfaction of physiological needs. When we hunger, ache with pain, or suffer from lack of sleep, our bodies demand attention. If these needs are not satisfied, little else matters and all social behavior is irrelevant. Starving people will fight one another for food.

Security ranks second to physiological demands. The instincts for physical security and self-preservation are strong in all individuals. A normally passive, mild-mannered individual will be transformed into a fighter when his or her life is threatened. Jobs and financial security are in this category. When people's livelihoods are endangered, their personalities change.

After the first two needs are satisfied, the need to be loved and to give love must be gratified. All humans need to feel loved and wanted. To people who feel that no one cares if they exist, life becomes meaningless—even suicide may seem an attractive alternative to their loneliness. Whether it is an intimate relationship or the friendship of many, some form of love must be present in everyone's life.

[1]Abraham H. Maslow, *Motivation and Personality* (New York: Harper & Row, 1970), pp. 35–46.

To a lonely person, life can become meaningless.

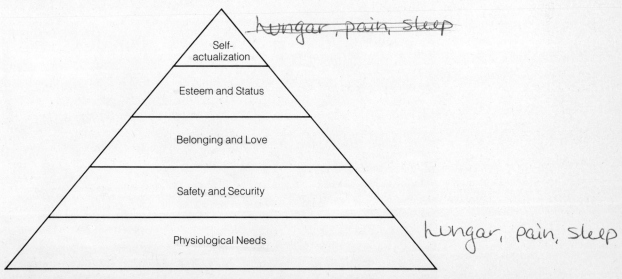

hungar, pain, sleep

hungar, pain, sleep

Figure 8–1
Maslow's Needs Hierarchy

- Self-actualization
- Esteem and Status
- Belonging and Love
- Safety and Security
- Physiological Needs

Only when an individual feels satisfaction in the first three areas can he or she pursue the fourth drive, recognition. People crave recognition in varying degrees. Some strive for graduation with honors, a national award, or the applause of a large crowd, whereas others can be happy with just a warm greeting from friends. Everyone thrives on recognition, and its giving and receiving is part of good human relationships.

The fifth level of the Needs Hierarchy is called self-actualization. This is sometimes called the "peak experience." Some people never reach this level. The peak experience is an almost mystical union of mind and body that can occur at a totally unpredictable time. A hunter might achieve self-actualization while watching the morning sun emerge over the horizon. A ballerina who has practiced for years may have a peak experience during a near-perfect performance. The sensation usually occurs as a result of reaching one's fullest potential; it is a rare and precious moment that involves total mind and body.

Maslow's Needs Hierarchy applies very directly to your understanding of your co-workers. The particular level at which each is functioning (and at which you are functioning) will influence your relationships. How effective is the worker who has been on a fasting diet for the last twenty-four hours? Try to give directions to someone who did not sleep the night before. A colleague whose job and financial security are threatened will be nervous and irritable. A large monetary loss to your firm will influence your boss's attitude

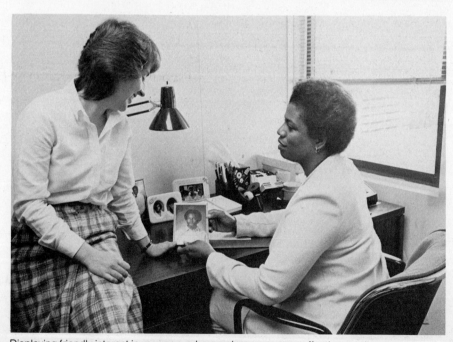

Displaying friendly interest in your co-workers makes you a more effective employee.

toward the whole staff. Any upset to the status quo can spell danger to an insecure person. If you can identify these basic needs in your fellow workers, perhaps you will not be so offended when they snarl back at your cheery "good morning."

The need to be loved and to give love also operates in the business world. To be an effective employee, you should take an interest in your colleagues. Ask about their weekends, their hobbies, and their families. Remember their birthdays and congratulate them on special occasions. You will find that your friendly concern is reciprocated.

Smart managers recognize the need in their subordinates for recognition. Large offices and fancy titles are often passed out in lieu of salary increases. Sincere compliments, friendly hellos, comments on appearance, thank-yous for assistance, pats on the back, and acknowledgment of well-performed tasks are ways of responding to people's needs for recognition.

"I'M OK—YOU'RE OK"

Thomas Harris's theory of the four life positions explains human behavior in terms of degrees of "OK-ness." The four classifications of OK-ness are placed into *life positions* as:

1. I'm not OK—you're OK.
2. I'm not OK—you're not OK.
3. I'm OK—you're not OK.
4. I'm OK—you're OK.

The ideal life position is the fourth position. Unlike the first three, it is arrived at through conscious choice. The first three ask "Why?"; the fourth, Harris says, asks "Why not?"

To help you identify these four life positions, a description of each is presented here.

I'm not OK—you're OK. Persons in this position need lots of approval from others. They often seek out important people to be near, and spend a great deal of time in social climbing. Their conversations are usually sprinkled with "if I" or "when I." Unfortunately, their constant striving for happiness is never successful; they never feel OK.

I'm not OK—you're not OK. This life position is one of existence, nothing more. People in this position travel through life without hope. Sometimes—through drugs, alcohol, or food—they find temporary release from the pain of life. Occasionally they withdraw completely, requiring psychiatric treatment or institutionalization.

I'm OK—you're not OK. Humans in the third position trust no one but themselves, usually as a result of childhood abuse. They may surround themselves with yes people who will pay them homage, but they have little respect for their followers. They seldom maintain a close relationship with anyone.

I'm OK—you're OK. This position is based on thought, faith, and action.[2] It results from a conscious decision to believe in oneself and one's fellow man. The self-assured individuals in this position can freely give and receive love. Not only do they have the respect and admiration of others, but they also have trust in their own innate powers. They have no need to join cliques to bolster self-esteem. It is a pleasure to work with people so self-confident. Colleagues like this are pleasant, interested in others, and progressive.

Harris explains that the four life positions are difficult to change once a pattern is set. But he, as well as other behavioral scientists, believes that change is not impossible. As he states, "What was once decided can be undecided." A not-OK person can become OK by conscious decision.

THE OFFICE FAMILY

The idea of an office family is a topic that has been receiving increasing attention. Recent studies show that today's office often resembles a family unit with corresponding familial relationships. This may be partly attributable to the increasing number of women in the work force. Whatever the reasons, you should be aware of the various types of office families and the relationships that can exist.

Although some companies may combine styles, most can be categorized as one of three family styles: paternal, maternal, and egalitarian.

The *paternal style* company has a central authority figure who uses competition for his or her attention as the motivating factor among employees. For example, a CEO (chief executive officer) may purposely promote rivalry among the top management team in order to see which executive will emerge with the most power. The winner will be rewarded accordingly.

The *maternal style* emphasizes employee welfare. In this kind of company, care and concern for the employee is expressed through the offering of a variety of fringe benefits, such as pension and educational assistance plans, fair work evaluation procedures, and employee recreation programs. The philosophy behind the maternal style is that employees who are treated fairly and with concern will be more motivated to return the favors through loyalty and hard work.

The *egalitarian style* emphasizes employee involvement in the development and growth of the company. It tends to offer a relaxed and casual environment versus a rigid atmosphere. For employees who thrive on discipline, dress codes, and set working hours, this style of management may be too permissive.

[2]Thomas A. Harris, *I'm OK—You're OK* (New York: Avon, 1973), p. 74.

Related to the family concept are the roles that employees may assume after working in a particular organization for several years. Be aware of these roles and the motivations behind the role playing. The most common roles are discussed below.

Father Figure—A male superior may enjoy playing the role of "big daddy" to a young employee. The young employee may represent to the father figure the daughter or son he never had. Because the employee fulfills a need in the man's personality, he or she may be given privileges and rights unavailable to other employees.

Mother Figure—This is the female counterpart to the father figure. A female superior may behave like a "doting" mother to one or more subordinates. The mother figure can often be identified by her concern for everyone's well-being.

Daughter and Son Figures—This is the female or male employee who responds to the attentions of either the father or mother figure. The behavior generally includes flattering and complimenting the superior who is lavishing attention on them.

Brother and Sister Figures—Sibling rivalry can emerge among co-workers as the result of the competition to gain acceptance and attention from the mother and father figures. This rivalry can create a lot of tension and interfere with constructive accomplishment.

Uncle and Aunt Figures—These roles are often played by long-time employees who have settled into their place within the organization. The role is generally one of an advisor offering information based on experience to a young or new employee.

A certain amount of loving and caring should exist between members of an organization. As mentioned in a previous chapter, you will probably spend most of your life in a work environment. Therefore, your co-workers will be the people that you associate with most frequently. As with familial ties, special office relationships can be good. However, becoming too involved in an office family or in a particular kind of office family relationship can also be dangerous and harmful. A special relationship between another person and yourself can subject you to hostility from co-workers. You should not allow yourself to depend on individuals in the office for acceptance and approval. Nor should you let the quality and the merit of your work be affected by reliance on a particular relationship. Relationships in the offices, as in life, change.

In general, the value of the various categories set out by Maslow, Harris, and other behavioral scientists is that they give you insights into your own motives and behavior and into the motives and behavior of others. Understanding yourself and others— knowing when to sympathize, when to praise, when to leave alone—will help you become more effective in both your business and social relationships. Awareness of human motives leads to empathy *and* self-respect.

The assertive person is firm and direct in conversation.

Assertion of Needs

Understanding yourself and others, however, is only half the formula for personal effectiveness. Once you recognize your needs, you must also assert your demands. Sometimes it is not difficult to fulfill a need; at other times, it will require some exertion of your will.

Assertiveness training—learning to stand up for your beliefs and rights—has gained such public interest that books and workshops on the subject are widely available. Two assertiveness training books—*Pulling Your Own Strings* by Wayne W. Dyer, and *When I Say No, I Feel Guilty* by Manuel J. Smith—provide excellent suggestions for the individual who wishes to become more effective in this area. Each author presents assertiveness in a different context.

WAYNE DYER: VICTIMS AND NONVICTIMS

Wayne Dyer sees people as assuming one of two positions, victim or nonvictim. Victims are persons who *let* others manipulate them. They are so frightened of bad things happening to them that they never attempt to assert themselves. They seem to be rolled up into a protective ball.

Victims can easily be identified: They look and act like victims. Their posture, clothing, and demeanor say, "I'm no good." Their nonassertive manner is evident in a conversation. They never contribute a new idea to a discussion because they are frightened of negative reactions.

Victims have ways of not accepting responsibility for their condition. Dyer has compiled a long list of excuses that victims use for placing the blame on someone or something else: "My mother was overprotective"; "My mother was underprotective"; "My father abandoned me"; "My father was too strict" are some examples.

Using the following statements, Dyer discusses a victim's feelings of inadequacy:

"I know I'm going to lose."

"I get upset whenever I have to confront someone."

"The little guy never has a chance."

"I hope they won't get mad at me for asking."

"They'll probably think I'm stupid if I tell them what I did."

"I'm afraid to. I'll hurt their feelings if I tell them what I want."

"I can't handle this alone: I'll get someone who isn't afraid to do it for me."

"They really shouldn't do this; it's not fair."[3]

A victim

With these notions floating around in a person's head, it is difficult to act assertively.

Dyer's bully theory illustrates how one can begin to move out of the victim trap. As a child, you probably encountered a bully at one time or another. If the bully discovered you were an easy pushover or a crybaby, you became a natural target for harassment. If you stood up against this tyrant, even though you lost the battle, the bully thought twice before bothering you again. You could no longer be considered an easy mark. In the adult world, as in childhood, you will discover bullies who will push you around *if* you let them.

Dyer offers some suggestions for changing your status from victim to nonvictim. First of all, you must believe you are a valuable person with something to contribute to the world. Each person is unique; each person has something special to offer to others. It is selfish to keep all this ability within yourself. Acknowledge your talents and learn to share them with others.

Below are some simple pointers to start you on the way to assertiveness:

- Don't start conversations apologetically: "I hate to bother you. . . ." State your purpose firmly and directly: "I have a problem I'd like to go over with you when you have time."

- Look directly into the other's eyes when speaking. Don't bow your head. In his book *Power,* Michael Korda stresses the value of making eye contact.

[3]Wayne W. Dyer, *Pulling Your Own Strings* (New York: Funk & Wagnalls, 1981), pp. 7–10.

A victimizer

- Consider your posture and body language. A hunched position does not impress anyone. Keep your body under control while speaking. Fidgeting, playing with your hair, and swinging your foot do not demonstrate that you have confidence in yourself, nor do they inspire confidence in others.

- Keep your composure when you say no. Sometimes when people feel pressured, they lose control and lash out at others, and so weaken their own position.

- If someone asks you for a favor and you don't wish to comply, don't make up excuses. Simply say politely, "I'm sorry, I can't do that."

Everyone makes mistakes, but victimizers delight in catching people in their mistakes. When such a person criticizes you, agree with your critic and then let it pass. If the person wants to continue dwelling on your error, don't let it make you irritable. Instead, a smile or a gesture of friendship will really unnerve the victimizer.

When you hear questions that start "Why do you always . . . ," "Why can't you . . . ," or "Why aren't you more like . . . ," you'll know you're in the presence of a victimizer.

Your response should never be defensive. Rather, turn the discussion to the victimizer's own motives: "Wait a minute. You're obviously upset. What makes you compare me to so-and-so? Why is it important to you that I behave like her?" Use sentences that begin with "you"; for example; "*You* think I should be more like Sally."[4]

[4]Dyer, *Pulling Your Own Strings*, p. 36.

Victims have fears that prevent them from functioning to their full capacity. It is normal to have fears, but it is abnormal to let these fears prevent you from participating in daily activities. Identify your fears and analyze them. Ask yourself what could possibly be the worst thing that could happen. Having answered that question, don't be afraid to act.

Learn to be quietly effective. You don't need to shout your accomplishments to others. If you are truly talented, people will recognize it.

MANUEL SMITH: YOUR ASSERTIVE RIGHTS

Manuel J. Smith has conducted assertiveness training sessions since the early 1970s. He has found that the nonassertive individual falls into one of three patterns: passive flight, frustration, or aggression.

Passive flight is practiced by the nonassertive type, who complies with a demand but inwardly rebels. For example, a young woman who resents the strong control of her supervisor may resist this dominance by consciously or unconsciously arriving at work every day just a few minutes late, thus causing constant irritation to the supervisor. *Frustration* can be described as the feeling of being torn between doing what one wants to do and doing what one should do—between, for example, going to a party and working overtime. *Aggression*—hostile action or behavior—may result when a manipulated person feels cornered or can no longer tolerate being abused. At this point, he or she may lose control and lash out in anger.

As a form of assertiveness training, Smith prescribes a *Bill of Assertive Rights* for his students. Each of the ten rights is presented and described here.

1. *You have the right to judge your own behavior, thoughts, and emotions, and to take the responsibility for their initiation and consequences upon yourself.* Whether you are choosing a career, initiating a change in your work routine, dealing with an unpleasant co-worker, or moving into your own apartment, you don't have to base your actions on what you think is expected of you or what other people tell you is best. Ultimately, the only person you have to answer to is yourself.

2. *You have the right to offer no reasons or excuses to justify your behavior.* You don't need to explain your actions to anyone. This, of course, does not apply to violent, hostile, or irrational behavior. But suppose a co-worker asks you to go out for cocktails after work. If you don't wish to go, simply reply no. It is not necessary to go into a dozen reasons why you don't want to go. In fact, it would be a subtle

form of manipulation should your co-worker insist on an explanation.

3. *You have the right to judge whether you are responsible for finding a solution to other people's problems.* Perhaps a co-worker is consistently behind on her work and is in danger of being fired. She asks you to help her out. If you do, you will find yourself behind on your own work. You have helped her in the past, but the situation seems to be ongoing. At this point, don't be intimidated. The problem is hers, not yours, and she will have to solve it.

4. *You have the right to change your mind.* Suppose you have accepted a job, but after reconsideration you realize that it would be the wrong one for you. If you want to change your mind, go ahead.

5. *You have the right to make mistakes and be responsible for them.* There is no need to feel guilty about making mistakes. Resolve to work harder and try to avoid making mistakes, but remember that an error-free human is an impossibility. For example, imagine you were told to arrange for a meeting of fourteen people for Thursday morning at 10:00. You sent memos, typed up an agenda, ordered coffee, but forgot to reserve a conference room. It's now 9:45, and all the conference rooms are taken. Admit your error, try to find an empty office, and promise yourself not to repeat the mistake.

6. *You have the right to say "I don't know."* People may try to manipulate you with such remarks as "What would hap-

A leader of an assertiveness-training seminar

pen if . . ." or "How would you feel if. . . ." Simply answer with an honest "I don't know." Whether the question has been asked by an angry customer looking for a missing shipment or by a demanding boss, "I don't know, but I'll find out" is a perfectly legitimate response.

7. *You have the right to be independent of the good will of others before coping with them.* People sometimes act out of fear of losing a friend. A friend who uses the friendship as a weapon isn't worth keeping. Smith's statement "You'll never be loved if you can't risk being disliked" is worth some thought. You may come home weary from a day at work, only to be greeted by a phone call from someone who wants to chat interminably about his or her problems. You have a right to say "I'm sorry, I just can't talk right now."

8. *You have the right to be illogical in making decisions.* Emotion is part of life and sometimes will overrule logic. This is not always wrong. Occasionally, you will want to do something because it is important to you. Maybe it is taking an art class during the evenings or buying a TV instead of a sofa for your new apartment. Others may never understand why it is important, but does that really matter?

9. *You have the right to say, "I don't understand."* Rules and regulations will sometimes dictate that people must behave in a ridiculous manner. If you find yourself complying with what seems like an infraction on your time and intelligence, question authorities about the ruling. Maybe

Hazel Hankin

One-on-one transactions in an assertiveness-training seminar.

To some people, a spotless office is not important.

your company has no cafeteria, yet forbids employees to eat at their desks, thus obliging them to buy lunches at coffee shops or restaurants. If someone asks "Why?" the rule may be revoked or revised to allow for a company eating area.

10. *You have the right to say "I don't care."* What is important to someone else may not be important to you. A co-worker may consider it imperative to keep the office in spotless condition. You may not place such emphasis on an immaculate office; therefore, it is not your responsibility to keep the surroundings sterile. You can say frankly "I don't care," and refuse to be manipulated into feeling guilty.[5]

Assertive Skills Manuel Smith teaches the use of such assertiveness skills as the broken record, fogging, negative assertion, and negative inquiry. The principle behind all of these is that you refuse to let other people coerce or manipulate you into doing what they wish, while at the same time refusing to allow yourself to lose control of your emotions.

The *broken record* is a tactic in which you state your position and repeat it as often as necessary. Look at this situation, in which a customer on a business trip checks into a hotel and finds no room available.

Customer: I have a reservation for tonight.
Hotel Clerk: I'm sorry. We have no record of your reservation, and we're filled up.

[5]Manuel J. Smith, *When I Say No, I Feel Guilty* (New York: Dial, 1975).

Customer:	But I have a confirmed reservation. I would like my room, please.
Hotel Clerk:	I'm sorry. I can't find a record of your reservation.
Customer:	I'm sorry too. I do have a reservation. May I see the manager?
Hotel Clerk:	The manager is out.
Customer:	In that case, if there is no one in charge to take care of my reservation, I'll just lie down here in the lobby on your couch.
Hotel Clerk:	I'll see what I can do.

"We have no record of your reservation."

Fogging and *negative assertion* are methods of dealing with criticism by offering no resistance to it, agreeing with it, and treating it calmly and perhaps even lightly. For example, Jim Black says to his colleague Joe Brown, "I see you've made your usual mistakes on the new graph." Joe answers, "I probably did. You know that I have a lot of trouble with graphs."

Instead of feeling intimidated, Joe admits the mistake but treats it lightly. If he had let Jim confuse and belittle him, the ridicule would probably have continued. Now, chances are good that Jim will find someone else to correct.

"I do have a reservation."

In *negative inquiry,* you question your critic. For instance, a co-worker may chide you for working later than the rest of the employees. Instead of trying to justify your actions, ask why it bothers her that you work overtime.[6]

The decision to act assertively means accepting both rights and responsibilities and refusing to feel guilty about saying no when you encounter manipulation.

Sexual Harassment on the Job

Particularly if you are a woman, you may encounter attempts at sexual harassment and victimization. Here, too, refuse to allow yourself to be manipulated. *Sexual harassment* has been described by the Alliance Against Sexual Coercion in the following paragraph:

> Sexual harassment can take the form of verbal abuse such as insults, suggestive comments and demands; leering and subtle forms of pressure for sexual activity; physical aggressiveness such as touching, pinching, and patting; and can end up as attempted rape and rape. . . .
> What we are talking about is unwanted sexual attention on the job. The fact that this attention is unwanted is what makes it harassment.[7]

[6]Based on Smith, *When I Say No.*

[7]Darrell Long Tillar, "Sexual Harassment in Employment: The Double Bind," *Equal Opportunity FORUM* (May 1979), pp. 4–12.

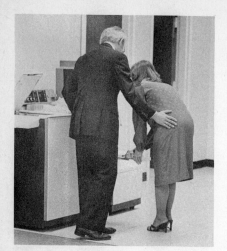
Sexual harassment can take the form of physical aggressiveness, such as touching or patting.

This encounter at the water cooler is an example of the sort of unwanted attention that constitutes sexual harassment.

In 1979, two federal cases were settled in favor of female employees who sued as the result of harassment. One case was settled out of court, after a five-year dispute, for $20,000 plus legal costs. At the time of the harassment, a young woman held a temporary position as executive secretary. She was told that if her evaluation was good after three months' trial, she could have the position permanently. At the end of the three months' trial period, her boss took her to lunch and informed her that in order to keep the position she must have relations with him. She resisted. She was fired shortly after the confrontation. She based her case on Title VII discrimination laws, and won.[8]

Title VII of the Civil Rights Act of 1964 does protect employees against such behavior; harassment is difficult to prove, however. As Darrell Long Tillar describes the situation in the article "Sexual Harassment in Employment: The Double Bind," the victim is in for problems whether he or she protests or not.

> If a woman takes a strong stand against the first evidence of harassment, she can face the humiliation of being told "not to flatter herself by imagining that she was being propositioned." If a woman tries not to overreact, and attempts to ignore the early warning signs or to put up with a minimum of harassment, she can find herself accused of "asking for it."[9]

It is not easy to resist attempts at sexual intimidation in an office situation: You need to have confidence in your worth as a person and in your abilities as a professional. On the other side of the coin, you also have a responsibility not to use your sexuality either as a tool or as a crutch. Certainly, sexuality is a part of the business world. It is expressed constantly in the clothes people wear, their conversation, and their attitudes. But even a casual flirtation requires mature judgment, and sexual liaisons within the office frequently result in a step out the door instead of up the ladder.

Self-Esteem and Sensitivity

The Bible verse "Love thy neighbor as thyself" is frequently misconstrued. In order to give to others, you must first have a high regard for yourself. People who lack self-esteem feel they have little to offer others. Personally effective people, on the other hand, have a sense of self-worth and want to contribute their talents to the world. As you move along in your career, it becomes increasingly more important to be sensitive to the needs and motives of others,

[8]Diane K. Shah and Susan Agrest, "A Steno Who Said No!" *Newsweek* (April 30, 1979), p. 72.

[9]Tillar, "Sexual Harassment."

and to be aware of your own motives and needs. Use this sensitivity and awareness as the basis for your daily business interrelationships and you will find that you perform more effectively as a person and as a professional.

KEY TERMS

Needs Hierarchy	passive flight	broken record
life positions	frustration	fogging
paternal style	aggression	negative assertion
maternal style	Bill of Assertive	negative inquiry
egalitarian style	Rights	sexual harassment
assertiveness training		

Your sexuality is expressed constantly in the clothes you wear. Don't make it a tool or a crutch.

TEST YOURSELF:
QUESTIONS FOR REVIEW AND DISCUSSION

1. Apply Maslow's Needs Hierarchy to *your* needs. List specific needs for each of the levels. Have you ever experienced self-actualization?
2. What life position are you in? Using a classroom or office setting, describe a person who possesses the characteristics of each position.
3. Identify the three company family styles and describe at least three familial relationships that can exist.
4. Describe some work situation in which you found yourself victimized. How did you handle the situation?
5. Have you ever fallen into any of the nonassertive patterns? If so, describe the situation.
6. Describe the last time you practiced assertiveness.
7. Explain some assertiveness techniques for dealing with attempts by others to manipulate you.

APPLICATION EXERCISES

1. Evaluate the following problem, then, based on the personal effectiveness training in chapter 8, describe your solution.

    You have been working very hard for two years on a research project for your company. You are near successful completion of the project and are about to present the findings and facts at a company board meeting. A young subordinate who has worked on the project for the last six months has made a minor discovery. He is excited about his findings, and he is eager to advance in the company.

    Through a memo to department heads and top executives, he announces his findings along with some of yours, which he passes off as his own. The memo makes him look like a "hero."

    Which of the following actions would you take?

    a. talk to him
    b. talk to your supervisor
    c. both
    d. ignore it
    e. other alternatives

    What, specifically, would you say if you chose to speak to your supervisor and/or him?

2. Identify each level of Maslow's Hierarchy of Needs, then list each level you have achieved and give an example of how that need was fulfilled.

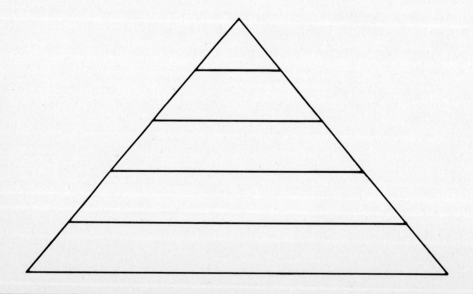

Suggested Readings

Berne, Eric. *Games People Play.* New York: Ballantine, 1978.

Bolles, Richard N. *The Three Boxes of Life.* Berkeley, Calif.: Ten Speed Press, 1980.

Dyer, Wayne W. *Pulling Your Own Strings.* New York: Funk & Wagnalls, 1981.

Harris, Thomas A. *I'm OK—You're OK.* New York: Avon, 1973.

Korda, Michael, *Power.* New York: Ballantine, 1976.

Maltz, Maxwell. *Psycho-Cybernetics.* New York: Pocket Books, 1969.

Maslow, Abraham H. *Motivation and Personality.* New York: Harper & Row, 1970.

Smith, Manuel J. *When I Say No, I Feel Guilty.* New York: Dial, 1975.

9

GROUP DYNAMICS

COMPREHENSIVE GOAL
To prepare you for effective group participation

SPECIFIC OBJECTIVES
After reading this chapter, you will be able to:

- identify group goals and group norms, and characterize group members

- understand the functions of an agenda

- define the terms "brainstorming" and "lateral thinking"

- list methods of group decision making

- define group intimidation, group cohesiveness, and "groupthink"

- diagram a communication pattern

- recognize power bases

- give advantages of competition and conflict

- explain the characteristics of a good meeting

Because so much of business operates on a group level, your professional success will depend to a great extent on how well you function as part of the group.

Speaking out in group situations will help you to advance in your career. If you consistently remain silent, your chances for promotion will be very slim. It is not always appearance, grades, or IQ that will impress your bosses and lead to the promotion you want; the verbal fluency you display is also important.

Functioning Within the Group

Responsible members of a group—large or small—will be alert to its intricate dynamics. They will recognize group goals, group norms, member types, power bases, and communication patterns.

GROUP GOALS

Each group has a common denominator or central purpose that moves it into action. This is the *group goal*. The goals of business groups are generally dictated by the head of the company. The goal of one business may be to save money, while another's is to increase production or to be the forerunner in the market. A wise member knows what the group goal is and acts accordingly. If the group goal is to save money, proposing a renovation of the company cafeteria could be a real blunder.

Group goals must be satisfying to the individual members. For example, progressive members may feel stifled within a conservative group. They may try to change the group's goal, or they may find it easier to quit the group. Agreement on the goals of a group makes for productive and smooth-running meetings.

Much business activity takes place on the group level.

GROUP ORGANIZATION

Jobs within a company are so interrelated that an employee cannot exist in an isolated environment, but must learn to interact with co-workers. A business organization is a team of people working together for a common goal. Figure 9–1 illustrates the interrelatedness of jobs within an organization.

Structures vary from one organization to another. A company can be organized according to the function of the work performed, the location where work takes place, or the product produced. Or it can combine approaches. Additionally, not every staff position in an organization requires the same amount of interaction with co-workers. Some employees will be required to attend every significant meeting, whereas others may never attend a single meeting. Nevertheless, every employee interacts with another co-worker to some degree.

GROUP NORMS

During your first few months in a new organization, you may feel reluctant to enter into discussions. This is a natural and wise reaction. Even freshmen legislators spend much of their first year in government getting acquainted with procedures and observing group norms.

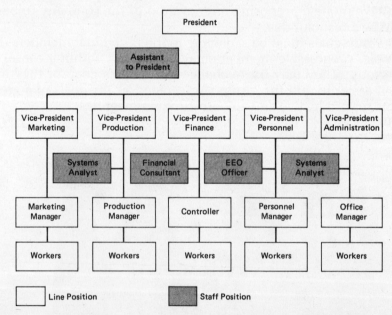

Figure 9–1
Interrelatedness of Jobs in an Organization

Source: Reproduced by permission of Harcourt Brace Jovanovich, Inc., from *Office Management,* by Burton S. Kaliski (p. 26), copyright © 1983.

Group norms determine whether your behavior is formal or casual.

Group norms define acceptable modes of conduct within a group; they are the unwritten rules that are seldom discussed but strongly enforced. For example, body language differs from group to group. In one group you can feel quite comfortable leaning back in your chair and putting your feet up on the table. In another, you are expected to sit up straight. The manner of speaking will vary from formality—addressing the leader as "Mr. (or Madame) Chairperson"—to casualness—"Hey, I've got a great idea." Appearance and clothing are also governed by group norms. A board of directors' meeting, for example, may require special attention to your wardrobe. In a formal atmosphere like this, a casual sports outfit does not convey the authority of a tailored suit. To sum up, your behavior, speech, and dress should be appropriate to your group's norms if you are to interact effectively with its other members.

GROUP MEMBERS

If you look around a group, you will be able to identify various personality types. Each group has its own blend, but certain types seem evident in most groups.

The Glory Seekers—These people speak frequently but have little to offer. They want to be heard and noticed and will dominate the floor if allowed. They make it difficult for others to participate.

The Silent Ones—Either as a result of shyness or apathy, these

The whisperers

individuals never contribute a thought. Unfortunately, silence is often interpreted as stupidity.

The Complainers—They have little good to say about anything, but frequently criticize people, projects, and material.

The Fanatics—These people take issues to extremes and can magnify an insignificant circumstance into a full-blown crisis.

The Thinkers—They seldom speak, but when they do their ideas are usually worthwhile.

The Creative Members—They look for and suggest new solutions for dead-end problems. They never take "no" for an answer.

The Workers—They volunteer for many duties and seem to be in most of the group activities. Their excess of energy may seem foolish to an outsider, but these industrious ones usually get the promotions.

The Supportive Members—Every group needs at least one member who adds to its cohesiveness. These people usually agree and say, "That's a good idea" or "I like your suggestion." Supportive members seldom make original contributions; nevertheless, they are an asset to any group.

The Latecomers—They disrupt the meeting by arriving ten or fifteen minutes late, managing to make their entrances fanfares of distracting noises.

The Early Leavers—The leavers are as disruptive as the latecomers. An early exit suggests to the rest of the group that the major issues of the meeting have been covered and that the remainder of the meeting is of no importance.

The Whisperers—These rude people irritate both the leader and the group members.

You can add other personalities to the list, or you may discover that some members of your group are composites of several characteristics.

Effective Group Members   The dominant personalities in the group are easy to identify, but the quietly effective members do not always stand out in a crowd. It will take several meetings before you can pinpoint them. Following are some of the traits of an effective group member.

Active Participation—Good group members contribute their expertise and background not by dominating the discussion but by constructively adding to it.

Active Listening—As you learned in chapter 7, active listeners do not daydream; they pay attention, evaluate, and frequently jot down key ideas. A member of the group who tunes out the speaker for even a moment finds it difficult to reenter the discussion for fear of expressing an idea that may have been covered during the mental retreat.

Objectivity—Confident members will remain objective even when someone attacks their ideas. When you submit an idea, it becomes the group's property. Consequently, an attack on your idea should not be considered an attack on you personally. If the group works collectively and objectively, a better idea may emerge from the discussion. Secure people realize

An active listener

this and will not feel upset when their suggestions are vetoed.

Sometimes a crisis will cause tension and pressure in a business meeting. This circumstance calls for objectivity, not outbursts of emotion. Fist-banging, crying, shouting, and swearing only cause the offending member to lose the respect of the others. Such antics get attention, but it is not favorable attention.

Relevance—Every idea a member contributes should relate to the central purpose of the meeting. An agenda (discussed in the following section) can help prevent the meeting from going off on a tangent.

Preparation—Good participants prepare themselves before walking into a meeting. This means studying the agenda, giving the topics some thought, and perhaps even researching the subjects under consideration and taking the applicable data to the meeting.

THE AGENDA

The *agenda* (list of topics to be discussed) should be published a few days in advance of the meeting. A typical agenda might look like the following:

```
                Executive Board Meeting

                  January 4, 1985

                        Agenda

    Proposal for Branch Office

    Open Discussion on New Work Rules

    Progress Report on June Open-House Ceremonies

    Report from Finance Committee on Interest Rates
```

Agendas are important for three reasons. First, they give the members an opportunity to prepare for the meeting. Second, they give direction to the meeting by indicating what and how much is to be covered, thus preventing digressions onto unimportant topics. Third, a published agenda eliminates *hidden agendas*—personal subjects that a member may want to discuss for selfish reasons.

When a group of people come together to solve a problem, the agenda form outlined in table 9–1 is particularly helpful. Each step in this agenda is important; if one or more are overlooked, an unsatisfactory solution may result.

BRAINSTORMING

As a student, you have been taught to think logically in a pattern of *vertical thinking*—reasoning from step to step in a straightforward progression of thought. Usually such reasoning is the best method for problem solving, but sometimes it can lead to dead-end or traditional solutions. *Lateral thinking* moves out from and around a problem and applies freely associated ideas to it. When lateral thinking is used in a group situation, it is usually called *brainstorming*.

To encourage the application of lateral thinking to corporation problems, Savo Bojicic developed the Think Tank™. A round ball with a clear plastic window on one side, the Think Tank™ contains

Table 9–1

PROBLEM-SOLVING AGENDA

I.   PREPARATION (The group clarifies the goal of the group and establishes atmosphere and format.)
     What is the specific group goal?
     What information and/or research will be necessary to reach the goal?
     What important question(s) must be answered in order to accomplish the group goal?
     Are there any specific barriers we may face in problem solving?
     —strong individual member attitudes toward problem?
     —an important point of view not being represented in the group?
     What procedures for participation will best lead to our goal?
     —time, seating, place
     —leadership; shared, designated, or leader-in-reserve

II. DESCRIPTION (The group determines the current status of the problem.)
     What terms within the problem question need to be defined and/or clarified?
     What are the facts related to the problem?
     What are the points of view of those involved in the problem?
     What previous action has been taken to attempt to solve the problem?
     What is unsatisfactory about the present situation?
     How serious is the problem?

III. ANALYSIS (The group understands why the problem exists.)
     Why did the problem develop?
     What specific factors have kept the problem from being solved already?
     What are the most basic causes of the problem?

IV. PROPOSALS (The group suggests many possible solutions.)
     What are all possible solutions (brainstorm without evaluation)?
     or
     What would be the ideal solution from the point of view of each person (or group) affected (useful in arbitration or when several definite views are in conflict)?

V.   SELECTION OF "BEST" SOLUTION (The group determines standards by which solutions can be judged and selects the "best" solution.)
     What specific criteria must the solution meet?
     —What are all the necessary standards which the solution to the problem must meet?
     What solution is "best" ("best" should answer all four below)?
     —Which solution solves the problem?
     —Which solution eliminates the basic causes?
     —Which solution meets the criteria?
     —Which solution does not create other problems?

VI. IMPLEMENTATION (The group works out approaches to implement the chosen solution.)
     How can the chosen solution be put into action?
     —Who must be involved? Cost of implementing? When is best time?
     —What is the best general approach to implementing the solution?
     What obstacles may come up to hinder the implementation?
     What approaches are most likely to overcome the stated obstacles?

Source: Linda R. Heun and Richard E. Heun, *Developing Skills for Human Interaction* (Columbus, Ohio: Merrill, 1978).

Every idea contributed should be relevant to the meeting's purpose.

A Think Tank

13,000 words, each printed on a plastic tab. By means of a knob on each side of the ball, the words are mixed and moved at random toward the clear window. You apply the first six words that appear in the window to the problem at hand.[1]

In business-meeting applications, brainstorming—lateral thinking in groups—is best done in groups of five or six people. Before the process begins, a time limit should be set and a recorder should be appointed to write down *all* the ideas. The participants should be reassured that any idea is welcome. Even the most absurd suggestion should not draw criticism: The essence of brainstorming is to consider all ideas regardless of logic. Many times out of the ridiculous comes the profound. Even a seemingly inane suggestion may spark insight for another member of the group.

DECISION MAKING

In general, a successful meeting is one in which a resolution is reached. Resolutions can be arrived at via many different methods, some good, some bad. The best resolutions are called win/win resolutions: All sides are relatively happy. In contrast, win/lose resolutions leave some members unhappy and therefore less likely to work wholeheartedly on the proposed plan.

[1]Edward de Bono, *Think Tank*™ (Toronto: Think Tank Corp./Imperial Press, 1973).

Group resolutions are typically arrived at by majority rule, compromise, dominant person, outside pressure, minority rule, and consensus.

Majority rule bases decision making on the vote. If 51 percent or more of the voters cast their votes in favor of a motion, it passes. Although the majority rule system is democratic, it is not always the best way to arrive at a solution. It frequently leaves the losers uncommitted to the plan.

Compromise is the give-and-take process that often goes on in legislatures before an actual vote is taken. One legislator will give up part of a proposal in order to secure votes from other legislators. Conceding one issue in exchange for a favor from another member is called "logrolling" in legislative circles. This is considered a win/win solution, because the members of the group work together until they reach a satisfactory conclusion. However, compromise sometimes means sacrificing good points for the sake of reaching a conclusion.

The *dominant person* method is perhaps the worst way to arrive at a conclusion. Many a group has reached a decision because its members let one person steamroll an idea through the discussion. One strong-willed individual can intimidate others to the point where power rather than discussion determines the decision.

Sometimes decisions are made because *outside pressure* is brought to bear on the group. A labor union, for example, might apply pressure to a management group by threatening a strike. In government, committee decisions are often influenced by lobbyists for outside groups, which apply pressure by threatening to withhold campaign support from the legislators involved if they do not

The majority of the participants favor the motion; therefore, it passes.

vote according to the wishes of the outside group whose interests are affected.

Minority rule sounds paradoxical, but it is common in business. A small board of executives often makes decisions that affect many people within an organization. While not a win/win solution, minority rule is sometimes the only practical form of decision making in a large corporation.

Consensus is considered the best method for arriving at a group decision. Consensus means that all members agree on all parts of the solution. Everyone feels involved and committed to making the decision work. Each segment of the problem is examined and discussed thoroughly; until all are satisfied with the first step of the problem-solving process, decision making does not proceed.

Although the best decision making results from consensus, it is a time-consuming system. Practicality will dictate what form of decision making your company chooses, but a wise leader will attempt to involve as many employees as feasible.

GROUP INTIMIDATION

The best decisions are reached when all members of a group participate, but sometimes the size of the group makes this impossible. In fact, it has been found that a five-member group can be more productive than larger groups.[2]

Maybe it is the fear of group intimidation that quiets all but the

[2]P. E. Slater, "Contrasting Correlates of Group Size," *Sociometry* 21 (1958): 129–39.

Sometimes a great deal of compromise has to take place in a meeting before a consensus can be reached.

A five-member group can be more productive than larger groups.

most outspoken members in a large group. *Group intimidation* is a situation in which the group verbally or nonverbally attacks one member. The person may have innocently volunteered an idea that offends the rest of the group, and they retaliate by turning on both the idea and its contributor.[3]

Sometime in your life, you have probably experienced group intimidation or witnessed such attacks. The embarrassment is enough to instill fear in anyone. However, with good leaders and cohesiveness, group intimidation can be prevented.

Communication Patterns

If you are a new member of a group, observe the communication flow to learn about its members and general mood. Each group will have its own distinctive communication pattern. At the next meeting you attend, see if you can chart its pattern using diagrams similar to the ones illustrated in figures 9–2, 9–3, and 9–4.

The ideal communication flow during a meeting is to and from all members, as in figure 9–2.

But the ideal seldom occurs, and the pattern may look more like figure 9–3.

The flow of ordinary daily business communication follows a consistent *communication pattern.* Typically, organizations use either the all-channel, the wheel, the Y, or the chain. (See figure 9–4 for an illustration of these four patterns.)

[3]Michael Doyle and David Straus, *How to Make Meetings Work* (New York: Wyden, 1976), p. 27.

The *all-channel* pattern is a casual, informal method of exchanging information. It seems to have no specific direction, but works well in small organizations with few employees. It also suits creative people who work together on common projects. In larger, more formal firms it is not a practical communication pattern.

In the *wheel* pattern, a central person controls the communication flow. An office manager with various subordinates might be the hub of the wheel structure. The dependence created by this pattern can be demoralizing for the subordinates.

You will find the Y pattern in firms in which there are two executive officers on an equal basis. The person situated at the juncture of the arms of the Y holds a powerful position, for he or she controls communication flowing both ways from the higher and lower levels of the business and has the power to decide what information is going to be passed along.

In the *chain* or *serial* pattern, communication flows upward or downward through certain channels. One drawback to this pattern is the chance that the message may become distorted as it flows.

As a newcomer to an organization, you would be wise to determine the pattern of communication. Then, for the sake of propriety, follow the correct channels. If you should decide on a specific occasion to bypass your immediate supervisor and talk to a department head, don't do it without serious thought. This decision should never be a casual choice, for it will strongly affect your supervisor's attitude toward you, for better or worse.

By the same token, if you neglect to pass on needed information to a co-worker or a subordinate, or if you communicate with them

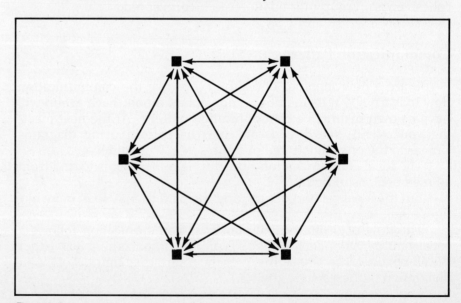

Figure 9–2
The Ideal Group Communication Pattern

via the wrong channels, you may cause offense and impair the functioning of the office.

POWER

The struggle for power within a group is constant and subtle. By watching the communication flow during a meeting, you can often decide who has power and who is trying to attain power. The best way to determine power bases is observation. Watch the members in a meeting and ask yourself these questions:

1. How does the leader address various members—warmly, hostilely, or impersonally?
2. Whom does the leader most frequently address?
3. How do the members address the leader?
4. Toward whom do the members face when speaking?
5. Does the nonverbal communication give any clues?

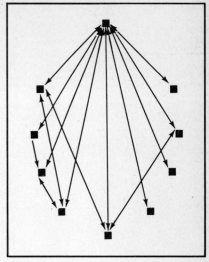

Figure 9–3
A Typical Group Communication Pattern

Power bases in a group are derived from qualities that have value to the group members. Common ones will be mentioned here. Among these are money, external contacts, seniority, expertise, recognition, and physical presence.

Monetary power tends to have a destructive effect on the dynamics of the group. Certainly, if a member of the group controls the budget for the project under discussion, he or she operates from a very strong position. The members of the group are going to think twice before disagreeing.

External contacts can give a group member power. Group mem-

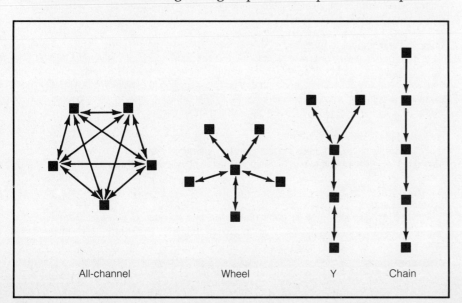

All-channel   Wheel   Y   Chain

Figure 9–4
Four Common Business Communication Patterns

bers with the right political or social contacts generally find them invaluable. A relative of the boss is in an enviable position during a company meeting.

Simply by virtue of being with the organization longer than anyone else, a member has *seniority* to use as a power base. The special knowledge seniority gives about the company's past policies, successes, failures, and politics can be an asset.

Expertise or public *recognition* can put a group member in a power position. A person who has specialized knowledge will be

---

In business, as in everyday life, it is easy for a message to become distorted as it moves along a channel. What can happen, if the participants in the passage of a message through a communication pattern are not alert, is illustrated in the following apocryphal story.

HOW'S THAT AGAIN?

A colonel issued the following directive to his executive officer:

"Tomorrow night at 2000 hours Halley's Comet will be visible in this area, an event occurring only once every 75 years. Have the men fall out in the battalion area in fatigues, and I will explain this rare phenomenon to them. In case of rain, we will not be able to see anything, so assemble the men in the theater and I will show films on it."

Executive officer to company commander:

"By order of the colonel who was in fatigues at 2000 hours tomorrow evening, the phenomenal Halley's Comet will appear above the battalion area. If it rains, fall the men out in fatigues and march to the theater where the rare phenomenon will take place, something which only occurs once every 75 years."

Company commander to lieutenant:

"By order of the colonel who was in fatigues at 2000 hours tomorrow evening the phenomenal Halley's Comet will appear in the theater. There is absolutely no explanation for this unusual event, and it is for that reason that the colonel is going to explain it to you in full. In case of rain in the battalion area, the colonel will give another order, something which occurs every 75 years."

Lieutenant to sergeant:

"Tomorrow at 2000 hours, the colonel will appear in the theater with Halley's Comet, something which happens every 75 years. If it rains, he will order the comet into the battalion area."

Sergeant to squad:

"When it rains tomorrow at 2000 hours, the phenomenal 75-year-old General Halley, accompanied by the colonel, will drive his Comet through the battalion area theater in his fatigues."

Source: "Permutation Personified," *Boles Letter* (E. D. Boles & Associates, 1962), quoted in Anita Taylor et al., *Communicating* (Englewood Cliffs, N.J.: Prentice-Hall), 1977), p. 246.

One way to determine power bases in a meeting is to observe toward whom the members face when speaking.

regarded with respect by others, as will one whose picture is often in the paper.

Even *physical presence* can constitute a power base. Tall men are more frequently promoted to executive positions than short men, one study has found. Posture and body control, as mentioned in chapter 4, also have an impact on others.

If you should happen to acquire, one way or another, one of these power bases, don't use it selfishly. The abuse of power can lead to failure instead of success.

COHESIVENESS

Cohesiveness is the natural relationship that develops when people work closely together, especially if the group is pitted against an adversary. When a crisis, such as a financial loss, threatens to dissolve the group, a strong common bond naturally forms. Cohesiveness, to a certain degree, is useful. All people need to feel warmth and affection from others. However, too much closeness may lead the group to poor decision making. If strong emotional ties develop, objectivity can be lost because the fear of hurting another member's feelings sometimes prevents a clear presentation of an issue.

When Irving Janis studied the subject of group cohesion, he found that the members of a strong, cohesive group may get along too well with each other. He named this condition *"groupthink."*

An expert in a field is in an excellent power position.

After a study of various governing bodies and international associations, Janis found eight symptoms of groupthink.[4] They are:

1. illusion of invulnerability
2. rationalization
3. morality
4. stereotype
5. direct pressure
6. group consensus
7. illusion of unanimity
8. mindguarding

To give a better understanding of groupthink, examine the dialogue in a meeting that takes place in a toy manufacturer's conference room. The members of the board are trying to reach a decision on adopting a new toy. The toy has not been fully tested, but the deadline for the Christmas toy market is only two weeks away and a decision has to be reached quickly.

Mr. Thatcher:	We always produce quality toys. We have never sold a poorly constructed toy. Our new Squawky will be another quality toy. (rationalization)
Ms. Wiacek:	We are a good company. We treat our clients fairly and squarely. We wouldn't sell a toy that would be harmful to children. (morality)
Ms. Cimino:	Perhaps we should run further tests?

[4]David W. Johnson and Frank P. Johnson, *Joining Together: Group Theory and Group Skills* (Englewood Cliffs, N.J.: Prentice-Hall, 1975), pp. 271–72.

Ms. Wiacek:	We have run tests and the safety results look good.
Ms. Cimino:	Who says the results are good? You or the safety inspector? We should get the inspector's report.
Ms. Wiacek:	I personally spoke with him, and he assures me the new Squawky is as safe as any other toy on the market. (mindguarding)
Mr. Dougherty:	We must make this decision soon. The Christmas deadline is two weeks away. (direct pressure)
Mr. Ludlow:	Our competitors are no threat. Company A is so conservative it would never come up with an idea like this one. The other company is run by a bunch of lame-brain women. (stereotype)
Mr. Dougherty:	We are a successful organization. We have survived other crises; we can face anything and succeed. (illusion of invulnerability)
Ms. Benjamin:	(To herself.) I wonder about the safety of such a toy. I really think it is risky to sell a toy without complete testing, but the rest of the group seems to be in favor of adopting this proposal. (illusion of unanimity)
Mr. Thatcher:	It appears that we are all in agreement here. Let's take a vote. (group consensus)

These symptoms of groupthink could lead the company to financial disaster if the product proves unsafe.

The desire to conform can hamper group effectiveness. Solomon Asch tested college classes and military groups to determine how strong group influence could be in the decision-making process. By using four white cards with various lengths of lines, he devised a simple test. He first presented to the group a card with a ten-inch black line. Then he presented three cards with lines of

Drawing by Lloyd Birmingham

Group consensus

three inches, ten inches, and twelve inches, respectively. He asked the group to match the first card with the one that matched it. This simple test had one controlling factor. Part of the group had been secretly instructed to pick the wrong card. When the choice of cards was presented, these individuals were able to influence many of the others to pick the wrong card. Asch then used this test on engineers, scientists, and architects, with the same results: People have a tendency to conform to group control.[5]

A certain amount of cohesiveness is good, but when it damages the effectiveness of the decision-making process, members need to reevaluate their methods.

COMPETITION AND CONFLICT

Rather than conformity, a healthy group should be characterized by competition and conflict. All sides of an issue in question are more likely to be examined if some dissension is present. The following dialogue in a business meeting illustrates beneficial conflict:

Chairman:	Is the new advertising campaign working well?
Various members:	(Their heads nod yes; all seem to be in agreement.)
Mr. Burke:	I hate to disagree, but I don't feel the campaign has the right appeal to our market.
Chairman:	What do you mean?
Ms. Koenig:	I think it is working well.
Ms. Johnson:	Maybe a year ago I would have thought it

[5]Solomon Asch, *Social Psychology* (Englewood Cliffs, N.J.: Prentice-Hall, 1952), pp. 450–51. Quoted in Kim Griffin and Bobby R. Patton, *Fundamentals of Inter-Personal Communication* (New York: Harper & Row, 1976), p. 141.

Drawing by Lloyd Birmingham

Sometimes it is important to resist pressure to conform to the group.

Deciding on the right advertising campaign can produce beneficial conflict.

	the wrong approach, but now that we have all the bugs out of it, I like the campaign.
Mr. Burke:	I can't put my finger on it, but I feel we are not saying what should be said.
Mr. Holland:	What do you mean?
Mr. Burke:	We are attracting only a certain segment of the market, even though this product has universal appeal. We need a campaign that attracts young and old, male and female. This may be an attractive campaign—but if it doesn't reach the total market, what good is it?
Ms. Koenig:	Maybe we need to analyze this further.
Mr. Holland:	But how are we going to decide what approach should be taken?
Ms. Johnson:	You mean after all the time and money put into this campaign, you now think we should change it all?
Ms. Koenig:	If it means more sales, yes.

The problem was not solved during this meeting, but a satisfactory campaign did emerge after several more meetings. Better advertising was produced as a result of the dissenting member's refusal to conform.

It is not easy playing the devil's advocate, perhaps because of the fear of group intimidation. Being a dissenter takes a great deal of self-confidence and a thorough understanding of the problem.

What makes a good meeting?

However, a responsible group member has the duty of occasionally saying, "Wait a minute; let's look at this from another angle."

Too much competition and conflict, on the other hand, will only produce tension. When a meeting reaches this point, it is time to break for a few minutes or even days until a better perspective can be achieved.

A GOOD MEETING

Too much cohesiveness or too much conflict can ruin a meeting. What, then, constitutes a good meeting?

Michael Doyle and David Straus give criteria for judging the success of a meeting in their book *How to Make Meetings Work*.

First, what happened? Did you get the results you wanted? What did you get done, what problems did you solve, what decisions did the group make? Were the solutions or decisions innovative? Obviously, you must judge the real importance of your meetings by the results you get from them. The results directly affect the functioning of your organization or group and its ability to achieve its objectives, whether the objectives are profits, delivery of services, survival, or member satisfaction.

Second, you will find it worthwhile to look at how the meeting went—the process of the meeting. How did problems get solved? How did decisions get made? How well did the group work together? How did people feel about the meeting? Did everyone get a chance to participate, or did one person dominate the meeting?

Was the meeting a pleasure to attend? Did you have fun? Were you stimulated or challenged? Did people draw and build on each other's ideas, or was the meeting a battle of egos?[6]

The big question is, "Was the meeting worthwhile?" Suppose Jane Smith misses a meeting and then asks Tom Jones what happened. If Tom shrugs his shoulders and says, "Nothing," it is some indication of the value of the meeting.

INTERACTION METHOD

Doyle and Straus, after years of business consulting, have developed a procedure for a good meeting. It is called the *interaction method*. An interesting aspect of the approach is the rule that prohibits the boss or manager of the group from acting as head of the meeting. All participants are on an equal basis, but a facilitator and a recorder are needed. The group sits in a semicircle facing the facilitator, recorder, and the recorder's papers (as shown in the illustration on this page). The whole group is expected to participate and work toward a consensus.

The *facilitator* is a neutral processor whose main function is to conduct a smooth meeting, not to interject personal thoughts and opinions. The facilitator calls on people, makes certain that one person does not dominate the floor, encourages constructive competition, and maintains a good atmosphere.

The *recorder* writes down every idea expressed during the meeting, on something that is visible to the whole group. The recorder

[6]Doyle and Straus, *Make Meetings Work,* p. 8.

The interaction method

does not editorialize, but tries to record accurately and act as the group's memory.[7]

The interaction method is very simple. What is difficult for the participants is adjusting to this different method of conducting a meeting.

Shakespeare's "All the world's a stage, and all the men and women merely players" can be applied to the intricacies of any meeting. Each meeting has a different scenario, and the roles change and adapt to circumstances and personalities. As a participant, you should constantly be aware of the significance of the roles and the purpose of the meeting.

[7]Doyle and Straus, *Make Meetings Work*, p. 83.

KEY TERMS

group goal	dominant person	Y
group norms	outside pressure	chain
agenda	minority rule	power bases
hidden agendas	consensus	cohesiveness
vertical thinking	group intimidation	groupthink
lateral thinking	communication	interaction method
brainstorming	pattern	facilitator
majority rule	all-channel	recorder
compromise	wheel	

TEST YOURSELF: QUESTIONS FOR REVIEW AND DISCUSSION

1. What type of group member are you? Do you make a point of participating at most meetings? Why? Why not? Can you add more personalities to the list of group members described in the text? Which types are effective members? Which types are detrimental to meetings?
2. What is lateral thinking? What are its advantages?
3. Was an agenda issued for your last meeting? If so, did the group follow the agenda? Did any members have a hidden agenda?
4. Was the goal of the meeting accomplished? If so, was it by consensus, majority rule, compromise, minority rule, dominant person, or outside pressure?
5. Were competition and conflict evident in your last meeting? Were they productive or unproductive? Did they lead to a form of group intimidation?
6. What is groupthink? Have you ever witnessed groupthink in a meeting? If so, describe the issue and how groupthink occurred.

APPLICATION EXERCISE

Observe a small meeting and chart the communication pattern. Put the names of each member in the circles provided. Each time a member speaks, draw a line from that member to whomever is addressed. What kind of communication pattern emerged?

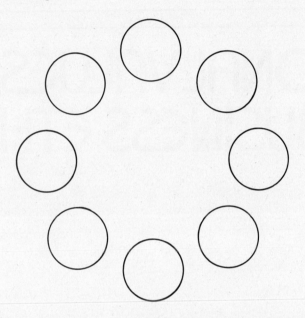

Suggested Readings

Doyle, Michael, and David Straus. *How to Make Meetings Work.* New York: Wyden, 1976.

Hall, C. Margaret. *Individual & Society: Basic Concepts.* Boonsboro, Md.: Antietam Press, 1982.

Hare, Paul A. *Social Interaction & Creativity in Small Groups.* Beverly Hills, Calif.: Sage, 1981.

Heiss, Jerold. *The Social Psychology of Interaction.* Englewood Cliffs, N.J.: Prentice-Hall, 1981.

Johnson, David W., and Frank P. Johnson. *Joining Together: Group Theory and Group Skills.* Englewood Cliffs, N.J.: Prentice-Hall, 1975.

Layder, Derek. *Structure, Interaction & Social Theory.* Boston, Mass.: Routledge & Kegan Paul, Ltd., 1981.

Schutz, William. *Here Comes Everybody: Bodymind & Encounter Culture.* New York: Irvington, 1982.

Taylor, Anita; Teresa Rosegrant; Arthur Meyer; and B. Thomas Samples. *Communicating.* Englewood Cliffs, N.J.: Prentice-Hall, 1977.

Verderber, Rudolph F. *Working Together: Fundamentals of Group Decision Making.* West Publishing, 1982.

10

PERSONAL VALUES AND BUSINESS ETHICS

COMPREHENSIVE GOAL
To provide guidelines to help you to assess personal values and to apply them to professional situations.

SPECIFIC OBJECTIVES
After reading this chapter, you will be able to:

- understand what is meant by *value* and *code of ethics*

- define personal values by means of the valuing process

- make use of the planning board

- identify areas of concern in the process of assessing business and personal problems

Its title may give the impression that this chapter will dictate *the* correct business behavior. But no person or textbook can give you a single correct answer to every situation. The *values*—things you consider important and desirable—that each of you has developed on the basis of your background, religious instruction, parental training, and intelligence will determine your personal *code of ethics*—the rules by which you conduct yourself. What this chapter will attempt to do is help you establish guidelines for clarifying your values and applying them to business situations.

What are your values? Unless you have given it a great deal of thought, this is a difficult question to answer; but it is an important one. Research has found that persons who have defined their values are more productive and purposeful, have better relationships, possess more zest for life, and develop stronger critical thinking skills.[1] Moreover, having a clearly thought-out value system will lessen your anxiety when you have difficult decisions to make.

Defining your values, making judgments about ethical professional behavior, and exercising your principles on business situations are the subjects of this chapter. Some of the material presented here may be disturbing, as will be some of the business practices you will encounter in the "real" world, but practicing these hypothetical situations in the classroom can, in a small way, prepare you for real confrontations.

Defining your Values

Many of your values have been implanted in you from childhood; they are the result of home environment, schoolbook lessons, peer

[1]Sheralyn Goldbecker, *Values Teaching* (Washington, D.C.: National Education Association, 1976), p. 11.

Your values are shaped by your home environment.

Television shapes modern values.

group influences, clergymen's sermons, and, of course, the media. But it is important from time to time to question them, to make sure that they are also based on firm conviction. Otherwise you may find yourself unsure of how to make the ethical decisions that will frequently be required of you during your professional career.

One method of examining your values has been developed by Louis Raths, Harmin Merrill, and Sidney Simon. The *valuing process*, according to Raths, is composed of the following seven subprocesses.[2]

PRIZING ONE'S BELIEFS AND BEHAVIORS
1. Prizing and cherishing
2. Publicly affirming, when appropriate

CHOOSING ONE'S BELIEFS AND BEHAVIORS
3. Choosing from alternatives
4. Choosing after consideration of consequences
5. Choosing freely

ACTING ON ONE'S BELIEFS
6. Acting
7. Acting with a pattern, consistency, and repetition

A practical tool for examining your values is the *values grid* (table 10–1) devised by Simon, Howe, and Kirschenbaum.[3]

[2]Cited in Louis Edward Raths et al., *Values and Teaching: Working With Values in the Classroom* (Columbus, Ohio: Merrill, 1966), p. 19.

[3]Sidney B. Simon et al., *Values Clarification: A Handbook of Practical Strategies for Teachers and Students* (New York: Hart, 1978), p. 35.

Schools and teachers implant values in children.

Using the grid, you can examine topics that range from world events to personal problems. Take a position on a particular topic; then apply the seven subprocesses to it, as follows:

1. Are you proud of (do you prize or cherish) your position?
2. Have you publicly affirmed your position?
3. Have you chosen your position from among alternatives?
4. Have you chosen your position after thoughtful consideration of the pros, cons, and consequences?
5. Have you chosen your position freely?
6. Have you acted on or done anything about your beliefs?
7. Have you acted with repetition, pattern, or consistency on this issue?

When you answer yes to a question, place a check mark in the corresponding numbered column on the grid. Before you can claim your stand on the issue as a personal value, you must have answered yes to at least six of the seven questions. For example, pretend you want to take a stand on nuclear energy. Perhaps there is a proposal to build a nuclear energy plant near your home. You take a stand opposing the plant. Now apply each of the questions to this position. If you can answer yes to six of the questions, you have a personal value.

The following topics are thought provokers that you might want to test against the values grid. Formulate an opinion on any of the general topics, and then ask the seven questions of your posi-

Acting on a belief

Table 10–1

VALUES GRID

	Issue	1	2	3	4	5	6	7
1								
2								
3								
4								
5								
Etc.								

Source: Reprinted by permission of A & W Publishers, Inc., from *Values Clarification: A Handbook of Practical Strategies for Teachers and Students, New Revised Edition*, by Sidney Simon, Leland Howe, and Howard Kirschenbaum, copyright © 1972, 1978 by Hart Publishing Company, Inc.

In some cities, public transportation is an important issue.

tion. If you can truthfully answer yes to six of the questions, you know the position is a personal value.

ecology	welfare
minority rights	foreign aid
nuclear energy	sex education in schools
solar energy	large families
public transportation	extramarital sex
Equal Rights Amendment	divorce
freedom of speech	child raising
communism	family vs. career
religion	financial security
nuclear weapons	dress codes in the office
taxes	alcohol
abortion	smoking
Social Security	legalizing marijuana
food stamps	drug use

Another excellent exercise for values clarification is called the *planning board*. It can be made by drawing a few lines on a sheet of paper, as shown in table 10–2.

Cut ten or twelve slips of paper approximately the same size as the slots in the planning board. When you finish, pick a question that is of personal interest to you. It can be frivolous or it can relate to a major life decision; the planning board is a very flexible device.

The question "What do I want from marriage?" will be used here as an example. On the slips of paper, write these suggestions: status, money, love, close relationship with mate, good-looking mate, home life, social life, religion, children, freedom for career growth. Or you may choose to list on the slips other qualities you think important in marriage. Then arrange the slips of paper in order according to your priorities, with the most important in the first slot and the least important in the last slot. Switch the papers around until you are satisfied with the order. Take your time. When you are finished, sit back and think about your planning board; then, if possible, talk it over with a close friend.

The planning board can be used in many ways, individually or in groups, as a game or as a serious decision-making aid. Following are some suggestions for your personal use.

Having a family is a value for many.

What do you want for yourself?

1. popularity
2. money
3. nice figure/physique
4. reputation as intellectual
5. outstanding friends
6. good looks
7. honors, awards
8. good health
9. one special person
10. lots of privacy

After college graduation, what do you want?

1. new car
2. job with high salary
3. travel
4. nice apartment
5. large wardrobe
6. marriage
7. a family
8. job with a future
9. benefit society
10. try new activity—sky diving, skiing, flying, etc.

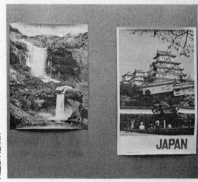
Travel is another value.

What do you want from your job?

1. status
2. good salary
3. satisfaction
4. good working conditions

Table 10–2

PLANNING BOARD

1.	6.
2.	7.
3.	8.
4.	9.
5.	10.

Source: Adapted from Values Clarification Workshop, conducted by Sid Simon, at South Dakota School of Mines and Technology.

5. pleasant co-workers
6. nice office
7. responsibility
8. variety of duties
9. chance for advancement
10. good boss

What do you want in a date?

1. good looks
2. good personality
3. good dancer
4. owns car
5. humor
6. intelligence
7. good figure/physique
8. money
9. quiet and serious
10. popularity

What do you want in a marriage partner?

1. consideration
2. understanding
3. sense of humor
4. equality
5. intelligence
6. college degree
7. good looks
8. nice figure/physique
9. career potential
10. large savings account

What do you like to do on your day off?

1. watch TV
2. participate in sports
3. be with friends
4. be alone
5. wash hair, do laundry
6. be with special person
7. movies or theater
8. do something very different
9. study
10. read a good book

Listing is an excellent way to clarify your values. Try to list ideas for each of the following questions:

■ What makes you smile?

Pleasant co-workers are important in a job.

What makes you laugh? An old Mack Sennett comedy?

You assess your values when you choose a marriage partner.

- What depresses you?
- What things can you do to get out of a depression?
- What are your favorite things?
- What are your favorite memories?

Or you can list ways to:

- Make a holiday special.
- Make your spouse feel important.
- Improve your appearance.
- Improve your personality.
- Become a better employee.

For other strategies defining your values, consult *Values Clarification*, by Simon, Howe, and Kirschenbaum.

Values defining is not a once-in-a-lifetime activity. It is an ongoing process. As you mature and change, so will your values; therefore, you must occasionally reassess them.

Business Ethics

The accepted mode of conduct has swung like a pendulum from one extreme to the other through the centuries of civilization. History records periods of behavior ranging from debauchery and corruption to rigid puritanical thought. *Blue laws*, many of which are still on

Some people value participation in sports.

Organizations such as the Women's Christian Temperance Union crusaded against social evils in the hopes of reforming human conduct.

state law books, were passed in hopes of controlling human conduct, but did little more than gain their nickname. While we are still affected today by legislation regulating the sale of alcoholic beverages and Sunday business hours, prohibitions against such relatively harmless activities as winking in public have proved fruitless.

It is hard to tell which way the pendulum is swinging today; certainly we tend to take a strict view on the way businesses and government conduct their affairs. How legislation affects business practices will be examined in chapter 16; here we will discuss the formation of a personal code of ethics for business.

LEARNING THE COMPANY'S CODE OF ETHICS

All professions and corporations have codes of ethics, written or unwritten. Professionals must practice according to the special codes of their associations: Doctors are bound by the Hippocratic oath; lawyers must function within the limits of their bar associations; soldiers have rules of military discipline. Corporations must operate within federal and state regulations in regard to business behavior. Moreover, they may establish their own networks of rules, often unwritten yet firmly enforced. For example, a firm may frown on smoking, drinking, and the wasting of supplies by its employees.

The corporate behavior of that same firm, however, may include the stacking of statistics, the condoning of tax evasion, the production of shoddy merchandise, and the overcharging of its customers.

This position can be termed the *double standard*. You will be faced with it in both your private and professional life. Occasionally you will discover that what is right for your boss may not be right for you, or vice versa. This ambiguity can lead to internal conflict unless you define "right" and "wrong" to your satisfaction.

SETTING PERSONAL GUIDELINES

The problem of right and wrong has perplexed philosophers since the time of Socrates and Plato, but has never been settled. You will have to determine for yourself what rules of conduct are important to you—a difficult task that is never completely finished.

To clarify your thoughts when you confront an ethical problem, ask yourself, "What is right for *me*—not for my best friend or my neighbor. How do *I* feel about this situation?" Then ask, "How will my actions affect other people? They have rights as well as I. If by exercising my rights I infringe on their rights, how should I act?"

You should recognize that each situation you encounter will be different. There is seldom a simple black and white or right and wrong solution. Most problems seem to fall into the gray areas—that's why they are problems.

If you do see a solution to an ethical problem, you should take action. Don't wring your hands and pace the floor in an agony of indecision. In chapter 8, you learned that it was a mistake to allow yourself to become a "victim." If you strongly believe that an injustice is occurring, you are a "victim" to stand by and let the wrong continue.

At some point in your career, you may have to determine to what degree you are a corporate person and to what degree a free and thinking individual. How much do you owe the corporation? How much of "you" are you going to give? Some people devote their entire lives to their firms. Are you willing to do that to become successful?

At what point do you become a corporate person?

Business Problems

The remaining pages of this chapter are devoted to hypothetical business situations that may arise during your career. There is no one correct answer to these problems. They are presented here to stimulate your thinking and to help you exercise your values. If they are used for group discussion, several answers should be presented. Examine all angles; use the brainstorming techniques you learned in chapter 9. For a good discussion, some members of the group should play devil's advocate and propose differing views.

1. You are a new employee. You find yourself in a department that lacks organization. Your fellow workers take long coffee breaks and two-hour lunch periods. There appears to be more play than work around the office. You

Long coffee breaks make it difficult to get work done.

find it difficult to get your work done because of all the interruptions. What would you do?

2. You are in a committee meeting. The entire committee seems in favor of passing a measure with which you strongly disagree. You realize that by speaking out against the measure you will place yourself in opposition to your supervisor. Remember, your job will be on the line if you speak out. You must present your position so well that you sway some members to your side. What would you do?

3. You have noticed that your immediate supervisor is seldom in the office. He stays home frequently because of personal problems. Because his department is somewhat isolated from others in the company, few of his colleagues are aware of his frequent absences. The executive to whom your supervisor reports is a good family friend of yours. You know that she is not aware of the problem. Should you tell her?

4. Two employees, one male, one female, started employment in the same department at nearly the same time. Both are involved in a new program for the company. He works very hard making outside contacts and consequently is out of the office a great deal. She stays in the office to manage his paperwork and attend meetings. When promotion time comes, she is appointed boss over him and given a raise. He feels he deserved the promotion more than she. What should he do?

5. As production manager, you are faced with a choice of marketing a product of poor quality at a low price or a

When you disagree in a meeting situation, it is sometimes hard to know whether to speak out.

| Date August 9, Wednesday | | | Date August 10 Thursday | | |
City Bowling Green, Ky			City Bowling Green		
Total Brought Forward			Total Brought Forward	123	15
Transportation			Transportation		
Hotel, Including Tips	54	00	Hotel, Including Tips	65	00
Meals, Including Tips	8	50	Meals, Including Tips	30	00
Telephone & Telegram	17	65	Telephone & Telegram		
Daily Mileage × Rate (only for cars on mileage basis)			Daily Mileage × Rate (only for cars on mileage basis)		
Other Items:*			Other Items:*		
Entertainment:	43	00			
D. Boyd. Discussed					
records management					
Iron Skillet					
Bowling Green, Ky					
*Entertainment must be detailed: persons and purpose TOTAL	123	15	*Entertainment must be detailed: persons and purpose TOTAL	218	15

A common ethical problem in business is padding expense accounts.

high-quality product at a higher price. This product is designed for a low-income market and the buyers cannot afford to pay a high price. What would you do?

6. As an assembly-line supervisor, you observe that one worker is not doing her job fast enough. She is slowing down production for the whole line. You learn that she has been sick and needs the job badly. She has used all her sick-leave benefits. What would you do?

7. You have returned from a company business trip. You are filling out an expense voucher. A colleague who has accompanied you on the trip encourages you to pad your expenses. He wants to exaggerate his own expenses, and if you don't exaggerate yours, his voucher will look strange. He tells you that everyone does it and that the company halfway expects it because the expenses provide a tax write-off. What would you do?

8. There is a woman in your office whom you cannot tolerate. She is a braggart and a busybody, and talks more than she works, but she is an expert apple polisher. The supervisor thinks this woman is doing a great job. You know better. One day, the head of personnel comes into the department and wants to speak with your colleague. She is taking the afternoon off, which is not unusual. Do you tell the supervisor the truth about her absence or do you look innocent and pretend you don't know where she is?

9. You have free access to company supplies—postage stamps, typewriter ribbons, mailing supplies, and pens.

Some people find it hard to resist taking company supplies for personal use.

You have gotten into the habit of helping yourself to these items for your personal use. Someone reports you to your boss, who harshly reprimands you. But you know that your boss, for his part, consistently cheats on his expense account because you have helped him with his end-of-month reports. You are angry and resentful, and you'd like to get even with him. What would you do?

10. One person in your office is an alcoholic. You cannot understand why the company tolerates his behavior. He acts fairly normal most of the time, but he is not dependable. He may go to lunch and never return. Because your jobs are interrelated, this impairs your work routine. What would you do?

11. You have a client who gives you an expensive gift for Christmas. It is against your company policy to accept such a gift. But you also know it will offend the client if you return the gift. What would you do?

12. What if you returned the gift described in problem 11 and the client said she understood. However, she continued by saying she could get around that problem by sending you on an expensive business trip to Bermuda. Would you accept?

13. You have regular contact with a customer whom you do not like. This person is rude and swears a great deal. You have always ignored his conduct and have tried to be pleasant. One day he really offends you. You feel you do not want to continue submitting to his discourtesy. Do you put him in his place by talking back, do you wait to discuss the problem with your boss, or do you continue to be pleasant?

14. Your career is surging upward. You enjoy your job very much, but it requires lots of time away from home. Your marriage seems to be suffering because of your frequent absences. You are afraid you will have to make a choice— get a divorce or quit the job. Which would you do? Are there other alternatives?

15. You have a difficult client. If you want to keep his account, you must wine and dine him. You don't mind entertaining this client, but he never knows when to end the evening. He usually continues drinking until the early hours of the morning. What would you do?

16. Your company is selling a product that you believe to be of poor quality. The product looks good and wears well, but is designed to deteriorate after the year's guarantee expires. You disapprove of this deception. What would you do if you were an assembly line worker? What would you do as production manager?

17. You are the public relations manager for a company whose advertising is dishonest. The company seldom returns money to a dissatisfied customer, but its advertising campaign implies that the company stands behind its products. You do not feel right about this type of advertisement. What would you do?

18. One of your associates is showering you with attention. He often stops in your office to chat and frequently asks you out to lunch. You do not care for this man, but he is the boss's son and has a great deal of influence with his father. What do you do?

19. Your company has a WATS (Wide Area Telephone Service) line which is to be used only for business purposes. If you call friends and relatives in another state, the company will never know. Should you make the calls?

Are you justified in using the company phone for personal calls?

20. Because you work in newspaper advertising, you know about special sales many days in advance. Your uncle, who has just opened a new furniture store, is planning an extensive ad campaign. You know what prices his largest competitor will have on certain items of furniture in an upcoming sale. Your uncle wants you to tell him so he can undercut this competitor by having prices that are lower. He also wants ads to run the same day as his competitor's. Would you tell him? Would you tell him if he offered you a percentage of the sales?

21. As an accountant for a firm, you must make monthly financial reports to the board. The board only likes to hear pleasant, glowing reports of financial success. However, if you paint a rosy picture, you will not be telling the entire truth. Should you ensure your job security by painting half-truths or should you give the board the sordid side of the financial story?

22. As an administrative assistant, part of your responsibility is to write speeches for your boss. Sometimes your views differ radically from hers. You do not like writing a speech that conveys ideas you cannot personally support. You don't want to quit the job because you realize that if you stay, you will someday have your boss's job. There are many other advantages and opportunities in this position. What can you do?

23. Your company has spent money training you for a specialized position. While at a training seminar, you are offered a better position with another company. The salary

An accountant may be asked to slant statistics to make the firm look good.

would be twice the salary you are now receiving. Would you quit your present job or would you feel obligated to stay?

24. You have been working for a company for several months. You were hired with the understanding that you would stay for three years. You hate the job. You are in a branch office in an old building and you only see one other person all day long. With your ability, you have a chance to go far in the company. However, right now you seem to be at the end of the line. What would you do?

25. You are offered a job in which you would have money, power, title, and a plush office. It is everything you want but, because the firm has a reputation for deceptive dealings with the public, the position represents a values conflict. Would you take the job?

As you can see, these questions are not simple to answer. But discussing them may stimulate your thinking and clarify your personal values for you. You may feel more comfortable with some solutions than with others. Neither this text nor another person can make decisions for you; you must arrive at them yourself.

KEY TERMS

values	values grid	blue laws
code of ethics	planning board	double standard
valuing process		

TEST YOURSELF:
QUESTIONS FOR REVIEW AND DISCUSSION

1. How can you determine if something is a value for you?
2. What is the difference between values and ethics?
3. Suppose you have been offered a raise and a transfer to another city. How would you respond to this offer if your primary value is family life? If it is financial security? Or career advancement?
4. What values do you possess that directly stem from parental training? From religious training? From schooling? What values have you arrived at by yourself?
5. Are your personal values today different from your personal values of five years ago? If so, give some examples.
6. Can you think of some values that all people hold in common? Of any that vary by age groups? By social status?
7. When you have a problem, do you turn to relatives and friends for advice? Do you find that their advice often does not "fit" your problem? Why? What are the advantages and disadvantages of talking your problems over with relatives and friends?

APPLICATION EXERCISES

Prioritizing

Use the spaces below to complete a list of 10 important goals that you wish to achieve in your lifetime. (For example: wealth, friends, prestige, loving spouse, job security, etc.)

1. _____   6. _____
2. _____   7. _____
3. _____   8. _____
4. _____   9. _____
5. _____   10. _____

Next, prioritize these goals by using the number grid below. Take item 1 and compare it with each of the remaining items you have selected. Using column A of the number grid, circle the number of the item which you consider the more important of the two. Then repeat the procedure in the respective columns with each consecutive item (item 2 use column B; item 3 use column C, etc.).

```
        A
    1   2   B
    1   3   2   3   C
    1   4   2   4   3   4   D
    1   5   2   5   3   5   4   5   E
    1   6   2   6   3   6   4   6   5   6   F
    1   7   2   7   3   7   4   7   5   7   6   7   G
    1   8   2   8   3   8   4   8   5   8   6   8   7   8   H
    1   9   2   9   3   9   4   9   5   9   6   9   7   9   8   9   I
    1  10   2  10   3  10   4  10   5  10   6  10   7  10   8  10   9  10
```

After completing the number grid, total the number of times each item was circled.

Item 1 _____   Item 6 _____
Item 2 _____   Item 7 _____
Item 3 _____   Item 8 _____
Item 4 _____   Item 9 _____
Item 5 _____   Item 10 _____

Now rewrite your list of priorities according to the number of times each item was circled. The item that received the most circles should be placed first, and the item that received the least would be in last position. Compare this list with your original to see if you prioritized your goals correctly.

1. _____   6. _____
2. _____   7. _____
3. _____   8. _____
4. _____   9. _____
5. _____   10. _____

This same activity can be done with innumerable subjects. For example, a student can chart the following job activities to evaluate personal career needs.

Item 1 Outdoor work   Item 6 Working with numbers
Item 2 Problem solving   Item 7 Conducting meetings
Item 3 Writing   Item 8 Creating new programs
Item 4 Helping others   Item 9 Supervising
Item 5 Researching   Item 10 Doing original work

Suggested Readings

Brooks, John. *The Game Players: Tales of Men & Money.* New York: Times Books, 1980.

Drucker, Peter F. *The Changing World of the Executive.* New York: Times Books, 1982.

Simon, Sidney B. et. al., *Values Clarification.* New York: Hart Publishing, 1978.

PART FOUR

PLANNING FOR SUCCESS

Growth in your career requires goal setting and time management. It involves coping with questions of social and business etiquette. It means encountering new opportunities for travel and dealing with new financial responsibilities. It means, in short, a new world with broad horizons.

11

SET YOUR GOALS-- MANAGE YOUR TIME

COMPREHENSIVE GOAL
To demonstrate how the pursuit of goals and the management of time
are integral units in the appreciation of life

SPECIFIC OBJECTIVES
After reading this chapter, you will be able to:

- list well-defined, long-range goals

- distinguish between outer direction and inner direction

- describe possible obstacles to achievement

- list steps for immediate goal planning

- plan a daily time schedule

Poor Richard's Alamanac asks, "Dost thou love life? Then do not squander time, for that's the stuff life is made of." Their material wealth and physical and mental attributes may differ, but all humans have only twenty-four hours to spend or waste each day. The management of those twenty-four hours is the responsibility of each individual.

Taking personal charge of your life in order to make each day count requires making decisions about your time, in terms of both long-range planning and daily scheduling. Long-range goals give you purpose and direction, while immediate daily plans are the means for arriving at these goals.

Long-Range Goals

Research shows that a long-range goal of four or five years is often achieved in half the time once an individual becomes dedicated to it. Moreover, sociologists have discovered that goal-oriented employees are more effective and aggressive than their goal-less colleagues. Many corporations, recognizing the value of goal planning, arrange planning seminars for their executives.

Who directs your life? You or others? The concepts of *outer direction* and *inner direction* may be helpful in providing an answer to this question. Outer-directed people let others tell them what to do and when. In contrast, inner-directed people decide for themselves what they want to do with their lives. Which type of personality do you suppose is more successful? Which type are you?

As Laurence Peter (author of *The Peter Principle*) states, "If you don't know where you are going, you will end up somewhere else." The purpose of this chapter is to help you end up somewhere, not "somewhere else."

SUCCESSFUL GOAL SETTING

Now stop reading and write down some things you want to accomplish in the next five years.

Study your list. Is it fairly short and loaded with generalities? If it is, you are a typical untrained goal planner. The following eight points can assist you in seriously planning how to get the most from life.

1. *Examine the goals you just listed.* Do any of them reflect a self-limiting attitude? Are you thinking small—letting preset boundaries hem you in? If you listed an estimated annual salary, did you limit it to what your friends, your parents, or even your boss earns? Why not set your sights higher? Did you express a desire to travel? Why not plan to go to Europe? Maybe no one else in your family has ever

Air France

A trip to Europe is not an unreachable goal.

been out of the state, but that doesn't mean you shouldn't want to see the world.

2. *Your goals should be challenging.* When you are goal planning, dare to dream big dreams. Would you like to own a car, a sailboat, a fur coat? Would you like to own your own business or run for public office? Quiet the inner voice that says "I can't." In terms of your immediate career planning, don't stop at entry level. Say "Where do I want to go from here? What do I visualize as the pinnacle of my success?" Why not plan to get to the top?

3. *Your goals should be realistic.* This point may seem to contradict the one above, but in essence it does not. True, you should be ambitious when goal planning, but your goals must fit your personality and aptitudes. It is not realistic for you to aspire to an executive position in a large corporation if you cannot tolerate paperwork or working indoors. Nor would it be wise for you to train for social work if people get on your nerves.

4. *Your goals should be specific.* Look through your list of goals for vague, general statements. Perhaps you stated that you would like to travel. Now be more specific and mention where you would like to go. Florida? Hawaii? A camping trip across the country? Maybe you indicated that you would like to live in an elaborate apartment. How many rooms will it have? Will it be a high-rise or a duplex? Will it have a balcony? Perhaps you wanted to own a pet. What kind? A Parrot? A black Scotty? A hamster? This specificity has a purpose: The more clearly you visualize your goals, the better your chances are for their actual achievement.

5. *Your goals should reflect a variety of interests.* If your five-year plan looks like the following, you may be headed for problems:

> Job with advancement opportunities
>
> $25,000 yearly salary
>
> Master's degree in business administration
>
> Plush office

The adage "Don't put all your eggs in one basket" is good advice for goal planning. Be careful not to fall into the error of setting your sights for a top position in only one corporation. Should the company become bankrupt or change ownership, or should you be forced to resign, you will suffer a great personal loss. Especially during the early years of your career, job changes are sometimes the best way to increase your salary and advance yourself professionally. When considering your life objectives, use the lateral thinking described in chapter 9. Explore all avenues; plan your life creatively. Perhaps a better list would resemble the following:

> Master's degree
>
> Job with advancement opportunities
>
> Pilot's license
>
> Vacation in Hawaii

Vary your goals: Don't put all of your eggs in one basket.

6. *Goals should be a pleasure to pursue.* A wise man once said: "Success is a journey, not a destination." It is not the pot of

gold at the end of the rainbow that is the true reward: It is the trip through the rainbow. Too many people have the mistaken belief that they will be happy when they earn a certain amount of money a year, only to find, when they reach that income level, that they are no happier. Anticipation of goals can be compared to a little child's birthday wish for a shiny new bicycle. He believes that the bicycle will make him so happy that he will never want another thing. But can a new bicycle, or any other form of material wealth, permanently satisfy all future wants? Don't wish your life away; enjoy each step toward your goal.

7. *Worthwhile goals should mirror the real you.* Be careful not to set goals to impress someone or to win respect. True goals are those you set for yourself.

8. *Keep in mind that goals are not meant to be chiseled in stone.* Sometimes you must "try on" goals for size. Occasionally you will find the goal does not fit. For example, Harry Jones may decide to become an engineer, but after a year in engineering school he may conclude that he really dislikes most of the courses required for the degree. This conclusion could be a mask for failure or laziness, or it could be an honest realization that he has selected an inappropriate goal. No one who has discovered an honest mistake should persist in it.

Return to the goals that you listed at the beginning of this section. By applying the eight suggestions for goal planning, can you now write a better set of goals?

Don't set goals merely to win someone else's respect.

After listing your goals, think about them and make a commitment to yourself to achieve them. You can, if you believe it to be possible. Self-trust is the first secret of success. ✳

Finally, be prepared to work hard for your goals. Without hard work, your goals will remain daydreams.

GOAL OBSTACLES

Planning is not all there is to achieving your goals. Obstacles of all kinds will block your way, and you will need patience, perseverance, determination, and hard work to overcome them.

If you openly declare a goal, expect criticism. Friends and family will tell you how foolish you are, or how crazy, to seek your dream. They will suggest that you lack capability or intelligence. Use this negativism to your advantage; turn your hurt and resentment into the energy that will ensure the success of your endeavor. Think of it this way: The more opposition you incur, the more glorious your achievement.

Fear of failure can hamper the best of plans. Accept failure as part of the course. Many times success is preceded by a series of failures; you have a choice of giving up or learning from the experience. There is a saying, "A failure is a man who has blundered, but is not able to cash in on the experience."

The waiting period between planning the goal and achieving it is an obstacle that can unnerve the strongest. In a world of instant food, instant replays, and instant news, people want fast results. A worthwhile goal doesn't come about quickly; it takes long hours of work, sacrifice, and self-denial. For example, dieting can be a most difficult form of self-denial. It takes continual willpower day after day.

DISCIPLINE, ADJUSTMENT, AND READJUSTMENT

Goal achievement requires self-discipline. This does not mean that you must turn into a hermit and set up housekeeping in the nearest cave. But there will be times when you would rather socialize, watch television, sleep late, or indulge in some personal luxury; yet you must deny yourself these pleasures in order to achieve your goal. Our contemporary life-style can still benefit from the wisdom of the ancient proverb, "He who loves pleasure will be a poor man."

Because life changes, you will be forced at times to modify or adjust your plans. Your goals of five years ago may not fit your needs of today. One college student set his sights on buying a sports car after his graduation. When the time finally arrived for him to purchase his dream car, he had taken a new job that meant relocation to a colder climate. He realized that a sports car would be

Courtesy Pacific Crest Outward Bound

Once you set a goal, be willing to work for it. Don't just daydream.

Richard Allouche

In a world of instant food, self-denial comes hard.

useless during the winter months, so he compromised and bought a more practical vehicle.

Other roadblocks will be thrown in your way—money shortages, health problems, unexpected moves to another city. Whatever the barrier, there is a way around it for the determined person. The story of Evanell Janousek, a well-known Midwest sculptor, exemplifies how misfortune can be turned into fortune. Because her son was born with a heart affliction, she had to be near him most of the time. To pass the time, she decided to start drawing. By the time her son had a successful heart operation at the age of two, she had become an accomplished artist. She then turned to sculpture, in time producing a series of delightful sculptures of children. She now has a profitable business creating her own line of sculptures.

Almost everyone experiences disappointment upon reaching a goal. Sometimes you work so long and hard that when the work is completed you almost feel a sense of loss. You may have experienced such a feeling the day after graduation, the 26th of December, or during the second week of ownership of a new car. One recently elected congressman privately confessed that his one week of glory after the election did not prepare him for the emotional letdown that followed when he was faced with the burdens of appeasing constituents, attending endless meetings, giving speeches, doing research, directing a large staff, and making wise decisions. Would the congressman give up his office, or the graduate his diploma? No, but both must undergo a readjustment period that calls for the planning of new goals.

Short-Range Planning

Some long-range goals look insurmountable until they are divided into smaller blocks of time.

Take apart your long-range goal and reassemble the required activities into yearly and seasonal plans. For example, suppose you must write a sixty-page research paper by next month. If you plan to write approximately fifteen pages a week, or two pages a day, the task does not seem so difficult. One administrative assistant, when faced with a large task such as organizing a regional business meeting, always divides the duties involved into weekly and daily schedules. For an example of her method of organization, see table 11–1.

As important as dividing the work into blocks of time is the setting of deadlines. Tell a friend, boss, or someone special that by a certain date you will have accomplished the task you plan. A deadline will give you a sense of obligation. Passing that deadline without completing the task may cause enough frustration to spur you into action.

Watch out for plateaus of contentment. As you advance toward your goal, don't get so comfortable with small accomplishments that you become lazy. A compliment on your appearance might be enough for you to forget your diet until "tomorrow." An "A" on one test might lessen the pressure to study for the next one. A promotion might influence you to relax and coast along in the job. Beware of such plateaus.

Daily Time Management

Books are written word by word, mountains are climbed step by step, and all major tasks are performed by means of miniscule actions. Accordingly, each minute of the day should be directed toward a purpose. The remaining portion of this chapter contains useful suggestions for effective daily time management.

THE NEED FOR STRUCTURE

Eric Berne, author of *Games People Play* and originator of transactional analysis, identified the need for structure as one of three basic human needs. *Time-structuring* is the organization of time into various segments. The two broad segments are action and inaction.

Inaction is the portion of the day spent in daydreaming, fantasizing, withdrawal, or planning for the future. This form of retreat should not occupy much of your time. The greater part of your day should be spent in action. According to Berne, action can be divided into five categories: rituals, pastimes, games, intimacy, and activity.

Rituals can be simple. Greetings—"Hi, how are you?" "Fine, how are you?"—are important American rituals. Religious cere-

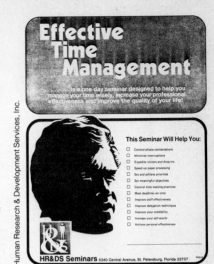

Many corporations, recognizing the value of time management, arrange seminars for their employees.

Table 11–1

PREPARATION FOR QUARTERLY BUSINESS MEETING

Four weeks prior to meeting	Confirm date, time, location of meeting. Reserve conference room. Send out meeting reminders.
Three weeks prior to meeting	Check with all participants for reproduction of materials to be used for meeting. Start reproduction of participants' materials. Order training film.
Week of meeting	Reconfirm meeting room reservation. Requisition chairs and tables. Check to make certain film has arrived. Check all reproductions.
Day of meeting	Have water, glasses, and ashtrays on tables. Check for sufficient chairs. Have projector and screen in room. Have materials on tables. Check room temperature. Have flip charts and other visual aids ready.

For a busy person, planning and organizing time is the only way to make sure that everything gets done.

monies, patriotic holidays, and fraternity rites are examples of rituals in which people are often expected to participate. Sometimes the origins of the rituals have been long forgotten, but their cultural and social significance persists.

Pastimes are forms of social exchange that serve to pass the time of day: for example, the jokes and banter exchanged during coffee breaks about topics ranging from the weather to working conditions.

Games are activities that sound like fun but are really traps. Games differ from pastimes in that they have the ulterior design of catching someone. Berne has given them descriptive titles such as "If It Weren't for You," "Kick Me," "Corner," and "Mine Is Better Than Yours." "See What You Made Me Do" is a game that is usually played with two people.[1] For example, if you interrupt a busy typist, the typist may make an error. In this situation, a game player will become upset and say, "See what you made me do!" In a more serious case, a wife may blame her husband for her failure to succeed in a career.

Games are not healthy social activities, and the time spent on them is ineffective action.

Intimacy is a form of interaction between two people who can freely relate to each other without fear of rejection. Each feels comfortable in the presence of the other, and mutual respect is evident. It is important for everyone to have at least one intimate relation-

[1]Material for this section is based upon Eric Berne, *Games People Play* (New York: Ballantine, 1964), p. 18.

ship. Intimacy does not necessarily mean sexual entanglement. Co-workers with similar interests may form an intimate working relationship and interact in a very productive manner.

Activity is the *core* of time-structuring, and the basis of all other transactions. Programming a computer, mailing a letter, washing clothes, conducting a survey, and writing a book are all examples of activity. Activity is the road to achievement of goals. ✳

CREATE A DAILY PLAN

The first step toward good time management is creating a daily plan. Follow this plan and cross off tasks as they are completed. The story of how Charles Schwab, former president of Bethlehem Steel, used a daily list illustrates the value of daily planning. Mr. Schwab asked Ivy Lee, a business consultant, to show him how to get more done with his time. Mr. Lee gave him a piece of paper and told him to write down the important tasks that he wanted to accomplish the next day. Then he was instructed to assign a "one" to the most pressing task, a "two" to the next most important, and so on down the list. Mr. Schwab was to work on task one until completed, then go to task two. If task two could not be finished within the remaining day's time, then it would become task one the next day. Mr. Lee told Mr. Schwab to use the method for a while and then send him a check for what he thought it was worth. Weeks later, Mr. Lee received a check for $25,000. Mr. Schwab had found the method so valuable that the plan was initiated for use throughout Bethlehem Steel.[2]

WRITE IT DOWN

Possibly you already practice some form of daily planning. Perhaps early in the morning, while shaving or driving your car to work, you mentally run through your plans for the day. This mental processing is good, but it is better to write the plans down on paper. By the act of writing you make a commitment to the plans. You need not be specific; merely note general ideas. Place the plans where you can see them during the day; as you complete a project, cross it off the list.

Besides your daily list of plans, you might occasionally want to keep track of how your waking hours are spent. Record all your activities on table 11–2. You will probably discover a few free hours that could be put to good use!

Planning and organizing are the first steps in using your time constructively. *Time engineering* is an additional way to make best use of your time. Essentially, time engineering is maneuvering projects toward completion with a minimum of wasted time and a

This is an advertisement for a time-management aid for executives.

[2]Cited in R. Alec Mackenzie, *The Time Trap* (New York: McGraw-Hill, 1975), p. 38.

Table 11–2

RECORD OF ACTIVITIES

Instructions: Place a check mark or **X** in a space to indicate how you have spent a full hour. Place fractions in the spaces to show parts of hours. Add columns to fit your own typical activities.

	Sleeping	Eating	Maintenance	Shifting Gears
1:00				
2:00				
3:00				
4:00				
5:00				
6:00				
7:00				
8:00				
9:00				
10:00				
11:00				
12 Noon				
1:00				
2:00				
3:00				
4:00				
5:00				
6:00				
7:00				
8:00				
9:00				
10:00				
11:00				
12 Midnight				

Definitions: Eating: includes preparation, clean-up
Maintenance: housework, yard work, care of clothes, car, etc.
Shifting Gears: includes changing clothes, showering, getting from one place to another

John H. Zenger et al., *How to Work for a Living and Like It: A Career Workbook,* © 1977 Syntex Laboratories. Published by Addison-Wesley, Reading, Massachusetts. Reprinted with permission.

maximum of concentration. It involves the basic principle of working smarter, not harder. The following are practical tips from an expert time engineer.

Never Be Caught Waiting When you have an appointment with a doctor, dentist, client, or whomever, expect to find yourself in the waiting room with a few free minutes. To avoid wasting time, bring reading material or work with you, or, if the waiting room is well stocked with up-to-date magazines that you usually wouldn't have time to read, take advantage of this chance to catch up on world events. Even reading a trade magazine that you normally don't have time for can widen your perspectives. Practicing isometric exercises while waiting for that appointment is another way of putting free time to good use.

Never be caught without reading material—make use of time spent waiting for appointments.

Don't Procrastinate Mañana isn't good enough for you. Don't wait for a thunderbolt from the clouds to act. Sometimes you may not feel like working: That is when it is most important to force yourself to get started. Perhaps you have a report that you really are not anxious to write. When you do, with a small amount of self-discipline, start writing, you may find second-grade words flowing from your pen. This is still no reason to stop. Keep at it—better words will eventually come.

Don't Be A Perfectionist There are times for thorough detailing of work and times for rough drafts. Learn the difference, and use your time accordingly. Exactness is important in computer programming, in mathematical computation, or in brain surgery. But when the boss asks for an estimate of the number of paper clips sold during the last year, don't attempt to arrive at an exact number by going through the vouchers. When instructions call for a paragraph summary, don't turn in a two-page report. The hairdresser who spends an extra fifteen minutes on one stubborn curl may be wasting both the client's and his or her own time. When the patron leaves the shop, the wind will probably rearrange the curls anyway.

Be A Speed Reader Precious time can be wasted in reading all the reports, memos, proposals, and letters that are a necessary part of office work. If you are a slow reader, you might invest in a speed-reading course that will help you to read faster and increase your comprehension.

For quicker newspaper reading, remember that reporters put the main ideas of a news story in the first three paragraphs. By reading the headline and the first three paragraphs, you will have covered the most important information. This way, you can inform yourself of the main news events in a very short time.

Hazel Hankin

There are books that can help you become a faster and more retentive reader.

A cluttered desk may cause you to waste time looking for important papers.

Avoid A Cluttered Desk Keep your desk organized in some workable fashion, so that you don't waste time searching for that one all-important paper. Establish priorities. This may entail periodic conferences with your boss or co-workers to decide which projects demand immediate attention, which can wait twenty-four hours, and which can be held till you have time.

Learn To Say No It is good to socialize occasionally, but when you have a project or deadline, you may have to conserve your time and energy and say no to fun. At times your friends will try to convince you that you should put your work away and join them; but if you have other time demands, apply your assertiveness training and say no.

Time Strategies Learn to foresee and avoid possible time wasters. Do you telephone the incessant talker or do you write a letter? Do you personally visit slow, time-consuming clients or speak to them on the telephone? Learn the best time to approach your boss with a new idea—is it early morning or late afternoon?

These time management suggestions are not intended to imply that you should rigidly schedule each minute, or run hurriedly from one project to another while ignoring valuable human relationships. But don't wander through life waiting for something good to happen. Lady Luck isn't going to smile on you unless you catch her attention. To make success happen, you must be the activating force in your own life, setting goals and managing your time wisely. ✳

KEY TERMS

outer direction	rituals	intimacy
inner direction	pastimes	activity
time-structuring	games	time engineering

TEST YOURSELF:
QUESTIONS FOR REVIEW AND DISCUSSION

1. What are some of your goals? How have your peers influenced your goals? Your family? Your teachers? Others?
2. Do you know a person whom you would consider successful? If so, does that person set goals? Is he or she inner-directed or outer-directed?
3. What is the relationship between goal setting and time management?
4. What are some time wasters in your life?
5. When is socializing a time waster and when isn't it?
6. Do you practice daily planning? What methods do you use?
7. Can you name some obstacles that could hinder goal achievement, other than the ones mentioned in the text? What are some ways around these obstacles?
8. Should all goals be of the tangible variety? Can you list some intangible goals?

APPLICATION EXERCISE

Create a pie chart by dividing the circle below according to the amount of time spent on your daily activities.

Suggested Readings

Davenport, Rita. *Making Time, Making Money: A Step-by-Step Program to Set Your Goals & Achieve Success.* New York: St. Martin's Press, 1982.

MacKenzie, Alec, and Kay C. Waldo. *About Time! A Woman's Guide to Time Management.* New York: McGraw-Hill, 1981.

McRae, Bradley. *Time Management.* Woodbury, N.Y.: Barron, 1982.

Scott, Dru. *How to Put More Time in Your Life.* New York: New American Library, 1981.

12

COURTESY AND COMMON SENSE

COMPREHENSIVE GOAL
To instruct you in some of the generally accepted modes of social behavior in order that you will feel at ease in social and business situations

SPECIFIC OBJECTIVES
After reading this chapter, you will be able to:
- make a proper introduction
- be aware of business situations that require good manners
- display a "you" attitude in business situations
- apply rules of telephone etiquette
- apply rules of restaurant etiquette
- define menu terms
- understand the proper placement and use of china and silverware
- know the correct amounts to tip for various services

You may possess the knowledge, skills, and training that could make you a real asset to a company; but if your dealings with co-workers, clients, and employers reveal ignorance of ordinary good manners, don't expect to be promoted.

The rules of social etiquette are more relaxed now than even a decade ago, but this is no excuse for a lack of consideration for others. The absence of prescribed rules calls for increased thoughtfulness and alertness to circumstances that require sincere gestures of courtesy.

This chapter will discuss both current business etiquette trends and situations that require you to use your own judgment.

Socio-Business Graces

The fast pace of the modern business world encourages less formality than was customary years ago. However, not all protocol has been abandoned, and some of the remaining observances will be covered in the following sections.

EXPRESSIONS OF COURTESY

Expressions of courtesy take both verbal and nonverbal forms. Sometimes they involve following rules, sometimes just using good sense.

Introductions In the business world, it is frequently necessary to introduce clients, new employees, visitors, and consultants. This ritual need not be confusing if you remember to consider age, rank, and sex when making introductions. In family and social situations, this means that you introduce a personal friend to your parents, a

As a professional, you need to make correct and graceful introductions.

A handshake is a common form of greeting among women as well as men.

younger person to an older, a man to a woman. At work you introduce a subordinate to a supervisor.

If you are still confused, remember to mention the name of the honored individual first. For example:

"Mother and Father, I would like to you to meet my friend, Jane Ellingson."

"Mr. Ritten [your boss], I would like you to meet our new receptionist, Ann Baylor."

"Mr. Hart [older person], I'd like you to meet Bob Anderson."

Include some information about each person to help the newly acquainted individuals start a conversation.

For example, when introducing the receptionist, Ann Baylor, to your boss, Mr. Ritten, you might add, "Ann has just moved here from New York. If I remember correctly, you were the sales manager in our New York office a few years ago. Is that right, Mr. Ritten?" Now Ms. Baylor and Mr. Ritten have some common ground for beginning a conversation.

Handshaking　When being introduced, men always shake hands. This ceremony is said to stem from an ancient ritual: Men would extend right hands to prove that they held no hidden weapons. Shaking hands among women is also becoming common today, as women assume more managerial positions.

Addressing Others　The question of how to address bosses and colleagues will arise soon after you begin a new job. When addressing your superior, use *Mr., Miss, Ms.,* or *Mrs.* before the last name until you are instructed to do otherwise. The use of first names is best left to the discretion of the person in authority. Your co-workers will soon inform you of their preferences regarding names. If they tell you they wish to be called by a certain name or nickname, it is courteous to comply.

The titles *Ms., Mrs.,* and *Miss* sometimes cause confusion. Mrs. refers to a married woman, and *Miss* to an unmarried woman. Because people felt these titles were sexist (there are no titles that distinguish between married and unmarried men), the title *Ms.* was coined. It can be applied to both unmarried and married women and is convenient when a woman's marital status is unknown. However, be careful when using *Ms.*—as many women greatly dislike it as prefer it.

Walking on Sidewalks   Custom used to dictate that a man escorting a woman should walk on the side nearest the street to protect her from sloppy street conditions. Many people still expect the custom to be observed. On the other hand, some women are insulted by this chivalry; they feel it is an act of male condescension. You may wonder what is correct. The only advice that can be given here is to assess the situation and personalities, then decide.

Opening Doors   Women's changing roles have also affected their attitude toward many social customs. For example, opening a door for a woman, once expected, now offends some women. This can leave a man confused.

Practicality and common sense dictate the acceptable action in this and many other situations. If a man is passing through a doorway at the same time as a woman, it is proper for him to hold the door for her and let her pass through first. However, there is no need for him to rush to the doorway and open it for her if she is ahead of him. Likewise, a woman should hold the door open for a man if his arms are full or if the door will otherwise slam back in his face just as he steps through.

Although some women dislike the term "Ms.," others prefer it.

Entering or Leaving the Elevator The same principle applies to entering and leaving an elevator. The person nearest the door should pass through first. It is sheer folly for a woman in the back of a packed elevator to expect men to part the way for her in order to let her out first.

Smoking Smokers must be considerate of nonsmokers. Smoke wafting across a nonsmoker's nose can be very irritating. If you smoke, observe no-smoking signs. Ask permission to smoke when in another person's office or in a social situation where your smoking may offend someone else. Don't smoke during meals, and don't talk with a cigarette or cigar in your mouth.

Nonsmokers should respect a smoker's wish to smoke. The smoker is well aware of the hazards of smoking and has made a personal choice. Nonsmokers should honor the personal rights of others and leave the health lectures for physicians.

WRITTEN AND VERBAL CONSIDERATIONS

"You" Attitude Good business correspondence and verbal communication utilize the *you attitude*. The "you" attitude means

In a crowded elevator, whoever is nearest the door should exit first.

Sending cards is a thoughtful gesture and a necessary part of business.

placing the other person's needs and problems before yours. In a business transaction, you might want to say, "Pay your bill by November first, or we will cut off your credit." But if you use the "you" attitude, you will say, "In order to protect your credit rating, you should pay your bill by November first."

In filling the order of a customer who forgot to include the model number on his order blank you might be inclined to say, "You forgot to give us the model number." But it would be better to say, "Please indicate the model number so we can send the order as soon as possible."

Passive Voice   A perceptive employee will sometimes put a statement in the passive voice to prevent placing the blame directly on someone. For example, a client comes in for a two o'clock appointment with Mr. Smith; however, Mr. Smith has forgotten about the appointment. To protect Mr. Smith, his secretary could use the passive voice: "Your name is not listed in the appointment book," rather than the active voice: "Mr. Smith forgot to put your name in the appointment book."

The secretary who can be tactful in circumstances such as this is an asset to an employer.

Written Messages   Thank-you notes; letters of appreciation, congratulation, and condolence; and birthday greetings are among the messages that a professional person frequently must send. Such messages can be time-consuming and difficult to write, but a wise person does not overlook these important occasions. The following are examples of necessary business notes.

Dear Ms. Swanson,

Congratulations on your promotion to vice-president of sales. I always felt you would go places at Acme Printing. I'm happy for you and wish you the best.

If I can be of help in any way when you assume your new duties, just give me a call.

Sincerely,

Bill Reynolds

Bill Reynolds

Dear Mr. Martin,

Thank you for speaking to our civic club. I wish you could have heard all of the favorable comments made about your speech after the meeting. You made us all think. Thanks again for sharing your time and thoughts with us.

Sincerely,

Cindy Myers

Cindy Myers

Special Favors Sincere compliments and praise can brighten an ordinary working day. A compliment to an associate who completes a difficult task will be much appreciated, but too many times it is forgotten in the rush of business.

Sending flowers is a thoughtful gesture at any time. One teacher sent rosebuds to male and female speakers in appreciation for their taking time out to speak to her class. Odd that a rosebud should be sent to a man? She didn't think so. A card that accompanied the flower suggested that the man present the rose to his wife or a female friend or co-worker. She never had difficulty getting a speaker to return to her class.

Telephone Etiquette

It is important always to project a professional image over the telephone. Since the visual impressions that so strongly influence people's judgments are absent when you use the telephone, only your voice and manners represent you and your company.

A good telephone voice is so essential that you should practice with a tape recorder to improve your voice quality. While listening to the tape playback, check for distracting mannerisms such as frequent use of "ah's" and "um's." Check also for clear diction. Do you pronounce each word clearly? Can you tell your vowels from your consonants? If you have a tendency to drone on in a monotone, practice raising and lowering your voice to add emphasis and interest. If you discover your voice to be high-pitched or whiny, get into the habit of lowering it. This takes conscious effort at first; but if you pause before speaking and train yourself to lower your voice, you can eliminate the irritating sound.

Your telephone voice and manners represent you and your company.

PHONE ANSWERING

If at all possible, let the telephone ring only once. Answering the telephone on the first ring gives an impression of efficiency, whereas a phone that rings six or more times leaves the caller with the impression that the employees either are overloaded with work or don't care about helping their customers.

When you answer the telephone, hold the receiver about an inch and a half from your mouth; holding it any closer causes a muffled sound. Clearly identify yourself.

For example:

"Good morning, the White Paper Company, Cindy Larson speaking."

Smiling during telephone conversations can add warmth and sparkle to vocal tone and help to project a professional image.

A typical telephone message form

or:

"Mrs. Bartlett's office. This is Mark Hanson speaking."

Stay away from confusing, lengthy identifications. If you answer the telephone frequently, guard against sounding bored or tired. Your "Hello, Miss Anderson speaking" can affect the caller's attitude about the entire company. Remember that your voice is sometimes the only connection that a distant customer or associate has with the company—and it can project very strong negative or positive images of the firm. Many telephone trainers instruct new employees to smile while talking into the telephone. It adds sparkle to their voices and prevents a boring monotone from creeping in.

If you must put a caller on hold, first ask his or her permission. Avoid leaving the caller on hold any longer than a minute. If it is going to take longer than a minute, give the caller a choice of continuing to stay on hold or accepting a return call as soon as possible. If the caller wishes to remain on hold, check back frequently to let him or her know you haven't forgotten.

Should the caller want someone who happens to be on a coffee break or down the hall, don't be specific about his or her whereabouts. Say that the person has stepped out of the office for a moment and offer to take a message.

Keep paper and pencil handy to jot down messages and telephone numbers. Most companies provide telephone memo pads, such as the one shown on this page. Repeat the caller's name and any important details the caller gave to be certain you have the information correct. If you are doubtful about the caller's name, ask how to spell it. It is worth the effort for you to take time to get the name right, rather than have it mispronounced during the return call.

Sometimes it may be necessary for you to screen calls to protect your boss from interruptions and undesirable callers. The following examples can be useful in handling this type of problem:

"Miss Wilson is in conference right now. Could I take your name and telephone number and have her call you?"

"I'm sorry, Mr. Reynolds is with a client. Could I take your name and number and have him return the call as soon as possible?"

"Mrs. Richards has just stepped out of the office. Let me take your name and number and I'll have her call as soon as she returns."

If the caller turns out to be someone your boss has been waiting to speak to, you can then say:

"Oh, one moment, Mrs. Richards has just returned to the office."

Sometimes it is necessary to screen calls.

Irate callers can require diplomacy on your part. Remember, their nastiness does not give you an excuse to be rude or tactless. Don't take the verbal attack personally; the caller is angry with the company, not you. You happened to be the person who took the call. As a representative of the company, you should listen attentively and try to get to the crux of the problem. If you do not have the authority to correct the problem, transfer the caller to someone who can help. When transferring the call, be careful not to give the impression that you are giving the caller the run-around. Explain your reason for transferring the call and ask the caller's permission to do so.

Thoughtlessness is magnified over the telephone. Gum chewing, eating or drinking, or clanging jewelry can become a real distraction, as can slang or poor grammar.

PLACING A CALL

Before you place a call, plan what you are going to say. Don't socialize too much on the telephone. Although it is fine to show interest in the other person, don't chat aimlessly about personal matters and then bring up business near the end of the conversation.

During the conversation, use the person's name once or twice. Whether you use the full name or the first name will depend upon your degree of familiarity.

Some executives consider it demeaning to dial their own calls, choosing instead to have a secretary perform that chore. This practice can offend the person on the other end of the line, who must

Before you place a call, plan what you will say.

then wait for the secretary to put her boss on. Executives who dial their own calls build better public images than those who are too busy for "lesser" persons. Busy executives can have telephone devices installed that program frequently used numbers. The executive has only to depress one button instead of the complete number and the automatic dial system completes the call.

Learn how to Direct Distance Dial (DDD), and keep a list of frequently used long-distance phone numbers. Be aware of time zones when calling long distance. Should you dial incorrectly and reach a wrong number, call the operator and inform the telephone company of the mistake. No charge will be made for the wrong number.

Try to terminate the conversation gracefully and courteously. Close with a polite and positive phrase such as, "It was nice talking to you," "Thank you for calling," "I won't keep you any longer," or "I know you must be busy, so I'll let you go." Don't replace the receiver so quickly that you hang up on the other party. One switchboard attendant nearly lost his job because of his way of abruptly depressing the switchboard button to disconnect the line. These sudden cutoffs were interpreted by clients as a lack of courtesy.

Be sure that your language usage is appropriate to the situation. The way in which you speak with your friends in telephone conversations is not necessarily the way in which you would address a client.

The following phrases are incorrect for business telephone conversations. How would you reword them?

He's not in yet.
He's gone for the day.
Bye-bye.
She's on a coffee break.
What's your name?
Repeat that, I didn't get it.
How do you spell it?

Who's calling?
Hang on a minute.
She didn't say where she was
  going.
I've gotta go now.
You know what I mean?

Correct telephone usage is not a trivial part of your job. Many employers will not hire applicants before conversing with them over the telephone.

Restaurant Etiquette

Certain social graces are expected of the professional person. Luncheon meetings and the entertainment of clients are all part of business. A person who feels at ease in such social situations has promotion potential.

Dining in a formal restaurant need not be a test of your social skills. It should be a time of pleasure and relaxation. The following suggestions can help make your next dining experience an enjoyable one.

Before going to the restaurant, call to find out if reservations are needed, and if jackets and ties are required for men. Some restaurants require reservations; others have a policy of first come, first served.

Federal Express Corp.

The way you speak to clients over the telephone must be appropriate to the situation.

The *maitre d'hotel* will show you to your table.

Upon entering the restaurant, you will be asked if you want to check your coats at the checkroom. A woman may want to take her wrap with her into the dining area—especially if it is an expensive fur or the air conditioning is too cool.

A captain (*maître d'hôtel*), or a host or hostess, will check your reservation if you have made one; then he or she will lead you to your table. The woman should follow first behind the captain or host or hostess. She will usually be seated so that her back is parallel to the wall.

A waiter or waitress will then arrive for your cocktail order. You can order a cocktail, an appetizer wine such as sherry or vermouth, or simply a sparkling water. Ask the waiter or waitress for suggestions if you are uncertain what to order. Do not feel it is necessary to have a cocktail or wine; no one should feel coerced into drinking to be sociable. Nor should you feel you must offer any explanation if you choose not to have a drink.

MENU TERMS

After an appropriate length of time, the captain or waiter or waitress will approach with a menu. Someone once commented that there seems to be a direct ratio between the size of the menu and the cost of the dinner. The larger the menu, the higher the price. But don't let the size of the menu or its foreign terms intimidate you. If there are no English translations printed below the terms, and you are in doubt about their meanings, your waiter or waitress will be happy to explain them to you. Remember, the attendants are there

Don't be afraid to ask the waiter to explain menu terms.

After reading the menu, a woman may tell a male companion her choice.

to be of service to you and to earn a good tip, so don't hesitate to make requests of them.

You may find some of the following terms on the menu. Their pronunciations and definitions can help familiarize you with some of the more common terms of fine dining.

à la carte (a la kart): each dish priced separately
au gratin (oh grah tan): with cheese
au jus (oh zhu): in its juice
au vin (oh van): in wine sauce
baked Alaska: frozen dessert of ice cream and cake served inside baked meringue
borscht (borsh): soup of beets and vegetables
buffet (buff ay): guests help themselves to array of foods
canapé (ka na pay): appetizer on bread or toast
caviar (kav i ar): fish eggs
champignons (shahm peen yon): mushrooms
cordon bleu (kor don blu): stuffed with cheese and ham
crêpe (krepp): thin pancake
croûtons (croo ton): small cubes of toasted bread
demitasse (demmy tass): small cup of black coffee
entrée (ahn tray): main course
escargots (es kar go): snails
filet mignon (fi lay meen yon): choice cut of beef, broiled
flan (flahn): egg custard
fois gras (fwah grah): goose liver
glace (glahss): ice cream
hors d'oeuvres (or durv): appetizers
legumes (lay gumes): vegetables

When the waiter takes your order, he will ask your preference in meal accompaniments.

You need not be a connoisseur to order wine.

mousse (moos): whipped dessert
poisson (pwa sohn): fish
pommes de terre (pum de tare): potatoes
potage du jour (poe tazh due zhoor): soup of the day
prix fixe (pree feeks): one set price for any complete meal on menu
shish kebab: meat and vegetables on skewer
table d'hôte (tah bul dote): complete meal (usually 3 courses)
Wiener schnitzel (ve ner shnit sil): veal cutlet

After reading the menu, the woman may inform her escort of her choice. He gives the order to the waiter or waitress. In many restaurants, however, the waiter or waitress will address the woman first, so be prepared for either situation. If applicable, you will also be asked your preference in salad dressing, and how you want your potatoes and meat cooked.

WINES

Before the meal is served, the wine steward, or *sommelier* (so mel yay), will present you with a wine list. Don't feel you must be a connoisseur to order wine. It helps to remember this simple guide: Red wine is generally served with red meats such as beef; white wines go well with white meats such as fish and poultry; rosé wine is appropriate for the lighter meats such as lamb or veal. For example, delicate meats in sauces usually go well with white wines. Turkey, game, and roast chicken taste better with light-bodied reds. Red wines will be served at room temperature or slightly cooler; white and rosé wines will be served chilled.

Following are examples of wines in each of the three classes.

Red Wine   Chianti (kee ahn tee)
                            Beaujolais (bo zha lay)
                            Bordeaux (bor doe)
                            Burgundy

White Wine   Chablis (sha blee)
                            Rhine
                            Chardonnay (shar duh nay)

Rosé   Rosé (roh zay)

A separate category of wines is the sparkling variety, of which champagne is the favorite. Champagne can accompany any type of meal and may be served any time of day; all you need to accompany it is a special occasion.

The terms listed below should answer some questions you may have about wines.

acidity: refers to the degree of tartness or sharpness—comparable to the varying degrees of taste in different apples
bouquet: the aroma of the wine
vintage: the year the grapes were grown and harvested
dry: not sweet; the natural sugar has been fermented out of the wine
smooth: refers to mature wines that have acquired silken texture

You may also order a carafe of house wine. The wine steward buys large quantities of good wines for a reasonable price; you benefit by this savings as well as the wine steward's knowledge of wines.

The wine steward will return with the wine and pour a small amount into the glass of the person who ordered it, who should sniff the bouquet of the wine and then taste it. If the wine is good, he or she will give permission to the wine steward to serve it to the other guests. Don't worry about not knowing whether the wine is good or not; if it has soured, it will taste vinegary, and without a doubt you will know. If the wine is bad, it will be replaced.

PLACE SETTINGS

The wine list may not be the only puzzle you encounter when dining. Many fine restaurants set their tables with elaborate arrangements of silverware, crystal, and china. Each piece is provided for a specific purpose. Whether or not you use all of the items provided depends on what foods you have ordered. For example, soup spoons and salad forks are often included in the place settings, but if you are not served these courses, you don't need to use this silverware. In general, silverware is arranged by course from the

Elaborate place settings won't be confusing if you are familiar with basic dining etiquette.

A typical place setting

outside in toward the plate. A few basic tips about dining etiquette will help you enjoy your meal without being concerned about which fork to use and other potential dining dilemmas.

DINING TIPS

Remember to put your napkin on your lap when you sit down. The cloth napkin should be folded in half and laid across the lap with the crease toward you. At the end of the meal, place the napkin on the table. Do not refold the napkin, but lay it slightly crumpled on the table.

Some restaurants serve hors d'oeuvres before you place your dinner order. These appetizers may be accompanied by a small fork; other appetizers—raw vegetable sticks, for example—are meant to be eaten with the fingers.

The soup or salad will be served after the appetizers. If the soup is served in a cup, it is permissible to pick up the cup and drink from it. If the soup is served in a bowl, use the soup spoon on your right. Spoon away from yourself and bring the spoon across the bowl to your mouth. Never tip the bowl to get the last drop. To eat salad, use the small fork on your left. If you find large pieces of lettuce in the salad, you may use your knife to cut them up.

The bread and butter plate to your upper left is to be used only for bread and butter. Your bread or rolls should not be cut with a knife, but torn into smaller pieces. After buttering the bread, place the knife across the plate. Soiled silverware should not be placed on the tablecloth.

There are two accepted methods of using eating utensils, the American and the Continental. In the *American method*, the fork is

You may use your knife to cut up large pieces of lettuce in your salad.

Notice the small fork and nutcracker that accompany this lobster.

held in the right hand to convey food to the mouth. You transfer the fork to your left hand to cut meat, then return it to the right hand for eating. In the *Continental method*, the fork remains in the left hand, and food is conveyed to the mouth with the tines downward.

Special Foods   Some foods require special utensils or techniques:

escargots	Snails are served with a silver clamp and a tiny fork. Hold the snail in the clamp with your left hand and use fork in the right to remove snail.
lobster	The lobster shell is split open before it is served. Use a small fork to lift meat out, then dip in melted butter or sauce.
crab legs	Similar to lobster. Sometimes a utensil resembling a nutcracker will accompany the dish. Crack the shell with this utensil, then remove the meat.
shrimp	Large shrimp can be eaten with the fingers. Pick them up by the tail, dip in sauce, and eat all but the tail.
clams	Use the small fork that accompanies clams. Usually the clams are served in half shells and are easy to remove.

Placement of silverware at completion of a course.

chicken	Depending upon the occasion, you can eat chicken with fingers.
corn on the cob	Often served with small spear in each end of the cob. Hold cob by these and eat the kernels from the cob. Do not cut the kernels onto your plate.
french fries	French fries should be eaten with a fork unless the occasion is an informal one.
shish kebab	Shish kebab arrives at the table on long skewers. Take skewer in one hand, and with fork in other hand push downward to remove the food from skewer.
artichokes	Remove a leaf from artichoke. Dip the leaf in sauce, place it between your teeth, and pull it out, leaving the pulp in your mouth. When all the leaves have been eaten, remove and discard the fuzzy center with knife and fork, and eat the best part, the heart.
olives	Olive pits can be removed from your mouth with your fingers.
caviar	Place a small amount on cracker or rye bread, and eat with fingers.
oysters	Usually served in shell or on half shell. Remove oyster with fork and eat.

The meal is generally served in courses. The waiter or waitress will serve you from the left and remove from the right. Be attentive to this procedure to avoid collision. After each course, if you have used a knife and fork, place the knife on plate with blade facing you. The fork is placed closer to the center of the plate. Spoons should be placed on saucers. Don't let silverware dangle off the side of the plate.

Water goblets and assorted wine goblets will complete the table setting. The goblet should be held by the stem and lower part of the bowl.

You may find the silverware for the dessert course at the top of your place setting, or clean utensils may be provided with each course. The silverware at the top of the plate can be confusing to a person who has never encountered such an arrangement. The grouping might consist of a fork, large or small spoon, and knife. What utensil you use depends on the dessert.

After dessert, a finger bowl may be placed in front of you. Sometimes a sliver of lemon will be floating in the warm water. Dip fingertips in bowl, one hand at a time, then dry on your napkin or on cloth provided.

Table 12–1

TIPPING GUIDE

Hotels
  Doormen
    50¢ to $1.00 per bag for luggage handling
    25¢ to 50¢ for hailing a taxi
  Bellmen
    50¢ to $1.00 per bag carried to room
  Chambermaids
    $1.00 per day per person occupying room
  Room Service
    15% of check

Restaurants and Nightclubs
  Hat and Coat Check Attendants
    50¢ to $1.00 per person
  Bartenders
    15% of check
  Waiters/Waitresses
    15%–20% of check (depends on quality of service)
  Busboys
    no tip; paid out of waiter's tip

Taxicabs
  15%–20% of fare; minimum of 50¢

Other Services
  Coffee Shops
    10¢–15¢ at counter if check is less than 50¢
    15¢–20¢ if check is 50¢ to $1.00
    15%–20% if check is over $1.00
  Washroom Attendants
    25¢–50¢
  Shoeshine
    25¢–50¢
  Parking Attendants
    15%–20% of daily parking charge; minimum 50¢
    Valet Parking—$1.00
  Barbers, Hairdressers, Manicurists
    15% of check

A good rule to follow: When in doubt tip 15%, but only for good service.

TIPPING

Tipping is expected in most restaurants. After deducting any sales tax, 15 to 20 percent of the bill is considered appropriate. For example, if your bill is $45.00, you would tip at least $6.75.

Usually the bill will be presented to you on a small tray. You then place the money for the bill and the tip on the tray. If you pay by credit card, place the card on the tray; the attendant will return with a credit slip for you to sign. When paying for bill by credit card,

Most people prefer to pay for business entertainment by credit card.

include the tip by adding it on to the bill or by leaving cash for it in the tray.

Sometimes attendants are stationed in the restrooms to provide extra services, such as towels and hair spray. If you use any of their services, you are expected to tip the attendants. A general guide to tipping appears in table 12–1.

ENJOY YOURSELF

Dining should be a pleasurable experience. Don't feel overwhelmed by the suggestions presented here. They are made only to make you feel more comfortable in an unfamiliar situation. If you do make mistakes, it is no disaster. Don't let excessive concern about rules spoil your pleasure.

KEY TERMS

"you" attitude *sommelier*   Continental method
maître d'hôtel American method

TEST YOURSELF:
QUESTIONS FOR REVIEW AND DISCUSSION

1. What are the guidelines to consider when making introductions?
2. Do traditional gestures of courtesy have a place in today's world?
3. Describe how the "you" attitude helps in business.
4. Describe the procedures usually followed when ordering wine.
5. Discuss the pros and cons of tipping.

APPLICATION EXERCISES

Supply the other half of these telephone dialogues.

1. Customer: I'm in need of some advertising.
   You: (You try to find out what type of advertising.)

   _____

   Customer: I don't know what I want yet. I do know I want some brochures
   created about our company's new program.
   You: (Sell your business or services at this point.)

   _____

   _____

   Customer: Are you expensive?
   You: (Yes, you are, but you do quality work.)

   _____

   _____

   Customer: Can I get an estimate?
   You: (You give estimates, but not over the phone. Encourage customer to
   make an appointment with you.

   _____

   _____

   Customer: Fine. Thank you.

2. Customer: This is Mr. Anderson. I placed my order a long time ago, and I want to know why I haven't received it.
You: (You first must determine what the order is and when it was placed; however, keep your message in the "you" attitude.)

_____

_____

Mr. Anderson: I placed an order for three Hanson typewriters some time during the week of October 22. That was over two weeks ago. I can't understand why this order is taking so long.
You: (You discover after checking the files that the order had to be back ordered and it will take another two weeks. You would like to keep Mr. Anderson's business and his goodwill.)

_____

_____

Suggested Readings

Donald, Elsie B., editor. *Debrett's Etiquette & Modern Manners.* New York: Viking Press, 1981.

Drobot, Eve. *Class Acts: Etiquette for Today.* New York: Van Nostrand Reinhold, 1982.

Ford, Charlotte. *Charlotte Ford's Book of Modern Manners.* New York: Simon & Schuster, 1980.

Post, Emily, and Anthony Stafferi. *The Complete Book of Entertaining from the Emily Post Institute.* New York: Harper & Row, 1981

Sutherland, Douglas. *The English Gentleman.* New York: Penguin, 1980.

13

WHEN YOU TRAVEL

COMPREHENSIVE GOAL
To provide basic guidelines to help you make efficient and enjoyable travel arrangements

SPECIFIC OBJECTIVES
After reading this chapter, you will be able to:

- plan a trip
- make reservations
- develop an itinerary
- understand passenger obligations
- manage travel time efficiently and effectively
- understand protections available to the traveler
- know procedures for settling claims against airlines
- understand terms associated with travel
- plan a travel wardrobe
- pack a suitcase properly

Travel has become an important aspect of today's business world, and you may at some time have to travel for business purposes, as well as for pleasure. Unless you understand the procedures, regulations, and demands associated with travel, however, the experience can become frustrating or even frightening. This chapter will present a few basic principles that should help you handle various aspects of travel with a minimum of inconvenience. Much of the chapter will emphasize air travel—now the most popular means of business travel. But many of the general hints presented are appropriate for proper travel management regardless of means of transportation.

A travel agency provides its services at no cost to you, saves you time, and spares you frustration.

Arrangements

Many large companies employ a specialist to aid in both personal and business travel arrangements for their employees. These people work directly with airlines, hotel chains, and other travel agencies and thus have access to the most up-to-date schedules, rates, and special requirements. If you are fortunate enough to have this service available, many of the headaches associated with arrangements can be avoided. When no travel specialist exists, you will either make arrangements through a travel agency or on your own.

TRAVEL AGENCIES

Travel agencies generally offer their service at no cost to you or your company. Most agencies have access to special unlisted telephone numbers for various airlines and hotels. Many will also hand-deliver tickets and other travel documents to your office.

MAKING YOUR OWN ARRANGEMENTS

Making travel arrangements on your own can be time consuming and sometimes frustrating; however, since you deal directly with the reservations agent, you can often get arrangements that will exactly correspond to your needs.

BE PREPARED

No matter which of the above sources you use, you must be prepared to supply complete and accurate information. Here are some pointers:

- Be precise about when and where you are going. Not all airlines serve all cities. Reservations clerks can help you more accurately when you inform them of your needs.

- State your preferred times of departure and arrival. Try to fit the time of your travel around the purpose of your travel. Keep return needs in mind also.

- Be as specific as possible on the accommodations you prefer. Indicate whether you plan to travel first class or coach, and if you want a nonstop, direct (some stops, but no change of plane), or change-of-plane flight. If a plane change is involved, investigate various routings. Some large airports have more than one terminal, and connections at these airports can entail lengthy delays. Heavy traffic at some airports can delay expected arrival time. Keep these possible delays in mind as you plan your trip.

- If hotels are involved, specify the type of room you prefer.

- If car rentals are necessary, be ready to indicate the type of automobile you require, when and where you will pick up the car, and when and where you will return it.

It is a good idea to have on file the schedule of airlines serving your location. If you travel frequently, you should become familiar with the *Official Airline Guide*, published by Official Airline Guides, Oak Brook, Illinois. This publication lists virtually all regularly scheduled flights in the United States, and contains detailed information on fares, frequency of service, possible routings, names of air carriers, and distances of airports from city centers.

Reservations Are Essential

Reservations, whether for air travel, hotel accommodations, or car rentals, are essential in today's crowded travel world. Airlines are carrying more passengers than at any time in history. Hotels, especially in large cities or popular convention areas, are booked weeks in advance. Car rental agencies usually have a limited number of vehicles available. Attempt to secure all of your reservations four to six weeks in advance.

AIRLINE BOOKINGS

Making advance reservations on airlines can save you or your company money. Often, special discounts are available to passengers who fulfill certain requirements: for example, purchasing tickets in advance and staying away a certain number of days. These special discounts, however, often apply to a limited number of seats. Once these seats are reserved, full fares go into effect. The earlier you reserve space, therefore, the better your chances of qualifying for a discount.

You can purchase your tickets and obtain a boarding pass at the time of check-in.

Airlines serving your area usually list a local telephone number or a toll-free 800 number for reservations. No matter how long the transaction takes, the charge involves only a local call. Reservations clerks are busiest during the working day, from 9 A.M. to 5 P.M. By calling early in the morning or late in the evening, you may avoid long phone delays.

Confirmed Reservations   Be prepared to make alterations in your schedule if a *confirmed reservation* is not available on your preferred flight. A confirmed reservation means that available space has been assigned to you. In most cases you will have to make an advance payment. Phoned reservations can be charged to a major credit card.

Realistically, long-range plans are not always possible. Urgent problems, unscheduled meetings, or unexpected emergencies can come up. On such occasions, it may not be possible to obtain confirmed reservations, and the airlines may offer you *wait list* or *standby* status.

Wait List Status and Standby Status   Under *wait list* status, all available seats are reserved but your name is added to a waiting list according to the date and time you make a request. If a confirmed passenger cancels a reservation before the day of the flight, the airline contacts the people on the list to offer them the canceled space. *Standby* status involves a bit more inconvenience and a bit more risk. Experience shows that every flight has a certain number of "no shows"—people who hold confirmed reservations but who, for some reason, are not able to make the flight. Obviously, the

Special fares may be accompanied by restrictions, so read advertisements carefully.

number of no-shows is not known until the flight is ready for departure. Five or ten minutes before departure, the airline will begin filling any empty seats with people "standing by" at the gate area. Thus a person on standby status must be at the gate before the scheduled departure time. There is no guarantee, however, that any standby passenger will get on his or her preferred flight.

If you are holding a confirmed reservation, it is your obligation to cancel it if your plans change. By doing so, you will make the space available to other people. If you do not cancel and become a no-show, you may have to pay a penalty. In many cases, the complete routing of a no-show is canceled, and you may find yourself without any reservations.

HOTEL RESERVATIONS

Available hotel space often fills up weeks in advance; therefore, it is good to confirm as early as possible. Airline reservations clerks can often secure hotel space for you at the time you make your flight requests. Many hotel chains offer a toll-free 800 number for making reservations if you prefer making your own reservations.

Some large hotels offer a wait-list service similar to that of the airlines, but securing alternate room reservations is usually safer than waiting for a cancellation.

Hotels usually expect you to check in before 6:00 P.M. on the date of your reservation. If your time schedule does not allow for this time requirement, you can guarantee a late arrival through a major credit card or by prepayment of one night's rental. Under the guarantee arrangement, the hotel will hold your room until you

Hazel Hankin

Checking in at a hotel

arrive—even all night long. If you do not claim your *guaranteed reservation* or cancel before 6:00 P.M., however, you will be charged for one night's rental. Avoid this charge by informing the hotel of changes in your plans.

CAR RENTALS

Again, an airline reservations clerk can often obtain car rental reservations for you. You can also make reservations on your own through a local or toll-free 800 reservations number.

If you inform the car rental agency of your expected arrival time, a car will usually be waiting for you when you arrive at your destination. When your plans change, inform the agency so that they can reschedule your reservations and free the car for some other customer.

Trans World Airlines Photo

Processing a ticket

The Itinerary

Once you have made your reservations, you should create an *itinerary* for your trip—a schedule of where you will be while you are away from your home base. It is a good idea to carry one copy with you for quick reference and to leave other copies in your office and at home so that you can be reached in case of emergencies or important messages.

Itineraries should include your airline flight numbers with times of departure and expected arrival, the cities you are visiting, the names of hotels where you are staying, and any phone numbers where you can be reached in case of emergencies or important messages. (See figure 13–1.)

It is often a good idea to keep old itineraries on file. If you make frequent trips to the same cities, you will have an idea of flight times and a record of hotels where you stayed. In some cases these old records can also be used for tax purposes to verify your business travels and expenses.

Tickets

Whenever possible, obtain your airline tickets prior to actual flight time. If you make your reservations far enough ahead of time, the airline will mail tickets to your home or business address. Most travel agencies have facilities for issuing tickets on their premises. In this way, you can avoid possible long waits at air terminal ticket counters.

Your ticket is a valuable document and should be protected from loss. It is a good idea to write your ticket numbers on a piece of paper that you keep separate from your luggage and tickets. If your tickets are misplaced, the airlines will want the numbers of the tickets to begin processing refunds. In most cases you will be required to purchase another ticket for the flight or portions of the flight misplaced.

Adjustments or refunds can take up to four months to process. If some other person uses the ticket you have lost, you may not get a refund. Airlines simply do not have the personnel or the facilities for checking the identity of each person using a prepaid ticket.

The Day of the Flight

Even small air terminals are now experiencing crowded conditions. Final check-in procedures can therefore be lengthy, so plan to arrive at the air terminal about an hour before flight time—earlier if you

NAME: Marie Sanchez

DATES: February 1 - 11, 1983

DATE	TRAVEL ARRANGEMENTS	BUSINESS	HOTEL	PHONE
Sun, 2/1	Republic Airlines #670 to WDC; lv 8:40am, arr 11:52am		Capitol Hilton, WDC	(211)555-1600
Mon, 2/2		Regional convention	Capitol Hilton	(211)555-1600
Tues, 2/3	American Airlines #563 WDC to Oklahoma City, lv 7:00am, arr 10:30am CST	Visit Okla City plant	Hilton Inn West, Oklahoma City	(405)555-7681
Wed, 2/4		Meeting with plant manager and staff	Hilton Inn West	(405)555-7681
Thurs, 2/5	AA #293/579 to Tucson, lv 3:30pm, arr 6:58pm	Meeting with Oklahoma salesman	Plaza, Tucson	(602)555-3741
Fri, 2/6		Call on Tucson customers	Plaza	(602)555-3741
Sat, 2/7	via rental car to Phoenix	Visit friends		(602)555-5081
Sun, 2/8	Western Airlines #723 to San Diego, lv 7pm, arr 6:58pm PST		Holiday Inn, San Diego	(714)555-5041
Mon, 2/9		San Diego office	Holiday Inn	(714)555-5041
Tues, 2/10		San Diego office	Holiday Inn	(714)555-5041
Wed, 2/11	RA #408, lv 3:10pm, arr MN/StP 9:25pm			

Figure 13–1
This is an itinerary for a business trip taken by an executive whose home office is in Minneapolis and who visits a regional meeting, branch offices, customers, and friends in various parts of the country. Itinerary forms vary, and the one shown here is only one of many possible versions.

When checking your luggage, be sure that the attendant tags each piece correctly and presents you with the proper claim stubs.

must purchase your ticket at the terminal. This cushion of time will allow for checking of baggage, passing through the security check, finding your departure gate, and selecting your seat. Remember that you *must* be at the departure gate at least ten minutes before departure time or your reservation is subject to cancellation.

LUGGAGE

If you have only carry-on luggage, you will usually proceed directly to the assigned departure gate. If you have baggage to be checked, however, there may be some delay. Larger airports have curbside check-in facilities that save you from having to carry your luggage into the terminal. In order to use this service, you have to present a valid ticket with confirmed reservation. Current airline regulations require that your name be visible on the outside of *each* piece of checked luggage.

Most airlines allow you to check up to three pieces of luggage at no charge. Pieces beyond that number are subject to an excess baggage charge. One or two pieces of carry-on luggage are usually allowed, provided that the pieces fit completely under the seat or can be stored in the limited closet space on board.

Claim Stubs   When checking your luggage, be sure that the attendant tags each piece correctly and presents you with the proper

Check-in counters at a large air terminal

claim stubs. Correct tagging simply means that the luggage is scheduled to be loaded on the correct flight number and scheduled to be unloaded at the correct destination. Retain the claim stubs until you claim your luggage at your destination. In many cities, security personnel will check your stub against the tag on your luggage. Without this stub, they may not allow you to remove your luggage from the baggage area. This practice is sometimes an inconvenience, but it is good protection against misidentified luggage or thievery. If your luggage gets lost or misdirected during your travels, you will be requested to surrender your claim check to aid the airline in recovering your property.

On a nonstop flight between two points, lost or misdirected luggage is seldom a problem. However, if a change of planes or airlines is required to complete your trip, the chance for temporary delay of your luggage increases.

There are three types of luggage tags commonly in use. The simple one-flight and final destination tag is used for nonstop and direct flights. The *online transfer* is used for change of plane flights while remaining on the same airline. The *interline transfer* is used for change of plane and change of airline. The latter two tags are illustrated in figure 13–2.

Spend a few extra seconds at the check-in counter to be sure that the attendant places the right tags on your luggage. He or she should complete this operation before handling another customer.

BOARDING

The attendant who checks in your luggage will also direct you to the concourse and gate number scheduled for your flight. Some airlines will also assign seats during check-in. Others will require you to proceed to the departure gate for seat selection. Not all flights have assigned seats: *Open seating* allows you to take any available seat once you board the plane.

By federal law, all airplanes must now identify smoking and nonsmoking sections. Usually passengers are accommodated according to their desires, but limited seating could put you in an area other than your choice. If you prefer the smoking section but are assigned to the nonsmoking section, you are absolutely forbidden to smoke. If you prefer the nonsmoking section and are assigned a seat in the smoking section, you have the right to request that there be no smoking in your area—federal legislation demands that all nonsmokers be accommodated. Arriving early will help insure that you obtain your preferred seating.

On your way to the boarding gate, you will be required to pass through a *security check*. All of your carry-on luggage, including handbags, must pass through an X-ray detection device. Each passenger must pass through a metal-detection passageway. These requirements are imposed for your safety and security. Several years

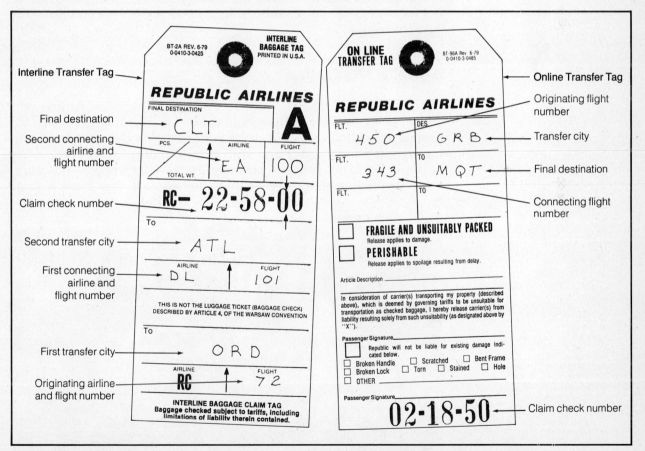

Figure 13–2
Airline Luggage Tags

A boarding pass

ago, there was a rash of "skyjackings" that caused potential danger and much inconvenience to passengers. In order to minimize the possibility of people carrying concealed weapons or other devices that could be used to intimidate passengers or crew, the federal government has imposed strict security checks.

Cooperate with the security personnel. Most important, don't jokingly suggest that you are in possession of a restricted item—you may be arrested or detained. To airport security personnel, there are no jokes, only potential hazards.

Plane Changes   When planning your trip, it is always best to schedule nonstop or *direct* flights. Restricted routings, unavailable space, or a variety of other reasons, however, may force you to accept a change of plane or a change of airline. These sometimes present complications, but most often go quite smoothly.

When making a connection, you must check in with the *connecting flight* just as you did with your originating flight. You will not be bothered with baggage check-in, however, and many times you will not have to go through another security check unless you leave the gate concourse.

Arrival at Destination

On arrival, you will first want to claim your luggage. Airline personnel or signs posted throughout the terminal will direct you to the proper unloading area. Check for your name on the outside of your luggage or match your claim stub with the number attached to the luggage. To make baggage claiming easier, some people put oversized distinctive markings on their luggage. If you have a large

A flight attendant will help you store carry-on luggage.

amount of luggage or heavy pieces to carry, porter service is almost always available.

GROUND TRANSPORTATION

Unless you have someone meeting you at your destination, you must find a means of transportation to your hotel or to your home. There are many services available, each offering different conveniences and costs.

Hotel Service   Many hotels, especially those located near an airport, provide a courtesy pickup and return service. Usually there is a bank of telephones near the baggage area with direct lines to hotels. Use the phone to request a pickup.

Airport Limousines   Most airports in large cities offer some sort of limousine or bus service to major hotels and to central locations throughout the city. Usually the limousine will load just outside the baggage claim area on a regular schedule. You may have a slight wait, but the fare is generally very reasonable. In some cases, you will have to hire a taxi to get from a downtown terminal to your hotel, thus adding a slight cost. These limousine services often offer return trips to the airport from either your hotel or a central terminal.

Taxis   Taxi service is usually abundant at all air terminals. It is convenient: The driver will take you to almost any location you require. It is also expensive. In many situations—for example, when time is a factor or a remote location is involved—the speed and convenience of a taxi far outweighs the cost factor.

Rental Cars   Rental cars provide you with the greatest mobility and freedom. When your final destination is miles away from the airport or when you require quick and frequent transportation around the area, a rental car may be the proper choice. The large car-rental companies have counters in every airport. Your firm may have a corporate account with one or more car rental companies, providing substantial discounts from the posted rates. It is a good idea to shop around, however, for rental rates vary greatly. Remember that you must present a valid driver's license and an acceptable credit card in order to rent a car. If you do not have an acceptable credit card, you will be expected to put down a large cash deposit to guarantee return of the car. Picking up a car involves much paperwork: The agency needs your car preference, home address, driver's license number, and billing reference. If you use rental cars frequently, it is a good idea to get this vital information into the agencies' permanent files.

Air Travel Problems

Air travel can be fun and convenient, but there are times when it can be frustrating. A federal agency, the *Civil Aeronautics Board* (CAB), has established basic rules to protect passengers, and each airline sets its own policies within the CAB guidelines. Knowledge of these basic rules and regulations can help you handle unfortunate situations in an informed and assertive manner. Possible problems and their resolutions include, but are not limited to, those listed below.

DELAYED OR CANCELED FLIGHTS

A variety of factors can cause delay or cancellation of flights. Airlines do not guarantee their time schedules. In cases of bad weather or equipment failure, a delay could be lengthy. If the delay is known far enough in advance, the airline will try to contact you. (This is why you are always asked for your local telephone number when you make an airplane reservation.)

If you are already at the airport, and the delay is likely to last over four hours, the airline will first attempt to make alternate flight arrangements for you on another carrier at no extra cost. If this cannot be arranged, most airlines will pay for a telephone call so you can inform people of your delay. They may also pay for a hotel room if you are stranded away from home overnight, pay transportation costs between the airport and the hotel, and provide funds for buying a meal either at the airport or the hotel.

Since delays and cancellations are often beyond the control of an airline, these services are mainly goodwill gestures and not required by law. Moreover, policies will differ from one airline to another in such situations.

OVERBOOKING AND "BUMPING"

In order to insure against no-shows, many airlines practice *overbooking*—the airline sells a few more confirmed reservations than there are seats on the plane.

Usually overbooking causes no problems, but on occasion all of the confirmed passengers show up for a flight. Obviously, there are not enough seats for everybody, and certain passengers then will be "bumped" from the flight. In such cases, the airline must follow procedures dictated by the CAB.

The gate attendant will seek out volunteers to give up their seats for compensation. There is no set amount of compensation for *voluntary bumping*, but it usually is equal to or greater than the price of the volunteer's ticket. The volunteer is allowed to keep the original ticket and the airline will help confirm another flight on which the original ticket may be used. Often, the overbooked airline will

Most airports offer limousine service to and from hotels.

also supply a meal voucher and even hotel and transportation expenses if the delay will be lengthy.

The rules are more stringent when *involuntary bumping* is involved. If there are no volunteers, the airline will decide who will be involuntarily bumped—in other words, which confirmed passenger will not be able to fly on their scheduled flight, but must wait until space can be found for them on a later flight.

An immediate cash payment equal to the price of the ticket is paid to each person denied boarding privileges. If alternate arrangements cannot be made that would ensure the passenger's arrival at the original destination within two hours of the originally scheduled time, the denied-boarding compensation is doubled. Again, you retain your original ticket and may use it on another flight. Extended delays may also entitle you to meal and/or hotel compensations.

DAMAGED, DELAYED, OR LOST BAGGAGE

Airlines move millions of pieces of baggage. Occasionally some luggage gets misdirected, lost, or damaged. Again, you have certain legal rights.

One of the statements included with your ticket informs you that the airline will insure your luggage and its contents to a certain limit for no extra charge. If your luggage and contents have a greater value than this, you should purchase "excess valuation" from the airline when you check your baggage. The cost is minimal. If your baggage is lost, then you can collect reimbursement up to the excess valuation you have declared.

Damaged Luggage Luggage damaged because of mishandling by the airline will be repaired, replaced, or paid for at a depreciated value. The same goes for any of the contents in the damaged luggage. The amount to be reimbursed is negotiated between you and the airlines. Small dents, scuffs, or scratches are usually not considered damage.

Delayed Luggage Delayed luggage can cause anxious moments, but the recovery rate is very high; usually baggage is located within a few hours.

You will be expected to fill out forms to help the airline trace your luggage. An airline representative will help you with the form. Generally, the airlines will absorb reasonable expenses you incur while they search for your luggage. In most cases, however, you must have prior authorization from the airline before making purchases against a claim. The liability limit also applies to delayed or lost baggage.

Lost Luggage If your luggage is indeed lost, you must continue to pursue your claim. The form you originally filled out is the basis for your claim. Processing this claim can take many weeks, so be sure to continue negotiations with the airline for reimbursement for immediate necessities.

Courtesy German Federal Railroad

Carting baggage in a railroad station

One final word: All claims for damaged, delayed, or lost luggage should be made before you leave the airport.

YOUR RIGHTS AND OBLIGATIONS

To become more fully aware of your rights and obligations when flying, obtain a copy of *Fly-Rights*, which is issued free of charge by the Civil Aeronautics Board. It is also a good idea to ask airline personnel whenever you feel the need for clarification. As a general rule, they will answer your questions quickly, fairly, and accurately.

Trains and Buses

Most areas of the United States can be reached by air. However, business trips sometimes take you to out-of-the-way places that do not have scheduled air service. In these instances, you may have to rely on train or bus service. Sometimes, also, the crowds at airports, the distance of airports from cities, and the advance-time requirements of airlines make train or bus travel a less expensive and more convenient choice. Moreover, if you are not pressed for time or are traveling for pleasure, you may prefer a more leisurely pace and a chance to enjoy the scenery.

TRAINS

Presently the U.S. government is attempting to revitalize passenger service on railroads through the National Rail Passenger Corporation *(Amtrak)*. Unfortunately, not all of the efforts have been equally successful. Along the East Coast from Washington to Boston, train traffic is frequent and usually reliable. Train stations are often located close to or within downtown areas, and if the places you intend to visit are located there, you will have little additional need for local transportation. Most trains do not require advance reservations, though some do, especially for long trips. What you trade off in speed of travel may be compensated for in lower costs, convenience of last-minute ticket purchases, and central locations of train stations.

BUSES

Bus travel is also an option not to be overlooked. Large, comfortable buses crisscross the United States and stop at many small towns not served by either train or air service. In addition, bus service tends to be frequent. Certain bus services are designated express, and the speed of their travel is often equal to that of train service. Finally, bus travel tends to be the least expensive of the

Many companies arrange for an employee's expenses to be paid by credit card.

options available to you. If your travels involve shorter, spur-of-the-moment trips to remote places, you should investigate bus services.

Funds for Travel

Whether for business or pleasure, travel entails numerous expenses. The cost of transportation, taxi fares, hotel expenses, and dining expenses can all easily add up to over $100 a day! You must plan and be prepared for these costs.

DIRECT BILLING

Businesses have various arrangements for supplying their employees with adequate funds to cover travel expenses. Many companies supply their employees with *direct bill credit cards*. This simply means that the employee is issued a credit card in the company's name and any charges made by the authorized employee will be billed directly to the company with no cash outlay required from the employee.

CASH ADVANCES

Other businesses will advance cash from special travel accounts so that employees will have money readily available for legitimate expenses. Still other companies will require an employee to pay expenses as they occur and submit vouchers for reimbursement.

Whatever method your company may use, you will be responsible for paying bills and must be prepared.

CREDIT CARDS

One of the simplest and most universally accepted methods of payment is the credit card. In fact, credit cards are usually more readily accepted than personal checks. Using a nationally recognized credit card also relieves you of the need to carry large amounts of cash. If you travel frequently, you will want to acquire one or more of the major credit cards.

TRAVELER'S CHECKS AND CASH

When cash is necessary, it is often a good idea to carry *traveler's checks*. The cost of purchasing these checks is minimal, and the protection they give you is worth the cost. Since the holder has already paid cash for the check, the recipient is also guaranteed immediate payment. If your traveler's checks are lost or stolen, you can be virtually assured of quick replacement of the funds. Remember to keep the serial numbers of traveler's checks in a safe place so that reimbursement can be expedited.

You should also have available a moderate amount of cash, since there are some establishments and services that do not accept either credit cards or traveler's checks. To avoid uncomfortable situations, you should have enough cash to cover these bills.

For security, make sure that your hotel door is locked at all times.

Travel Security

Protection of yourself and your valuables is always a serious consideration. When alone in a hotel room, do not open the door for anyone unless you are certain it is safe. Even a person claiming to be from room service or a maid may not be legitimate. If you are in doubt, ask for identification. In some states, the law specifies that each hotel door must have a peephole so that the occupant can see the caller. Some travelers prefer staying in hotels with a 24-hour desk attendant. This permits calling the desk if trouble should arise.

If you must carry valuable items when you travel, use the hotel safe-deposit facilities. This service is usually free. You should avoid leaving valuables of any kind, including airline tickets, in your room. Anything of exceptional value and not needed on your trip should be left at home.

Most homeowners' or property insurance will cover any losses you sustain while away from home. If your property is not covered, you may wish to purchase special insurance that covers the period of your travels.

The Travel Wardrobe

There is no need to bring your entire wardrobe with you on a business trip. If you have ever lugged a heavy suitcase around for a day, you already know the value of a limited travel wardrobe—a few good basic articles and several accessories.

Here is a variety of useful, lightweight business luggage, ranging from carry-on to weekender to garment bag.

SELECTING TRAVEL CLOTHES

When selecting clothes for travel, choose dark colors that do not show soil. Wrinkle-free polyesters and polyester blends are a blessing for travelers. For travel days, wear casual loose-fitting dark clothes and comfortable walking shoes.

Below are some ideas for a travel wardrobe for a five-day business trip, with actual travel on the first and fifth days.

WOMAN'S WARDROBE	MAN'S WARDROBE
1 suit	2 suits
1 blazer	1 sport jacket
1 coordinated skirt or pants	1 coordinated trousers
3 blouses	4 shirts
1 sweater	4 ties
1 dress	1 casual outfit for travel
scarves	1 pr. dark shoes
1 casual outfit for travel	
1 pr. dark pumps	

Both wardrobes should include some type of all-weather coat. Even warm climates have cold spells.

EXTRAS

In addition to clothing, remember to take along such vital but often forgotten items as aspirin, adhesive bandages, alarm clock, safety pins, medication, razor, needle and thread, and small scissors. Folding umbrella, travel iron, lint remover, laundry soap are all nice extras. Your grooming aids, of course, must be packed. Frequent travelers often keep a second set of grooming aids packed in a travel kit. This extra set lessens the chance of forgetting something when in a hurry.

PACKING TIPS

Many travelers use only two bags so that they are not dependent on porters. Really efficient travelers pack all their clothing into a garment bag and one piece of under-the-seat luggage, which they can carry aboard the plane. The garment bag can be hung in the aisle closet, and the carry-on piece will slide under the seat, making it possible to avoid baggage claim lines altogether.

If you must take additional baggage, pack carefully, so that your clothing will arrive at your destination unwrinkled and ready to wear.

Samsonite has developed a packing method called *interfolding*, which is illustrated in these pages. Following are additional, basic guidelines to help you pack like an expert traveler.

- Put heavy items on the bottom of soft bags, or next to the hinge in hard-shelled suitcases.

- Place shoes in plastic bags, shoe bags, or old socks to prevent polish from rubbing off on other items.

- Put all breakables or spillables in a separate piece of luggage or in a sealed, heavy duty plastic bag so that minimal damage will occur if something accidentally breaks or spills.

- For women's suits, lay buttoned suit jacket in suitcase; bring sleeves slightly across front, place folded skirt on top of jacket; then fold other half of jacket over top of skirt.

- For men's suits, put trousers in first with legs extending beyond side of suitcase. Place unbuttoned jacket on top with sleeves across front. Fold trouser legs over jacket, then rest of jacket over top of trousers.

- If you prefer to pack shirts or blouses on top of each other, alternate the collars.

- Unless you are interfolding, place each folded garment in a plastic bag to further prevent wrinkling.

- Tightly roll soft items such as socks, hose, and underwear when you place them at the folds of your garments. This will prevent lines where the clothes are folded.

- The tighter the clothes are packed, the less chance for wrinkling. Most suitcases have interior ribbon or leather straps to hold clothing in place.

Making reservations, catching planes or trains, changing time zones, remembering details, and walking into rooms full of total strangers can make travel a strain. But travel can be an opportunity to meet new and potentially valuable clients for your company.

Laying clothing in from alternating sides is the first step of the *interfolding* method of packing for travel.

Place shirts and light sweaters with collars toward the hinge, cushioning folds with rolled undergarments.

Fold sleeves of blouses and jackets back along the natural seams.

Starting with top garment, fold into the case, smoothing wrinkles as you go.

KEY TERMS

confirmed reservation
wait list status
standby status
guaranteed
   reservation
itinerary
online transfer
interline transfer

open seating
security check
direct flight
connecting flight
Civil Aeronautics
   Board (CAB)
overbooking

voluntary bumping
involuntary bumping
Amtrak
direct-bill credit
   cards
traveler's checks

TEST YOURSELF:
QUESTIONS FOR REVIEW AND DISCUSSION

1. Name some advantages and disadvantages of using a travel agency.
2. Explain the difference between wait list status and standby status.
3. What is the purpose of an itinerary?
4. What security precautions, other than the ones mentioned in the text, should be taken by you personally while traveling?
5. What is the purpose of the airport security check?
6. What are the advantages of credit cards? Of traveler's checks?
7. Can you list additional items, not mentioned in the chapter, that should be packed in either the suitcase or attaché case?
8. Based on your travel experience, what advice can you give others?
9. If you are involuntarily bumped, what are your rights?

APPLICATION EXERCISE

Plan an imaginary business trip. Determine a destination city in which you would conduct your business appointment. Then call a travel agency to find out the costs for a round-trip ticket and the suggested times for your departure and arrival. Check with one of the major hotel chains and find out the cost of the accommodations and the various types of accommodations.

Suggested Readings

Fly-Rights: A Guide to Air Travel in the U.S. Washington, D.C.: Civil Aeronautics Board.

Kaye, Dena. *The Traveling Woman.* New York: Bantam, 1981.

Lerner, Elaine, and C. B. Abbott. *The Way to Go: A Woman's Guide to Careers in Travel.* New York: Warner Books, 1982.

Pletcher, Barbara. *A Travel Sense: A Guide for Business & Professional Women.* California: Harbor Publications, 1980.

Travel Unraveled. Minneapolis, Minn.: Republic Airlines.

Woolridge, Susanna. *Travelling Alone: A Practical Guide for Business Women:* New York: Simon & Schuster, 1979.

14

MANAGING YOUR MONEY

COMPREHENSIVE GOAL

To assist you in making the best use of your earnings and in managing your business expenses.

SPECIFIC OBJECTIVES

After reading this chapter, you will be able to:

- make responsible use of an expense account

- prepare an income and expenditures budget

- select the types of insurance coverage you most need

- explain the risks and rewards of using credit

- describe how taxes affect financial planning

- plan an investment strategy

- discuss the tax implications and features of Individual Retirement Accounts

When you accept your first job, you assume a responsibility not only for your own performance on the job, but also for the management of the money you earn. Moreover, it is very likely that at some point you will be asked to be responsible for your company's expenditures. This chapter will offer suggestions to help you manage money successfully both on the job and off.

Expense Accounts

More and more today, employees at all levels are involved in travel, entertainment, and other company activities for which they must be reimbursed. Although guidelines have been established by the Internal Revenue Service for the reporting and reimbursing of business-related expenses, the management of these expenditures is usually left up to you. Part of your job performance evaluation may be based on how well you control your expenses and how accurately you report those expenses.

EXPENSE DIARY

An *expense diary* is a daily record of the dates, places, purposes, and amounts of legitimate business expenses. It may be a simple sheet of paper or an elaborate, detailed expense book. Expenses may be reported daily, weekly, monthly, or yearly, depending on company practice. Since most business expenses are deductible from corporate taxes, the IRS will ask for proof of the amounts being deducted. The expense diary and your receipts serve as this proof.

There are many different forms of expense diaries: Examples of various kinds are shown below. Note that it is necessary to record

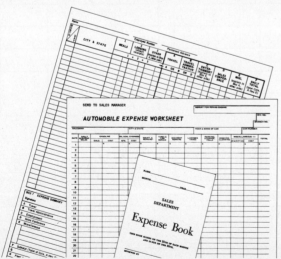

You may have occasion to keep a record of expenses during your business career.

EXPENSE REPORT
MISCELLANEOUS

Name Lynn Fisher	Employee No. 555000	Department	Period From 10/31 To 11/1

Purpose of Trip Sales Travel

Date	City of Expense	(1) Own Meals	(2) Lodging	(3) Air/RR/ Bus Fare	(4) Local Fares	(5) Other Explain	(6) Daily Total
10/31	N.Y. – Manchester, N.H.	$24.00	$50.00	$47.50	$21.50		$32.25
11/1	Manchester, N.H. – N.Y.	$ 8.75		$47.50	$25.50	$38.00	$51.30
	Column Total	$32.75	$50.00	$96.00	$47.00	$38.00	$83.55

(5) DETAIL OTHER EXPENSES

Date	Explanation	Amount	Date	Explanation	Amount
11/1	Lunch with clients	$ 38 00			

Expense Summary			Office Use Only	Record of Advance		
(A) Travel	143	00		Date	Office	Amount
(B) Entertainment	—	—				
(C) Other						
Own meals	32	75				
Lunch with clients	38	00				
Hotel	50	00			Total	
(D) Total	263	75				
(E) Less Advances	100	00	Proofed	Lynn Fisher		
				Signature		
(F) Amount Due You	163	75	Recorded	S. Rethod	1/23	
(G) Amount Due Company				Approved by	Date	

Figure 14–1
An Expense Report

the date of the expenditure, where you were when the expenditure occurred, and the amount and category of the expenditure. Some expenditures require verified receipts. To reduce the possibility of not having a required receipt, try to get receipts for *all* of your cash outlays. Your expense diary should be updated on a daily basis so that you won't overlook any expenses.

METHODS OF REIMBURSEMENT

Companies vary in their methods of providing employees with expense money, as well as in the amount of expense money that is reimbursed. Some of the more common policies are described here.

You should get reimbursed for a business expense.

Advance   A company advances the employee an amount of money, in the form of cash or check, based on the employee's or the company's estimate of expenses. The employee pays his or her expenses and submits a report. If the estimate was too high, the employee returns the excess. If the estimate was too low, the company reimburses the employee for the extra expenses.

Corporate Credit Cards   Many companies issue travel credit cards to their employees. These credit cards represent corporate accounts. Whenever an expenditure is made with a corporate card, the bill is sent directly to the company for payment. This procedure saves a lot of paperwork for the company, since it can pay all bills on a periodic basis and frees the employee from the necessity of writing many individual checks. If you use a corporate credit card, you must submit all receipts for verification. Of course, you may use the cards only for business-related expenses.

Credit Letters   This procedure is a cross between the advance and the corporate credit card. Employees are issued a *letter of credit* with a pre-established limit. The amount of money advanced is guaranteed by a bank or credit card company. When an employee needs cash, the letter is presented to an authorized agent who advances cash and records the transaction on the letter.

Cash Reimbursement   In many businesses the employee must spend money out of pocket and then submit receipts for his or her expenses. After the expenses have been reviewed, the employee is reimbursed for money advanced to the company. This procedure obviously places a financial burden upon the employee; therefore, it is most often used only for small incidental expenses.

Per Diem   Many companies establish a fixed daily rate for reimbursable expenses. This *per diem* rate usually sets an upper limit per day for such major expense categories as food, lodging, and entertainment. Any costs above this limit must be absorbed by the employee. If expenses do not reach the per diem limit, however, the employee reports the actual expenses, not the maximum limit.

Whatever plan your employer uses, it is important that you understand the company policy and follow it to the letter. Don't jeopardize your career by attempting to hedge on company-paid expenses. Most companies have a firm idea of what constitutes necessary expenses, and you may find yourself in an embarrassing situation if your expenses are above the average.

CAR EXPENSES

Most companies provide reimbursement for the expenses of using an automobile for business purposes. In some cases, the company provides employees with a company-owned or -leased car. When the car is used for business, all costs associated with operating it are reimbursed. When this company car is used for personal reasons, the employee usually pays the company a fixed rate per mile for the privilege. The car remains the property of the company, which may establish restrictions on its use.

Many companies also reimburse employees who use their personal cars on company business. Under this arrangement, you keep track of all business-related mileage and report this with your regular expense account. You are then paid a certain rate for each mile associated with business. Whichever method your company may use, it is important to record your automobile expenses daily and accurately.

Courtesy of San Diego Gas & Electric

If you drive a company car, record your automobile expenses daily and accurately.

Personal Money Management

Proper management of your employer's money is an important aspect of on-the-job responsibilities. As important to your professional growth, however, is wise management of your wages. The remainder of this chapter will deal with suggestions about living within your earnings and planning for the future as your financial rewards and your personal responsibilities grow.

Budgeting

A budget is a planning tool—assisting you to make the best decisions regarding the spending of your available funds. Few among us have all the money we need. It's important, therefore, to establish spending priorities.

GROSS VS. NET INCOME

The total amount you have available for budgeting is your *net income*—the actual amount of your paycheck. This will be less than the *gross income* offered when you were interviewed for the job, because certain deductions are made from your salary before you are paid. On your check stub you may expect to find the following deductions itemized: income tax (federal, usually state, and sometimes local), Social Security, pension contributions, and group insurance (life and/or death). Depending upon your place of employment, you may find such additional voluntary "automatic withdrawals" as charitable contributions and savings plans (credit union, U.S. government savings bonds, or stock purchases).

SAVINGS

Earlier chapters have emphasized the importance of goal setting to professional success. Before considering how you want to spend your paycheck, you should review your savings goals. Following is a list of possible savings goals. Take a few moments to consider how you would rank them.

- down payment on a home

- annual vacation expenses

- flexibility in an emergency

- anticipation of a major purchase

- protection against long-term needs, such as education, medical expenses, and retirement

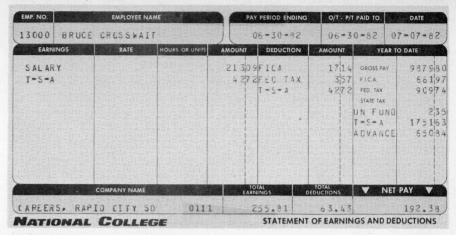

EMP. NO.	EMPLOYEE NAME			PAY PERIOD ENDING	O/T - P/T PAID TO	DATE
13000	BRUCE CROSSWAIT			06-30-82	06-30-82	07-07-82

EARNINGS	RATE	HOURS OR UNITS	AMOUNT	DEDUCTION	AMOUNT	YEAR TO DATE	
SALARY			213.09	FICA	17.14	GROSS PAY	9879.80
T-S-A			42.72	FED TAX	3.57	F.I.C.A.	661.97
				T-S-A	42.72	FED. TAX	909.74
						STATE TAX	
						UN FUND	2.35
						T-S-A	1751.63
						ADVANCE	650.84

COMPANY NAME		TOTAL EARNINGS	TOTAL DEDUCTIONS	▼ NET PAY ▼
CAREERS, RAPID CITY SD 0111		255.81	63.43	192.38

NATIONAL COLLEGE   STATEMENT OF EARNINGS AND DEDUCTIONS

Here are some typical payroll deductions itemized.

As you progress in your career, acquiring material possessions and perhaps family responsibilities, these priorities will no doubt change. If you think you won't be able to save money without help, you may want to commit yourself to a systematic forced savings plan. It may be payroll savings, automatic transfer from checking to savings accounts, or automatic withdrawals from checking to purchase life insurance or mutual funds.

PREPARING A BUDGET

When you draw up a budget, it is a good idea to start by keeping a record of everything you spend over a period of two or three months. Include even your small cash outlays for items such as cosmetics, candy, and newspapers. Then look over your expenditures. You will see that some of them are *fixed expenditures:* They are the same from month to month, or they occur bimonthly, quarterly, or yearly. Other expenditures will vary from one period to another: These are flexible or *discretionary expenditures.* You have control over them.

Your fixed expenditures will include rent (for homeowners, taxes and mortgage payments), insurance, and regular payments on loans. Utility payments should also be considered fixed expenditures, even though their amounts may vary somewhat. Flexible expenditures will include food (at home and out); household expenses (repairs and maintenance, cleaning supplies, furniture and appliance purchases); car repairs, gas and oil; medical and dental expenses over and above health insurance; recreation (vacations and leisure activities); clothing; and personal expenses (grooming, medications, and newspapers).

Add up your fixed expenditures for each month. Keep in mind that fixed expenses that occur less frequently than monthly, such as automobile insurance, must be estimated on a monthly basis so that you can put aside money to pay for them. Subtract your fixed expenditures from your monthly income. What is left is what you will have for your flexible or discretionary expenditures.

Now, on the basis of your spending record, estimate how much you can spend on each flexible category each month. Some categories could be large one month and negligible another. However, even though you take a vacation in July and do Christmas shopping in December, if you don't budget for these expenses throughout the year, you won't have the money when you need it.

Remember, a budget is a planning device. As such, it needn't be thought of as unchangeable. But keep in mind that if you increase your spending in one category, you must make adjustments in one or more other categories.

You will have to review your budget from time to time. For example, suppose at the end of March you find that your expenses have exceeded your income by 10 percent. You must take steps during the remaining months of the year to compensate for this overspending.

A monthly budget for a single working person whose net monthly income is $1,200 might look something like that shown in figure 14–2.

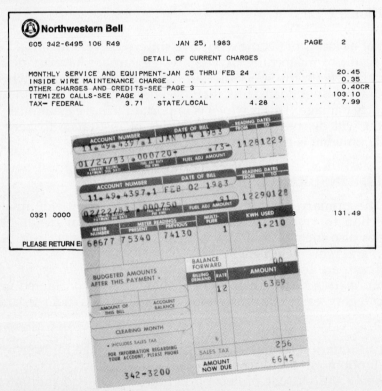

These are samples of bills for fixed expenditures.

Net Income = $1200.00

Fixed Expenditures		Discretionary Expenditures	
rent	$350.00	food	$160.00
gas	30.00	gas, oil, car repairs	80.00
electricity	40.00	clothes	70.00
phone	25.00	recreation	70.00
car loan	13.00	personal	25.00
car insurance	32.00	medical/dental	40.00
life insurance	10.00	contributions	10.00
	$622.00		$455.00

Total Expenditures = $1077.00
Savings for month = 123.00

Figure 14–2
A One-Month Budget

Insurance

Most of us know of people who have suffered severe financial losses as a result of misfortune. Average wage earners have no place in their budgets for the shock of a sudden and large expense, whether it be the result of death, fire, theft, sickness, disability, or accidental property damage. This is why it is important to have insurance. This section will discuss the four categories of insurance to help you decide on what is best for you.

LIFE INSURANCE

The primary purpose of life insurance is to provide financial protection to your beneficiary in the event of your death. Some policies also include disability benefits, savings plans, loan provisions, and retirement benefits.

There are four types of life insurance: *term, endowment, whole life,* and *universal.* Although the last three can be considered under one category, cash value insurance, we will discuss them separately here.

Term Insurance Term insurance provides coverage for only a specific amount of time. The *premium*—the cost to you—is raised whenever the current protection period expires and the policy is renewed. A *beneficiary* (the person named to receive the benefits) is designated to receive the *face amount* (the amount for which the policy is insured) upon the death of the insured. Often there is a maximum age after which the policy can no longer be renewed.

The lowest-cost term insurance is sold only to groups. If you have the opportunity to participate in a *group life* plan, don't pass it up. Sometimes this insurance is available through your employer, your union, or even savings banks.

Endowment Insurance   An endowment insurance plan is a kind of savings plan. It is more expensive than either term insurance or whole life insurance, because you pay premiums for a short time and you are eligible to receive the face amount after a shorter period. This may be ten years, twenty years, thirty years, or at age 65. You pay premiums for the time indicated. When the plan expires, the face amount is payable in cash. If you die before the plan expires, the policy pays the face amount.

Whole Life Or Straight Life Insurance   Whole life policies cost a fixed premium over your lifetime, and accumulate cash value against which you can borrow. You pay proportionately more for coverage, compared with term insurance, during your early years, and proportionately less during your later years. It is not likely that premiums would ever exceed the death benefit.

Universal Life Insurance   In response to the high interest rates of the 1970s and 1980s, the insurance industry has offered an alternative to whole life insurance. This insurance, universal life, combines the concepts of term life with an *annuity*—the amount payable yearly. The term insurance feature provides protection in the event of the death of the insured. The annuity feature provides more flexibility of earnings from the investment of the premium. Typically, the interest rate earned on the annuity is related to prevailing short-term interest rates. In addition, as long as the term insurance premium is maintained, there is no interest charged should the policyholder need to borrow on the policy. The same is not true of whole life.

When interest rates are above 10 percent, the universal insurance concept would seem to be a worthwhile alternative to whole life. This is because the annuity portion of the policy would tend to accumulate significant savings. Should interest rates fall below 10 percent, the features of whole life insurance which provide guaranteed cash values would take on greater importance.

HEALTH INSURANCE

You are going to need medical attention regularly throughout your life. But medical costs can sometimes be too much for anyone's

An insurance advertisement

Health Insurance Plan of Greater New York

This is a health insurance option.

income to absorb. Health insurance levels out those costs so that you can budget for them regularly, rather than find yourself confronted with a sudden overwhelming expense.

Most companies offer medical insurance plans to their employees; the cost of this insurance is paid for in part, and sometimes in full, by the company.

Individual health insurance plans are more expensive than group insurance plans. Therefore, if your employer offers a group plan, sign up. Read the policy when it is sent to you—no health insurance covers every risk. Your policy will probably include a basic plan and a major medical plan. Basic health insurance pays all or part of hospital, surgical, and medical costs up to a certain specified limit. After that, major medical insurance takes over up to a higher specified limit.

Many health insurance plans offer *deductible* and *coinsurance* provisions. The deductible provision of an insurance plan is the amount you have to pay in the event of a claim before the insurance company incurs any liability. The higher the deductible, the lower the premium.

The coinsurance provision splits the liability for a claim between you and the insurance company. If you assume a percentage of the cost of all future claims, the insurance company will reduce your premium. Typical plans are 80/20, 75/25, and 70/30.

For example, Bill Cain has a $500 deductible, 80/20 major medical plan. He undergoes physical and drug therapy for leg and back injuries. The total cost is $3,639. Bill pays $500, plus 20 percent of the remainder, or $627.80. His total payments are $1,127.80. The insurance company pays the balance of $2,511.20.

The federal government has also entered the health protection field through Medicare and Medicaid. You can inquire at your Social Security Administration office to determine whether you qualify for special assistance.

AUTO INSURANCE

In 1981, motor vehicle accidents accounted for 50,800 deaths, 1.9 million disabling injuries, and $40.6 billion in direct costs.[1] Fortunately, most of these costs were covered by insurance.

In practically all states, it is a legal requirement that all auto owners carry a minimum of liability coverage. In all states, financial responsibility laws require perpetrators of accidents to show proof of ability to assume the cost of the accident, at the risk of losing their driver's licenses and/or paying heavy fines. Before beginning to drive your car you should check with your insurance agent as to the legal requirements in your state, as well as considering his recommendations as to coverage. It is "penny-wise and pound foolish" to

[1]*The World Almanac and Book of Facts 1983* (New York: Newspaper Enterprise Association, 1983).

be without liability insurance. One lawsuit finding you negligent could financially ruin your entire life.

Your options then seem to be limited to how much or what type of coverage to buy. There are four major categories of risk coverage.

Liability   Liability coverage protects you up to stated limits from claims of others for restitution of property damage, mental anguish, legal costs, or other expenses associated with accidental damages for which you are to blame. This coverage is often sold in *split limits* with a maximum payable by the underwriter—for example, a maximum of $250,000 payable to each injured person, $500,000 total bodily injury per accident, and a maximum of $50,000 property damage per accident.

If you can buy liability coverage with a firm that offers a single limit instead of split limits, your risk of being underinsured in any one category is minimized. In either case, liability coverage protects you against the possibility of a catastrophic claim. You should acquire as much automobile liability insurance as you can afford, and ideally you should protect yourself up to what you perceive to be your future net worth.

Medical   Medical coverage provides payment of medical expenses for you and your immediate family if they result from an automobile-related accident. All reasonable costs incurred up to one year after the accident (up to a stated dollar limit) are covered, regardless of who was at fault.

Collision   This coverage provides reimbursement for damage to your own automobile. It can be expensive, unless you are willing to

Automobile insurance protects you against liability in major accidents, like this one, or in minor fender-benders.

accept a deductible clause. Moreover, if your auto has a market value below $3,000, you must seriously evaluate whether collision insurance is worth the expense. For example, if the cost of collision insurance for your car is $200 per year and the car is worth $2,000, unless you totally destroy it once every ten years ($200 divided into $2,000), you will be losing money on your insurance.

Comprehensive This is an inexpensive protection against certain *named perils*, such as fire, theft, vandalism, and natural disaster. It is usually offered with a small deductible that spares the insurance company paperwork on millions of small claims. If the market value of your auto is $1,000 or greater, this coverage can be acquired at a reasonable cost.

PROPERTY AND CASUALTY INSURANCE

You can acquire coverage on specific items of personal property either against specified risks (named perils) or against any risk excluding certain specified perils (e.g., earthquakes, war, nuclear accidents). Although named peril plans are less expensive, you will probably feel more comfortable with an all-risk plan that covers against *any* uncertainty.

Homeowner's Insurance If you are a homeowner, you will find that many insurance companies offer comprehensive packages to satisfy your needs. Renters can also purchase insurance for protection against the loss of their personal belongings.

An important additional feature of homeowner's and renter's coverage is protection against the risk of causing property damage or bodily injury to others. If negligence on your part can be proven, you are financially responsible for the consequences.

HOW DO YOU GET INSURED?

You are now aware of the principal items on the insurance supermarket shelf. What are you going to buy? Consumers Union publishes a monthly magazine, *Consumer Reports,* which from time to time reviews the quality of underwriters and their products in the various insurance categories. Begin your shopping with a visit to the library.

Life insurance agents aggressively pursue your business. Talk to more than one agent before you sign anything. If you need auto coverage, use the telephone to gather quotes from reputable companies. Ask about discounts (good student, nonsmoker, no history of accidents). Remember to buy a generous amount of liability insurance before you purchase any other coverage.

The Yellow Pages will also provide leads to property, life, and casualty and health insurance companies. Always compare two or more companies before you buy. The differences in annual premium costs are often as much as 50 percent.

Credit

Credit is the use of someone else's money for a certain period of time. It is most often associated with borrowing at an interest cost. It is financially wise to take advantage of credit opportunities, and equally unwise to take indiscriminate advantage of each offer that is made to you. When enticing offers of credit do not fit your budget, refuse them.

This section will describe the costs and types of credit available to you as an average wage earner.

CREDIT CARDS

The credit cards we are all familiar with include travel cards (American Express, Diner's Club, and Carte Blanche), gasoline cards, and bank cards (Visa and MasterCard). These are obtained by application and may be used as a substitute for cash or checks. As you use the cards, the balance you owe is accumulated and billed to you monthly. Most issuers of credit cards assess an annual fee.

If you pay the amount owed without delay, you have used the card for its convenience—you don't need to carry cash, you have use of the money for thirty or more days, and you can easily keep a record of your expenses. On the other hand, if you do not pay the bill in full, the card issuer lends you the outstanding balance at a

Consumer Reports annually reviews various insurance plans.

Credit cards

high interest rate (which varies from state to state) until such time as you have no further carry-over. Be careful to make payments within the time period specified on your bill; otherwise, a charge will be carried over.

If you lose a credit card and someone uses it in your name, you are liable for the first $50 but insured thereafter. To absolve yourself of liability, you should notify the issuer immediately of the loss.

BORROWING

Financial institutions make loans with an interest charge and sometimes require the pledging of property or securities to guarantee the repayment of the loan—*collateral*. To obtain a loan, you must prove your financial reliability. The lending institution investigates, for example, your history of check writing, utility payments, length of residence at one address, and prior loan experience.

A credit bureau in your community maintains a central record of your credit history. The law permits you to have access to this file. If you dispute the validity of any of the contents of your credit record, you may submit a 100-word statement to that effect. Moreover, adverse information must be removed after seven years elapse.

THE COST OF CREDIT

Whether you are borrowing from a bank, savings and loan institution, credit union, or finance company, you should be aware of how much the credit costs are. The Truth in Lending Law requires

creditors to give you certain basic information regarding finance charges and annual percentage rates.

The *finance charge* is the total dollar amount you pay to use the credit. It includes interest charges and sometimes service charges of various sorts.

The *annual percentage rate* (APR) is the percentage cost of credit on a yearly basis. All creditors, whether they are banks, stores, car dealers, credit card companies, or finance companies, are obliged by law to give you in writing both the finance charge and the APR for your loan. It is your responsibility to use this knowledge to select the credit that is least expensive.

Of course, you want to get the loan or use the credit card that involves the lowest cost or interest rate. But if this loan entails a higher monthly payment than your budget will allow, you must consider whether the purchase is really necessary.

Open-End Credit   If you have a credit card or a charge account, you are using open-end credit. You can use *open-end credit* again and again, up to a preset limit. Your costs will be affected by two factors, both of which must, under the Truth in Lending Law, be explained to you by your creditor. First, creditors must tell you how they calculate the finance charge. The method used can affect your bill by several dollars a month. Second, they must let you know when finance charges begin on your credit account. If you are charging a large purchase, you will want to compare the billing methods of various stores and take them into account when calculating the total cost of the item.

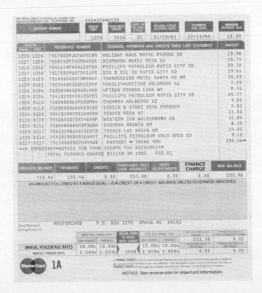

If you use a credit card, your monthly statement will reveal the real cost of your credit, as well as itemizing each purchase and payment.

A monthly checking account statement

CHECKING ACCOUNTS

When you begin to pay your own bills, you will most likely decide to open a checking account. Again, you should comparison shop. There are some accounts that carry a monthly service charge and/or a charge per check; others, if you combine them with a savings account in which you maintain a specified balance, will allow you to write checks at no cost at all. In any case, it is your responsibility to keep accurate records of your checks. Overdrawing on a checking account will cause you expense and embarrassment, and possibly damage your credit rating.

INSTALLMENT LOANS

If you purchase an expensive item—a car, for example—you may be able to sign an installment purchase agreement.

This agreement is a legal contract giving the vendor title to the purchased item (the collateral) until you have paid the loan balance and interest charges in full. If you fail to maintain periodic payments as promised, the consequences may include:

Acceleration—If you miss a payment, the entire amount is due.

Repossession—In the event of default, the merchandise can be taken away without notice.

Garnishment—Up to 25 percent of your take-home pay can be collected by the lender directly from your employer until the loan is repaid.

Before you decide on the financing of a large purchase, ask to take home the installment agreement. Compare the interest cost and percentage with alternative sources of credit. Get out the budget to see how you can squeeze in this new obligation!

RETAIL CREDIT

This source of financing is sometimes called *revolving credit*. Many companies offer their customers the opportunity to open a *charge account*, in which the accumulated monthly balance will be billed to you much as a credit card statement is billed. If you pay the balance in full, the account costs you nothing and provides you with considerable convenience. If you wish to carry over some of the balance, be aware of the interest charge and the effect of the monthly payment on your budget.

REGULATION OF CREDIT

In response to the consumer movement, the federal government has legislated constraints on the credit market. The 1971 Fair Credit Reporting Act protects consumers with respect to the collec-

Department store credit cards

tion and publication of credit information. The 1975 Fair Credit Billing Act requires lenders to mail statements fourteen days before the payment-due date, and gives the borrower recourse against unfair practices by a creditor.

Regulation Z of the 1975 Consumer Credit Protection Act (also known as the Truth in Lending Law), which is supervised by the Federal Reserve Board, requires lenders to disclose both the dollar amount of finance charges and the annual percentage rate that dollar amount represents.

The Equal Credit Opportunity Act of 1975 made it illegal to discriminate on the basis of sex or marital status when considering a credit application. If you feel you have been treated unjustly insofar as credit approval is concerned, contact the local office of the Federal Trade Commission.

SO WHAT SHOULD YOU DO?

"Borrowing is a sin," preached past generations. And it is true that by going into debt you assume a greater risk of future financial problems than you do by paying cash. On the other hand, consider the advantages of utilizing our modern credit systems:

■ You carry less cash and risk less loss.

■ You can acquire goods and services when you need them.

■ You can take advantage of bargains at sales.

■ You can return unsatisfactory merchandise with minimal problems.

- Your debts will be repaid with less valuable dollars in a time of inflation.

When you have decided to go into debt, make your first move carefully. A low-cost loan might be available within your family. If you offer to pay a higher interest rate than that earned on a savings account, the lender profits. Also, consider a credit union or bank financing, either of which may be cheaper than signing an installment agreement. The balance due on your credit cards or charge accounts can sometimes be paid off with a loan from a cheaper source. Lastly, stay within your budget!

Banking Opportunities

Until recently, the wage earner had only two opportunities for depositing paychecks—checking and savings accounts. Savings accounts pay the depositor a modest rate of interest, which is usually 5½ percent. Traditionally, checking accounts did not pay interest and were usually designed as alternatives to paying cash for financial obligations. Some banks charge a monthly fee or a per transaction assessment.

Deregulation of the banking industry by federal legislation has allowed banking institutions to innovate in their efforts to attract customers. Because of the rapidity with which the investing options are being added and revised, only the more popular of these options will be discussed.

If you have a credit card, you can take advantage of unexpected bargains.

INTEREST PLUS CHECKING

Since 1981, customers have been able to earn interest on money in checking accounts. These are referred to as *NOW accounts* (Negotiable Order of Withdrawal). While many banks offer interest-bearing checking accounts unconditionally, others impose service charges. For example, some banks charge $8 per month on accounts of less than $2,000. Some require a minimum balance, while others require a minimum average balance.

These varied requirements should serve as a caution to the person considering a NOW account. The possibility exists that a substantially greater return could be realized by another investment, since the interest rate on NOW accounts is 5¼ percent. Credit unions often offer more attractive rates of return, and service charges are often nonexistent.

SUPER NOW ACCOUNTS

A further effort to deregulate the banking industry occurred on January 5, 1983. As of that date, financial institutions were authorized to establish the Super NOW account for their customers. As with the NOW account, the *Super NOW account* is a checking account. But there are significant differences. While the NOW account returns 5¼ percent interest, the Super NOW account's interest rate is approximately that of the money market, which in recent years has been consistently higher than 5¼ percent. The minimum balance required for the Super NOW account is considerably higher than in the NOW account—often it is $2,500. If the balance falls below this minimum the interest rate drops automatically to 5¼ percent. As with the NOW account, there is no limit to checking privileges. Investments up to $100,000 are insured by the federal government.

INDIVIDUAL RETIREMENT ACCOUNTS

How would you like to have an "extra" $350,000 when you retire at age 65? Of course you would! The *Individual Retirement Account* (IRA) makes this possible. An IRA is a tax-sheltered plan that is available to an individual who is under the age of 70½ and who has *earned income*—wages earned as an employee. A 1980 revision of the tax laws removed a restriction which previously made the IRA available to only those wage earners not under a pension or retirement plan, public or private. In other words, the IRA is available to wage earners irrespective of their participation in any retirement plan.

The IRA offers a means of accumulating tax-deductible deposits in a savings plan, either with banks, savings and loans organizations, insurance companies, or in other financial institutions. Deposits can be in stocks, bonds, mutual funds, or in other money-related areas. Acquisitions of antiques or "collectibles" are not allowed. As long as the IRA remains in force, the earnings on those deposits accumulate tax free. Deposits can be withdrawn after the age of 59½ without penalty, absent disability. You must begin withdrawal of deposits by the age of 70½. Thus, IRAs provide an opportunity to build or add to your own retirement fund on a *tax-sheltered* basis.

Contributions by an individual cannot exceed $2,000 annually. However, a wage-earning spouse can also invest $2,000 annually. A married person with a nonworking spouse can invest $2,250 annually.

You can see how the "extra" $350,000 comes about. If you were to invest the maximum $2,000 each year for thirty years, this would grow to $361,000, assuming an annual interest rate of 10 percent.

Sounds easy doesn't it? Saving money is never easy. Our needs and wants seem to outgrow our income levels. One must establish a pattern of saving part of that which is earned. After all, you have made a commitment to complete your education for a career in business. The rewards received from putting aside a part of your earnings are worth the sacrifices made along the way.

This discussion reflects the early efforts to deregulate the banking industry. As this trend continues, certain changes will occur in opportunities and requirements. As you consider investment decisions, you should thoroughly research all of the options. These deliberations will be worth the time and effort expended.

Taxation

Responsible financial planning includes tax planning. This section will focus on personal income tax and legal methods of minimizing your tax liability. If you want more information, study the material that accompanies your tax return forms or consult an authority on income tax laws. Tax offices (IRS) also provide free tax information as well as a toll-free number you may use.

Federal Income Tax

Residents of the United States are required to file a tax return if their annual earnings are $3,300 or more. The return is due April 15 of the year following the period in which income was received. Taxable income includes wages, tips, fees, business profits, dividends, interest, royalties, and even alimony. Certain distributions from government and insurance companies are tax exempt. These include Social Security pensions, unemployment insurance benefits, life insurance death benefits, and settlements of liability insurance claims.

Responsible financial planning includes figuring out your income tax.

Until 1977, a taxpayer could elect to itemize deductions or apply what was referred to as a "standard deduction." Since 1977, the standard deduction has been replaced by the *zero bracket amount*. Every taxpayer has the benefit of the zero bracket amount: $2,300 for a single person, $3,400 for a married couple filing jointly, and $1,700 for a married person filing separately is exempt from taxation automatically.

THE SHORT FORM

Figure 14–3 shows Form 1040A. You can use this if your sources of taxable income are confined to employee benefits, dividends and interest are less than $400 each, and your itemized deductions do not exceed the zero bracket amount.

FORM 1040 AND SCHEDULES

In all other cases, *Form 1040,* the long form, must be filed, with schedules attached itemizing the exact sources of the entries. You need complete only the schedules that apply to your tax return.

The most frequently used schedules are: Schedule A, Itemized Deductions; Schedule B, Dividend and Interest Income; Schedule C, Business Profits or Losses; Schedule D, Capital Gains or Losses; Schedule E, Additional Income Sources. To use these, you will have to keep precise, accurate records—receipts, canceled checks, and bank and dividend statements.

1 Control number		OMB No. 1545-0008		

2 Employer's name, address, and ZIP code	3 Employer's identification number 13 1925377	4 Employer's State number 13-1925377

Ann M. Zimmerman
69 E. Charles Avenue
Any State 57325

5 Stat. em-ployee ☐	De-ceased ☐	Pension plan ☒	Legal rep. ☐	942 emp. ☐	Sub-total ☐	Cor-rection ☐	Void ☐

6	7 Advance EIC payment

8 Employee's social security number 523 45 7699	9 Federal income tax withheld 1,670	10 Wages, tips, other compensation 12,000	11 FICA tax withheld 804.00

12 Employee's name, address, and ZIP code	13 FICA wages 12,000	14 FICA tips 0.00

Consolidated Enterprises, Inc.
1949 Rothsay St.
Johnsberg, NY 10235

16 Employer's use

Form **W-2 Wage and Tax Statement 1982**   Copy B To be filed with employee's FEDERAL tax return   Department of the Treasury
This information is being furnished to the Internal Revenue Service.   Internal Revenue Service

A W–2 form

TAX WITHHOLDING

Your employer is required by law to collect state and federal taxes "at the source." The size of this withholding from your gross income will depend on the *W–4* form that you completed at the time of your employment. The total amount of taxes withheld will be reported to you on a *W–2* form at the year's end and will be credited against the taxes you owe for that year.

TAX STRATEGIES

Your motto should be: "Avoid, not evade, taxes." Here are three methods of avoiding paying more taxes than necessary.

- You may file a joint return with your spouse and combine deductions, exemptions, and sources of income, or you may file separate returns. Joint returns generally prove more advantageous to married taxpayers than filing separately. Try calculating your family's tax liability both ways to check it out.

- If you can foresee unusual deductible expenses (under Schedule A), it pays to concentrate them in one tax year. The following and preceding years you can "overdeduct" under the shelter of the zero bracket amount. For example, if you have suffered a large casualty or theft loss, you may concentrate other deductible expenses into the same year— perhaps making your charitable or political contributions on January 1, July 1, and December 31 instead of once in each of three years, or having that medical or dental work that you have been putting off.

1982

Department of the Treasury—Internal Revenue Service

Form 1040A US Individual Income Tax Return (0)

OMB No. 1545-0085

Step 1
Name and address

Use the IRS mailing label. Otherwise, print or type.

Your first name and initial (if joint return, also give spouse's name and initial) — Last name

Ann M. Zimmerman

Present home address

69 E. Charles Ave

City, town or post office, State, and ZIP code

Illinois   57325

Your social security no.

523-45-7649

Spouse's social security no.

Your occupation *Secretary*

Spouse's occupation

Presidential Election Campaign Fund

Do you want $1 to go to this fund?...................☒Yes ☐No

If joint return, does your spouse want $1 to go to this fund? ☐Yes ☐No

Step 2
Filing status
(Check only one)
and
Exemptions

1 ☒ Single (See if you can use Form 1040EZ.)
2 ☐ Married filing joint return (even if only one had income)
3 ☐ Married filing separate return. Enter spouse's social security no. above and full name here.
4 ☐ Head of household (with qualifying person). If the qualifying person is your unmarried child but not your dependent, write this child's name here.

Always check the exemption box labeled Yourself. Check other boxes if they apply.

5a ☒ Yourself   ☐ 65 or over   ☐ Blind
 b ☐ Spouse   ☐ 65 or over   ☐ Blind
 c First names of your dependent children who lived with you

Attach Copy B of Forms W-2 here

 d Other dependents:
 (1) Name   (2) Relationship   (3) Number of months lived in your home.   (4) Did dependent have income of $1,000 or more?   (5) Did you provide more than one-half of dependent's support?

 e Total number of exemptions claimed.................

Write number of boxes checked on 5a and b *1*

Write number of children listed on 5c

Write number of other dependents listed on 5d

Add numbers entered in boxes above *1*

Step 3
Adjusted gross income

6 Wages, salaries, tips, etc. (Attach Forms W-2)............ 6 | *12,000* | *00*
7 Interest income (Complete page 2 if over $400 or you have any All-Savers interest)...... 7 | *150* | *00*
8a Dividends *200 00* (Complete page 2 if over $400) 8b Exclusion *100 00* Subtract line 8b from 8a 8c | *100* | *00*
9a Unemployment compensation (insurance). Total from Form(s) 1099-UC.
 b Taxable amount, if any, from worksheet on page 16 of Instructions.............. 9b
10 Add lines 6, 7, 8c, and 9b. This is your total income............ 10 | *12,250* | *00*
11 Deduction for a married couple when both work. Complete the worksheet on page 17...... 11
12 Subtract line 11 from line 10. This is your adjusted gross income......... 12 | *12,250* | *00*

Step 4
Taxable income

13 Allowable part of your charitable contributions. Complete the worksheet on page 18..... 13
14 Subtract line 13 from line 12........... 14
15 Multiply $1,000 by the total number of exemptions claimed in box 5e........... 15 | *1000* | *00*
16 Subtract line 15 from line 14. This is your taxable income............. 16 | *11,250* | *00*

Step 5
Tax, credits, and payments

Attach check or money order here

17a Partial credit for political contributions. See page 19...... ■17a | *25 00*
 b Total Federal income tax withheld, from W-2 form(s). (If line 6 is more than $32,400, see page 19.)..... 17b | *1670 00*

Stop Here and Sign Below if You Want IRS to Figure Your Tax

 c Earned income credit, from worksheet on page 21......... 17c
18 Add lines 17a, b, and c. These are your total credits and payments................ 18 | *1,695* | *00*
19a Find tax on amount on line 16. Use tax table, pages 26-31.... 19a | *1710 00*
 b Advance EIC payment (from W-2 form(s))........... 19b
20 Add lines 19a and 19b. This is your total tax............ 20 | *1710* | *00*

Step 6
Refund or amount you owe

21 If line 18 is larger than line 20, subtract line 20 from line 18. Enter the amount to be **refunded to you**........ 21
22 If line 20 is larger than line 18, subtract line 18 from line 20. Enter the **amount you owe**. Attach payment for full amount payable to "Internal Revenue Service." 22 | *15* | *00*

Step 7
Sign your return

I have read this return and any attachments filed with it. Under penalties of perjury, I declare that to the best of my knowledge and belief, the return and attachments are correct and complete.

Ann M. Zimmerman   4-10-85
Your signature   Date   Spouse's signature (If filing jointly, BOTH must sign)

Paid preparer's signature   Date   Check if self-employed ☐   Preparer's social security no.

Firm's name (or yours, if self-employed)
Address and Zip code   E.I. no.

For **Privacy Act and Paperwork Reduction Act Notice,** see page 34.

Figure 14–3

Form 1040A is the short tax form.

- Income averaging and income splitting are methods employed by taxpayers with fluctuating incomes. If your income has jumped, you can spread the addition over five tax returns (prior or future years). If you have unearned income, you can give away the source (e.g., real estate, investments, or copyrights) to a family member or trust in a lower tax bracket.

Other Taxes

Federal and state income taxes are not the only personal taxes to be considered when you are planning your finances. People who make profits by investing in the stock market or in real estate may have to pay capital gains taxes. When there is a death in the family, estate taxes may have to be paid. You may never have occasion to pay these taxes, but there are two other taxes you will certainly have to deal with: social security taxes and sales taxes.

SOCIAL SECURITY TAXES

Federal Insurance Contributions Act *(FICA)* taxes are levied as a percentage of your gross earned income. These taxes fund a national insurance plan that offers retirement, disability, and health benefits to wage earners and their families.

SALES TAXES

In most states, you have to pay sales taxes. If you are making a large purchase—for example, a major appliance or a car—the sales tax can make a considerable difference in the price you pay. Remember, sales taxes can be deducted from your federal income tax if you itemize deductions. For this reason, you should keep receipts of your large purchases.

Investing

Among the financial decisions you will be making in the years ahead will be how to invest your long-term savings.

HOME OWNERSHIP

After the acquisition of an automobile, the first major investment you are likely to make is a home, whether it is a house, a condominium, or a co-op apartment. Home ownership is a symbolic aspiration as well as a financial investment—a major feature of the American dream. Since this is often the first major commitment in a family's financial growth, it is crucial that the decision be well managed. The following guidelines deserve consideration:

- Begin with a small, affordable house rather than stretching for the "dream home."

- Don't let monthly payments of principal, interest, taxes, and insurance exceed 30 percent of the family's *net* income.

- Be prepared for many additional expenses when comparing the monthly payment to a monthly rent. Homeowners have to pay for the upkeep of a complex structure (e.g., its plumbing, roofing, driveway, and garden).

- Don't borrow more than 2½ times the family's gross annual income.

- The closing costs of a home sale are often so great as to erase any advantage of buying over renting unless the property can be held for several years.

Home ownership is part of the American dream.

OTHER INVESTMENT POSSIBILITIES

Later in your career, you may want to look at other ways in which to invest your money. Among these will be stocks and bonds, mutual funds, and real estate (land, residential rentals, or commercial property). You may even want to investigate the futures market, options, collectibles, and precious metals. All of these can be risky. Remember, it is not wise to make any speculative investment unless you can afford to lose money on it.

You can get help with your taxes from the Internal Revenue Service.

A fisheye view of the
stock exchange trading floor.

Your Financial Future

Financial planning is a skill that will demand your continuous attention throughout your professional career. This chapter has given you guidelines for dealing with the various kinds of financial problems and opportunities you will encounter as a professional. These will likely be smaller in scope early in your career than later on. Nevertheless, if you develop a responsible attitude toward your practical day-to-day concerns of budgeting, planning, and investing now, you will be more able to cope with those that arise in the years to come.

KEY TERMS

expense diary	beneficiary	open-end credit
letter of credit	face amount	revolving credit
per diem	group life	charge account
net income	annuity	NOW Account
gross income	deductible	Super NOW Account
fixed expenditures	coinsurance	Individual Retirement
discretionary	split limits	Account
expenditures	named perils	earned income
term insurance	credit	zero bracket amount
endowment insurance	collateral	Form 1040
whole life insurance	finance charge	W-4 form
universal life	annual percentage	W-2 form
insurance	rate	FICA
premium		

TEST YOURSELF:
QUESTIONS FOR REVIEW AND DISCUSSION

1. Explain why term insurance carries a lower premium than other life insurance.
2. What do you consider the most useful form of insurance for a young person?
3. Discuss the importance of developing a good credit rating.
4. Describe the difference between NOW and Super NOW Accounts.
5. What are the main purposes of developing and utilizing a personal budget?
6. "Buy now and pay later" has become the theme of much of the advertising effort in this country. What are the pitfalls of such a practice? Are there any advantages to such a philosophy?
7. Describe the tax advantages of an Individual Retirement Account (IRA).
8. Compare the advantages of owning versus renting a home.

APPLICATION EXERCISES

1. Assume that you have just graduated and that you have accepted a position as office manager with a construction firm at a monthly salary of $1,500. Develop a personal budget of your anticipated fixed and discretionary expenditures for one month. Be sure that you don't overlook the fact that the $1,500 is a gross figure and not net. You can assume that income tax deductions and other fixed deductions, such as Social Security and retirement, will amount to approximately 25 percent of the gross salary.

2. Interview the director of the local credit bureau. Obtain information as to the methods by which the bureau establishes credit ratings, what purposes credit ratings serve, and the importance of maintaining a good credit rating.

Suggested Readings

Bailard, Thomas E., et al. *Personal Money Management,* 3rd ed. Palo Alto, Calif: Science Research Associates, 1980.

Consumer Handbook to Credit Protection Laws. Washington, D.C.: Board of Governors of the Federal Reserve System, 1979.

D'Ambrosio, Charles A. *Principles of Modern Investments.* Palo Alto, Calif.: Science Research Associates, 1976.

Insurance. St. Paul, Minn.: Changing Times Educational Service Editors, 1982.

Mehr, Robert I., and Emerson Cammack. *Principles of Insurance.* Homewood, Ill.: Irwin, 1980.

Rosefsky, Robert S. *Personal Finance and Money Management.* New York: Wiley & Sons, 1978.

Rosefsky, Robert S. *Money Talks: Bob Rosefsky's Complete Program for Financial Success.* New York: Wiley & Sons, 1982.

PART FIVE

MOVING UP THE LADDER

As you develop as a professional, you will be able to view your career in a broad, corporate context. You will be affected by the management policies of your employer; these management policies will in turn be affected by government regulations.

Sooner or later, you may be considered for a management position. Will you want that responsibility? And how will you behave in that role? It's not too early for you to start developing a managerial point of view.

15

TAKING CHARGE

COMPREHENSIVE GOAL
To assist you in considering a career in management through an increased understanding of management principles and leadership theory

SPECIFIC OBJECTIVES
After reading this chapter, you will be able to:

- explain the importance of goals and objectives to the success of an organization

- define and explain the four management functions—planning, organizing, directing, and controlling

- compare and contrast the relative effectiveness of team and unilateral decision making

- describe the philosophic differences between scientific management and human relations

- explain how management by objectives is a merger of scientific management and human relations

- demonstrate an understanding of Theory X and Theory Y

- describe how situational leadership operates

- explain how Theory Z goes beyond Theories X and Y

- trace the evolution of leadership theory

The subject matter in chapters 15 and 16 is of a different and more technical nature from that contained in previous chapters; and you will notice that the writing style is, accordingly, also more precise and technical. But the information these chapters contain about the broad principles and concerns of business is important to your professional development. Therefore, we have decided to include it despite its difficulty—but we have tried to limit our discussion to that material necessary for a basic understanding of our topics.

Even though your first professional position is not likely to be in management, you will be affected by managers from your first day on the job. Your immediate impression of those who bear management responsibilities may be one of awe. Soon, however, you will realize that these men and women have duties to perform just as you do, that they are held accountable for the results of their efforts just as you are, and that the weight of their responsibilities can create enormous strain and pressure.

As you adjust to your position, you may become curious about the profession of management. You may wonder why some administrators seem to lead more successfully than others—why Ms. Jones, in charge of purchasing, accomplishes results with little fanfare while Mr. Anderson, accounting supervisor, must constantly be ordering, directing, and "watching over" those in his department. You may wonder how some managers made it to the top and speculate that others will never advance beyond their present positions. Finally, you may fantasize about the day when you will be promoted to a management position and assume managerial responsibilities of your own.

The information in this chapter will help you decide whether or not you are interested in a career in management. You will develop a greater awareness of the complexities of decision making and an appreciation of people who make decisions. You will also develop a greater understanding of how your job fits into your organization. Because of this awareness, you will be a better-adjusted and a more valuable employee.

On the job, you will become aware of how management affects you and what makes a good manager.

Management and Leadership

Before we discuss management and leadership, it is necessary to define and explain the two terms. *Management* is the authority vested in a person who has a designated administrative title. This title may be "supervisor," "foreman," "plant manager," or "president." Management refers to an administrative position. On the other hand, *leadership* refers to a trait rather than to a position. A person who has leadership qualities is someone whom people will want to follow. Whether this person actually leads will depend upon whether the opportunity to lead and the desire to lead are both present.

Chrysler-Plymouth

Today's automobile industry is attempting to maintain its goal of making a profit while producing more economical cars.

Leadership can be either formal (associated with a managerial position) or informal. Formal leadership is awarded by higher authority, but informal leadership is awarded by the powerless, the followers. In your first position, you will report to people who have managerial positions. Ideally, they will also have the leadership traits that will cause you and others to accept their supervision willingly.

In your new job, you will also become aware of an informal structure that is present in almost every organization. Certain employees, without having administrative authority, may exercise such strong influence that other employees will carry out their wishes. The astute manager recognizes these informal leaders, enlisting their support so that their efforts are complementary rather than competitive. For example, suppose there is a need to prohibit smoking in an area of the plant near a paint room because of explosive fumes. Instead of merely posting "No Smoking" signs, the supervisor will explain the need for the change to the informal leaders, requesting that they support the policy.

The Responsibilities of Management

Management's responsibility is to get the job done. However, a problem arises in determining what constitutes "getting the job done" and in selecting appropriate techniques.

Courtesy of IBM

Competition among manufacturers of computer software is intense. Thus, a manufacturer needs to establish clear-cut objectives for achieving its goal with regard to the share of the marketplace it wants to secure.

The basic responsibilities of management are to establish organizational goals and objectives and to marshal the various available resources toward meeting those goals and objectives. This is a large order, but it is the primary concern of management in all organizations—profit or nonprofit enterprises, sole proprietorships, partnerships, or huge corporations.

GOALS

Organizational *goals* constitute the "reason for being" of the enterprise. They are long-term, and they seldom change. How they are achieved, however, may change from time to time, as economic and social conditions warrant. For example, the goals of the American automobile industry may be to produce automobiles and to make a profit. How these are achieved is undergoing drastic changes because of the competition of foreign manufacturers and of the energy situation. Suddenly "economy" has replaced the once popular "the bigger, the better." Nevertheless, the goals of the industry remain unchanged.

OBJECTIVES

When Lewis Carroll's Alice, in *Alice's Adventures in Wonderland*, asks the Cheshire Cat where the road leads, the answer is "Where do you want to go?" Alice replies, "I don't really know." The Cheshire Cat concludes the conversation by saying, "Then it really doesn't matter, does it? If you don't know where you are going, then any road will do."

Objectives are the guideposts used by an organization to chart the course of the enterprise in terms of products, service, and marketing. They serve as the standards by which managers measure the effectiveness of the organization.

Objectives are generally short-range, and are more specific than goals. They describe those activities that will meet a goal. Suppose that the Apricot Computer Company has made the decision to enter the personal computer market. This is the organizational goal. The objectives might be as follows:

- to produce a microcomputer with small business applications and for personal use
- to meet the competitor's pricing practices
- to develop the software that will serve the needs of small businesses and families
- to establish area centers that will provide the sales force and the technical expertise to assist buyers in utilizing their computers

- to establish and maintain a testing and research arm of the company for evaluating and improving products

Once objectives have been determined, a set of specific activities are developed for achieving each objective. Typically, a broad-based involvement of company employees in setting these activities occurs. This has the effect of personalizing these activities, which in turn produces a greater commitment toward meeting the overall goals of the organization.

RESOURCES

The tools of production—working capital, raw materials, quality and nature of plants and equipment, and number and size of qualified and trained work force—are the resources that must be considered in determining the goals of the organization. For example, it would be foolhardy to attempt to produce a complicated piece of equipment, such as a video tape recorder, without highly trained electronics technicians.

Management Functions

Management's role is seeing that organizational goals are achieved. In doing this, management performs four functions: planning, organizing, directing, and controlling.

Planning is the process of forecasting the future and then determining the appropriate strategies and activities (objectives) that will attain the company's goals. Variables that a manager must consider include anticipated consumer demands and expectations; societal, political, and economic constraints; and competitor's products. In other words, planning involves answering "who," "when," "what," and "how" questions. The planning function must precede the other functions.

Organizing follows the planning function. Once plans have been developed and functions determined, management's responsibility is to group the work to be done into efficient units, to assign employees to their areas of greatest expertise, and to delegate responsibility.

Directing involves guiding and supervising the efforts of subordinates toward the attainment of the organization's objectives. This requires the ability to communicate both verbally and in writing.

The last function, *controlling*, is concerned with evaluating performance and making adjustments in the other three functions. Controlling serves as the rudder of the organization. As the results of evaluation emerge, adjustments in direction and focus can occur. For example, if the production level of a work group diminishes rapidly, management will be alerted to investigate the causes for the change. Maybe incompatibility between members of the group and the foreman indicates a need for a restructuring of the work group or a reassignment of the foreman.

DECISION MAKING

In the past, supply-and-demand relationships were simple to define. A company executive could easily set production rates to meet an established and stable demand. However, the complexities of today's changing society have brought about the need for a change in the way decisions are made.

The buying habits of the American public do not remain stable and predictable. Consumer preferences are shaped by a number of factors, including advertising and economic conditions. During a period of continued inflation, generic products were introduced to consumers. These items were sold in plain packages simply labeled with the content's name. By eliminating the expenses associated with advertising and fancy packaging, generic products could be sold at a far lower cost than their name-brand counterparts.

Or consider the upheaval which was created in the American automobile industry by rapidly escalating gasoline prices and the subsequent oil glut and decline in gasoline prices. Management must anticipate changing consumer demands, but it would be highly unusual for one person both to be skilled at consumer analysis and to have the expertise required to make the corresponding adjustments in the planning, directing, and controlling functions.

Courtesy of King Soopers, Denver, Colo.

Consumer preferences are shaped by a number of factors, including advertising and economic conditions.

Management Teams   As a result, single decision makers have been replaced by management teams, whose members bring expertise from their own areas of responsibility to the decision-making scene. The underlying assumption of management-team decision making is that "none of us is wiser than all of us."

Management-team decision making is not without drawbacks, some of which were pointed out in chapter 9. One of these hazards, groupthink, is particularly risky. The tragedy of the Bay of Pigs, an effort organized by the CIA in 1960–61 to overthrow Cuban leader Fidel Castro, was attributed to the human phenomenon of groupthink. Several of President Kennedy's advisers had reservations about the planned attack but refrained from expressing them. Each assumed that he was the only dissenting voice, when in fact the decision to invade Cuba never would have achieved consensus had group members spoken out. You may have been in a class situation where you assumed you were the only one who didn't understand a point, when in fact many in the class had the same problem.

Group decision making, despite the problems associated with it, will probably continue to be a management tool for some time to come.

Machiavelli

Leadership and Management Theory

Current leadership and management theory can best be understood by tracing its historical development. In the following section, the ideas of some of the best-known thinkers in this field will be discussed.

MACHIAVELLI

Perhaps the most famous early leadership theorist was Machiavelli. In the sixteenth century he wrote *The Prince*, which was based on his study of the ruling structure in the Italian states. Machiavelli observed that a leader ought to be both feared and loved. If there must be a choice, however, it is better to be feared than loved. Love is an obligation that selfish people can break when it serves their purpose, but, he said, fear is a power relationship maintained by threat of punishment.

Machiavellian philosophy was based upon manipulation, power, and fear. Even though few leaders would care to admit it, much of what Machiavelli wrote in the 1500s is practiced today. Certain leaders, acting most times out of a desire for the general good but at other times for selfish reasons, believe that an organization or "cause" is all important. They consider people simply pawns to be used in bringing about the goals of the organization or cause.

One need not look to the history of great and powerful people to identify Machiavellian leadership styles. In many contemporary business organizations, there are people in positions of power who accomplish their goals through threatened or actual reprisal in the form of discharge or demotion.

A worker caught in the complexities of mass production and mechanization (Charlie Chaplin in *Modern Times*).

SCIENTIFIC MANAGEMENT

The Industrial Revolution of the early 1800s, which brought about mass production, job specialization, and mechanization, greatly increased the need for a more scientific approach to the study of worker productivity. In the late nineteenth century Frederick W. Taylor became the best known among those who examined human work efficiency.

A laborer with the Midvale Steel Company, Taylor became interested in worker accomplishment. His research resulted in changes in the work force that, in turn, produced increased productivity and higher pay for workers.

Taylor emphasized the scientific rather than the human approach to productivity, and his movement became known as *scientific management*. Among the principles of Taylor's scientific management theory were the following:[1]

1. All managers must be trained to use scientific principles, instead of rule-of-thumb methods to solve problems.
2. Managers should select and then train and develop their personnel rather than letting the workers choose their own work habits.
3. There must be an almost equal division of work responsibility between management and workers.

A contemporary of Taylor was Mary Parker Follett, one of the few women leadership theorists. Follett contributed much to the concepts of leadership and management.

"Stronger than all armies is an idea whose time has come," says Victor Hugo. The Industrial Revolution was the "time" that generated the "idea" of scientific management. Taylor's proposals were widely adopted in American industry. Efficiency experts equipped with stopwatches and clipboards became prominent management fixtures.

Around the period of World War I (1914–18) labor unions, on behalf of their members, began expressing their opposition to what they considered to be the demands of scientific management for a speedup of production and a reduction of the work force. As a result, the federal government enacted a prohibition of the use of time and motion studies in all federal construction contracts. This prohibition continued to be enacted each year from 1916 to 1949. Pressure from organized labor provided the impetus for a change in emphasis from production-line efficiency to a concern for the individual. This change was to be reflected in the writings of later leadership and management theorists.

[1]Frederick W. Taylor, *The Principles of Scientific Management* (New York: Harper & Brothers, 1911), pp. 36–37.

HUMAN RELATIONS

The shift away from scientific management came slowly and began quite by accident.

A group of Harvard researchers in 1927, under the leadership of G. Elton Mayo, studied the effects of changes in physical working conditions on productivity at the Hawthorne Electric Plant in Illinois. They discovered that changes in physical working conditions, such as reducing the amount of light, had almost no effect on productivity. Even when the lighting was reduced to almost the candle power of moonlight, productivity was unaffected. This greatly puzzled Mayo and his associates.

Finally, the researchers concluded that it was the attention paid to the workers and their involvement in the project that caused the greater productivity, and not the physical working conditions at all. By segregating the working crew and asking for their cooperation and recommendations, the researchers had converted them from "cogs in a machine" to a productive group. This gave rise to the phrase *Hawthorne Effect*, which explains increased results when people are involved in decision making.

The results of the Hawthorne studies initiated an entirely new management theory that became known as *human relations*. This theory emphasizes the importance of the worker's self-esteem and morale to business productivity.

MORALE FACTORS

Human relations theorists point to a survey that has been conducted over and over with nearly the same results each time. The person completing the questionnaire is asked to rank ten morale factors (1 = high, 10 = low). The ten factors are listed below, in the order in which they are usually ranked.[2]

1. appreciation of work done
2. feeling "in" on things
3. sympathetic help with personal problems
4. job security
5. good wages
6. work that keeps employee interested
7. promotion and growth within company
8. personal loyalty to workers
9. good working conditions
10. tactful disciplining

Notice that human relationship items—appreciation of work done, feeling "in" on things, and sympathetic help—appear toward the top of the scale. This, according to the human relations school of thought, demonstrates that managers need to be concerned with the personal aspects of their employees' performance.

[2]Paul Hersey and Kenneth Blanchard, *Management of Organizational Behavior: Utilizing Human Resources*, 4th ed. (Englewood Cliffs, N.J.: Prentice-Hall, 1982), pp. 41–42.

The "human relations" theory emphasized the importance of worker morale to business productivity

THEORY X AND THEORY Y

One of the greatest contributions to human relations was made by Douglas McGregor. McGregor believed that all organizations and leaders could be categorized by what he referred to as *Theory X* or *Theory Y*. In his book, *The Human Side of Enterprise*,[3] McGregor summarized Theory X assumptions:

- The average person has an inherent dislike of work and will avoid it if he or she can.

- Because of this dislike for work, people must be coerced, controlled, directed, or threatened with punishment to get them to put forth adequate effort toward the achievement of organizational objectives.

- The average person prefers to be directed and wishes to avoid responsibility, has relatively little ambition, and wants security above all.

Work is as natural as play or rest.

Theory Y assumptions, on the other hand, were:

- Work is as natural as play or rest.

- External control and the threat of punishment are not the only means for bringing about efforts toward organizational objectives. People will exercise responsibility in the service of objectives to which they are committed.

- Workers' commitment to objectives will correspond to the rewards associated with their achievement.

- Under proper conditions the average person learns not only to accept but also to seek responsibility.

- The capacity for imagination and creativity is widely, not narrowly, distributed in the population.

- Under the conditions of modern industrial life, the intellectual potential of the average person is only partially fulfilled.[4]

McGregor believed that organizational success could be reached most effectively through the human element present in Theory Y. Frederick Taylor and his scientific management would more likely have operated under Theory X. Which theory do you prefer? What do you believe about people and their motivations?

[3]Douglas McGregor, *The Human Side of Enterprise* (New York: McGraw-Hill, 1960), pp. 33–34.

[4]McGregor, *The Human Side of Enterprise*, pp. 47–48.

Personnel policies may be communicated verbally and nonverbally.

What do you believe about yourself? Which approach to management would you prefer in an organization in which you were considering accepting employment? Ask yourself these questions as you consider various job opportunities.

This is not intended to mean that you should not accept employment in an organization that you perceive to be a Theory X type organization. Some people, some situations, and some leadership environments demand a Theory X type of treatment. Theory Y is not always applicable and "good," Theory X is not always inappropriate and totally "bad," and managers will never fall entirely within either category.

The Self-Fulfilling Prophecy   McGregor added another concept to leadership theory—the self-fulfilling prophecy. McGregor observed that people live up to or down to the level that is expected of them. If management believes that its employees are lazy and untrustworthy, and communicates this belief, then they will tend to become lazy and untrustworthy. If, on the other hand, management believes that its employees are energetic and want to be productive, then they will tend to become energetic and productive.

How does management communicate that people are lazy and untrustworthy? It communicates this most obviously in personnel policies. For example, what does management communicate to employees when they are expected to punch a time clock for coffee breaks in addition to their morning arrival and afternoon departure? Would you feel trusted in such an organization? Wouldn't you be more apt to complete your work if management allowed you some flexibility in adjusting your time schedule within the overall framework of the company's schedule?

Personnel policies and practices are not always communicated in writing. Many are never found in a company policy manual, but they are nevertheless communicated verbally and occasionally nonverbally, as you discovered in chapter 7.

MANAGEMENT BY OBJECTIVES

Our discussion of leadership theory has taken us from scientific management to human relations. Scientific management places an emphasis on organization, efficiency, and worker productivity. Human relationists believe that the goals of the organization can best be met by personal involvement and by a concern for the individual.

A marriage of the two extremes would seem to be the next logical sequence. Such a marriage appears in *management by objectives* (MBO). Made popular by Peter F. Drucker and George S. Odiorne in the late 1950s, MBO is defined as a "program designed to improve employees' motivation through having them participate in

Management by objectives involves employee participation in goal setting and personnel evaluation.

setting their goals and letting them know exactly how they will be evaluated."[5]

Notice the elements of human relations in the above statement. That employees "participate in setting their goals" presumes that employees are both capable of and interested in having a part in determining what is expected of them (Theory Y). Notice also the element of scientific management: "Letting them know exactly how they will be evaluated." This evaluation may depend upon the number of units produced per hour or upon the results of a time and motion study analyzing production problems.

Employee Participation How do employees participate in setting their goals? For example, suppose that in order to meet the deadline for bids on a project, an architectural firm must have its plans and specifications in the hands of the prospective bidders thirty days prior to the bid opening. This is the objective. Each division within the firm must fit its activities into this time frame. The engineers and draftsmen responsible for the preparation of the specifications must have their material dictated and to the typists by a certain date. The project manager must coordinate the entire operation, meeting with the various supervisors and providing them with certain objectives for their unit, and cooperatively setting performance standards and

[5]George S. Odiorne, *Management by Objectives: A System of Managerial Leadership* (New York: Pitman, 1965), p. 55.

deadlines. These supervisors deal in the same way with those they supervise until everyone in the organization is involved. Evaluation occurs periodically during the life of the project at various checkpoints and upon completion of the project. The final MBO evaluation will answer the question, "Were plans and specifications delivered to the prospective bidders at least thirty days prior to the bid opening in sufficient quantity to assure competitive bidding on the project?"

Flexibility   MBO can be either a Theory X or a Theory Y device. The personnel director may view it as an individual performance appraisal (Theory X), whereas the office manager may hope that it will get the office staff moving as a team, thereby increasing production (Theory Y). Indeed, it is being used with varying degrees of success in both ways. Those who advocate its use as a management tool claim that it both increases productivity and improves employee morale.

SITUATIONAL LEADERSHIP

Concerned with what they viewed as a lack of consideration for managerial behavior in other theories, Paul Hersey and Kenneth Blanchard have proposed *situational leadership*.[6] This theory describes appropriate managerial behavior as either *task-* or *relationship*-oriented. Task-oriented behavior emphasizes the duties of the employee in accomplishing the defined job. Relationship-oriented behavior injects a human element in the supervision process. The assumption is that there are periods when the achievement of the organization's goals must take precedent over any personal concerns; at other times the human needs of employees are given priority. Hersey and Blanchard believe that the decision as to task- or relationship-oriented managerial behavior is largely determined by the maturity of the group being supervised. *Maturity* is defined as the ability and willingness to set high but attainable goals.

The successful leader has the skill to utilize both task and relationship styles. The higher the maturity of the group, the more the leader emphasizes relationship behavior. A further responsibility of the leader is to assist the group to become more mature.

THEORY Z

After World War II, Japanese businessmen journeyed to America to learn why American industry was so successful. They

[6]Hersey and Blanchard, *Management of Organizational Behavior: Utilizing Human Resources*, pp. 41–42.

apparently learned their lesson well, since Japanese worker productivity has become the envy of the world. Today, American industrialists are visiting Japanese businesses to learn from the Japanese success story. This success has been attributed in large part to a leadership philosophy.

This philosophy has been described as *Theory Z*.[7] Intending to go beyond McGregor's Theory Y, the theory places a great deal of emphasis on worker participation in decision making. For example, employees and their immediate supervisors are grouped in what is referred to as *quality circles*. The purpose of these quality circles is to assign areas of responsibility and to decide the methods of achieving the forthcoming work tasks. Contrast this to the typical American system of the supervisors handing out work assignments without any involvement of the worker.

Workers in Japan are assured of lifetime employment with a company, with the opportunity for retraining for another job with the company, if necessary. Workers are trusted and allowed to work with a minimum of supervision. Many of these features are being incorporated into American industry.

As the Japanese are to be admired for their employee consideration, so should the American system for its development and use of technology. No nation can approach America in the sophistication and utilization of technology. However, some authorities believe that technological advancement has been at the expense of consideration for worker participation in decision making. The current economic and social conditions in this country would seem to support the conviction that now is the time for American management to incorporate elements of the Japanese model into the ongoing operation of industry and business without sacrificing productivity or technology. When and if this occurs, American industry should regain its former pre-eminence throughout the world.

The Challenge for Management

As technology becomes more complex and the use of computers as a business tool expands, the need for improved ways of dealing with the human side of enterprise also increases. Leadership theory must not be built around the computer to the extent that human needs will be neglected. Management's challenge will be to retain the human concerns advanced by Mayo, McGregor, and others, while utilizing the almost unlimited potential of the computer as an information-gathering, storing, and interpreting tool.

[7]William G. Ouchi, *Theory Z* (New York: Avon Books, 1982).

KEY TERMS

management
leadership
goals
objectives
planning
organizing
directing
controlling
scientific
  management

Hawthorne Effect
human relations
Theory X
Theory Y
management by
  objectives
situational leadership

task-oriented
  behavior
relationship-oriented
  behavior
maturity
Theory Z
quality circles

TEST YOURSELF:
QUESTIONS FOR REVIEW AND DISCUSSION

1. "To fail to plan is to plan to fail" is a popular saying in modern management circles. Apply this to a business with which you are familiar.
2. Give some examples of Machiavellian philosophies that you have personally been affected by or that you have witnessed.
3. What are some work situations where strict Theory X decisions would be called for? Theory Y?
4. Discuss this statement: "Not all leaders are managers but all managers should be leaders."
5. Describe what you think will be the leadership theory of the future.
6. A commonly accepted principle of good management is that employees should be involved in making those decisions that affect them. Discuss some ways that employees at the following levels can be involved: (a) production line; (b) clerical and office; (c) lower level management; (d) top level management.
7. What is the single important leadership trait that you would like to see in your immediate supervisor? Is this trait one that is common to leaders only or is it one that you would like to see in all people?
8. What are the two elements of situational leadership as far as leader behavior is concerned? What determines which leadership style should be utilized?
9. Discuss the statement: "Theory Z is putting Theory Y to practical use."

APPLICATION EXERCISE

Categorize each of the following hypothetical personnel policies as either "Theory X," "Theory Y," or "Theory Z," or "Machiavellian." (A policy may fit in more than one category.) Discuss your decisions with other members of your class. Be sure to state the basis for your decisions.

1. Employees are expected to complete their assigned duties in an eight-hour day with reasonable breaks for refreshments and meals.
2. Employees are required to punch in on the time clock no later than ten minutes prior to the beginning of their scheduled work day and must not check out prior to the completion of their work day.
3. Radios are not permitted at an employee's work station.
4. Employees desiring to have radios at their work stations are reminded to be considerate of their co-workers and to avoid distracting them from their work.
5. Employees and their immediate supervisors are responsible for scheduling their quality circle meetings at times that would minimize interruptions of production.
6. Employees are reminded that company policies are to be followed to the letter. It is the responsibility of each employee to become familiar with all policies. Violation of policies is cause for immediate suspension or discharge.

Suggested Readings

Drucker, Peter F. *The Effective Executive.* New York: Harper & Row, 1967.

Drucker, Peter F. *The Changing World of the Executive.* New York: Harper & Row, 1982.

Hersey, Paul, and Kenneth Blanchard. *Management of Organizational Behavior: Utilizing Human Resources,* 4th ed. Englewood Cliffs, N.J.: Prentice-Hall, 1982.

McGregor, Douglas. *The Human Side of Enterprise.* New York: McGraw-Hill, 1960.

Odiorne, George S. *Management by Objectives: A System of Managerial Leadership.* New York: Pitman, 1965.

Ouchi, William G. *Theory Z.* New York: Avon Books, 1982.

Taylor, Frederick W. *The Principles of Scientific Management.* New York: Harper, 1911.

This, Leslie E. *A Guide to Effective Management: Practical Applications from Behavioral Science.* Reading, Mass.: Addison–Wesley, 1974.

16

MANAGEMENT AS A CAREER

COMPREHENSIVE GOAL
To help you asess your suitability for management.

SPECIFIC OBJECTIVES
After reading this chapter, you will be able to:

■ assess your personal interests and aptitudes and identify a career field based on this assessment

■ describe the future need for managers

■ list the ten qualities that top management contenders possess

■ describe impingements upon unilateral managerial authority created by federal acts

■ describe the areas that cause executives to fail

Chapter 15 was intended to arouse your interest in leadership theory and its importance in managerial decision making. If you want to build on this interest by considering a career in management, this chapter will provide you with a greater understanding of the practical aspects of and the opportunities in the field.

Before you can make an intelligent decision on this matter, however, you will need to conduct a thorough assessment of yourself and your goals. Basing your answers on your interests, your employment history, and what you have learned from previous chapters, ask yourself the following questions:

- Am I a decision maker?

- Am I a people-oriented person?

- Am I challenged by the opportunity to solve a problem?

- Am I willing to assume the burden of management?

- Am I willing to devote many more working hours to my job than do those whom I supervise?

- Can I share the responsibility for the actions and decisions of others?

- Can I work effectively in a team effort?

- Am I an effective communicator?

- Am I challenged by a changing environment?

Do you think that you could become a manager? Assess your aptitudes and goals.

Management Prerequisites

Those who occupy management positions would almost unanimously answer *yes* to the above questions. If you also answered most of them affirmatively, you may be suited for a career in management. However, it is a good idea to expand upon the above questions in order for you to develop a more complete understanding of the job requirements for managerial positions.

Many employees' impression of a manager is someone who sits in a big office and bosses people. Certainly, management is a "people" job. If you have an aversion toward making decisions regarding other people's futures, perhaps you should reconsider pursuing a career in management.

The *desire* to manage is a vital prerequisite. Not everyone has the aptitude, interest, or personality to become a manager. As with most endeavors, the desire to become successful at something is an important indicator.

Since management deals primarily with people, the ability to communicate orally and in writing is a necessary quality. Every manager must communicate with those to whom he or she is responsible, as well as to those at the same and higher managerial levels. Vague, misunderstood directions issued to those being supervised may cause mistakes, production slowdowns, confusion, and even accidents.

The image of the tough, hard-driven, lonely person at the top has largely been replaced by the management team. Successful managers cannot be inflexible; they must be able to work as a team member.

The results of a recent study provide further insight into the skills and aptitudes necessary to be successful in the field of management.[1] Researchers surveyed twenty-one executives who were forced to resign or take early retirement, along with twenty other executives who had made it all the way to the top. The report identified sixty-five factors that were instrumental in contributing to the failure of the twenty-one executives. These sixty-five factors were grouped into the ten following categories:

1. Insensitivity to others
2. Coldness, aloofness, and arrogance
3. Betrayal of trust
4. Overly ambitious
5. Specific performance problems
6. Inability to delegate
7. Inability to staff effectively
8. Inability to think strategically
9. Inability to adapt
10. Overly dependent upon superiors

Notice how many of the above items deal with the ability to get along and work with other people. The most frequently stated cause for failure was insensitivity to other people.

INTERESTS AND APTITUDES

Suppose that you have decided to consider a career in management. How do you proceed? Presumably, this decision is based on your perception of your personality, interests, and aptitudes. How do you make this determination? First, your *interests*. How do you like to spend your spare time—reading, working with your hands, communicating with people? These are clues as to what you are best suited for. If you want more information, there are at least two valid measures of interest available—the *Kuder Occupational Interest Survey* and the *Strong-Campbell Interest Inventory*. Most school and college counselors administer these assessments.

Do not confuse interests with *aptitudes*. Simply liking to be with people does not necessarily mean that your personality and ability

[1]Morgan W. McCall, Jr., and Michael M. Lombardo, "What Makes a Top Executive?," *Psychology Today* (February 1983), pp. 26–31.

indicate that politics or sales are your wisest career choices. Aptitudes—those abilities with which you were born—are a more reliable yardstick of your academic success than your interests. Your aptitudes are measured by such examinations as the *ACT* (American College Test) and the *SAT* (Scholastic Aptitude Test). These aptitude tests are usually administered to high school juniors and seniors.

Aptitudes are also indicated by your grades in various high-school and college courses. Naturally, the courses you elected are an indication of your interests as well as your aptitudes. If you enrolled in accounting, economics, and other business courses, you indicated an interest in these fields. If you achieved high grades, you indicated an aptitude. Having taken the appropriate courses, you have some insight into two measures of your management potential—your interests and your aptitudes. Talk with people who are successful in the fields that appeal to you. See if your interests and aptitudes indeed qualify you for the opportunities available in those fields. It is said that selecting a career is one of the most important decisions a person will make in a lifetime. Take the time and make the effort necessary to do this properly.

Courtesy of Sea World

An interest in animals combined with an aptitude for psychology could produce a career as an animal trainer.

EDUCATION

A question you must be asking is "How important is a formal education to my success in a management career?" The answer is—very important! In a study conducted by Christopher Jencks and reported upon in *Psychology Today*, Daniel Yankelovich stated, "Beside family background, the single most important factor contributing to. . .economic success is finishing college. . . . Completing college gives whites a whopping 49 percent advantage over those who do not—the percentage is even larger for blacks."[2] Moreover, according to Sylvia Porter, "Virtually all newly appointed company executives are college graduates and more than one in three have advanced degrees. Most majored in business or engineering and among those with master's degrees most are in business."[3]

WHERE ARE THE JOBS?

"Management" exists in almost every occupational field—transportation, medicine, manufacturing, education, etc. Your interests, aptitudes, and goals will determine your choice among them.

Statistics indicate, however, that you will make a major change of job at least six times during your working life. Therefore, you

[2]Daniel Yankelovich, "Who Gets Ahead in America," *Psychology Today* (July 1979), p. 40.

[3]Sylvia Porter, "What Factors Send Some to the Top?" Rapid City *Journal* (May 4, 1979), p. 22.

The help-wanted ads contain dozens of management-level positions.

should think of your career planning as a continuous building process, not as one "fixed-in-concrete" decision.

Unless you marry the boss's son or daughter, it is unlikely that you will obtain a management position as your first job. However, the potential for promotion into management positions should be a part of your first job decision. To avoid getting into a dead-end situation where management promotions are blocked, you should examine the company's management structure. Look at the company's *organizational chart.* It will illustrate the various levels and areas of responsibility in the company and will reveal the range of opportunities for management promotions. For example, the sample organizational chart shown in figure 16–1 shows that the vice president in charge of marketing has the sales manager and the product research director reporting to him. They in turn supervise sales personnel and the research department, respectively.

Rising to the Top   Let us assume that you have completed your formal education and that you have obtained a position in a firm that offers management potential. How do you rise to management level? By maintaining a learning attitude. Learn all you can about the firm—its products, goals, problems, personnel, and its management philosophy. Ask questions of your supervisor. Observe company executives in action and learn from their years of experience. How do they make decisions? What is their management philosophy? Volunteer your time and talents when opportunities arise. In other words, be a good employee—one who is trusted and responsible. Then, when a management position opens, make a formal application to the appropriate administrator.

Career Opportunities in Management   According to the U.S. Department of Labor, the need for managers during the 1980–1990 decade will grow by approximately ten million.[4] Within this figure the number of self-employed managers is likely to decrease, as the number of large corporations and chains continue to increase. The greatest increase in management positions is projected to be in the highly technical areas, such as information management and computers. The need for management personnel in this field will increase by twenty-one percent. These statistics should be kept in mind as you contemplate your future in a management career.

If you are a woman or a member of a minority, your future in management is even brighter. *Title VII of the Civil Rights Act of 1964* bans discrimination in employment on the basis of race, color, religion, sex, or national origin. Many companies, under affirmative action directives, actively seek out women and minorities to fill management positions.

[4]*Occupational Outlook Handbook,* U.S. Government Printing Office Washington, D.C.: 1982–83), p. 22.

In 1969, only 46 women served on the board of major companies. In 1979, the figure was nearly 300, and it continues to grow. The nation's top ten corporations all have at least one woman on their governing boards. Similar strides are being reported for minority group members.

The vast majority of promotions into management positions are made from within the organization, so you generally have an edge on outside applicants. However, you may not get the managerial appointment even though you might be the best qualified applicant within the firm. Occasionally, a firm's top leaders will want to bring in "new blood." They may do this for a variety of reasons; usually they want a change in management philosophy. If you are not selected, you should not let this affect your work and your attitude. Other opportunities will very likely present themselves.

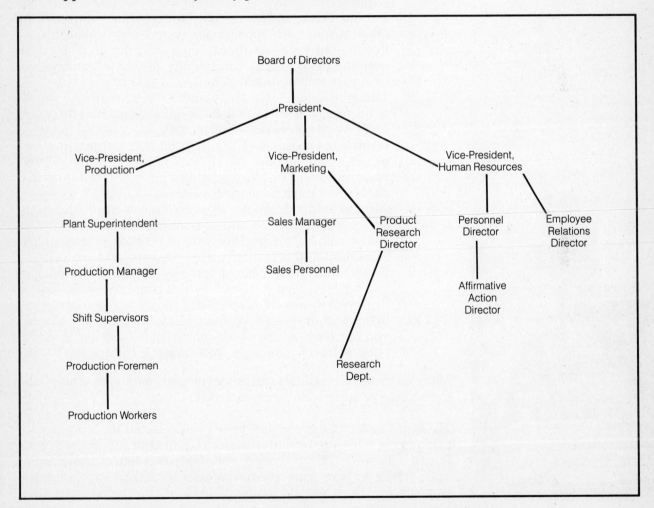

Figure 16–1
A Sample Organizational Chart

The qualities of a good manager include diplomacy and thoughtfulness.

What Makes A Good Manager   The qualities that top management contenders possess have been described as follows.[5] They are:

1. Appearance—Conspicuous obesity or extreme emaciation are negative marks. In men, conservative dress can't be faulted. In women, a good quality suit with a fresh, bright-colored blouse is excellent. Jewelry should be muted, hair neat.
2. Personality, style—You can learn manners and poise, adopt diplomatic approach, act with proper deference.
3. Articulateness—This category is increasingly important because even if you have the proper educational background, superb dress and manners, good looks, etc., you will ruin your chances if you come across as a "linguistic cripple."
4. Energy, drive, ambition—Easy to recognize—through the quick stride, fresh appearance, superb physical health.
5. Positive attitude—Without being an utter fool, you can beat the pessimist by consistently displaying a constructive, cheerful outlook on life.
6. Thoughtfulness—No one wants a "yes" man. An intelligent man or woman usually weighs a question for a second or two before responding.
7. Overall composure—The nail biter, hair twirler, foot tapper, or chain smoker rarely goes beyond an initial interview unless his or her credentials are so outstanding that allowances must be made for nervous habits.
8. Aura of leadership—An erect carriage, a head held high, an agreeable manner, and self-confidence connote leadership qualities. You must be sure of yourself to lead others. Important in this is that you inspire trust and are likable.
9. Bright, informed, a bit of sparkle—If you are intelligent and well rounded, you usually will come across as such. A degree of humor adds sparkle.
10. Breadth of interests—Without being the least bit pedantic, you can learn a little about many fields—art, architecture, politics, travel, languages, economics, literature, music, etc.

Many of these ten qualities can be developed, whatever your goals, to enhance your personal and career life.

The Best Leader   Suppose you have been selected for a position in management. This represents a major step in your career road. Your formal education has provided you with theoretical background upon which to base your day-to-day decisions. You have a knowledge of the firm and its goals. You have developed your own

Another desirable quality in a manager is articulateness.

[5]Sylvia Porter, p. 22.

management theory. How will you proceed? You might keep in mind the words of the ancient Chinese philosopher Lao-tse:

> A leader is best when people barely know he exists, not so good when people obey and applaud him, worst when they dislike him. Fail to honor people, they fail to honor you. But of a good leader, who talks little, when his work is done, his aim fulfilled, they will say, "We did this ourselves."

Impingements on Managerial Authority

To the casual observer, it may seem that top-level management has complete control over company employees. On the contrary, federal legislation controls a lot of American business operations, and many of these laws have existed since the late 1800s and the early 1900s.

A number of laws governing the rights of workers to organize for the purpose of collective bargaining with their employers began in the 1930s. Not all of this legislation works to the disadvantage of the employer. For example, more than twenty states have enacted *right to work laws*, which prohibit forced union membership as a condition for keeping one's job. The Taft-Hartley Act of 1947 outlines six unfair labor practices for which unions and their members may be found guilty.

The Civil Rights Act of 1964, the Fair Labor Standards Act, the Equal Pay Act, and the Occupational Safety and Health Act (OSHA) are but a few of the various legislative enactments which regulate the way managers may or may not conduct the affairs of the company. Individual states have their own set of laws corresponding to those at the federal level.

It would benefit you to become familiar with the provisions of these and other laws of a similar nature. This information can be obtained from a local, state, or federal Labor Relations Board. The Suggested Readings at the end of this chapter also list sources of this information.

Legislation and court decisions have created constraints on managerial decision making. However, this trend seems to be slowing and, in some situations, reversing.

What's Ahead for You?

If you are considering a career in management, there are several matters to include in your decision. Management positions require a special blend of personality traits that thrive on the challenge of working with people and all of their peculiarities. The future need for management personnel appears to be expanding, particularly in the growth industries, such as electronics and information transmis-

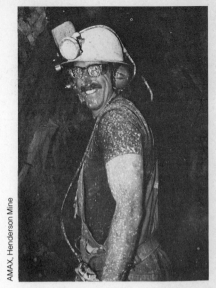

AMAX, Henderson Mine

A miner's hard hat, safety glasses, ear muffs, and emergency breathing apparatus—sample precautions the federal government is concerned with when it monitors safety in the workplace.

Hazel Hankin

A union grievance meeting

sion. Opportunities for women and minority members are also increasing.

In light of the rapidly changing social and economic environment, a managerial career is certain to become more accessible, more complicated, more challenging, and more satisfying.

KEY TERMS

Kuder Occupational Interest Survey
Strong-Campbell Interest Inventory

aptitudes
ACT
SAT
interests

organizational chart
Title VII of the Civil Rights Act of 1964
right to work laws

TEST YOURSELF:
QUESTIONS FOR REVIEW AND DISCUSSION

1. Explain why management is often described as a "people" job.
2. List the personal characteristics that successful managers should possess. How many of these do you possess?
3. Of the characteristics listed above that you do *not* possess, how can you overcome your shortfallings?
4. Would you like a career in management? Why? Why not?
5. What do you see as the most effective procedure for gaining entry into the field of management?

APPLICATION EXERCISES

1. Suppose that you are a department head who is considering promoting one of your workers to a management position. What qualities would you look for in a potential manager?

2. Identify a successful manager in your community. This person might be the head of a manufacturing firm, a college president, or the local superintendent of schools. Arrange an interview with this person. The following are suggested questions for you to discuss.

   A. How long have you been in your present position?
   B. How long have you been with this firm?
   C. What is your educational background?
   D. Describe the duties performed in your first managerial position. In your present position.
   E. To what do you attribute your success?
   F. What do you see as the main responsibilities of those in managerial positions?
   G. What parts of your job provide you with the greatest challenges? The greatest satisfactions?
   H. What advice would you offer young people who are interested in a management career?

   Share the results of your interview with your classmates.

Suggested Readings

McCall, Morgan W., and Michael M. Lombardo. "What Makes a Top Executive?" *Psychology Today* (February 1983), pp. 26–32.

National Labor Relations Board. *A Layman's Guide to Basic Law Under the National Labor Relations Act.* Washington, D.C.: U.S. Government Printing Office, 1971.

Occupational Outlook Handbook. Washington, D.C.: U.S. Government Printing Office, 1982–83.

Porter, Sylvia. *Sylvia Porter's New Money Book for the 80s.* New York: Avon, 1980.

Taylor, Benjamin J., and Fred Witney. *Labor Relations Law.* Englewood Cliffs, N.J.: Prentice-Hall, 1979.

GLOSSARY

acceleration A provision in an installment purchase contract stipulating that the entire amount owed must be paid immediately if one payment is missed (*p. 348*).

acid mantle Chemical properties on the surface of the skin (*p. 56*).

acne A skin disorder characterized by chronic inflammation of the sebaceous glands resulting in the appearance of pimples and blemishes on the face, neck, and shoulders (*p. 62*).

ACT. *See* American College Test.

activity In transactional analysis, the core of time-structuring and the basis of all other transactions. It is purposeful work directed toward the achievement of a goal (*p. 279*).

additive A substance, such as artificial flavoring, artificial coloring, or sweeteners, added to many commercial foods (*p. 115*).

advance Money a company advances to an employee based on an estimate of business expenses to be incurred and for which the employee must be reimbursed (*p. 335*).

aerobic dance Exercise set to music, combining the fun of dance with the benefits of jogging (*p. 90*).

aerobics A form of exercise involving steady, sustained, and vigorous physical activity that improves oxygen intake, aids the circulatory system, strengthens the body, and helps burn up calories (*p. 88*).

Age Discrimination in Employment Act of 1967 Prohibits job discrimination (refusal to hire, or firing) against individuals 40 to 65 years old simply because of their age. An amendment to the act in 1979 raised from 65 to 70 the age at which an employer may require mandatory retirement (*p. 47*).

agenda A list of topics to be discussed at a meeting (*p. 232*).

aggression A reaction to manipulation in which the victim turns on the victimizer (*p. 217*).

all-channel pattern A casual, informal method of exchanging information that seems to have no specific direction (*p. 238*).

American College Test (ACT) A standardized aptitude test usually administered to high school juniors or seniors, used to help determine which collegiate pursuits would be most successful (*p. 381*).

American method A manner of using eating utensils in which the fork is held in the right hand to convey food to the mouth, is transferred to the left hand to cut food, and returned to the right hand for eating (*p. 302*).

Amtrak The National Railroad Passenger Corporation, a quasi-public corporation established by Congress under the Rail Passenger Service Act of 1970 in an attempt to revitalize passenger service on railroads (*p. 325*).

analogous color scheme Related colors, e.g., red and orange, blue and violet, yellow and green, placed together in a range of shades, tints, and tones (*p. 127*).

androgens Male hormones that cause skin to become thicker and oilier during puberty (*p. 58*).

annual percentage rate (APR) The percentage cost of credit on a yearly basis (*p. 347*).

annual report A yearly summary issued by a company giving the firm's financial standing, growth, types of products, and proposals for new products; its corporate officers; and the location of its home and branch offices (*p. 37*).

annuity An investment yielding fixed payments during the holder's lifetime or for a fixed number of years (*p. 341*).

antibacterial soap A soap product with extra chemicals added to inhibit bacterial growth (*p. 60*).

antiperspirant A deodorant preparation that contains special chemicals to retard the flow of perspiration (*p. 78*).

application form A printed form relating to personal, educational, and employment information that an organization requests a prospective employee to fill out before an interview (*p. 22*).

application letter A carefully constructed letter applying for a particular position and containing a description of major qualifications relating to the job, a reference to the enclosed résumé that presents other qualifications, a request for an interview, and a statement of where the applicant can be reached (*p. 17*).

APR. *See* annual percentage rate.

aptitude Special ability or talent for achievement in learning or developing skills (*p. 380*).

assertiveness training Various methods of teaching people how to be effective, to stand up for their rights, and not let others coerce or manipulate them (*p. 214*).

astringent A skin product, generally containing

alcohol and other ingredients, used to remove excess oil and refresh skin (p. 61).

balanced diet Daily menus that provide all the necessary nutrients by including food from each of four categories: protein-rich foods; fruit and vegetables; breads, cereals, and pasta; milk and milk products (p. 105).

beneficiary In insurance, the person designated to receive the amount for which a policy holder is insured (p. 340).

BFOQ. See bona fide occupational qualification.

Bill of Assertive Rights Ten rights of the individual prescribed by Manuel J. Smith for his students as a form of assertiveness training (p. 217).

block of silence The point in an interview when the interviewer deliberately discontinues the dialogue to see how the interviewee handles the situation (p. 45).

blue laws Strict laws designed to control human behavior by regulating such activities as Sunday business hours, amusements, and sale of alcoholic beverages (p. 257).

body language Messages conveyed by bodily movements and facial expressions (p. 185).

bona fide occupational qualification (BFOQ) Personal information that relates directly to a job being sought (as certain physical standards for modeling)—under civil rights legislation, the only personal data that may be required of a job applicant (p. 15).

brainstorming A method of solving problems in which members of a group freely contribute ideas and suggestions and all ideas are welcome regardless of their logic (p. 233).

broken record An assertiveness tactic in which an individual states a position and repeats it as often as necessary (p. 220).

budget An estimate of income and expenditures over a particular period of time (p. 337).

CAB. See Civil Aeronautics Board.

calorie A unit used to measure the energy produced by food. One food calorie is equal to the amount of heat required to raise the temperature of one kilogram of water one degree centigrade (p. 107).

cancer A disorder of cells of the body in which malignant cells reproduce rapidly (p. 159).

carbohydrates A food source, such as starches and sugar, for supplying energy and heat to the body (p. 103).

cardiopulmonary system The body system involving the heart and lungs. Also called cardiorespiratory (p. 88).

care labels The labels sewn to a garment detailing proper cleaning and handling care (p. 149).

carry-on luggage Hand luggage airline passengers take on board themselves and store under their seats (p. 317).

CEO. See chief executive officer.

chain A serial pattern by which communication flows upward or downward through certain channels (p. 238).

chancre A small, hard, painless sore, usually in the genitals, mouth, or anus, whose appearance is the first symptom of syphilis (p. 162).

charge account A credit arrangement whereby a customer may purchase goods or services and pay for them at a later date (p. 348).

Chief executive officer (CEO) The top officer in a corporation (p. 212).

chroma A term referring to the purity of a color determined by its freedom from white (p. 125).

chronological résumé A résumé that lists the most recent job or education experience first and the remaining data in reverse chronological order (p. 11).

cilia Hairlike extensions that fill the lining of the lungs. Their action of whipping back and forth at 900 times a minute forces pollutants and mucus from the lungs (p. 164).

Civil Aeronautics Board (CAB) A federal agency that regulates economic activities of U.S. airlines in interstate, overseas, and international travel and establishes basic rules and guidelines to protect passengers (p. 322).

Civil Rights Act of 1964 Law that prevents employers, employment agencies, and unions from discriminating because of race, color, religion, sex, or national origin (p. 385).

classic A style of clothing that has been accepted for years and that probably will never go off the market (p. 147).

clearinghouse A service that provides information on job vacancies in a field for a specified geographical area (p. 7).

close-ended questions Narrow, specific questions that zero in on one specific point and can be answered briefly (p. 43).

closing costs Various taxes, insurance, survey,

and appraisal fees that must be paid in addition to the basic purchase price when a real-estate deal is closed (*p. 357*).

club tie A tie with a minute repeating pattern woven in the material (*p. 141*).

code of ethics The set of rules by which people conduct themselves (*p. 251*).

cohesiveness The natural relationship that develops when people work closely together, especially if the group is pitted against an adversary (*p. 241*).

coinsurance A provision in a health insurance policy that splits the liability for a claim between the insured and the insurance company. If the insured assumes a percentage of the cost of all future claims, the company will reduce the premium (*p. 342*).

collateral A pledge of property or securities to guarantee repayment of a loan (*p. 346*).

College Placement Annual A directory, published yearly by the College Placement Council, of occupational needs anticipated by corporate and governmental employers who normally recruit college graduates (*p. 6*).

college placement office A college agency providing assistance to students and alumni in finding jobs (*p. 6*).

communication cycle A complex transaction of thought in which two or more people can take part. Four basic components are necessary to complete the cycle: the sender, the message, the receiver, and the feedback (*p. 180*).

communication pattern The distinctive manner in which a group or organization communicates (*p. 237*).

complementary color scheme Two colors that complement and intensify each other, as green and red (*p. 126*).

comprehensive Automobile insurance that provides protection against certain "named perils," such as fire, theft, vandalism, and natural disaster. It is usually offered with a small deductible (*p. 344*).

compromise The give-and-take process that often goes on in legislatures before an actual vote is taken. Each group modifies its position in order to reach a conclusion (*p. 235*).

conditioner A rinse, cream, lotion, or other product used to alleviate a hair problem (*p. 73*).

confirmed reservation A term indicating the traveler has been assigned available space for which advance payment is generally required (*p. 313*).

connecting flight The flight to which a passenger transfers from the originating flight to complete a journey. The passenger must check in with the connecting flight as with the originating flight (*p. 320*).

consensus The general agreement of all members of a group on all parts of a decision (*p. 236*).

contact lens A small, thin lens of glass or plastic fitted over the cornea of the eye to correct a vision problem (*p. 142*).

Continental method A manner of using eating utensils in which the fork remains in the left hand after cutting meat and the food is conveyed to the mouth with tines held downward (*p. 303*).

controlling The process of evaluating performance to see if organizational goals are being achieved and making the necessary adjustments in planning, organizing, and directing if these goals are not being met (*p. 366*).

corporate credit card A credit card in a company's name issued to its employees for business-related expenses. The bills for these expenditures are sent directly to the company for payment (*p. 335*).

corporate image The mental conception the public has of a company's values and attitudes (*p. 37*).

cortex The middle layer of the hair shaft; it is responsible for hair's elasticity, and contains the pigment that gives hair its color (*p. 69*).

cortisone A drug useful in controlling inflammation, sometimes used by a dermatologist to help clear skin of acne (*p. 63*).

credit The authority to spend someone else's money under certain conditions of time and/or up to a certain limit (*p. 345*).

credit cards Travel cards, gasoline cards, bank cards, and department store cards identifying the holder and allowing him or her to charge goods or services instead of paying by cash or check. The balance is accumulated and billed monthly (*p. 345*).

cryosurgery A surgical procedure used to treat severe acne or other skin disorders by freezing (*p. 63*).

cryotherapy A medical treatment using extremely cold temperatures, sometimes used to clear up acne (*p. 63*).

DDD. *See* Direct Distance Dial.

deductible In an insurance plan, the amount a

person has to pay in the event of a claim before the insurance company incurs any liability (*p. 342*).

dental floss Thin thread used to clean between the teeth where toothbrushes often can't reach (*p. 158*).

deodorant A cream or liquid preparation applied to the skin to reduce or prevent body odor (*p. 78*).

deodorant soap A soap that contains a fragrance, and sometimes an antiseptic agent to reduce body odor (*p. 60*).

depilatory A chemical product applied for the purpose of removing unwanted hair (*p. 77*).

dermatologist A doctor who deals with the skin and its diseases (*p. 63*).

dermis Living tissue, below the epidermis, containing nerves, blood vessels, smooth muscles, hair follicles, sweat glands, and sebaceous glands (*p. 56*).

detergent soap Synthetic soap that does not contain fats (*p. 60*).

detoxify To remove poison or toxin (for example, alcohol from the liver) from something (*p. 167*).

direct bill credit cards A credit card issued in a company's name that allows charges made by an authorized employee to be billed directly to the company, with no cash outlay required from the employee (*p. 326*).

Direct Distance Dial (DDD) Dialing a desired long distance number directly, with no operator assistance required. This results in a lower toll rate (*p. 296*).

direct flight A flight from one city to another with intermediate stops but no change of planes (*p. 320*).

directing A function of management that involves guiding and supervising the efforts of subordinates toward the attainment of the organization's objectives (*p. 366*).

discretionary expenditures Flexible expenditures, such as for food, household, car maintenance, clothing, and recreation, that vary from one period to another and over which a person has some control (*p. 338*).

DOE In job-advertising jargon, an abbreviation for "depends on experience"(*p. 8*).

dominant person method In decision making, the domination of a group discussion by one strong-willed member who steamrollers an idea through the meeting (*p. 235*).

double standard A particular code of conduct applied more strictly to one group or person than to another (*p. 258*).

dress code Company policy that spells out acceptable office attire (*p. 31*).

drug In *Beyond Drugs*, by Stanley Einstein, defined as: "Any substance that by its chemical nature alters the structure or functioning of the living organism" (*p. 168*).

drug abuse According to the World Health Organization, "Persistent or sporadic excessive drug use inconsistent with or unrelated to acceptable medical practice" (*p. 168*).

drug dependence According to the World Health Organization, "A state of psychic or physical dependence, or both, on a drug, arising in a person following administration of that drug on a periodic or continuous basis" (*p. 168*).

earned income Wages that are earned through employment (*p. 351*).

egalitarian style A company philosophy that emphasizes employee involvement in decision making as a motivator (*p. 212*).

electrolysis A process for removing unwanted hair, generally permanently, by inserting an electric needle into the hair follicle in order to destroy the root (*p. 76*).

empathy The projection of one's personality into the personality of another in order to understand him or her better (*p. 181*).

empty-calorie foods Foods, such as soda pop, potato chips, candy and cake, with high caloric value but little nutritional worth (*p. 111*).

endowment insurance A policy on which premiums are paid over a specified period of time, at the end of which the face amount is paid to the insured or to a beneficiary if the insured dies prior to maturity date (*p. 341*).

EOE An abbreviation for Equal Opportunity Employer (*p. 8*).

epidermis The outer surface of the skin, containing a layer of dead cells for the protection of the living tissue underneath (*p. 56*).

Equal Credit Opportunity Act of 1975 Federal legislation making it illegal to discriminate on the basis of sex or marital status when considering a credit application (*p. 349*).

Equal Pay Act of 1963 Federal legislation requiring that men and women performing under similar working conditions receive the same benefits and pay for substantially equal skills, efforts, and responsibilities (*p. 385*).

exfoliation The removal of dead skin from the epidermis by rubbing a terry washcloth over the skin or by scrubbing it with an abrasive sponge or soft-bristled complexion brush (*p. 60*).

expense diary A daily record of the dates, places, purposes, and amounts of legitimate business expenses (*p. 333*).

face amount The amount for which a policy holder is insured (*p. 341*).

facial contouring The use of makeup to give the face dimension by accenting certain areas by means of light tones and de-emphasizing others by means of dark tones (*p. 81*).

facial undertones Color in the skin that can have an effect on colors of clothing (*p. 128*).

facilitator A neutral processor in a meeting whose main function is to see that the meeting runs smoothly (*p. 247*).

facts Statements that can be readily supported by proof or evidence (*p. 189*).

fad A clothing concept that becomes enormously popular but is generally of short duration (*p. 147*).

Fair Credit Billing Act A law requiring lenders to mail statements 14 days before the payment-due date; the law provides borrowers with some recourse against unfair practices by creditors (*p. 349*).

Fair Credit Reporting Act Protects consumers with respect to the collection and publication of credit information (*p. 348*).

Fair Labor Standards Act Also known as the Wages and Hours Law. Passed by Congress in 1938 to improve the standard of living of workers, it established a minimum wage, a maximum work week, and time-and-a-half-pay for overtime (*p. 385*).

fashion A style of clothing that stays popular for several years (*p. 147*).

FDA. *See* Food and Drug Administration.

Federal Insurance Contributions Act taxes (FICA taxes) Social security taxes levied as a percentage of gross earned income that fund a national insurance plan offering retirement, disability, and health benefits to wage earners and their families (*p. 356*).

fee paid A term indicating that the fee ordinarily charged a successful job applicant by a professional placement service will be paid by the employer (*p. 7*).

feedback The verbal or nonverbal response a receiver returns to the sender as a necessary part of the communication cycle (*p. 192*).

FICA taxes. *See* Federal Insurance Contributions Act taxes.

finance charge The total dollar amount, including interest charges and sometimes service charges, that a person pays to use credit (*p. 347*).

fixed expenditures Regularly occurring expenses that have to be paid each month or at some other set interval (*p. 338*).

fluoride A substance added to drinking water to help prevent tooth decay (*p. 158*).

Fly-Rights A publication issued free of charge by the CAB to acquaint passengers with their rights and obligations when flying (*p. 325*).

fogging In assertiveness training, a method of dealing with criticism by offering no resistance to it, agreeing with it, and treating it calmly and perhaps even lightly (*p. 221*).

Food and Drug Administration (FDA) A federal agency enforcing laws protecting the public against impure and harmful foods, drugs, and cosmetics (*p. 115*).

Form 1040 "Long form" federal income tax return (*p. 353*).

formal balance In fashion design, having a garment identical on each side of an imaginary line drawn vertically down the middle of the figure (*p. 146*).

foulard A tie usually having a small geometrical pattern imprinted in the design (*p. 141*).

foundation A product available in liquid, cream, pancake, or solid form that is applied to improve the natural appearance and texture of the skin and to provide a base for makeup (*p. 81*).

fringe benefits Benefits such as pensions, medical and life insurance, paid vacations and holidays, sick-leave policy, profit sharing, and tuition payments that a company offers its employees in addition to salary (*p. 41*).

frosting A hair-coloring process that adds highlights by applying bleach to strands of hair pulled through holes in a tight rubber cap (*p. 75*).

frustration A feeling of being torn between doing what one wants to do and what one should do (*p. 217*).

functional résumé A résumé that concentrates on duties performed or skills acquired (*p. 11*).

games Activities that manipulate people and

have the ulterior design of trapping someone (*p. 278*).

garnishment Attachment of a debtor's assets, by court order, to pay a debt. Some installment purchase contracts include a provision for garnisheeing the creditor's wages (up to 25 percent of his take-home pay) if a payment is missed (*p. 348*).

generalizations The grouping of people, things, or ideas under one label, making no exception for individuality (*p. 197*).

genital herpes A venereal disease, commonly called herpes 2, caused by a virus and characterized by small, painful blisters in the genital area (*p. 162*).

goals Long-term, generally unchanging aims of an organization—its "reason for being" (*p. 365*).

Golden Mean The principle of proportion that the smaller space should have the same relationship to the larger space as the larger space to the whole (*p. 146*).

gonococci The microorganisms that cause gonorrhea (*p. 161*).

gonorrhea A contagious, pus-producing inflammation of the mucous membranes of the genitals caused by microorganisms called gonococci. Perhaps the most common of all venereal diseases (*p. 161*).

GPA. *See* grade point average.

grade point average (GPA) A measure of a student's overall scholastic achievements (*p. 10*).

gross income Total income or salary before any deductions (*p. 337*).

group goal The common denominator or central purpose that moves a group into action (*p. 227*).

group intimidation A situation in which a group verbally or nonverbally retaliates against a member whose idea has offended the others (*p. 237*).

group life Low-cost term insurance sold only to groups; it may be available through a person's employer or union (*p. 341*).

group norms Unwritten rules, seldom discussed but strongly enforced, that define acceptable modes of conduct within a group (*p. 229*).

groupthink A condition occurring when members of a strong, cohesive group get along too well with one another. Too much closeness can lead to a lack of objectivity, and hamper the group's effectiveness in making decisions (*p. 241*).

guaranteed reservation An arrangement whereby travelers who cannot arrive by a hotel's check-in time can guarantee that their room will be held for them by prepaying a night's rental or using a major credit card (*p. 315*).

hair cuticle The protective outer layer of scales on a hair shaft (*p. 70*).

Hawthorne Effect A term (derived from studies at the Hawthorne Electric plant in Illinois) referring to the increased results when people are involved in decision making. The study found that change in physical working conditions had almost no effect on productivity, but the attention paid to the workers and their involvement in the project stimulated greater production (*p. 370*).

health food A broad term applied to a variety of foods claimed to be organically grown and/or free of chemicals, but whose superior nutritional value is unsubstantiated (*p. 115*).

herpes simplex virus type 1 A virus that causes cold sores, fever blisters, and other lesions above the waist (*p. 163*).

herpes simplex virus type 2 The virus that causes genital herpes, a venereal disease (*p. 162*).

hidden agendas Personal subjects, as opposed to topics listed on the regular agenda, that a member of a group may want to discuss for selfish reasons (*p. 232*).

hue Color, or the characteristics that differentiate one color from another (*p. 125*).

human relations A management theory that emphasizes human and social factors affecting employee performance (*p. 370*).

hydrate In skin care, to apply moisture to the face (*p. 62*).

Individual Retirement Account (IRA) A savings plan that defers tax on the investment until the investor reaches retirement age (*p. 351*).

inference A conclusion that is drawn from something assumed but that needs additional information before it is recognized as a fact (*p. 190*).

informal balance When the left and right sides of a garment are not identical, but are balanced in their proportions (*p. 147*).

inner direction The manner in which a person's life is directed. Inner-directed persons decide for themselves what they want to do with their lives (*p. 271*).

installment loan A loan repaid in periodic installments. For large expenditures, an install-ment purchase agreement gives the vendor title to the purchased item (the collateral) until the balance of the loan and interest charges are paid in full (*p. 348*).

interaction method A procedure for a meeting in which all participants are on an equal basis and the boss or manager is prohibited from acting as the head. A facilitator conducts the meeting, and a recorder records every idea expressed (*p. 247*).

interline transfer A change from a plane on one airline to another on a different airline (*p. 318*).

intermediate colors Orange, green, and violet colors (*p. 126*).

internal static Interference with communication, caused by different knowledge, emotions, and backgrounds of the sender and receiver (*p. 193*).

interview A face-to-face meeting between a job applicant and a representative of a company for the purpose of evaluating the qualifications of the person applying for a job (*p. 29*).

intimacy A form of interaction between two people who can freely relate to each other with-out fear of rejection because each feels comfort-able with the other and mutual respect is evident (*p. 278*).

involuntary bumping The decision made by an airline as to which passengers with confirmed reservations will be taken off a flight when more seats have been sold than are available on the plane. A refund of the full price of the ticket must be awarded to each person denied board-ing privileges (*p. 323*).

IRA. *See* Individual Retirement Account.

isometrics A method of exercising that pits one set of muscles against another or against an im-movable object and requires no noticeable movement (*p. 88*).

isotonics Exercises, such as calisthenics and weight lifting, that require movement to create muscle contractions (*p. 88*).

itinerary The detailed outline of a trip, including airline flight number, time of departure and ar-rival, cities to be visited, names of hotels, and telephone numbers where the traveler can be reached (*p. 315*).

job objective A statement in a résumé that tells the employment goal or position a person is seeking (*p. 11*).

Job Services Center A state employment service that provides free job placement, along with vo-cational counseling, testing, and statewide placement (*p. 6*).

Johari Window A comparison of the human per-sonality to a four-paned window, with each pane representing a segment of the total indi-vidual (*p. 201*).

keratin A protein substance of which hair is made (*p. 69*).

kinesics The study of body language—the mes-sages conveyed by bodily movements and facial expressions (*p. 185*).

Kuder Occupational Interest Survey A standard-ized test designed to help individuals make oc-cupational choices based on interest priorities (*p. 380*).

lateral thinking A method of problem solving by moving out from and around the problem and applying freely associated ideas to it (*p. 233*).

leadership The quality or trait of being able to lead or influence the behavior of others in a particular direction (*p. 363*).

letter of credit A letter an employee can present to an authorized agent who will advance a pre-established amount of cash or credit authorized by the employer and then record the transaction on the letter (*p. 335*).

liability Automobile insurance coverage offering protection up to stated limits from claims of others for restitution of property damage, bodily injury, mental anguish, legal costs, or other ex-penses associated with accidental damages (*p. 343*).

life positions Classification of human behavior in terms of OK-ness: I'm not OK—you're OK; I'm not OK—you're not OK; I'm OK—you're not OK; and I'm OK—you're OK (*p. 211*).

lines Optical illusions created by placement of seams, button rows, contrasting colors on clothes, resulting in a shorter, fatter, slimmer, or taller effect (*p. 144*).

maitre d'hôtel The headwaiter or person in charge of the dining room, who acts as host, takes reservations, greets diners, and shows them to their tables (*p. 298*).

majority rule A voting process in which the deci-sion is binding on the whole group if 51 percent or more of its members vote in its favor (*p. 235*).

major medical   A health insurance policy providing protection, up to a specified limit beyond a basic health plan, against the high expense of long-term serious illness or injury (*p. 342*).

management   The authority vested in a person who has a designated administrative title. Management's basic responsibilities are to establish organizational goals and objectives and to marshal the various available resources toward meeting those goals and objectives (*p. 363*).

management by objectives (MBO)   A program designed to motivate employees through having them participate in setting of goals, and subsequently evaluating them in terms of their success in meeting those goals (*p. 40, 372*).

maternal style   A company philosophy that emphasizes employee welfare as a motivator (*p. 212*).

maturity   A term used in situational leadership theory, which is measured by the ability and willingness of employees to set high, but attainable goals (*p. 374*).

MBO.   *See* management by objectives.

Medicaid   A program funded jointly by the state and federal governments to provide medical aid for people with low incomes (*p. 342*).

Medicare   A program financed under Social Security Administration funds to provide medical care for the aged (*p. 342*).

medulla   The inner, tubelike core of a shaft of hair (*p. 69*).

melanin   A brown pigment that determines the darkness of the skin (*p. 56*).

message   In communications, the spoken or written word, gestures, facial expression, or other means by which the sender transmits his or her thoughts (*p. 182*).

minority rule   A form of decision making, commonly found in business, in which a small board of executives makes decisions that affect many people in an organization (*p. 236*).

mirror technique   An interview technique in which the interviewer picks a key concept in a job applicant's statement, repeats it or rephrases it, and develops it into another question (*p. 44*).

moisturizer   A skin conditioner applied after an astringent or skin freshener to act as a seal and prevent moisture loss (*p. 62*).

moniliasis   A yeast type of fungus infection that causes severe itching and a white, curdy discharge. It spreads to sex partners and frequently recurs. In males, the infection affects the oral, penile, and anal areas (*p. 163*).

monochromatic   A color scheme that uses various tints, shades, and tones of a single color (*p. 126*).

muscle relaxation   A process of reducing muscle tension by means of deep breathing and serially tensing and relaxing muscles of the arms, legs, and body (*p. 100*).

nail cuticle   The small strip of hardened skin that touches the fingernail or toenail (*p. 79*).

named perils   Itemized dangers specified for coverage or exclusion in an insurance policy (*p. 344*).

Needs Hierarchy   A theory developed by Dr. Abraham Maslow that arranges the basic human needs and drives that motivate all people in a pyramidlike scale (*p. 209*).

negative assertion   A method of dealing with criticism by offering no resistance to it, agreeing with it, and treating it calmly and perhaps even lightly (*p. 221*).

negative inquiry   A form of assertiveness in which an individual does not try to justify his or her actions but instead questions critics by asking why they are bothered (*p. 221*).

net income   The actual amount of a paycheck available for budgeting after deductions have been made for income tax, Social Security, pension contributions, group insurance, and the like (*p. 337*).

neutralizer   An agent that stops the action of the chemical solution applied to the hair in both permanent curling and in straightening the hair (*p. 75*).

nonspecific vaginitis   A bacterial infection that causes increased vaginal secretions, a white or gray discharge, inflammation and swelling of the vagina, and pain during intercourse (*p. 163*).

nonstop flight   *See* Direct Flight.

nonverbal communication   Transmitting a message by means of body language, vocal intonation or inflection, physical objects, or space, rather than by written or spoken word (*p. 185*).

NOW Accounts (Negotiable Order of Withdrawal)   A checking account that earns interest (*p. 351*).

nutrition   The process by which food is taken in and used to promote growth and replacement of tissues (*p. 102*).

objectives   Guideposts used by managers to

chart the course of an enterprise in terms of products, service, and profitability. They serve as standards by which managers measure the effectiveness of the organization, are generally short-range and more specific than goals, and describe activities that will meet a goal (*p. 365*).

Occupational Safety and Health Act (OSHA) A federal law passed in 1970 to provide for the establishment and enforcement of safety and health standards to protect workers (*p. 385*).

Official Airline Guide A publication that lists virtually all regularly scheduled flights in the United States, and contains detailed information on fares, frequency of service, possible routings, types of aircraft used, and distances of airports from city centers (*p. 312*).

online transfer A transfer from one plane flight to another on the same airline (*p. 318*).

open-end credit Credit that can be used again and again, up to a preset limit, as with a credit card or charge account (*p. 347*).

open-ended questions Broad, general questions that give a job seeker an opportunity to speak freely about his or her strong points or special skills and provide the interviewer with information that might not otherwise be revealed (*p. 43*).

open seating An airline policy that allows a passenger to occupy any seat that has not already been taken (*p. 319*).

ophthalmologist A physician who deals with diseases of the eye (*p. 142*).

opinion A personal judgment, appraisal, or belief (*p. 190*).

optician A person who makes and sells eyeglasses (*p. 142*).

organically grown Foods grown without chemical fertilizers or pesticides (*p. 115*).

organizational chart A chart or diagram of the management structure of an organization illustrating the various levels and areas of authority and responsibility. A study of the chart can reveal the range of opportunity for management promotions (*p. 382*).

organizing A function of management to implement a company's plans by grouping the work to be done into efficient units, assigning employees to their areas of greatest expertise, and delegating responsibility (*p. 366*).

OSHA. *See* Occupational Safety and Health Act.

outer direction A concept relating to how a person's life is directed. Outer-directed people let others tell them what to do and when (*p. 271*).

outside pressure The strong threats or pressures brought to bear on a decision-making group by outsiders who wish to influence a vote in their own interest (*p. 235*).

overbooking The selling by an airline of more confirmed reservations than there are seats on a plane (*p. 322*).

painting A bleaching process that changes hair color minimally and is done with a brush to highlight random areas (*p. 75*).

paisley tie A tie designed with many colors in a teardrop-shaped motif (*p. 141*).

passive flight The practice of a nonassertive individual who complies with a demand but inwardly rebels (*p. 217*).

paternal style A company philosophy that emphasizes competition as a motivator (*p. 212*).

pastimes Forms of social exchange that serve to pass the time of day (*p. 278*).

per diem A fixed daily rate a company establishes for an employee's reimbursable expenses (*p. 335*).

pH balance The acid-alkaline balance of the skin (*p. 56*).

planning A function of management that involves forecasting the future and then determining the appropriate strategies and activities (objectives) that will attain the company's goals (*p. 366*).

planning board An aid for values clarification and decision making that involves listing desirable goals or qualities in order of priority (*p. 254*).

plaque A thin, transparent film, containing bacteria, on the enamel of a tooth (*p. 157*).

podiatrist A foot doctor (*p. 78*).

poise A quality that expresses itself physically in grace of movement and mentally in the assurance of looking and feeling good (*p. 87*).

power bases Quality, such as money, external contacts, seniority, expertise, and public recognition, that have value to group members and enable their possessor to operate from a strong position (*p. 239*).

premium The cost of an insurance policy, usually payable monthly or annually (*p. 340*).

primary colors Yellow, blue, and red, colors that can be used in various combinations to produce the secondary colors of green, violet, and orange (*p. 126*).

probationary period The trial period a new employee must undergo before being considered a regular member of the staff (*p. 40*).

probing questions Technique used by an interviewer who suspects information is being withheld and who asks varied questions to determine the extent of the problem (*p. 43*).

professional placement services Privately owned agencies that provide job placement services for a fee (*p. 7*).

promotion policy The plan a company folows in giving its employees an opportunity to advance to a better job within the company (*p. 40*).

proof The percentage of alcohol contained in a beverage (*p. 166*).

proteins Essential nutrients, often called the building blocks of the body, necessary for the healthy growth, maintenance, and repair of body tissue (*p. 102*).

proxemics In business communications, relating to unwritten rules about the use of space (*p. 186*).

pure soap Soap made from animal and vegetable fats (*p. 59*).

quality circles Groups of employees with immediate supervisors, who work together to assign areas of responsibility and to decide the methods of achieving the forthcoming work tasks (*p. 375*).

RDA. *See* recommended daily allowance.

recommended daily allowance (RDA) The essential nutrients that should be consumed each day to maintain good health (*p. 116*).

receiver The person in the communication cycle who absorbs the message directed toward him or her by the sender (*p. 189*).

recorder In an interaction meeting, the person who records accurately every idea expressed during the meeting (*p. 247*).

references Individuals who can supply a prospective employer with complete information about an applicant's quality of work, ability, character, and potential (*p. 15*).

Regulation Z A provision of the 1975 Consumer Credit Protection Act (also known as the Truth in Lending Law) requiring lenders to disclose both the dollar amount of finance charges and the annual percentage rate that dollar amount represents (*p. 349*).

relationship-oriented behavior A part of situational leadership theory that calls for the supervisor to deal with employees in personal ways rather than in a task-related manner (*p. 374*).

repossession If a buyer fails to meet the periodic payments on an installment purchase, the merchandise can be repossessed, or taken away without notice (*p. 348*).

rep tie A conservatively colored tie with diagonal stripes (*p. 141*).

resting heart rate The rate at which a person's heart beats when he or she is not engaging in exercise (*p. 89*).

résumé A well-organized summary of educational background, work experience, and pertinent personal data that gives a prospective employer an overview of your entire work history, education, and skills. Sometimes called a data sheet or *vita* (*p. 9*).

revolving credit Retail credit that sets a limit on what may be owed; when payment is made, the credit is automatically renewed. Interest must be paid on any unpaid balance (*p. 348*).

right to work laws State laws that prohibit requiring a worker to belong to a union in order to get or keep a job (*p. 385*).

rituals Greetings, religious ceremonies, patriotic holidays, and fraternity rites that have cultural and social significance (*p. 277*).

Rule of Fourteen A method of preventing overdressing by using a point system to count color and pattern of all visible clothes and accessories. The recommended total should not exceed fourteen or fall below eight points (*p. 143*).

SAT. *See* Scholastic Aptitude Test.

saturated fats Those fats found in meats, dairy products, and lard that have the characteristic of hardening at room temperature (*p. 103*).

Scholastic Aptitude Test (SAT) A standardized test that measures the individual's potential for success in different kinds of academic pursuits (*p. 381*).

scientific management An approach to production, developed by Frederick W. Taylor, that places emphasis on organization, efficiency, and worker productivity (*p. 369*).

sebaceous glands Skin glands that secrete oil through pores containing hair follicles (*p. 56*).

secondary colors Violet, orange, and green, produced by combining the primary colors: blue and red to produce violet; red and yellow to produce orange; and yellow and blue to produce green (*p. 126*).

security check Examination of carry-on luggage and handbags with an x-ray detection device at airports, while passengers walk through a metal-detection passageway. This is to prevent concealed weapons or other devices from being carried aboard a plane (*p. 319*).

self-fulfilling prophecy A theory that people live up to or down to the level that is expected of them (*p. 372*).

semi-fast diet A diet that includes a large breakfast and a very late lunch, and eliminates the evening meal (*p. 113*).

sender The person who begins the communication cycle when he or she wants someone to react, respond, or behave in some manner (*p. 180*).

sexual harassment Unwanted and unwarranted sexual attention on the job. In may include verbal comments and abuse, suggestiveness, or physical aggressiveness (*p. 221*).

shade The amount of black that has been added to pure pigment (*p. 125*).

single limit In automobile liability coverage, a policy that offers a single limit instead of split limits so the risk of being underinsured in any one category is minimized (*p. 343*).

singular perception Looking at events, persons, or ideas from an extremely narrow viewpoint that doesn't allow for other people's perceptions of them (*p. 196*).

situational leadership theory A theory that describes the appropriate behavior for a supervisor to adopt, depending on the maturity level of the subordinates (*p. 374*).

slanting Shading the truth a bit to benefit a particular point of view or person (*p. 198*).

sommelier A wine steward (*p. 300*).

SPF. *See* Sun Protection Factor.

split-complement color scheme A combination of one color with another next to its complement on the color wheel; for example, blue matched with red or yellow (*p. 127*).

split limits Automobile liability coverage sold in split limits, as 250/500/50—a maximum of $250,000 payable to each injured person, $500,000 total bodily injury per accident, and a maximum of $50,000 property damage per accident (*p. 343*).

standby status Waiting at the airline gate area in the hope that some passengers with confirmed reservations will not appear and the airline will begin to fill these empty seats a few minutes before departure time (*p. 313*).

static Any interference with the exchanges between sender and receiver that distorts the intended message or feedback in such a way that misinterpretation results (*p. 193*).

stress The body's reaction to any demand made upon it (*p. 171*).

Strong-Campbell Interest Inventory A standardized test designed to assist individuals in making career choices based on interest (*p. 380*).

subcutaneous Beneath the skin (*p. 56*).

Sun Protection Factor (SPF) The amount of protection a sunscreen product will give as shown by a number on the container. The number ranges from 2 (minimal sun protection) to 15 (maximum sun protection) (*p. 64*).

sunscreens Various preparations designed to protect particular skin types from sunburn (*p. 64*).

Super NOW Account Differs from the NOW account in that a minimum balance is required and there is no restriction on the interest rates that may be imposed (*p. 351*).

surprise questions An interview technique in which a question is posed at an unexpected point in an interview for the purpose of judging how well a person can handle pressure (*p. 44*).

sweat glands Small glands that secrete liquid waste material through the pores and act as a cooling system for the body (*p. 56*).

syphilis A highly infectious venereal disease caused by microorganisms whose technical term is *Treponema pallidum*. It is acquired by kissing or sexual intercourse or congenitally (*p. 161*).

Taft-Hartley Act A federal law (Labor Management Relations Act) intended to equalize an imbalance of power between labor and management resulting from earlier legislation many believed favored labor (*p. 385*).

target zone The range of heart beats per minute that a person engaging in aerobic exercise should stay within in order to achieve a safe, but effective workout (*p. 89*).

task-oriented behavior A situational leadership concept that says the leader should deal with employees in task-related ways if the group maturity level is low (*p. 374*).

term insurance Life insurance that provides

coverage for only a specific amount of time but is renewable at a higher premium (*p. 340*).

Theory X One of two opposite sets of assumptions (X and Y) about managerial approach to supervision offered by Douglas McGregor. Theory X assumes that (1) the average person has an inherent dislike of work, (2) most people must be coerced, controlled, directed, or threatened to get them to put forth adequate effort toward the achievement of organizational goals, and (3) the average person prefers to be directed, avoids responsibility, has little ambition, and wants security (*p. 371*).

Theory Y One of two opposite theories (X and Y) presented by Douglas McGregor relating to assumptions affecting the management of human resources. Theory Y assumptions are that (1) work is natural, (2) people will exercise responsibility in the service of objectives to which they are committed, (3) workers' commitment to objectives will correspond to the rewards associated with achievement, (4) under proper conditions the average person learns to accept and seek responsibility, (5) the capacity for imagination and creativity is widely, not narrowly, distributed, and (6) under the conditions of modern industrial life, the intellectual potential of the average person is only partly fulfilled (*p. 371*).

Theory Z A management philosophy applied by the Japanese, which emphasizes worker involvement in decision making, lifetime employment, and the use of quality circles (*p. 375*).

thinging The dehumanization of personal relationships by thinking of people only in terms of their usefulness or service, regarding them as "things" or machines, rather than as human beings with feelings, attitudes, strengths, weaknesses, likes, and dislikes (*p. 197*).

Think Tank™ A device developed to help in applying freely associated ideas to corporate problems. A round ball with a clear plastic window on the side contains 13,000 separate words that are mixed and moved at random toward the window. The first six to appear are applied to the problem (*p. 233*).

thoracic Of or relating to the chest (*p. 94*).

time engineering Process of maneuvering projects toward completion with a minimum of wasted time and a maximum of concentration (*p. 279*).

time management The process of planning and organizing to make the most effective use of time (*p. 277*).

time structuring The organization of time into segments, action and inaction, as applied in transactional analysis (*p. 277*).

tint A gradation of color according to the amount of white added to it (*p. 125*).

tipping Adding a percentage of the bill as a gratuity for services rendered (*p. 305*).

tipping process A bleaching process in which just the ends of the hair are lightened (*p. 75*).

tone The various modifications of a particular color according to the amount of gray added (*p. 125*).

trade association A group of business firms in a field of common interest organized to promote the exchange of information and ideas and to cooperate in activities beneficial to its members (*p. 6*).

trade and professional journals Magazines published in the interest of a business, trade, or profession. Their classified ad sections are a good source of information about jobs available in a specific field (*p. 6*).

transactional analysis According to a theory by Eric Berne, people's personalities are divided into three parts—parent (the authoritarian part), child (spontaneous and emotional part), and adult (who listens, assesses the situation, and takes appropriate action) (*p. 200*).

transparent soap A mild soap that dissolves rapidly, has added fat and glycerin for translucency (*p. 59*).

travel agency An agency that arranges transportation, itineraries, and accommodations for travelers, generally with no charge for service because the agency receives its commission from airlines and hotels (*p. 311*).

traveler's checks Issued by a bank, travel, or express agency in various denominations. The traveler signs them at the time of purchase and when cashed. They can be replaced if lost or stolen, and allow people to travel without having to carry large amounts of cash (*p. 327*).

Treponema pallidum The microorganism that causes syphilis (*p. 161*).

triadic color scheme A color scheme using three colors that are an equal distance apart on the color wheel, as yellow, blue, and red. One color should be the basic one, with the other two as accents (*p. 127*).

trichomoniasis A form of vaginitis caused by a

single-cell parasite that lives in the vagina or urethra. The symptoms in women (usually absent in men) are a foul-smelling greenish-yellow discharge, together with itching and irritation (*p. 163*).

Truth in Lending Law   The Consumer Credit Protection Act of 1975. Its Regulation Z requires lenders to disclose both the dollar amount of finance charges and the annual percentage rate that dollar amount represents (*p. 349*).

two-value thinking   The belief that if a particular quality does not exist in someone or something, then its opposite must. It may permit one desirable or undesirable trait to distort the whole picture (*p. 195*).

universal life insurance   A type of life insurance that combines the features of whole life with an annuity (*p. 341*).

unsaturated fats   Oils, such as sunflower oil, safflower oil, and corn oil, considered by many nutritionists to be better for people than saturated fats (*p. 103*).

vaginitis   An overall term, meaning inflammation of the vagina, encompassing a number of diseases and disorders that are not venereal but may be transmitted sexually. Most prominent among them are moniliasis, trichomoniasis, and nonspecific vaginitis (*p. 163*).

value   The range of light and dark in a color (*p. 125*).

values   Things a person considers important or desirable (*p. 251*).

values grid   A tool for examining values by answering seven question regarding methods of affirmation, choice, and action on any topic from personal problems to world events (*p. 252*).

valuing process   A method of examining values developed by Louis Raths, Harmin Merrill, and Sidney Simon. It includes prizing one's beliefs and affirming, choosing, and acting on them (*p. 252*).

vascular system   The blood vessels of the body (*p. 88*).

venereal disease   A disease, such as gonorrhea or syphilis, transmitted primarily by sexual intercourse (*p. 160*).

vertical thinking   Reasoning from step to step in a straightforward progression of thought (*p. 233*).

vitamin overdose   Taking too many vitamins in the mistaken belief that they will be beneficial can lead to various ailments and cause serious damage to some body organs (*p. 105*).

vitamins   Organic substances found in most foods and necessary in small quantities for the maintenance and regulation of bodily functions (*p. 104*).

voluntary bumping   When a flight is overbooked because the airline has sold more reservations than there are seats, passengers will be asked to volunteer to give up their places for compensation (*p. 322*).

W–2 form   End-of-year report from employer to employee showing taxes withheld during the year (*p. 354*).

W–4 form   Statement of employee's tax status filed with employer; from it, the employee's taxes to be withheld are calculated (*p. 354*).

wait list status   The status of travelers whose names are added to a waiting list after all available seats on a flight have been reserved. If a confirmed reservation is canceled, the seat is offered to those on the waiting list according to the date and time of their initial request (*p. 313*).

waxing   A process for removing unwanted hair by applying warm wax to the skin, letting it dry, and then pulling it away with hair imbedded in it (*p. 76*).

wheel pattern   A pattern in which the flow of communication is controlled by a central person. An office manager with various subordinates might be the hub of the wheel structure (*p. 238*).

whole life insurance   Life insurance policies that cost a fixed premium over a person's lifetime and accumulate cash value against which he or she can borrow. Also called straight life (*p. 341*).

Yellow Pages   The section of a telephone directory, generally printed on yellow paper, containing listings of firms or individuals classified according to type of business or profession (*p. 8*).

yoga   A series of postures and exercises that are designed to stretch the muscles, induce deep breathing, and promote mental relaxation (*p. 95*).

"you" attitude   Placing another person's needs and problems before your own (*p. 290*).

Y pattern   A pattern of communicating in firms with two executive officers on an equal basis. The person at the junction of the arms of the Y controls the flow of communications from both higher and lower levels and has power to decide what information will be passed along (*p. 238*).

zero bracket amount   A federal income tax provision whereby, if deductions are not itemized, the first $2,300 of a single person's income is automatically exempt from taxation. For a married couple filing jointly, the amount is $3,400; for a married person filing separately, the amount is $1,700 (*p. 353*).

INDEX

Acceleration, installment loans and, 348
Accessories, shopping for, 140–42
Acid mantle, 56
Acne, 62–63
Addressing others, 288–89
Aerobics:
  dancing, 90
  exercise, 89–93
Age Discrimination in Employment Act of 1967, 47
Agendas, of meetings, 233
Aggression, 217
Air travel, 312–14, 315–25
  arrival at destination, 320–22
  baggage problems, 323–25
  bookings, 312–14
  canceled and delayed flights, 322
  day of the flight, 316–20
  ground transportation, 321–22
  overbooking, 322–23
  preparation for, 311–12
  tickets, 315–16
Alcohol, 165–68
  alcohol abuse, 167–68
All-channel pattern, of communication, 238
American College Test (ACT), 381
American Dental Dictionary, 156
American method, use of eating utensils, 302–303
Amtrak, 325
Analogous color scheme, 127
Androgens, 58
Annual percentage rate (APR), 347
Annual report, 37
Annuity, 341
Antibacterial soap, 60
Antiperspirant, 78
Appearance, for interviews, 31–33
Application forms, 22–24
Application letters, 17–21
Aptitude tests, 380–81
Asch, Solomon, 243–44
Assertiveness, 214–17
  assertiveness training, 217–21
  Bill of Assertive Rights, 217
  victims and nonvictims theory, 214–17

Astringent, 61
Attitude:
  in interviews, 33–34
  posture and, 98
Auto insurance, 342–44
Automobiles. *See* Cars.

Bach, George R., 197
Background static, in communication, 195
Baggage, air travel and, 317–18, 323–25
Balance, clothing, 146–47
Bandy, Way, 80
Banking:
  checking accounts, 349
  Individual Retirement Accounts, 351–52
  interest plus checking, 351
  Super NOW accounts, 351
Belts, 141
Beneficiary, 340
Berne, Eric, 200, 277–78
Bill of Assertive Rights, 217
Blanchard, Kenneth, 374
Block of silence, used in interviews, 45
Blouses and shirts, 138–39
Blue laws, 257–58
Boarding, airplane, 318–20
Body care, 77–79
  dental hygiene, 157–58
  foot care, 78
  hand care, 78–79
  hair removal and shaving, 75–77
  skin care, 55–69
Body language, 185–86
Bojicic, Savo, 233
Bona fide occupational qualification (BFOQ), 15
Bookings, airline, 312–14
Borrowing, credit, 346
Brainstorming, 233–34
Broken record, assertiveness skill, 220–21
Bronzing gels, 80
Brushing the hair, 72
Budgeting, 337–40
  gross vs. net income, 337
  preparation of the budget, 338–39
  savings, 337–38
Bumping, airline, 322–23
Bus travel, 325–26
Business ethics. *See* Ethics.
Business etiquette, 290–92
Business expenses, 333–36

Calories, 107, 109
Cancer, 159–60
Cars:

provided by business, 336
  rental of, 315
  rental of, at airports, 321
Carbohydrates, 103
Cardiopulmonary system, 88
Care labels, 149, 150–51
Carr, Rachael, 95
Cash advances:
  expense accounts and, 335
  travel, 326–27
Cash reimbursement, 335
Chain (serial) pattern, of communication, 238
Chancre, 162
Charge account, 348
Checking accounts, 349
Chroma, of color, 125
Chronological résumé, 11
Civil Aeronautics Board (CAB), 322
Civil Rights Act of 1964:
  discriminatory questions, 47
  implications for management positions, 382–83
  personal data and, 15
  sexual harassment, 222
Civil service exams, state and federal, 6–7
Claim stubs, luggage, 317–18
Classic, clothing, 147
Clearinghouse, 7
Close-ended questions, used in interviews, 43
Co-workers, needs hierarchy and interactions with, 210–11
Coats, 139–40
Cohesiveness, group, 241–44
Coinsurance provision, insurance plan, 342
Collateral, 346
College Placement Annual, 6
College placement office, 6
Collision coverage, 343–44
Color:
  complexion and, 128, 129
  psychology of, 128
  wardrobe and, 125–29
Color Me Beautiful (Jackson), 129
Combination skin, 57–58
  cleansing, 61
Communicating, 179–202
  breakdown in, 193–99
  communication cycle, 179–93
  self-awareness and, 199–203
Communication cycle, 179–93
  feedback in, 192–93
  message in, 182–88

receiver in, 189–91
  sender in, 180–81
Companies:
  code of ethics, 258–59
  family styles of, 212
Competition, group, 244–46
Complementary color scheme, 126
Complete Medical Exam, The, (Rosenfeld), 156
Complexion, color, 128, 129
Comprehensive coverage, of insurance, 344
Compromise, 235
Conditioning, hair, 73
Confirmed reservations, 313–314
Conformity, group, 243–44
Congenital syphilis, 162–63
Connecting flights, 320
Consensus, 236
Contact lenses, 142
Continental method, use of eating utensils, 302–303
Controlling, management function of, 366
Corporate image, 37–38
Cortex, 69
Contouring, facial, 81
Courtesy. *See also* Etiquette.
  expressions of, 287–90
  in interviews, 35–37
Credit, 345–50
  borrowing, 346
  checking accounts and, 348
  cost of, 346–47
  credit cards, 345–46
  installment loans, 348
  regulation of, 348–49
  retail credit, 348
Credit cards:
  corporate, 335
  travel and, 327
Cross-country skiing, 91–92
Cuticle:
  of hair, 70
  of nail, 79
Cycling, 92

Dandruff, 74
Decision making:
  in groups, 234–36
  management team, 367
Deductible provision, insurance plan, 342
Dental hygiene, 157–58
Dentists, evaluation of, 156–57
Deodorant, 78
Deodorant soap, 60
Depilatory, 77
Dermatologist, 63